CW01567104

HISTORIA

Zeitschrift für Alte Geschichte
Revue d'histoire ancienne
Journal of Ancient History
Rivista di storia antica

— — — — — — — — — — — — — — — —

EINZELSCHRIFTEN

Herausgegeben von
Kai Brodersen/Mannheim
Mortimer Chambers/Los Angeles
Martin Jehne/Dresden
François Paschoud/Geneve
Aloys Winterling/Freiburg

HEFT 194

Michael B. Charles

Vegetius in Context

Establishing the Date
of the *Epitoma Rei Militaris*

Franz Steiner Verlag Stuttgart 2007

Bibliografische Information der Deutschen Nationalbibliothek
Die Deutsche Nationalbibliothek verzeichnet diese
Publikation in der Deutschen Nationalbibliografie;
detaillierte bibliografische Daten sind im Internet über
<http://dnb.d-nb.de> abrufbar.

ISBN 978-3-515-08989-0

ISO 9706

© 2007 Franz Steiner Verlag, Stuttgart.
Gedruckt auf säurefreiem, alterungsbeständigem
Papier. Druck: Printservice Decker & Bokor, München
Printed in Germany

This volume is dedicated to the
memory of my grandmother

Imelda Dorothy Charles (née Fenlon)

1921–2002

CONTENTS

8   Contents

ACKNOWLEDGEMENTS

This work began in 2000 as a doctoral thesis and, after a number of years, has finally emerged in what I hope is a publishable format. Along the way, many hardy souls have had to withstand innumerable papers, lectures and general pontificating about the importance of Vegetius and his writings. Chief among this cohort must surely number my erstwhile doctoral supervisor and now good friend Dr Brian Jones.

Warm thanks must also be expressed to Professor A. R. Birley, one of my examiners and the person most responsible for encouraging me to turn my originally somewhat overweight thesis into a far crisper monograph. Professor Birley's unfailing critical assistance, not only with this work but also with several others, is greatly appreciated. Also responsible for shaping the final product is Professor François Paschoud, who demonstrated to me the inestimable value of clear argumentation.

Other individuals have also provided assistance on points of detail. These include the anonymous reviewers of three now-published articles touching on Vegetian themes, in addition to Miss Yvette Hunt, Professor R.D. Milns, Dr Philip Rance, Dr Tom Stevenson and Dr John Whitehorne. Errors inevitably remain, but all the aforementioned persons should be absolved of any complicity. I should also like to thank Dr Suzanne Dixon and the late Mr Bruce Gollan for inculcating in me an appreciation of the Latin language during my undergraduate studies at the University of Queensland. And one should never forget those tireless (and extraordinarily patient) library staff members dedicated to finding copies of obscure articles hidden away since time immemorial.

On a more personal note, my parents Gail and Hedley Charles provided much support during the formative stages of this work's compilation, a duty taken over in more recent times by my wife Cinthya Paredes Castillo, who has been incredibly indulgent with regard to the innumerable hours spent on revising this volume instead of attending to household chores.

Thanks must also be expressed to Professor Neal Ryan, Head of the School of Management, Queensland University Technology, for granting me the time needed to revise this text. Finally, thanks to the members of *Historia*'s Editorial Committee, especially Professors Kai Brodersen and François Paschoud, for giving me the opportunity to place this monograph in their Einzelschriften series.

A NOTE ON LATIN AND GREEK NAMES

It is always difficult to make choices with regard to the way in which Latin and Greek proper names should be written. While some might choose to maintain strict standards of internal consistency, I chose to depart from this philosophy. Instead of Gratianus and Ambrosius, I use Gratian and Ambrose, the forms most commonly found in historical treatments written in English. Consistency would mean that the emperor Trajan would appear as Traianus, which would unduly confuse matters given that this was also the name of his father. Likewise, the use of Claudianus in place of Claudian would surely smack of pedantry. Thus I have opted for Latinate and often anglicized forms of proper names. Greek names pose even further difficulties when transliterated. Once again, I have preferred Latinate and, where appropriate, anglicized forms, thus Arbogast and Sozomen instead of Sozomenus (or Sozomenos) and Arbogastes. This 'system', or lack thereof, may not please some readers. In view of this, I beg their indulgence.

ABBREVIATIONS

Abbreviations for ancient sources and collections of ancient sources follow the norms of the *Oxford Classical Dictionary*[3], eds. S. Hornblower and A. Spawforth, Oxford/New York, 1996 (*OCD*[3]); and, for journals, *l'Année philologique*. *Carm.*, *Chron.*, *Ep.*, *Pan.*, etc., are used with their normal meanings. Note the following exceptions:

Alcib.	*Alcibiades* (Nep.)
ALL	*Archiv für Lateinische Lexikographie und Grammatik mit Einschluss des älteren Mittellateins*
Ambros.	Ambrose
ANRW	*Aufstieg und Niedergang der römischen Welt: Geschichte und Kultur Roms im Spiegel der neueren Forschung* (Berlin/New York)
Arist.	Aristides
Or.	*Orationes*
BAR	British Archaeological Reports
Bell. Gild.	*De Bello Gildonico* (Claud.)
Bell. Goth.	*De Bello Gothico* (Claud.)
BJRUL	*Bulletin of the John Rylands University Library*
BMC	*Coins of the Roman Empire in the British Museum*, 6 vols. (ed. H. Mattingly, London, 1965–1976)
Car.	*Carus, Carinus et Numerianus* (*HA*)
Carm. min. corp.	*Carminum Minorum Corpusculum* (Claud.)
CB	*The Classical Bulletin*
CC	*Corpus Christianorum: Series Latina* (Turnholt)
CIG	*Corpus Inscriptionum Graecarum* (ed. A. Boeckhius, *et al.*, Hildesheim/New York, 4 vols.)
Cons. Constant.	*Consularia Constantinopolitana*
Cons. Ital.	*Consularia Italica*
Cons. Manl. Theod.	*De Consulatu Fl. Manlii Theodori* (Claud.)
Cons. Olyb. et Prob.	*De Consulatu Olybrii et Probini* (Claud.)
Coripp.	Corippus
Ioh.	*Iohannis*
DRB	*De Rebus Bellicis*
Epit.	*Epitoma Rei Militaris* (Veg.)
Epith.	*Epithalamium* (Claud.)
Euseb. Werk. 7	*Eusebius Werke 7. Die Chronik des Hieronymus*, ed. R. Helm (Berlin, 1984)
Eutrop.	Eutropius
Brev.	*Breuiarium*
Evag.	Evagrius
HA	*Historia Augusta*
H.F.	*Historia Francorum* (Gregory of Tours)
H.E.	*Historia Ecclesiastica*
Hist. Goth.	*Historia Gothorum Wandalorum Sueborum* (Isid.)
John Lydus	
De magist.	*De Magistratibus*
In Eutrop.	*In Eutropium* (Claud.)

In Rufin.	*In Rufinum* (Claud.)
Lewis & Short	*A Latin Dictionary* (C.T. Lewis and C. Short, Oxford, 1879)
Malal.	John Malalas
Mamert.	Mamertinus
Marcell.	Marcellinus Comes
Merob.	Merobaudes
Milt.	*Miltiades* (Nep.)
Mul.	*Mulomedicina* (Veg.)
NJKA	*Neue Jahrbucher für das Klassische Altertum*
NPhM	*Neuphilologische Mitteilungen*
Nov. Marc.	*Leges Nouellae Marciani*
Nov. Valent.	*Leges Nouellae Diui Valentiniani*
Nupt. Hon. et Mar.	*De Nuptiis Honorii et Mariae* (Claud.)
OLD	*Oxford Latin Dictionary* (ed. P. Glare, Oxford, 1986)
Olympiod.	Olympiodorus
Pacat.	Pacatus
Paulin.	Paulinus of Milan
Vit. Amb.	*Vita Ambrosii*
Paul. Nol.	Paulinus of Nola
Pers.	*De Bello Persico* (Procop.)
PES	*Publications of the Princeton University Archaeological Expeditions to Syria in 1904–1905 and 1909*, 4 vols. in many parts (eds. H.C. Butler, *et al.*, Leyden, 1907–1949)
Philostorg.	Philostorgius
PhW	*Philologische Wochenschrift*
Prosp.	Prosper
Ps.-Aur. Vict.	Pseudo-Aurelius Victor
Epit.	*Epitome de Caesaribus*
RG	*Res Gestae Diui Augusti*
RIC	*The Roman Imperial Coinage*, 10 vols. (ed. H. Mattingly, *et al.*, London, 1923–1994)
RMG	*Revue Militaire Générale*
Rom.	*Romana* (Jord.)
Salv.	Salvianus
Gub.	*De Gubernatione Dei*
SGS	*Scottish Gaelic Studies*
Socrat.	Socrates Scholasticus
Symm.	Symmachus
Rel.	*Relationes*
TAASDN	*Transactions of the Architectural and Archaeological Society of Durham and Northumberland*
Tac.	*Tacitus* (*HA*)
Them.	Themistius
Orat.	*Orationes*
Theod.	Theodoret
Val. Flacc.	Valerius Flaccus
V.C.	*Vita Constantini* (Eus.)
Vict.	Victor Tonnensis

INTRODUCTION

An attempt to date Vegetius' *Epitoma Rei Militaris*? It may seem strange that, after more than a century and a half of Vegetian scholarship, no one has yet produced a monograph on the topic. Several articles have been written on the theme and the introductions to the various Teubner editions of the Latin text, in addition to those that accompany the English, Italian and German editions of the work,[1] have all had something to offer. Many scholars, too, have thought it necessary to provide a date for the *Epitoma* (occasionally referred to as the *De Re Militari*) in more general works on Roman military history. But much speculation remains. A survey of military thought in the Late Empire was the initial plan. Yet, as work progressed, it soon became apparent that a diversity of thought accompanied the present understanding of Vegetius' *Epitoma*, a text which, in the main, endeavours to restore Roman military prestige by reverting to the military discipline and formations of the early Principate through to the early Dominate. Initial confidence in the general scholarly consensus that the text was addressed to Theodosius I soon gave way to increasing disquiet. Much, it appeared, remained to be said, while no one treatment seemed to provide all the answers. Thus it seemed necessary to turn a minor historiographical sortie into a campaign, a battle to be fought on manifold fronts.

A secondary aim is to exploit more fully the potential of the *Epitoma* as a source for the Late Empire, rather than merely as a source for military formations, tactics and traditions of the more distant past. This, so far as can be established, has not yet been attempted on a large scale. Obviously, this investigation not only enables the text itself to be dated with greater precision (which, of course, must remain this volume's primary aim), but also allows us to corroborate and validate the information provided by the epitomator's contemporaries. Ideology is as important as the nuts and bolts of history. Thus it is important to remember that the value, first and foremost, of any literary source is that it reflects the views and intentions of the author rather than any particular historical reality. Vegetius must be viewed in this fashion or we risk creating pseudo-history. In short, this is not merely the study of one text in isolation, but the study of any text that might relate to the themes and language employed by Vegetius. A firm tenet of the research methodology employed is that it is necessary to draw a picture of the late-Roman world as accurately as possible in order to divine the military and political atmosphere into which we can slot the *Epitoma* – thus "Vegetius in context", as the title suggests.

---

[1] At present, there is no Collection Budé edition of the *Epitoma* available, even though such a text was reported to have been in preparation many years ago. A new edition in Spanish (Paniagua Aguilar 2006) has now appeared, but its contents have not been incorporated into this volume on account of its very recent appearance. For a bibliography on Vegetius, see Sablayrolles 1984, 139–146. The Latin text used in this work is that of Reeve 2003.

1. AIMS AND METHODOLOGY

It is important to introduce a brief history of Vegetian scholarship. A great deal of discussion has been occasioned by Seeck's nineteenth-century attempt to date the *Epitoma*. Seeck, following a brief comment by Gibbon, placed the *Epitoma* in a fifth-century context and held that the work must have been addressed to Valentinian III (western emperor 425–455).[2] Although Seeck's view was initially accepted, some twentieth-century scholars, among them Barnes, Chastagnol, Mazzarino, Sabbah and Sirago, have attempted to prove that the *Epitoma* was a product of the reign of Theodosius I, the last emperor to rule both *partes imperii*. So influential were these scholars that the majority of standard reference works, such as the *OCD*, Pauly-Wissowa's *RE* and *PLRE* nominate Theodosius I (eastern emperor 379–395, emperor of both East and West 394–395) as the most likely recipient of Vegetius' treatise. Still, proponents of the Gibbonian view have occasionally surfaced, such as Goffart, Gordon and E. Birley. More recently, attempts have been made to associate the text with other late-Roman emperors such as Valentinian II and Honorius.

As a consequence, the principal aim of this discussion is to demonstrate that the popular contention that the text was addressed to Theodosius the Great has much less merit than is generally supposed. While it is clearly impossible to 'prove' beyond question that the treatise was addressed to *any* particular emperor, it will be shown that the balance of probability tips the scales in favour of Valentinian III. In short, it will be demonstrated that the *Epitoma* finds its most likely historical niche in the second quarter of the fifth century rather than in the late fourth century, and, more specifically, in that period of time when Theodosius II and Valentinian III ruled the Roman world, i.e., *post* 425.

Instead of looking at the problem from a purely 'military' perspective, as the majority of the above-mentioned authorities have done, I shall attempt to place the treatise in its cultural, economic, historical and, of course, military context. In part, this will be achieved by means of an extensive analysis of sources not often used by military scholars. Take the case of Claudian, a writer of panegyrical works and court propaganda in the first years of the reign of Honorius (emperor of the West, 395–423). Claudian, who might initially seem to be of little value for Vegetian studies, deserves more attention than is usually accorded by military historians of late antiquity. Although the 'testimony' of a western courtier[3] might not initially seem to be of great value, the present discussion will show that Claudian's works ought not be discounted as evidence for the Roman military of

---

[2] Except in cases where ambiguity might ensue, dates in this thesis are A.D. unless otherwise signalled.

[3] It appears, however, that Claudian was born in Egypt, perhaps even Alexandria as the Suda tells us s.v. Κλαυδιανός. On this, see Conte 1987, 658–659; Levy 1948, 90–91; Schamp 2001, 971–991; Rolfe 1919, 136–137; Teuffel 1892, 419 (vol. 2). Cameron (1970, 1) even entitles the first chapter of his monograph "The Poet from Egypt". For ancient evidence, see Sid. Apoll. *Carm.* 9.274–276; Claud. *Carm. min. corp.* 19.3, 22.19–20, 41.12–13. But cf. Christiansen 1997, 79–95; and see also Gnilka 1976, 96–123.

his day. Since Claudian owed an enormous stylistic debt to Latin poets such as Statius, Horace and Vergil,[4] it stands to reason that some essential 'truth' is revealed whenever he departs from the standard and hackneyed epic machinery that he was accustomed to employ. So, if we can establish a reasonable understanding of the military environment in those years between the reigns of Theodosius I and Valentinian III, we will have a far greater chance of establishing the principal differences between Claudian's time and that of Vegetius. A similar approach will be applied to the poetical works of Merobaudes and Sidonius Apollinaris, and the output of Christian writers such as Ambrose, Augustine, Orosius, Prudentius, Philostorgius and Sozomen, in addition to the various Latin and Greek chroniclers.

The present work, then, is not just an attempt to assign a date to a text. Rather, it is an analysis of Vegetius and his world. Only when the various aspects of the Vegetian world are suitably understood can we nominate the era in which he may have written. Of course, the contextual approach is far from new, and such an approach has had manifold applications in the Humanities. While the most important tool in the investigation of any text, be it ancient or modern, is obviously the work itself, one must be awake to the possibilities of recreating, as far as resources allow, the atmosphere and cultural milieu in which the author lived and wrote. For example, the contextual approach has been used to study the verse and drama of the Andalusian poet and dramatist Federico García Lorca (1898–1936). Josephs and Caballero argue that the critic of Lorca's work must be acquainted with the "contexto cultural" in which he wrote, "sin el cual la obra de Lorca nos parece indescifrable".[5] One might say the same of Charles Dickens' work and the social injustices of the Victorian age, or of Shakespeare's *Macbeth* and contemporary Jacobean fears of the supernatural. The same holds true for any study of Vegetius – the date of the *Epitoma* is equally indecipherable without a thorough appreciation of the values, beliefs and interests that men of his ilk held in the Late Empire. Just as one must adequately comprehend the *fenómeno andaluz* in order to achieve a greater understanding of Lorca's world of love, death, honour, and, above all, the coalescence of cultures, so too must one arrive at an understanding, in the broadest possible sense, of all the contemporary matters of which Vegetius treats in his *Epitoma*. Our mission is to divine the chronological 'niche' in which the *Epitoma* belongs.

Chronological pointers can be found in the text, and some scholars have used these in diverse ways with a view to bolstering their respective arguments. The traditional arguments for and against a Theodosian date have revolved around these axes. It is thus difficult not to offer commentary on these old standards. Failure to do so would be inexcusable, even if the task is more revisitation than discovery. To understand Vegetius' world is to comprehend the manner in which he would have responded to any given situation. As noted above, Vegetius has often been assessed as a source for the past. In the present work, he will be

[4] On this, see Martin 1960, 72.
[5] Josephs/Caballero 1992, 53.

discussed almost exclusively as a witness to his own time. There is much to learn from the *Epitoma* about the Late Empire. We learn not only about terrestrial combat, but also about contemporary attitudes to various subjects of importance. Vegetius is our departure-point for brief investigations into attitudes to recruitment and barbarization, siege-craft, attitudes to the East, naval policy, Christianity, perceptions of Empire, and the rôle of the emperor in late antiquity – all of which, when analysed and understood, should enable us to date the text with greater precision.

2. THE *TERMINI*: 383 AND 450

The *terminus post quem* for the *Epitoma*'s composition is generally held to be the death of the western emperor Gratian in 383 (he is called *diuus Gratianus* by Vegetius at *Epit*. 1.20.3). Despite this, Sabbah discerns a reference to calculating the date of Easter at *Epit*. 4.35. If true, this may give us a slightly later *terminus*.[6] The entire chapter, which concerns the material with which ships should be built, reads as follows:

> obseruandum praecipue ut a quinta decima luna usque ad uicesimam secundam arbores praecidantur ex quibus liburnae contexendae sunt. his enim tantum octo diebus caesa materies immunis seruatur a carie, reliquis autem diebus praecisa etiam eodem anno interna uermium labe exesa in puluerem uertitur, quod ars ipsa et omnium architectorum cotidianus usus edocuit et contemplatione ipsius religionis agnoscimus quam pro aeternitate his tantum diebus placuit celebrari (*Epit*. 4.35.1–3).

The last phrase (beginning with *et*) is what especially concerns us. Stelten translates this as "and we know from the study of religion itself how only on these days was it pleasing that anything concerning eternity be celebrated".[7] This is a very literal translation and forces Stelten to conclude that "What Vegetius means by the reference to religion is not clear".[8] But Sabbah believes that the reference should be associated with a theological reform of "387–388".[9] He points out that Theophilus, the bishop of Alexandria, developed a paschal calendar for one hundred years based on Theodosius' first consulship in 380. Milner seems to accept Sabbah's finding and lists it with "personal arguments" that can be used to reinforce the supposition that the *Epitoma* was dedicated to Theodosius I.[10]

---

[6] Sabbah 1980, 145.

[7] Stelten 1990, *ad loc*.

[8] Stelten 1990, 274 n. 'b'. Milner (1996, 143) provides: "and we recognize it too when we contemplate the very religious festival which it has been decided to celebrate forever more on these days alone". Note also Formisano 2003, *ad loc*.: "e anche noi ne veniamo a conoscenza se consideriamo questo rituale che si è stabilito di celebrare solo in quei giorni"; Manmana Giuffrida 1997, *ad loc*.: "e ne riceviamo conferma dallo studio della stessa religione a cui piacque che si celebrasse solo in quei giorni la festa dell'eternità"; Müller 1997, *ad loc*.: "und unter Beachtung gerade dieses Brauchs sollte man nach unserem Erkennen Holz um der Haltbarkeit willen nur an diesen Tagen fällen".

[9] Sabbah 1980, 146. Formisano (2003, 345 n. 30) and Milner (1996, xli) agree.

[10] Milner 1996, xli; see also 143 n. 2 of the same work.

Sabbah's argument is not unconvincing and there seems to be no reason to object. But does the reference at *Epit.* 4.35 necessarily mean that it was written to please the emperor Theodosius? Of course not. In any case, why did Vegetius not mention that the new calculation was developed under the auspices of this pious emperor? Certainly, there is no reason why the reference could not have been written under Theodosius' successors, i.e., up until the reign of Valentinian III. The Latin, too, gives us no reason to imagine that Theophilus' calculations were "[un] ... événement récent", as Sabbah maintains (witness the tense of *placere* in Vegetius' *placuit celebrari*).[11]

Less contentious is that the *terminus ante quem* must be 450. The editor of a Vegetian text, one Flavius Eutropius,[12] signed a *subscriptio* with details of the consular date: "Fl. Eutropius emendaui sine exemplario Constantinopolim consul. Valentiniano Augusto VII. et Avieni [*sic*] (i.e., 450)".[13] Happily enough, this *subscriptio* was retained in several of the subsequent manuscripts. The date of the *Epitoma*, quite obviously, must fall between these two points – a period of some seventy years. During this period of time, there were no less than thirteen possible recipients of the text, if the more insignificant usurpers are excluded.[14] The relevant Augusti are listed below. Note that the names written in italics are important usurpers, and that the dates do not necessarily correspond to an ordered succession of rulers. For example, Theodosius' two sons, viz., Arcadius and Honorius, were Augusti during the lifetime of their imperial father.

WEST	EAST
Valentinian II (375–392)	Theodosius I (379–395)
Magnus Maximus (383–388)	
Eugenius (392–394)	
Theodosius I (394–395)	Arcadius (383–408)
Honorius (393–423)	Theodosius II (402–450)
Constantine III (407–411)	
Constantius III (421)	
John (Iohannes) (423–424)	
Valentinian III (425–455)	

[11] Sabbah 1980, 146.

[12] We know nothing of the life or identity of this particular Flavius Eutropius.

[13] Lang 1885, vi.

[14] Constantine III was preceded by two others rebellious generals, namely Marcus and Gratian, both of whom had been proclaimed by their troops; see Stevens 1957, 316–347; *PLRE* II, Constantinus 21, Gratianus 3, Marcus 2. Constantine himself raised his son Constans to the purple. Other would-be emperors were used as puppets by barbarian rulers. Priscus Attalus was proclaimed by Visigothic kings on two separate occasions; once by Alaric in 409 (Zos. 6.7.1; Sozom. 9.8.2), and again by Athaulf in 414. Jovinus was proclaimed Augustus by the Burgundian Gundahar and the Alan Goar in 412 and, in the following year, made his brother Sebastianus a colleague (Olympiod. frgs. 18, 20; on this, see Matthews 1975, 313–315). Even more bizarre is the case of Gerontius, a general of Constantine and Constans, who, after revolting against the two 'Augusti' (409 or 411), did not proclaim himself emperor but conferred that honour on an individual called Maximus. On Gerontius, see Demougeot 1951, 454 n. 71; O'Flynn 1983, 64, 170 n. 3; Seeck 1912, 1270; Stevens 1957, 343 and n. 159.

From this list, we might readily exclude Constantius III, husband of Galla
Placidia and the father of the future emperor Valentinian III. This individual,
Stilicho's[15] replacement and western generalissimo from 410–421, was Augustus for only a year. In any case, Honorius, at the time, was senior Augustus of the
West. The *Epitoma*, if it had been composed during the period of Constantius'
military pre-eminence, would probably have been submitted to Honorius rather
than to his 'junior' colleague.[16] It is always pertinent to note that Vegetius addresses his work to an *imperator inuictus*, not *imperatores inuicti*. Of the more
significant western usurpers, Eugenius and John might readily be excluded, if
only because they enjoyed power for a very short time. Maximus, though proclaimed Augustus by his troops in 383, only took Italy in 387, the year in which
Valentinian II was forced to flee to Constantinople. It is unlikely that Vegetius
would have presented his work to an emperor who did not control one of the
imperial seats (viz., Rome, Milan or Ravenna in the West, or Constantinople in
the East). Constantine III deserves little attention, for our author would have
surely viewed Honorius as the legitimate ruler of the West. His official tenure of
the purple, in any case, was ephemeral. This leaves us with six principal contenders, viz., Theodosius I, Valentinian II, Honorius, Arcadius, Theodosius II and
Valentinian III.

Önnerfors, the editor of the latest Teubner edition of the text, disappointingly
offers little to the debate.[17] Reeve might be said to do likewise in his recent
Oxford edition.[18] But many authorities, as mentioned above, have suggested that
the emperor to whom the work was addressed is Theodosius I, emperor of the
East and emperor of the whole Empire from 394–395.[19] Indeed, as Goffart relates, "the opinion most actively expressed at present [at least in 1977] is that the
De re militari [*sic*] was a late fourth-century production meant for the eyes of

---

[15] As Cameron (1970, xiii) points out, 'Stilico' is probably the more correct orthography,
but 'Stilicho' is used throughout this work owing to its greater frequency in scholarly literature.

[16] Constantius, of course, was older than Honorius.

[17] In his brief treatment of the *termini*, Önnerfors (1995, vi) writes "de ea quaestione ...
maxima est inter uiros doctos dissensio; ex ipso opere re uera nihil certi concludi licet"; see also
vi n. 4: "complexus sum", with id. 1991, 150–151, where Önnerfors concludes that we have
"Eine sehr breite Palette von komplexen Theorien, die für den Militärhistoriker sicherlich von
größerer Gewichtigkeit sind als für den Philologen .... Hier soll kein Versuch unternommen
werden, in der leidigen 'Kaiserfrage' Stellung zu beziehen".

[18] Reeve 2003, see especially vi–viii.

[19] e.g., Barnes 1979, 255; Baatz 1997, 5; Bennett 1991, 59; Degen 1992, 139–140; Formisano 2003, 10; Gauld 1990, 402–403; Harvey 1937, 444; Jähns 1966, 110; Lippold 1980, 150–151,
166, 199 ("um 390"); MacCracken 1913, 390 (see also 390 n. 1); Neumann 1965, 992–993;
Paschoud 1967, 110; Planck 1877, 53; Richardot 2003, 537; Sabbah 1980, 131–155; id. 2004,
32; Schöner 1888, 34–44; Sherwood 1980, 18–19; Shrader 1979, 280; id. 1976, 9, 11–12; id.
1981, 168 (on this occasion, however, he does qualify his assertion with "probably"); Silhanek
1972, 13; Sirago 1961, 467–475, 493; Stelten 1990, xv (yet, at id. 1968, 70, he merely states that
it was written "In the decade before the year 400 A.D."); Teuffel 1892, 400–401 (vol. 2) (since
Teuffel seems to believe in the authenticity of the heading *ad Theodosium imperatorem*, he does
not discount the possibility that the work was addressed to Theodosius II). The above list is by
no means exhaustive.

Theodosius I".[20] This statement continues to reflect the current state of opinion, especially since the latest edition of the oft-consulted *OCD* maintains a Theodosian date.[21] True, some have used the words "likely" or "very likely" when stating their contention that the *Epitoma* was addressed to Theodosius.[22] Yet it is perhaps symptomatic of the uncertainty surrounding the text's date that many who have nominated this emperor have done so in a tentative fashion, often with the word "probably" or "possibly" (or its non-English equivalent) in attendance.[23] Alternatively, some scholars, who have not the temerity to nominate a specific emperor but believe that the *Epitoma* must have been written in the Theodosian era, propose either Theodosius I or Valentinian II and invite the reader to flip a coin in order to divine the true recipient.[24] Syme simply proposes that "Vegetius belongs to the time of Valentinian or Theodosius".[25]

Even more circumspect are those who contend that the text belongs to the last decade or so of the fourth century.[26] This, of course, could mean that Vegetius was writing under no less than four emperors, viz., Arcadius, Honorius, Theodosius I and Valentinian II. Stephenson assigns a "late-fourth/early-fifth century" date to the treatise,[27] as do Bishop and Coulston, in addition to Daly and Holmes.[28] If we assume that this means 383–*c*. 425, a field of seven possible recipients presents itself, although it must be said that the reign of Valentinian III does not really belong to the "early fifth century". In similar fashion, Jullian writes that "Végèce ... écrivait sous Théodose ou ses fils",[29] while Goldsworthy offers the "late fourth/very early fifth century", an opinion which excludes Valentinian III.[30] More unsatisfactory still is the view of Collingwood and Myres – shared, amongst others, by Dixon and Southern and most recently by Feugère –

---

[20] Goffart 1977, 71.

[21] *OCD*[3], 1110–1111.

[22] Marcone 1981, 123, 138; Mazzarino, 1956, 489 (cf. id. 1942, 238: "contemporaneo al nostro periodo", a comment which pertains to the era of Stilicho); Milner 1996, xix; Viré 1998, 260. Watson (1969, 26) holds that, out of Theodosius I and Valentinian III, "the former seems the more likely".

[23] Adams 1995, 3; Cameron 1998, 686; Chastagnol 1974, 62; Dove 1971, 17; Hartke 1951, 409 n. 4; Schanz 1914, 194 (see also 195, s.v. "Die Zeit des Vegetius"); Hermann 2000, 259.

[24] e.g., *PLRE* I, 763. De Jonge (1955, 101, 105) believes that Ammianus was a contemporary of Vegetius, i.e., that he was writing under either Theodosius I or Valentinian II. Elton (1996, 269) merely states that "scholarly opinion is divided between Theodosius and Valentinian III" and that "the former is preferred here". Cherry (2001, 176) uses "possibly" for both Theodosius I and Valentinian III.

[25] Syme 1968, 113.

[26] Bachrach 1973, 36; Conte 1987, 637; Cowan 2003, 32; Dobson 1989, 221; Gilliver 1999, 177 (but cf. id. 1996, 56: "fourth-century"); Junkelmann 1986, 106; Mezzabotta 2000, 53; Spaulding 1975, 153; Tomlin 1989, 249; von Albrecht 1994, 454 (vol. 1); but, in vol. 2, "etwa zwischen 383 und 450" (1172); Wheeler 2004, 310.

[27] Stephenson 1999, 21.

[28] Bishop/Coulston 1993, 42; Daly 2002, 53; Holmes 2002, 359.

[29] Jullian 1884, 4.

[30] Goldsworthy 2000, 217; but, in a later work, we find "Near the end of the 4th century" (2003, 12).

that Vegetius was simply a "fourth-century ... writer".[31] This sort of statement could lead unsuspecting readers to imagine that the *Epitoma* might have been written in the days of Julian or, what is even worse, Constantine and his sons.

Other scholars, most notably E. Birley, Goffart, Gordon, Lang and Seeck,[32] hold that Valentinian III (emperor of the West 425–455) was the likely recipient of the *Epitoma*.[33] Indeed, Gibbon, in his eighteenth-century *Decline and Fall of the Roman Empire*, wrote that "the series of calamities which [Vegetius] ... marks, compel us to believe that the *Hero*, to whom he dedicates his book, is the last and most inglorious of the Valentinians".[34] This opinion could well be regarded as the first word in the continuing modern debate. It is notable that Müller, in his recent German translation and commentary on the text (1997), also leans in favour of Seeck's belief that the text belongs to the reign of Valentinian III.[35] Valentinian II, half-brother of Gratian and son of his imperial namesake, has also had some advocates (most recently Zuckerman), but scholars have largely ignored this possibility.[36]

The only other real contender is Honorius, son of Theodosius I and emperor of the West from 395 to 423. The case for Honorius, however, is comparatively weak and has been generally disregarded.[37] The most significant proponent of a dating under Honorius is Giuffrida Manmana, who first introduced her thoughts on the matter in 1981 and has since published an Italian edition (with translation) of the *Epitoma*, in which the case for Honorius receives an expanded treatment.[38] Other scholars merely specify a fifth-century date,[39] or ascribe the work to "the

[31] Collingwood/Myres 1937, 279; Dixon/Southern 1992, 12; Feugère 2002, 18, 90, 171; but cf. 178: "end of the fourth century AD". See also C.W. Jones 1932, 248; Montross 1960, 84; Rankov 1994, 47.

[32] E. Birley 1988, 58–68 = id. 1985, 57–67; Goffart 1977, 65–100; Gordon 1974, 35–55; Lang 1885, x. Lang, who had originally preferred Theodosius I, admitted to having been convinced by the argument of Seeck, as did Grosse 1913, 96 (see also id. 1920, 24).

[33] *Inter alios*, Frank 1969, 135; Richter 1865, 66; Rowell 1967, 304; Thompson 1952, 52; Várady 1961, 343. A.H.M. Jones (1964, 642 [vol. 2]) confusingly writes that Vegetius was "writing under Valentinian", yet Barnes (1979, 254) assumes that he was referring to the latter. See also Ferrill 1986, 129 and n. 195 (178–179). Rebuffat (1978, 832) also seems to favour a fifth-century date, for he accepts Fournel's conclusion (found in his *État de la Gaule au Ve siècle* [1805]) that Vegetius was writing in the fifth century. Dorjahn and Born (1934, 148–158) write that the *Epitoma* was written in the West some twenty or twenty-five years after the sack of Rome in 410, which takes us firmly into the reign of Valentinian III. Lindsay (1993, 41) also steers toward Valentinian III. Burns (1994, 35) holds that Vegetius was writing "ca 435", but does not say whether in the East or in the West.

[34] Gibbon 1994, 70 n. 125 (vol. 2).

[35] Müller 1997, 11.

[36] That is, apart from Oman (1905, 17; see also 17 n. 2) and Ramsay (1867, 1235).

[37] But cf. Förster 1895, 7–9.

[38] Giuffrida Manmana 1981, 25–56 (this article was published under the name Giuffrida); id. 1997, 15–45. Fischer (1991a, 288) writes that Vegetius "is believed to have been active" between 383 and 450; he also notes that Pelagonius was one of Vegetius' main sources for the *Mulomedicina* and that "Pelagonius ... was writing between 200 and 400". Fischer, then, seems to think that the *Mulomedicina* was not written while Theodosius I was alive. Of course, this does not necessarily imply that he believes that the *Epitoma*, too, was not composed before 400.

[39] MacDowall 1994, 14.

beginning of the fifth century", i.e., the time of Honorius or Arcadius.[40] If Vegetius *did* write after the sack of Rome in 410, as will be postulated, it seems rather improbable that the work would have been addressed to Honorius, an emperor who was too incompetent to prevent the Goths from ravaging Italy. Vegetius' *imperator inuictus* seems to be insulated, by the passage of time, from the military disasters that followed the death of Theodosius the Great (alluded to at *Epit.* 1.20.4–5). In the *Epitoma*, the honorand is conveniently absolved from any sort of responsibility – it is not in his reign that the problems began. Of course, that is not to say that the emperor to whom the *Epitoma* was addressed was any more martial in spirit than Honorius.

Lastly, Chadwick describes the *Epitoma* as a "late third century work [*sic*]" dedicated "to the Emperor Valentinian I (A.D. 364–375)".[41] Richmond writes likewise.[42] As explained previously, Valentinian I's son is described as *diuus* at *Epit.* 1.20.3. Certainly, the way in which Vegetius introduces *diuus Gratianus* clearly shows that that Gratian had been emperor – witness *ab urbe condita usque ad tempus diui Gratiani*. Vegetius uses the phrase in question as a period of time. This would not have happened while Valentinian I was alive. In addition, Vegetius mentions the Huns on two occasions (*Epit.* 1.20.2, 3.26.36). The Huns played no significant rôle in Roman history until they forced the Goths to escape from their depredations during the reigns of Gratian and Valens. In any case, Theodosius I and his generals were probably the first Romans to meet the Huns in combat. Chadwick and Richmond's assignation of the treatise to the reign of Valentinian I remains little short of nonsensical. Still, it does illustrate the confusion that exists regarding the date of Vegetius' *Epitoma* and the need for a more comprehensive treatment of the problem. Lastly, and most surprisingly of all, Gabriel and Boose contend that Vegetius was writing "two centuries after Teutoburg" (i.e., A.D. 9),[43] a statement which would put the epitomator at the beginning of the third century A.D.

---

[40] Wolfram 1988, 304.

[41] Chadwick 1958, 146–176. Chadwick (1968, 166), in her treatment of *Epit.* 4.37, also writes that "his work appears to be more or less contemporary with the reconstruction of the fleet by Theodosius [i.e., the father of Theodosius I] at Boulogne after the great raid of 367, and with the transportation of the Heruli and other troops to Richborough for the attack on London, in which the fleet played an important part".

[42] Richmond 1963, 61.

[43] Gabriel/Boose 1994, 417.

CHAPTER 1

IDENTITY AND PROVENANCE

Vegetius, who lived at a time when the spectre of barbarian invasion loomed large over the Empire, wrote his treatise in order to revive Rome's flagging martial prowess. Rather than a history, the *Epitoma* appears to be, as Milner describes it, a 'scissors-and-paste' mosaic of the works of others augmented with material of the epitomator's own composition.[1] Vegetius specifically mentions, *inter alios*, Cato the Elder, Cornelius Celsus, Frontinus and Paternus, in addition to the *constitutiones* of the emperors Augustus, Trajan and Hadrian. What becomes quite clear is that Vegetius essentially belongs to a western (i.e., Latin) literary and ideological tradition. But can this be demonstrated to a convincing degree? With respect to this problem, the identity of Vegetius should obviously be discussed in some detail. What this chapter will attempt to show is that our subject did indeed hail from the Western Empire and that, at the very least, his material was decidedly more relevant to an Italian Augustus than to one based at Constantinople, the capital of the Eastern Empire. Of course, Vegetius' provenance has always been an important aspect of the principal problem that concerns us here. As a consequence, material relating to this question has been marshalled together in this chapter so that the most likely solution can be established.

1. THE TWO VEGETII

Nothing is known of Vegetius except what may be discovered from his writings, viz., the *Epitoma Rei Militaris* and the *Digesta Artis Mulomedicinae*, the latter being a veterinary work on the care of livestock.[2] One might well ask why the two works are attributed to authors of different names, thus Flavius Vegetius Renatus and Publius Vegetius Renatus for the *Epitoma* and *Mulomedicina* respectively. As is well known, the name Flavius, in the Late Empire, indicated that its bearer belonged to the imperial civil service, or was a military officer. Much work has been done on this theme.[3] The appearance of Flavius in connection with the

---

[1] Milner 1996, xv–xvi; see also ch. 7 of the same work. Paschoud (1967, 111) agrees: "[l'Abrégé d'art militaire est] ... une mosaïque d'extraits qu'il résume, compile, contamine". Cf. Schenk 1930, 5, 60–61.

[2] The standard edition of the text remains Lommatzsch 1903.

[3] Cameron 1988, 26–33; Keenan 1973, 33–63; id. 1974, 283–304; id. 1983, 245–250; Mócsy 1964, 257–263.

Epitoma and not with the veterinary work may signify that the former was written by Vegetius as *comes* (as manuscript tradition tells us), and that the latter was composed on his own private account. This seems feasible enough.

Vegetius' full name, then, may have been Flavius Publius Vegetius Renatus, or simply Publius Vegetius Renatus. For Cameron, Flavius became "little more than a courtesy title functioning something like Mr in Modern English usage".[4] What is even more important for the present discussion is that Cameron's research has led him to conclude that

> there is ... an unusually large and unanimous body of evidence suggesting that Flavius was correctly used with the diacritical name alone. Thus Fl. Symmachus, but not Q. Fl. Aurelius Symmachus; Fl. Senator, but not Fl. Magnus Aurelius Cassiodorus Senator.[5]

This line of reasoning helps to explain why Publius went missing from our subject's name, but not why we are left with Vegetius and Renatus. Despite this, Cameron does note a series of consular men, albeit easterners, whose nomenclature reminds us in some small way of that of Vegetius, viz., Fl. Anthemius Isidorus *cos.* 436; Fl. Taurus Seleucus Cyrus *cos.* 441; Fl. Flor. Romanus Protogenes *cos.* 449; and Fl. Appalius Illus Trocundes *cos.* 482.[6] While these are obviously the consuls' full names, it is important to note the appearance of Fl. with names other than the diacritical. One might also adduce *CIL* 6.1783 (= *ILS* 2948), where Valentinian III is himself called Fl. Placidus Valentinianus: *imperatores Caess. Fl. Theodosius et Fl. Placidus Valentinianus semper Augg.*

It is not entirely improbable that, in the epitomator's case, the *praenomen* was removed from some manuscripts, but the *nomen*, contrary to normal practice, was retained. This would give Fl. Vegetius Renatus, which could obviously have been expanded to the familiar Flavius Vegetius Renatus. Despite the difference in subject matter, it is now generally accepted that both works were written by the same Vegetius, a thesis first suggested by Schwabe,[7] and later demonstrated by Schöner.[8] After a linguistic comparison of the two works, Schöner concluded that "die beiden Vegetius identisch sind".[9] I find no cause to differ.[10] Although the compilation of abridgements and summaries was a popular élite pastime in the Late Empire,[11] witness Eutropius' *Breuiarium*, Festus' *Breuiarium* (a *breuiarium*

---

[4] Cameron 1998, 28.

[5] Cameron 1998, 29.

[6] Cameron, 1998, 31.

[7] Schwabe 1913, 317.

[8] Schöner 1888, 19–25. See also von Albrecht 1994, 454 (vol. 1), 1172 (vol. 2); Neumann 1965, 1018; Schanz 1994, 198ff. This view is supported, *inter alios*, by Adams 1995, 2–3; Chastagnol 1974, 59; Fischer 1981a, 288; Formisano 2003, 8; Goffart 1977, 68, 89ff.; Holmes 2002, 360; de Jonge 1955, 104; Mezzabotta 2000, 54; Sherwood 1980, 8, 15; Shrader 1979, 280; id. 1976, 7; Viré 1998, 260–261; Zaffagno 1990, 259. The *Epitoma* and *Mulomedicina* are grouped together in Blackman/Betts 1989. Andersson (1938, *passim*) uses the *Mulomedicina* throughout his work for the purpose of comparison with the *Epitoma*.

[9] Schöner 1888, 25.

[10] But cf. Jähns 1966, 126; Southern/Dixon 1992, 15.

[11] See von Wölfflin 1902, 333–344; Galdi 1922, 229; Malcovati 1942, 5–11.

de breuiario[12]) and Ps.-Aurelius Victor's *Epitome de Caesaribus*, it seems more than coincidental that two such works were written by a 'Vegetius'. In sum, Vegetius' full name might best be written as Fl. Publius Vegetius Renatus.

At this point, it is worth noting that the words *breuiarium* and *epitome* (ἐπιτομή) were probably not synonymous in the classical world, even though the terms seem to have meant the same thing to medieval bibliophiles.[13] *Breuiarium* referred to a species of *chronicon* that spanned *ab urbe condita* to the author's own time.[14] *Epitome*, on the other hand, originally meant an abridgement of a work written in another language. By the early Empire, the term came to refer to any adapted version of a previous work – witness the lost *Epitome Liuiana*, a text which seemingly dates to the reign of Tiberius.[15] Of course, the names we give to ancient works are generally adapted from manuscript titles that perhaps bear little resemblance to the text's original name.

To return to our problem, Viré believes it significant that the *praefationes* of both 'Vegetian' works describe a similar *modus operandi*. Indeed, she writes that "la présentation est identique ... dans chacun des deux traités".[16] Viré notes, furthermore, that Vegetius uses the terms *breuiter* (*Epit.* 2 prol. 3[17]; *Mul.* 1 prol. 6)[18] and *adbreuiare* (*Epit.* 3 prol. 4)[19] "pour définer la forme qu'il a donnée à son oeuvre"; in addition, he employs the verbs *enucleare* (*Epit.* 1.28.1; *Mul.* 1 prol. 6) and *digerere* (*Epit.* 4 prol. 8; *Mul.* 1 prol. 6) "pour qualifier le travail auquel il s'est livré".[20] Viré also demonstrates that the author of the two works alludes to his *mediocritas* at *Epit.* 3 prol. 4, and again at *Mul.* 1 prol. 6.[21] Shrader presents us with what he believes to be a further piece of 'evidence' for the assimilation of the two Vegetii: "the earliest known manuscript containing the *De re militari* [*sic*], Vatican MS Reg. Lat. 2077, identifies the author of the *De re militari* [*sic*] excerpts there as Publius Vegetius Renatus".[22] Although this hardly represents conclusive evidence, it is still worthy of consideration.

---

[12] See Momigliano 1977, 85–86, but cf. Cameron 1969a, 305; den Boer 1972, 173 and n. 3; von Wölfflin 1904, 69ff., 173ff.

[13] On this, see Opelt 1960, 944ff.; Eadie 1967, 11 n. 1. Vegetius' work on military matters, being compiled from Latin rather than foreign (i.e., Greek) works, is not really an *epitome* but a *breuiarium*.

[14] See Eadie 1967, 12–13.

[15] See Sanders 1904, 255–260, which largely follows id. 1897, 48. Eadie (1967, 11) concurs. Cf. Suet. *Gram.* 10; Sen. *Ep.* 39.1.

[16] Viré 1998, 261.

[17] I have used the abbreviation 'prol.' instead of '*praef.*' throughout this volume in order to accord with Reeve's 2004 edition of the *Epitoma* (the text of which I have generally followed), and because Lommatzsch's 1903 edition of the *Mulomedicina* does likewise. Despite this, I have often used *praefatio/praefationes* in the text when discussing Latin works, and 'prologue/prologues' when dealing with Greek ones.

[18] Festus also uses this word in his *Breuiarium* (3.1) in order to stress the nature of his work (witness *breuiter intimabo*); see den Boer 1972, 175.

[19] Önnerfors (1995, *ad loc.*) and Reeve (2004, *ad loc.*) prefer *adbreuiare*, while Stelten (1990, *ad loc.*) elects *abbreuiare*.

[20] Viré 1998, 261.

[21] Viré 1998, 261 and n. 9.

[22] Shrader 1976, 8. See Lang 1885, xi.

Generally accepted, too, is that Vegetius was not a military man.[23] Indeed, Vegetius disclaims any personal knowledge of military affairs and only claims to be compiling relevant military information from earlier material.[24] From manuscript *subscriptiones* – which may be apocryphal – we discover that Vegetius was supposedly a *uir inlustris* (or *illustris*) and *comes*. Using the version of *comes* found in MS Vat. Lat. 4497, Schöner argues that Vegetius held the rank of *comes sacrarum largitionum*.[25] If this is so, the titles *uir inlustris* and *comes* are compatible, something which adds a degree of authenticity to the *subscriptiones* in question. Even if Schöner's identification of Vegetius as an imperial finance minister is inaccurate, we should remember that the rank of *comes*, the frequent appearance of which perhaps adds some small weight to its authenticity, was reserved either for senior members of the imperial bureaucracy, or for military chiefs of staff.[26] That Vegetius was a man of some financial means is difficult to refute. With the aid of the scant information provided by the *Epitoma*, we may conclude, with a fair degree of confidence, that he was a bureaucrat of some importance.[27] Still, it is not necessary for the present purpose to nominate precisely which post Vegetius held in the rather complex imperial administration of the Late Empire.

2. VEGETIUS THE FAITHFUL

One might immediately think that religion would have little to do with military matters in the late fourth and fifth century, yet one should not underestimate the importance of faith to both soldier and commander. The religiosity of Vegetius poses no apparent problems. He was some sort of Christian.[28] Whether he took his purported faith seriously is another matter entirely. It will be well to review some instances in the *Epitoma* where references to Christianity are found.[29]

The epitomator's first reference to divinity, in the *praefatio* of book 1, does not indicate anything, other than that he acknowledges the existence of a god (or

[23] On this, see Gordon 1974, 45; Grosse 1913, 96; Paschoud 1967, 112ff.; Schöner 1888, 12. Shrader (1976, 9–10) holds that, while Vegetius had "no practical military experience and held no high office", his position as *comes sacrarum largitionum* enabled him to gain some knowledge of military matters ("such as recruiting"). Cf. Silhanek 1972, 1, 8 and n. 15.

[24] See Veg. *Epit.* 1 prol. 3–4, 1.8.7–12, 1.28.1, 2 prol. 2–3, 2.3.8, 2.4.1–4, 3.6.1.

[25] Schöner 1888, 9: "Reichsfinanzminister". Shrader (1976, 9; 1979, 280) concurs, while similar thoughts are expressed at Sherwood 1980, 17.

[26] See A.H.M. Jones (1964, 104–105 [vol. 1]). As Jones relates, "Constantine was the first to bestow the title [of *comes*] by official codicil". Of course, the companions of the emperor had always been styled, in a rather semi-official fashion, *comites*.

[27] Goffart (1977, 88) writes that Vegetius was a "government official of highest rank".

[28] Shrader (1976, 6–7) holds that "internal evidence suggests that Vegetius was a Christian or was at least familiar with that faith". Mazzarino (1956, 488) writes that "Vegezio è, almeno formalmente, cristiano". See also Formisano 2003, 9; Müller 1997, 11 n. 8.

[29] In addition, Vegetius tells us, at *Epit.* 3.5.4, that '*Deus nobiscum*' is the sort of phrase that one might employ as a *signum uocale*. Likewise, he writes, at *Epit.* 4.40.5, that the course of heavenly bodies is dictated *Dei arbitrio creatoris*.

'God') – witness the presence of *Deus* (*Epit.* 1 prol. 1). Much has been made of Vegetius' description of a military oath. The relevant passage reads as follows:

> [milites] ... iurare solent, et ideo militiae sacramenta dicuntur. iurant autem per Deum et Christum et Sanctum Spiritum et per maiestatem imperatoris, quae secundum Deum generi humano diligenda est et colenda. nam imperator cum Augusti nomen accepit, tamquam praesenti et corporali Deo fidelis est praestanda deuotio et impendendus peruigil famulatus; Deo enim uel priuatus uel militans seruit cum fideliter eum diligit qui Deo regnat auctore (*Epit.* 2.5.2–4).[30]

Stelten, for one, finds it difficult to understand how such an oath could have had any meaning to those who took it:

> It is extremely difficult to picture a Roman soldier taking such an oath; even though Christianity had entered into the lives of the Roman people, such devotion to a transcendent God does not quite suit the character of the pragmatic Roman mind. Loyalty to a Marius because he was a Marius; yes! Loyalty to Caesar because he was Caesar; yes! But loyalty to the emperor because he represented God! Is that possible?[31]

Yet it is difficult to envisage what other oath the soldiers could have taken. The *milites* would certainly not have been allowed to swear allegiance to their individual commanders as in Republican times – such a suggestion would have been tantamount to treason. Rather, imperial troops would have had to swear in the name of their *imperator*. This is only to be expected, for "the soldier was bound to the legitimately reigning Emperor in a very personal way by the military oath, the *sacramentum militare*"[32] – a procedure which had been the norm since Augustus' reign. But swearing in the name of the three persons of the Trinity? The reference to *per Deum et Christum et Sanctum Spiritum* should not seem as puzzling as Stelten would have us believe. Christianity had been the official religion of the Empire since the days of Constantine.[33] So why should it surprise that soldiers had to swear by what was, to all intents and purposes, the state god? Such a connection must have intensified under Theodosius I, the emperor who attempted to end pagan influence in the Empire's administration. Since the Christian god was the god of the state, i.e., the Empire's divine protector, it is logical that the emperor would have claimed that he ruled by the grace of God.

The real problem with Vegetius' discussion of the military oath is not the authenticity of his testimony. Instead, the issue of contention lies in dating the source(s) for 2.5.2–4 of the *Epitoma*, if indeed Vegetius required sources for this *locus*. One should bear in mind that a Christian-flavoured military oath could not have existed before the accession of Constantine the Great. It is difficult to establish whether Vegetius describes the contemporary situation (which would indicate that it met with his approval) or whether he is stating a) that this was the norm in the past, and b) that this situation should be revived. The tense of the verbs does not help, for Vegetius often uses the present to describe situations that

---

[30] On the oath, see Förster 1879, 6–7.
[31] Stelten 1990, xviii. This repeats almost verbatim what he had written at id. 1968, 71.
[32] Rowell 1967, 304.
[33] With a brief lapse, of course, during the reign of Julian the Apostate.

most certainly did not exist at the time of the *Epitoma*'s composition. So what *can* we make of *iurant per Deum* etc.? Was this still the case when Vegetius wrote his treatise?

There is no evidence that the tradition of a Christian-flavoured military oath had lapsed by the time of the *Epitoma*'s composition. Indeed, it is far more likely that soldiers would have sworn such an oath at the close of the fourth century (if it is accepted that the work *was* written under Theodosius I or Honorius), or in the fifth century, rather than in the reign of Constantine the Great and his immediate successors. After all, the Christian faith, in the first half of the fourth century, was yet to acquire the singular importance that it evidently enjoyed by the time of Vegetius. One should also consider that, if such an oath had been sworn in the past, yet was now in disuse, this would indicate that the influence of Christianity had waned. This was hardly the case from the reign of Theodosius onwards. Apart from the 'reign' of Eugenius, the orthodox Christian faith went from strength to strength. The problem remains: when would Vegetius' military oath have come into being? Would Theodosius I have ever demanded such an oath? This was possible in the East, but the same could hardly be said about the much more religiously diverse West of the late fourth century. With this presumably in mind, Rowell holds that the oath properly belongs to a fifth-century context and contends that the form of the *sacramentum militare* of Ammianus' day, i.e., that of Theodosius I, may be ascertained if the Christian elements of the Vegetian oath are removed.[34] Unfortunately, Rowell refrains from explaining his conclusions.[35]

A final point regarding religiosity must be made. In the introduction to his German translation of the text, Müller draws our attention to a passage from the *Epitoma* where reference is made to gladiatorial combat: *palorum enim usus non solum militibus sed etiam gladiatoribus plurimum prodest* (1.11.3). He places this in the context of Vegetius' faith.[36] Müller believes that the reference to gladiators, which he thinks would have been offensive to Theodosius I and his immediate successors, would have been a much lesser aggravation at a later time, i.e., under Valentinian III (or perhaps even Theodosius II). But this seems less than convincing, for the statement is timeless and tells us that the use of 'stakes', a dummy-like target for practice, is of benefit to both soldiers *and* gladiators. Still, Vegetius describes the use of *pali* in the imperfect tense, witness *defigebantur, eminerent, se exercebat, minaretur*, etc. (*Epit.* 1.11.4–8), as if practice at the stake with *gladii* were no longer carried out. It does seem, though, that Vegetius acknowledges the possibility of the continued existence of gladiatorial combats (*munera*) in his own day. It should be clear, too, that his aphorism at *Epit.* 1.11.4 that *nec umquam aut harena aut campus inuictum armis uirum probauit* [note perfect tense] *nisi qui diligenter exercitatus docebatur ad palum* need not mean

---

[34] Rowell 1967, 304.

[35] Still, the oath is clearly meant to be sworn by members of Vegetius' revivified *antiqua legio*. Barbarian *foederati*, in any case, would surely not have been forced to accept the military mark – *nam uicturis in cute punctis milites scripti, cum matriculis inseruntur* (*Epit.* 2.5.2).

[36] Müller 1997, 11–12.

that gladiatorial combat was no longer practised – it simply means that no gladiator or soldier was successful who did not train with swords *ad palum*.

Of course, it is difficult to believe that *munera* had died out completely at any point during the period in question, although the rise of Christianity as the religion of state did pave the way for the eventual demise of gladiatorial combat.[37] Games in the West of some sort would not have been unknown in the reign of Valentinian III,[38] although one should take care to distinguish *uenationes* (which continued throughout the fifth century[39]) from mortal combat between trained individuals (of which there is little, if any, evidence for this period). Constantine initiated this process in 325 with an edict, addressed to Maximus, Vicar of the Orient, proscribing the practice throughout the Empire (*Cod. Theod.* 15.12.1 = *Cod. Iust.* 11.44.1).[40] But the decree's inefficacy is clearly demonstrated by continued mention of gladiatorial contests in literature, and even in imperial rescripts.[41]

So, would the *locus* in question have been pleasing to Theodosius I and his successors?[42] Honorius, as Müller points out, took active steps to put an end to gladiatorial combat. The gladiatorial schools (*ludi*) at Rome were apparently closed in 399,[43] and the emperor appears to have banned the practice altogether in 404 after the monk Telemachus apparently tried to stop a *munus* at Rome and was torn to pieces by the crowd (Theod. *H.E.* 5.26). The force of this 'ban' is debatable – Wiedemann suggests that it was "a temporary punishment of one particular community, like that of Pompeii in the reign of Nero".[44] However, Wiedemann points out that, aside from contorniates dating to the "430s or 440s" depicting gladiators in combat, the last written reference to *munera* comes from a contorniate of "410 or later".[45] This contorniate bears the inscription *reparatio muneris feliciter*. After this, no more references are found. Gladiatorial combat in the arena was closely linked to paganism and it is probably for this reason, rather than the inherent cruelty of the 'sport', that the Church opposed its existence.[46]

[37] On the last days of gladiatorial exhibitions, see Grant 1971, 115–119; Wiedemann 1992, 128–164.

[38] Grant 1971, 118: "perhaps they continued as late as 439–40".

[39] See Robert 1940, 330; Wiedemann 1992, 158.

[40] See also Wiedemann 1992, 156–157. Maximus later became Praetorian Prefect (see *PLRE* I, Maximus 49).

[41] e.g., *Cod. Theod.* 15.12.2 of 357 and *Cod. Theod.* 9.40.8 of 365.

[42] Theodosius I seemed to have been particularly keen to reduce senatorial expenditure on games, especially at Rome (see *Cod. Theod.* 15.9.1 of 384; Symm. *Rel.* 8–9, and especially 8.3: *gladiatorio muneri … sumptuum*). But this may have had more to do with wanting to reduce the influence of pagan senators (who, like their forebears, used the games as a means to increase or solidify their social position) rather than humanitarian or theological concerns; see Hopkins 1983, 9.

[43] According to Wiedemann (1992, 164 n. 74), this "depends on a highly speculative interpretation of CIL XIV.300".

[44] Wiedemann 1992, 158.

[45] Wiedemann 1992, 158. See Alföldi 1943, no. 176 (and cf. no. 204).

[46] Wiedemann (1992, 155–156) suggests that "Unlike the chariot-racing and *venationes*, gladiatorial games could not be tolerated by Christians, not because of any residual pagan rituals

Christian rulers, after all, have never been strangers to the application of 'cruel and unusual' punishments.[47]

In any case, the *locus* in question need not be taken as a sign of Vegetius' approval of gladiatorial combat. Thus Milner's observation that "Gladiatorial games called forth no sanctimonious denunciation from Vegetius" (which he sees as a further indication that the text could not have been written after Honorius' closed the *ludi*) has little relevance.[48] Vegetius is not interested in throwing criminals to the lions. He is concerned primarily with swordsmanship. It is for this reason – and this reason alone – that he introduces gladiators into the *Epitoma*. The gladiator, i.e., a man who fights with the *gladius* (as the word originally meant),[49] obviously needed to be adept at his deadly craft. Vegetius hopes that Rome's soldiery, by employing the traditional military and gladiatorial exercise of fighting *ad palum*, might regain the skill-level of the past. He does not condone the bloodshed of the arena. Rather, he is merely referring to what one might anachronistically call 'fencing'. In view of this, it hardly seems fitting to use *Epit.* 1.11.3 as evidence for the text's date.

3. DEDICATIONS AND MANUSCRIPT TRADITION

Vegetius dedicated his text to a ruler who is addressed, among other titles, as *imperator inuictus* (*Epit.* 1 prol. 6, 1.28.1, 2 prol. 2, 2.18.4, 3 prol. 4, 3.26.35, 4.31.1) and *domitor omnium gentium barbararum* (*Epit.* 2 prol. 4).[50] Unfortunately, the name of Vegetius' emperor has survived in only a few of the extant manuscripts. And what has survived, viz., *ad Iustinianum, ad Theodosium* and *ad Valentinianum*, is of very little use. The dedication *ad Iustinianum*, which undoubtedly refers to the Byzantine emperor Justinian I (*regnauit* 527–565), is certainly an anachronistic interpolation. That the text was dedicated to the seventh-century Byzantine ruler Justinian II (*regnauit* 685–695) is even more fanciful. Indeed, almost all the scholarly output on Vegetius' *Epitoma* completely ignores this dedication, for a sixth-century date is little short of ludicrous and can readily be set aside.

... but because they usurped the symbolism of Christian religious sacraments in providing salvation". But cf. Prudent. *c. Symm.* 1.379ff., where we are told that gladiators are "sacrificed" to the god of the underworld (*terrifici scelerata sacraria Ditis*).

[47] For example, while Constantine the Great disapproved of *munera*, he apparently had no qualms about sending captured prisoners of war to the beasts; see *Pan. Lat.* 12(9).23.3.

[48] Milner 1996, xl. Milner also observes that "this type of entertainment was dying out after 410 even in Rome".

[49] For example, the well-known Thracians, *murmillones* (or *mirmillones*, pre-Augustus: *galli*) and *secutores* fought with sword and shield. Other types of 'gladiator' used a variety of weapons including tridents, nets and lances.

[50] It seems that the first book was written and dedicated to the emperor, and that the remaining three books were supposedly written at the emperor's request; on this, see E. Birley 1988, 58.

Now that we have dismissed Justinian I, what can be done with the more credible dedications? At some point in the textual transmission, the title of some versions of the *Epitoma* acquired the words *ad Valentinianum imperatorem*. *Inscriptiones* of Laurentianus IV, 175 and Laurentianus II, 316 place the text in the era of a 'Valentinian', while one of the *subscriptiones*, viz., that of Harleianus 2551, is notable for the presence of the words *ualentino augusto consuli* [*sic*]. According to Goffart, the words of the two *inscriptiones* referred to above "were added by a copyist but entered into the early printed editions".[51] This, of course, must remain pure conjecture. But, in later years, the reference *ad Valentinianum* was held to be apocryphal and was consequently removed from most subsequent emendations of the text.[52]

Perhaps more compelling is that, in two of the earlier manuscripts, viz., Palatinus Latinus 909 of the tenth century and Vaticanus Latinus 4493 of the twelfth century, the emperor is referred to as Theodosius (I or II?).[53] These dedications are also found in later manuscripts.[54] Yet, as Gordon describes, these manuscripts may be of an "inferior quality".[55] In any case, there is no real evidence to suggest that such a name ever appeared in the ancient editions of the *Epitoma*. Indeed, it is quite possible that the dedication *ad Theodosium*, together with the highly unlikely *ad Iustinianium* and the dubious *ad Valentinianam*, was a later interpolation. Theodosius I was lauded by Christian writers. It should not surprise us, then, that later Christian copyists may have appended his exalted name to the manuscripts on which they were working. Moreover, that later copyists should attempt to identify Vegetius' honorand as one of the great champions of the faith might also explain the otherwise inexplicable appearance of *ad Iustinianum*.

Lang, who prepared the original Teubner editions of the *Epitoma* (1869 and 1885, now replaced by Önnerfors' 1995 text) held that a copyist was ultimately responsible for the dedication *ad Theodosium*. He divided the manuscript tradition into descendants of two lost hyparchetypes and called the resulting families ε and π.[56] This tradition continued until 1995, when Önnerfors made the assertion that Π of the tenth/eleventh century (Val. Pat. Lat. 909) was not a heavily

---

[51] Goffart 1977, 69; see also Lang 1885, ix n. 1.

[52] Note that the dedication to Valentinian is retained in an edition of Vegetius printed as late as 1985; see Phillips 1985, 12.

[53] See Lang 1885, vii; Stelten 1990, xxvii–xxviii. The *Epitoma* was extremely popular in the Middle Ages. It was also widely translated into the vernacular tongues; see Meyer 1896, 401–423; Thorpe 1952, 39–50; Legge 1953, 262–264; Knowles 1954, 353–383; Löfstedt 1976, 449–470; MacCracken 1913, 389–403; Springer 1979, 85–90; Wisman 1979, 17–23.

[54] e.g., Ambrosianus G 83: "incipit liber Flavii Vegetii Renati Viri Illustris Epithomatum Institutorium Rei Militaris ad Theodosium imperatorem feliciter"; Laurentianus v. II 358: "Fl. Veg. Ren. V. Ill. De Re Militari ad Theodosium felicem imperatorum libri IIII"; Monacensis 522: "Flauii Vegetii Renati Epitomatum Institutorum Rei Mil. ad Theod. imp. libri IV". Note the orthographical errors or, what might be more accurate, departures from the classical form.

[55] Gordon 1974, 36.

[56] On this, see Finch 1962, 22–23.

corrupted descendant of π, as Lang initially supposed,[57] but was derived from an entirely different manuscript tradition. Thus Önnerfors, in his 1995 edition, proposed that Π, which he renamed T, was a descendant of a lost hyparchetype, which he called β. In order to accord with Önnerfors' new stemma, Lang's two manuscript families, viz., ε and π, were held to be the descendants of α, a hyparchetype which had existed at the same level as β.[58] Still, Önnerfors, like Lang, provides an essentially bipartite stemma for the *Epitoma*'s textual tradition. In response to Önnerfors' views, Reeve has subsequently – and logically – argued that the stemma should be regarded as tripartite: ε, δ (a part of π) and β (which is essentially T and another manuscript called *Z*). This system is valid up until *Epit.* 4.39.1, a point where δ breaks off and, as Holmes conveniently summarizes, "is replaced for the remaining chapters by a fourth family φ, which descends from a member of δ (*R*) up to 4.39.1, and then makes use of a different manuscript, which is independent of both ε and β, to supply the missing ending".[59]

To return to our problem, Lang sought to demonstrate that the π-class manuscripts (I will continue to use Lang's system, if only for the sake of clarity), in which *ad Theodosium* is found, contain a large number of deliberate corrections in comparison with those of the ε-class.[60] Andersson,[61] who conducted a thorough reappraisal of the manuscript tradition, also preferred the readings of the ε-class.[62] On the other hand, Barnes contends that the issue of corrections is irrelevant and that Lang's two manuscript traditions can, in fact, be used to demonstrate a late-fourth-century date for the *Epitoma*.

As Barnes' argument would be difficult to summarize, the more substantial part must be cited:

> Manuscripts of one [i.e., π] of the two classes into which Lang divides the primary witnesses to the text of *De re militari* [*sic*] state that Vegetius dedicated the work *ad Theodosium imperatorem*.[63] There is no call to disallow this evidence on the grounds (in any event debatable) that this class of manuscripts "contains many deliberate corrections" [a quotation from Goffart[64]] in the text. On the contrary, the fact that these manuscripts lack the subscription noting a revision in the text in 450 (which the other class has) *prima facie* implies that the bifurcation of the manuscript tradition had already occurred before 450: one class of

---

[57] Finch (1962, 22–23) does not appear to disagree with Lang on this point.

[58] Still, Önnerfors (1995, *ad loc.*) almost always prefers the readings of α to those of T. He believes that T is full of *errores* and *somnia* (xxii).

[59] Holmes 2002, 360 (Holmes seems to support Reeve's conclusions and indeed criticizes Önnerfors' text). For a summary, see Reeve 1998, 183. For the arguments leading to his conclusion, see id. 1995, 479–499. Most of this material is presented in a more accessible and less-specialized format in Reeve's edition of the text (2003); see especially xiv–xxxiv.

[60] Lang 1885, vii, xvii. Lang also recognizes a third class of manuscript, of poorer quality than either ε or π, and assigns it the name λ.

[61] Andersson 1938, 1. Cf. Finch 1962, 22–23, who notes that "it is somewhat more difficult to determine the readings of π than of ε by reason of the fact that, whereas ε is represented by a number of ninth and tenth century manuscripts, there are very few early π manuscripts".

[62] See also Goffart 1977, 71; Shrader 1976, 15–16.

[63] Lang 1885, xi, 3, 5, 32, 63, 125, 166.

[64] Goffart 1977, 71.

manuscript preserves the subscription which Fl. Eutropius added to its ancestor at Constantinople in 450, the other the annotation of a scribe or editor that Vegetius' addressee was Theodosius. This scribe or editor probably belongs to the first half of the fifth century – at which date he either was or may have been in a position to know which emperor Vegetius addressed. If the name is correct, a fourth-century date follows. [65]

Although relatively cogent, Barnes' argument is impossible to prove. On the surface, it makes sense to hold that, because the *Epitoma* was edited in 450, the text must have been in circulation for some time (and had therefore become corrupted). Yet no evidence exists to support this. Dorjahn and Born, in their discussion of the text's *terminus post quem*, think that we should allow a "modest period of ten years after completion before the work of Eutropius would be needed".[66] As a consequence, they propose a window of fifty-seven years (383–440) in which the treatise could have been written.[67] Contrary to Barnes' belief, the Eutropian recension carried by examples of one class of manuscript (ε) does not mean that the other class (π) (examples of which carry *ad Theodosium*) had necessarily come into being before 450. Indeed, it is possible, as Reeve points out, that the entire medieval manuscript tradition of the *Epitoma* may derive from copies of Flavius Eutropius' text.[68] That certain manuscripts retain the Eutropian recension – while others bearing *ad Theodosium* do not – may be no more than an accident of history.[69]

However, Richardot, who supports a Theodosian date for the text, would see the recension of 450 as a direct consequence of the danger posed by Attila:

> À cette date [i.e., 450] les Goths Amales (Ostrogoths) étaient soumis à Attila et ils furent vaincus avec lui à la bataille du *Campus Mauriacus* en 451. Le danger alain, goth et hunnique dénoncé par Végèce [1.20], et renouvelé par Attila, justifiait la réédition de Végèce par Eutropius.[70]

This argument represents a *non sequitur*, for the Alans, by 450, had long ceased to exist as a separate military threat. The majority of this group had made its way to Spain by 409 and was subsequently absorbed by the Vandals.[71] Moreover, one group of Goths, namely the Visigoths, was instrumental in the defeat of the Huns

---

[65] Barnes 1979, 255. Sabbah (1980, 134) argues in a similar fashion.

[66] Dorjahn/Born 1934, 149–150.

[67] Dorjahn/Born 1934, 150.

[68] Reeve 2000, 248.

[69] On this, see Reeve 2003, viii. Reeve points out that "Some manuscripts that do not mention Theodosius have descendants that do, and these can only owe the name to conjecture or contamination". The original *ad Theodosium*, therefore, might have no factual basis whatsoever.

[70] Richardot 1998, 139.

[71] That the Alans were associated with the Vandals by the second half of the fifth century is demonstrated by Sidonius at *Carm.* 2.379–380: *consanguineo me Vandalus hostis Halano / diripuit radente.* In addition, Sidonius, describing military events of 416–418, writes as follows: *simul et reminiscitur illud, / quod Tartesiacis auus huius Vallia terris / Vandalicas turmas et iuncti Martis Halanos / strauit et occiduam texere cadauera Calpen* (*Carm.* 2.362–365). Note that the subject of the deponent verb *reminiscitur* is the Vandal foe *qui pacem pugnamque negat* (*Carm.* 2.356).

by Valentinian III's general Aëtius in the following year.[72] In his panegyric on Avitus, Sidonius devotes considerable attention to Theodoric's rôle in the defeat of the Huns.[73] Perhaps Richardot intended to state simply that "un danger" – rather than any specific danger – was "renouvelé par Attila". If this is so, it would appear that Richardot forgets a) the depredations of Alaric's Visigoths during the first decade of the fifth century, b) the danger of the Franks after their partial invasion of Gaul (c. 425), and c) the threat posed by the Vandals in subsequent decades. But the adjectival use of "alain, goth et hunnique" (which words qualify "danger" and, in particular, that which was "dénoncé par Végèce") does suggest, from a grammatical perspective, that he is referring to a Hunnic revivification of this tripartite military force. His reference to the Ostrogoths and their association with the Huns reinforces this interpretation.[74] Thus it might reasonably be concluded that Richardot's suggestion has no real historical basis.

In addition, another problem needs to be raised, viz., when was the first book of the *Epitoma* joined to the latter books? That the last three books were published separately from book 1 is easy to demonstrate:[75] *nam libellum de dilectu atque exercitio tironum dudum tamquam famulus optuli, non tamen culpatus abscessi* (*Epit.* 2 prol. 9). Note that Vegetius describes book 1 as a *libellus*,[76] while, elsewhere in the same *praefatio*, he describes his latest composition as an *opus*.[77] This represents a clear indication that book 1 was more pamphlet than tome. Interesting, too, is Rubio's assertion that the chapter numbering in book 4 of Scorialensis L.III.3 may point to a possible third military work, i.e., a *Liber belli naualis* (books 31–46 of book 4), that was joined to the other sections at some indeterminate date.[78] A specialized naval book would have had far more relevance in the Vandal era of naval supremacy than in the reign of Theodosius I. Still, the existence of five books of military science rather than four has enjoyed little modern support. That a 'book 5' appears rarely in the manuscripts would seem to militate against the antiquity of the hypothetical fifth book. If a) the separate military writings of Vegetius were joined together in antiquity (as is generally supposed), and b) there really were five books rather than four (if it is assumed that a separate naval manual never existed), it might be expected that a solid manuscript tradition of five books would be the inevitable result.

---

[72] Cassiod. *Chron.* 1253 (*MGH:AA* 11, *Chron. min.* 2, 157); Isid. *Hist. Goth.* 25 (*MGH:AA* 11, *Chron. min.* 2, 277); Prosp. 1364 (*MGH:AA* 9, *Chron. min.* 1, 481–482).

[73] Sid. Apoll. *Carm.* 7.295ff., and especially 319ff. Sidonius recounts the way in which Avitus' influence over the Visigoths enabled an alliance to be formed against the common enemy *cum rupta tumultu / barbaries totas in te transfuderat Arctos, / Gallia* (*Carm* 7.319–321). These lines obviously refer to the Huns and their many allies.

[74] Richardot draws our attention to Wolfram 1988, 262–273.

[75] Various scholars have attempted to divine the chronology of publication. Such attempts are based more on opinion than reliable evidence; e.g., Schöner 1888, 37, 44; Shrader 1976, 11–12.

[76] Vegetius also uses this word at *Epit.* 1 prol. 6, 1.28.1. He also describes book 1 as an *opusculum* at *Epit.* 1. prol. 4.

[77] This word occurs at *Epit.* 2. prol. 9.

[78] Rubio 1973, 215–219.

While the sequence of composition has been established to some degree, the period in which Vegetius' military works were welded together has never been properly discussed. Vegetius' first military book may be viewed as a polemic on the recruitment of soldiers and their training. The second 'work' (i.e., books 2–4), whilst also advocating the *consuetudo antiqua*, is less rigid in form and wider in scope – one need only witness the inclusion of chapters on food-supply, military stratagems and siege-craft. What is more, some time may have elapsed before the final compilation of Vegetius' military works was effected. So, if we adhere to the thesis that these texts were addressed to Valentinian III, it is not entirely beyond the bounds of possibility that the separate books, which would have been initiated at some time after 425 (and perhaps closer to 440), had found their way to the East midway through the fifth century and were then re-edited as a complete volume by the mysterious Flavius Eutropius (or someone else shortly before he added his subscription). A similar procedure, quite conceivably, could also have happened in the West.

Of course, it must be admitted that the above suggestion is *completely* hypothetical and is mooted primarily to expose the inconsistencies of Barnes' argument. Such a hypothesis, nevertheless, might be used to explain the words *sine exemplario*. This feature of the Eutropian recension at Constantinople has also never been explained adequately, at least by Vegetian commentators.[79] Indeed, the whole Eutropian formula, viz., "Fl. Eutropius emendaui sine exemplario Constantinopolim[80] consul. Valentiniano Augusto VII. et Avieni [*sic*]",[81] presents considerable problems.

That *libri* were *emendati* without a 'copy' or 'model', i.e., *sine exemplario*,[82] is clearly of interest.[83] Richardot provides the explanation that "La formule *sine exemplario* sur laquelle la critique est restée muette, pourrait signifier qu'Eutropius ne disposait que d'un manuscrit du *De Re Militari* [*sic*], sans un autre exemplaire de contrôle".[84] Richardot seems to suggest that Eutropius' task was to correct the (presumably orthographic) errors that had supposedly marred one example of the text, and that he did this without the benefit of a more 'perfect' example.[85] If Eutropius' task involved correcting the errors of "un manuscrit", on what basis, then, could he justify his emendations? Cameron reminds us that *subscriptiones* from the late Empire often "prove no more and no less than that Sallustius, Asterius or whoever *corrected his own copy*, usually though not always with the

---

[79] Reeve (2004, xvii) believes that "There is no way of telling what differences his intervention made".

[80] This locative is found in many late-Latin texts, sometimes in company with *apud*, e.g., at Marcell. *Chron.* 399.3 (*MGH:AA* 11, *Chron. min.* 2, 66) and Prosp. 1177 (*MGH:AA* 9, *Chron. min.* 1, 461).

[81] On such subscriptions, see Haase 1860, 3–24, and especially 9, 13.

[82] Lewis & Short, s.v. *exemplarium*, define the word as I, "A copy" or II, "A model, pattern, original". The *OLD*, s.v. *exemplarium*, gives "A copy, transcript".

[83] Note that *exemplarium* is the post-classical form of the older *exemplar*, and that both words share essentially the same meaning.

[84] Richardot 1998, 136.

[85] For some thoughts on *subscriptiones* in the Late Empire, see Cameron 1977, 26–28.

aid of a professional *grammaticus*".[86] This could also be done "*sine antigrapho* or *sine magistro*".[87] Thus the activity of recension was "at once a standard academic exercise and the normal way of checking the work of a not always very literate copyist or calligrapher".[88] What Cameron describes is perhaps the most likely – and least controversial – explanation of the Eutropian subscription, although we cannot be certain with regard to whether our Eutropius should be placed in the category of those who sought to correct a badly executed copy of a text. The earliest post-antique fragment of the *Epitoma* (from chapter 39 of book 4) dates to the seventh century – two centuries or so after Eutropius' recension.[89] We have little evidence of its popularity before that time. Other 'dark age' evidence that the text was used before the ninth century is presented by Bede.[90] Although he never cites Vegetius by name, material derived from the *Epitoma* appears to be found in several works written in the first half of the eighth century, viz., the *De Temporum Ratione*, the *Retractiones in Acta*, the *Historia Ecclesiastica*,[91] and the *Vita Cuthberti*.[92]

Traditional interpretations of the Eutropian formula thus shed some light on the nature of Eutropius' task. However, if the verb *emendare* means, in this context, something other than 'to correct errors' and is not simply a substitute for *corrigere*, the problem might be placed in a rather different context. Perhaps it was the *form* rather than the contents of the text that was revised or improved. Lewis and Short, for one, allow "improve" as a possible translation for *emendare*.[93] While the ancient *exempla* in the *OLD* are generally used to stress the 'corrective' nature of the verb, the compilers of the work offer examples where the word is associated with making a text ready for publication.[94] In particular, Aulus Gellius writes the following: *librum ... Lampadionis manu emendatum*

---

[86] Cameron 1977, 26–27. These thoughts are repeated at id. 2004, 504.

[87] Cameron 2004, 504.

[88] Cameron 1977, 27.

[89] Lang 1885, xi, xxxiii. Shrader (1976, 18) notes that "The only extant fragment of Vegetius' *De re militari* [*sic*] which antedates the Carolingian era is a short extract contained on ff. 99v–100v of Vatican MS Reg. Lat. 2077, a seventh century book written in uncials with a fourth or fifth century palimpsest of Cicero's *Verrines* in rustic capitals beneath one portion". On this, see also Reeve 2004, xi–xii; Reynolds 1983, xvi.

[90] See C.W. Jones 1932, 248–249; Shrader 1976, 19–20.

[91] According to C.W. Jones (1932, 248–249), a quotation from *Epit.* 4.35–36 appears at *De Temp. Rat.* 28; a quotation from *Epit.* 2.25 appears at *Retract. in Acta* 28; and a paraphrase of *Epit.* 1.24 appears at *Hist. Eccles.* 1.5. Familiarity with *Epit.* 4.42.2 may also be divined at *De Temp. Rat.* 29.

[92] Ogilvy (1967, 254) observes that Bede quotes Vegetius at *Vita Cuthberti* 17, as does Colgrave 1940, 214. Furthermore, Ogilvy (1967, 254) points out that Alcuin of York, writing in Charlemagne's time, also used the *Epitoma*.

[93] Lewis & Short, s.v. *emendo*.

[94] *OLD*, s.v. *emendo* 2. Some particularly fine examples of this sense of the verb are presented by the following: Val. Max. 4.1.10a: *in publicis tabulis ... carmen emendari iussit*; Quint. *Inst.* 7.6.11: *cum emendaret testamentum*; Mart. 6.64.6: *emendare meos ... libellos*; Pliny, *Ep.* 4.26.1: *petis ut libellos meos, quos studiosissime comparasti, recognoscendos emendandosque curem.*

(*N.A.* 18.5.11). Now C. Octavius Lampadio is said to have edited the *Bellum Punicum* of Naevius and, in doing so, divided the poem *in septem libros* from what was previously one continuous volume (Suet. *Gram.* 2). This represents a not dissimilar action to Eutropius' hypothetical work on the Vegetian text.

So, Eutropius' use of *emendare* need not necessarily be associated with the correction of errors (although this, considering the inclusion of *sine exemplario*, does remain by far the most likely possibility). What, then, might one deduce from this? Two admittedly tenuous possibilities are as follows: a) that book 1 was joined together in 450 or thereabouts with the other military books, and b) that the text, if it had already been put into its present form, was augmented by the inclusion of chapter headings, tables of contents, etc.[95] While there is, of course, no evidence that the chapter headings and sequence of the books were not the product of the work's original author, the fact that the books of the *Epitoma* are most definitely numbered 1–4 in the vast majority of the extant manuscripts *does* indicate that further work was carried out on the Vegetian military corpus as a whole after the initially separate publication of what we now denominate book 1 and books 2–4 (something which happened with countless other works in antiquity). Obviously, we will never know the time frame in which these activities were carried out. However, the various conjectures presented above clearly demonstrate that alternative histories for the compilation and emendation of the *Epitoma* are not necessarily *completely* misguided. Barnes' version of the supposed "bifurcation of the manuscript tradition" is just one of many possible scenarios. It can hardly be cited as firm evidence that the text was written in the fourth century.

Even if we accept the apparently dubious reading of Lang's π-class manuscripts, to which of the two Theodosii does *ad Theodosium* refer? Goffart holds that "the attribution would perhaps have to be decided by establishing whether Vegetius wrote for an eastern or a western emperor".[96] Certainly, it is not impossible that a military treatise, though written in Latin rather than in Greek, could have been meant for an emperor of the East. Indeed, the dynasty in the East, at the time, was Latin-speaking.[97] Thus if we use the criterion of language alone (which, in any case, would seem rather ill advised), there is no real reason to exclude any of the eastern emperors from our list of candidates. In particular, this consideration does not allow us to discount Theodosius II, who reigned in the East from 408 to 450. Despite this, it is most widely held that the *Epitoma* was directed to an emperor of the West. This is the view adopted here.[98]

[95] It is pertinent to note that Shrader (1976, 15) holds that "It was probably at that time [i.e., 450] that the chapters were provided with summaries". This statement is repeated by the same author in a later work (1979, 282). On the chapter headings, see also Schröder 1999, 144–145; Reeve 2000, 276–277. Reeves' brief discussion of the chapter headings and accompanying tables appears to be inconclusive, and he himself writes that "The answer ... remains *non liquet*" (2000, 277). These thoughts are repeated at id. 2004, xxxviii.

[96] Goffart 1977, 71.

[97] On the continued use of Latin at Constantinople, see Dagron 1969, 23–56.

[98] For an overview of the various arguments for a western rather than eastern emperor, see Goffart 1977, 82ff.

Silhanek, however, is a marked exception. He attempts to demonstrate the eastern origin of the *Epitoma* on the basis of two separate and highly implausible arguments.[99] First, he writes that Vegetius must have lived in the East because of his "relationship with the emperor Theodosius".[100] He goes on to claim that, if "[Vegetius] ... remained in Theodosius' retinue from the time of Gratian's death through the composition and publication of the *Epitoma*, he would have lived more in Thessalonika and Constantinople than in Rome".[101] According to Silhanek, this was because "Theodosius made these cities his capitals while he was gaining a rapprochement with the Goths".[102] That Vegetius was in the "retinue" of Theodosius I cannot be proved, a factor which relegates the first argument to the realm of historical fiction.

Second, Silhanek attempts to show that the *Epitoma* was written in Constantinople: "three of [the] manuscripts speak distinctly of 'Our Officer in Constantinople', *Comitem Constantinopolitanum Nostrum*".[103] This represents rather dubious evidence, especially when one remembers that some manuscripts dedicate the text *ad Theodosium*, and that others bear *ad Valentinianum* (in addition to dedications to more improbable rulers). Moreover, the three fourteenth-century manuscripts in which we find *Comitem Constantinopolitanum Nostrum*, viz., Harleianus 2551, Vaticanus 2193 and Vaticanus 4494, should not be connected without qualification to the class of manuscripts that hail from the tenth century, one of which preserves the Eutropian record of a textual recension at the very end of the fourth book (i.e., Lang's class ε). To solve this question, Dorjahn and Born point out that the appearance of *Comitem Constantinopolitanum Nostrum* in the fourteenth-century texts "is probably due to a confusion at some time caused by the subscription [*Fl. Eutropius* etc.] in one class of manuscripts".[104] In view of this, one should probably place little authority in late-medieval titles such as those found in Harleianus 2551 and Vaticanus 4494, titles which even Silhanek admits "confuse and combine the usual title, Eutropius' subscription [only found in ε-class manuscripts] and additional material as well".[105]

Ultimately, all that the recension of the ε-class manuscripts proves is that the text of the *Epitoma* was present in the East by 450. Manuscript titles, therefore, should not be used with any certainty to establish the text's addressee.

---

[99] Silhanek 1972, 10–11.
[100] Silhanek 1972, 10–11.
[101] Silhanek 1972, 10.
[102] Silhanek 1972, 10.
[103] Silhanek 1972, 10.
[104] Dorjahn/Born 1934, 148.
[105] Silhanek 1972, 11. *Vaticanus* 4494: "Eutropii Flauii Vegetii Renati uiri illustris comitis Constantinopolitani Valentino Augusto Consuli epithoma institutorum rei militaris de commentatiis traiani et adriani fortuni".

4. AUDIENCE AND ORIGIN

Why, then, a western rather than an eastern emperor? Seeck held that the mention of Gratian (*Epit.* 1.20.3) is important. According to him, Vegetius would not have mentioned this emperor if his work had been directed to an eastern emperor (Gratian had never ruled in the East, only the West).[106] Seeck's argument can only be accepted if one accepts his primary contention, i.e., that the *Epitoma* was addressed to Valentinian III. If Vegetius' work were addressed to Theodosius I, his belief that Vegetius would not have mentioned a western Augustus is made redundant, for Theodosius not only ruled both parts of the Empire from 394–395, but also was present in Italy from August 388 to June 391. As a consequence, if Vegetius addressed his *Epitoma* to Theodosius, the mention of Gratian would hardly have been out of place – if, of course, one accepts that Vegetius would have dared to criticize Gratian at *Epit.* 1.20.2–5. It is worth bearing in mind that Gratian was the half-brother of Galla, Theodosius' supposedly beloved wife, and the woman with whom Zosimus (4.44.3) tells us that the emperor became besotted at first sight.[107] Of course, this might be little more than historical romance. Richardot even holds that Theodosius' relationship with Gratian is immaterial.[108] Yet, as will be demonstrated, a considerable body of evidence exists to cast strong doubts on the notion that the *Epitoma* was addressed to Theodosius I. Seeck's observation, therefore, may not be without some merit.[109]

In addition, the lack of any textual reference – direct *or* indirect – to Constantinople points to a western emperor, or at least an emperor who had interests in the West, as well as in the East. On this criterion, at least, Theodosius I cannot be excluded from our list of possible recipients. In a similar fashion, lack of reference to the eastern capital might also be used to exclude Theodosius II. Although Vegetius makes no reference to Constantinople, Rome, the symbolic capital of the West and indeed the whole Empire,[110] is alluded to or directly invoked on five occasions. At *Epit.* 1.3.4, we find the reference *post urbem conditam*, which, in this context, most certainly refers to Rome,[111] in addition to a reference to the

[106] Seeck 1876, 63.

[107] Theodosius and Galla married in 388, i.e., five years after Gratian's death; see Zos. 4.44–47. Zosimus tells us that Justina would not allow Theodosius to marry her daughter until Gratian's death had been suitably avenged (4.44.4), a task which the emperor duly accomplished after the capture of Maximus in August 388 (4.46.3).

[108] Richardot 1998, 140: "L'absence de liens de parenté entre Gratian et Théodose Ier explique certainement la franchise de Végèce dans la critique".

[109] Förster (1895, 7), though he contends that the *Epitoma* was addressed to Honorius, writes that "Recte mihi quoque ostendisse videtur Seeck Vegetium et in occidentali imperii parte fuisse neque Theodosio libros obtulisse". Yet he qualifies his support with the following words: "Argumenta autem, quibus Valentinianum III fuisse Vegetii imperatorem efficere studet, non satis firma mihi esse videntur".

[110] See *Nov. Valent.* 5: *urbis Romae, quam merito caput nostri ueneramur imperii.* This Novel dates to March 440. At this time, the western emperor was firmly ensconced in the highly defensible town of Ravenna in northern Italy.

[111] Veg. *Epit.* 1.3.4: *nec inficiandum est post urbem conditam Romanos ex ciuitate profectos semper ad bellum.*

Tiber. Another reference to the Tiber is found at *Epit.* 1.10.3, this time accompanied by a description of the Campus Martius. At *Epit.* 4 prol. 7 and *Epit.* 4.9.3, we find references to Rome and the Capitol. Finally, at *Epit.* 4.26.5–6, we read that a nocturnal Gallic attack on the *arx Capitolina* was betrayed by the cackling of geese. The 'Italocentric' nature of the *Epitoma* is also emphasized by Vegetius' discussion of the Augustan fleets at Misemum and Ravenna, and the way in which these fleets controlled the Mediterranean from their central locations (*Epit.* 4.31.4–6).[112] By writing thus, our author appears to express the hope that the present emperor might effect similar naval dispositions. But this could only have been carried out by an Augustus who controlled Italy, normally the emperor of the West. It could be argued that Theodosius I had effectively controlled the Italian peninsula from 388. However, that Vegetius believes that an Augustus based in Italy could effectively control the entire Roman world from its traditional 'hub' suggests that his honorand was officially – and not just physically – based in the West, i.e., Vegetius' emperor was the actual western Augustus, and not just an emperor who happened to be residing temporarily in that part of the Empire. Theodosius I, it should be remembered, only achieved the official stewardship of both *partes imperii* in 394.

An alternative theory could be propounded: Vegetius, if he were writing under Theodosius I, may have been intimating that the emperor should withdraw from Constantinople and permanently grace the Italian peninsula. This theory has its drawbacks. A transferral of power to Rome could only have been conceivable after Valentinian II's death. It would surely have been treasonable to suggest that Theodosius become sole ruler while Gratian's direct successor still lived. That Valentinian II, although the 'senior' Augustus, was a mere puppet in the hands of his older eastern colleague matters little. Such advice, it might readily be imagined, would not have pleased Theodosius, a man keen to preserve the fiction that Valentinian II was the real western emperor. This is demonstrated by the energy that he showed in crushing Maximus, and the good faith that he demonstrated in restoring the young Augustus. It seems, then, that any thoughts of Theodosius permanently residing in Italy as sole emperor of a united empire would have been inconceivable before Valentinian II's assassination in 392. What is more, the most likely opportunity for such a suggestion would have occurred only after the emperor's victory over Eugenius and Arbogast in September 394. In any case, while Theodosius *did* remain in Italy after his victory in 394, he almost certainly never intended to stay there. It was fate, rather than any human design, that he would never again see the walls of Constantinople.[113]

At this juncture, it is necessary to consider Vegetius' birthplace. Modern scholars almost unanimously believe that Vegetius was born (or at least lived the greater part of his life) in the western, Latin-speaking half of the Empire.[114] This,

---

[112] See also Veg. *Epit.* 4.32.1.

[113] On this, see Cameron 1969, 270. But cf. Grumel 1951, 24: "Théodose serait resté en Italie pour gouverner directement à la place d'Honorius encore trop jeune".

[114] Dorjahn/Born 1934, 148. Teuffel (1892, 400–401 [vol. 2]) assumes that Vegetius lived in the West. Milner (1996, xxxiv) points out that "the name [Vegetius] though rare derives from

perhaps, is mainly because he wrote in Latin. Yet it could be argued that this proves nothing whatsoever other than that our author enjoyed what might be termed a 'classical' education[115] – no reason exists why a suitably trained Greek-speaker could not have written a military treatise in Latin. Indeed, all highly placed officials in the East would have needed a thorough understanding of Latin in both its written *and* spoken forms. A good portion of these public servants, of course, would have spoken Greek as their first language. Thus Dorjahn and Born's claim that the "Latinity" of the treatise demonstrates that Vegetius was from the West is without any real foundation.[116] In its edited form, Vegetius' Latin is clear, precise and presents few problems. Instead of 'proving' that Vegetius' first language was Latin, this could be used to indicate precisely the opposite, i.e., that its author was more a student of the language than a native speaker. Prose composed in a person's acquired tongue often seems far more comprehensible to a reader with an imperfect grasp of the same idiom. Idiomatic expressions are reduced, vocabulary is not especially difficult, and sentence structure conforms as much as possible to the author's 'mother-tongue'.[117] In sum, the language is not as 'foreign' as it might otherwise be.[118] Vegetius' 'Latinity', therefore, cannot be used to prove anything about the birthplace of the author – it is merely a *possible* indication that Latin was his first language.

Despite the above, it is highly significant that almost all the sources that Vegetius mentions wrote their *opera* in Latin. Indeed, Vergil is specifically mentioned at *Epit.* 1.6.2 (*Mantuanus auctor*) and *Epit.* 4.41.6 (*Vergilius*). He is also clearly alluded to at *Epit.* 2.1.1: *res igitur militaris, sicut Latinorum egregius auctor carminis sui testatur exordio, armis constat et uiris*. The latter represents an obvious allusion to the very beginning of the *Aeneid*. Yet Lang and Gemoll believe that *sicut Latinorum egregius auctor*, etc. (*Epit.* 2.1.1) is not Vegetian.[119]

---

the *cognomen* 'Vegetus' which is commonest in Spain, and next commonest in Gallia Narbonensis"; see Mócsy 1983, 303, s.v. UEGETUS. According to Milner (1996, xxxiv n. 6), "when [Mócsy's] ... figures are adjusted to take account of the different sizes of the samples in each western province, Spain still comes first with 34%, Gallia Narbonensis second with 16%, Noricum, Gallia Belgica and the two Germanies, and Britannia third with around 10–12%. Thus a 'Vegetus' was twice as likely to come from Spain as from Narbonensis". More recently, Lőrincz (2002, 151) records that forty-two (roughly half) of the attested Vegeti are known to come from Spain, the next highest region of provenance being Narbonensis with twelve; and, of the four inscriptions bearing 'Vegetius', two are from the Rhineland, and one each from Spain and Narbonensis. While this may be very interesting, it does not get us particularly far in our search for Vegetius' birthplace.

[115] Thompson (1952, 2–3) applies the same logic in determining the birthplace of the Anonymus, the author of the fourth-century *De Rebus Bellicis*.

[116] Dorjahn/Born 1934, 148.

[117] This last factor, however, would hardly pertain to a language such as German, an idiom which places a strong emphasis on word order.

[118] For example, the introductory notes to Lang's Teubner edition of the *Epitoma* (to cite an immediately relevant example) are rather more comprehensible to the non-Latin speaker than anything that Tacitus ever wrote.

[119] Lang 1885, *ad loc.*; Gemoll 1872, 118. Cf. Andersson 1938, 27–32, where a rather more balanced discussion of the references to Vergil is provided (see especially 29–30).

Gemoll holds that these words, which he thinks must have first been written as *marginalia*, were allowed to creep into the text itself at some stage in the process of textual transmission.[120] Likewise, Gemoll holds that the words *quod etiam in apibus Mantuanus auctor dicit esse seruandum*, along with the following three lines of verse (*Epit.* 1.6.2–3), "non sunt Vegeti [*sic*]", a position followed by Lang.[121] De Jonge dismisses this sort of statement as "an example of hypercriticism" and writes that both scholars "have not paid sufficient attention to the general style and colour of the work".[122] I am inclined to agree. Even more significant is that certain sections of the *Epitoma* appear to imitate lines from both the *Aeneid* and the *Georgics*.[123] Although such 'borrowings' may have come from a second-hand source, such as Celsus or Frontinus, Andersson writes that he can see no reason "cur non Vegetius ipse Vergilium imitari potuerit".[124]

Cato the Elder is mentioned on several occasions (*Epit.* 1.8.10, 1.13.6, 1.15.4, 2.3.6). Vegetius also writes that his sources include Cornelius Celsus (*Epit.* 1.8.11), Frontinus (*Epit.* 1.8.11, 2.3.7), Tarruntenus Paternus (*Epit.* 1.8.11), Sallust (*Epit.* 1.4.4, 1.9.8), Varro (*Epit.* 4.41.6) and the *constitutiones* of Augustus (*Epit.* 1.8.11, 1.27.1), Trajan (*Epit.* 1.8.11) and Hadrian (*Epit.* 1.8.11, 1.27.1). Apart from these named sources, there are several occasions where it is possible to discern a resemblance between the words and thoughts of Vegetius and those of other Latin authors. One such occasion is presented by *Epit.* 4.44.9, where Vegetius laments the fate of unburied sailors: *qui acerrimus casus est, absumenda piscibus insepulta sunt corpora* (*Epit.* 4.44.9). Could he have had 1.2.56 of Ovid's *Tristia* in mind?[125] It is impossible to reach any firm conclusion, and one maintains doubts about the worth of establishing *rapprochements*. Stelten points out that "the need for a proper burial was a very important aspect of both pagan and Christian beliefs and practices".[126] The similarity between Vegetius and Ovid, therefore, may be nothing more than coincidence. In addition, one modern commentator sees the influence of the late-first-century B.C. architectural and engineering writer Vitruvius Pollio, author of the *De Architectura*, in certain sections of the *Epitoma*.[127]

The impact of Latin literature on Vegetius' treatise is undoubted, but what of Greek works? The only Greek author mentioned by name is Homer (*Epit.* 1.5.4).

---

[120] Gemoll 1872, 118.

[121] Gemoll 1872, 118, with Lang 1885, *ad loc.* (Lang puts the supposedly non-Vegetian words between brackets).

[122] De Jonge 1955, 104.

[123] On these similarities, see Andersson 1938, 29–31. While some of these *imitationes* are extremely similar to sections of Vergil, others, however, appear somewhat dubious and could have come from a variety of sources. Of especial interest is that *Epit.* 4.41 shows similarities to lines from book 1 of the *Georgics* on three occasions; on this, see Sander 1928, 908–910.

[124] Andersson 1938, 30.

[125] Ov. *Tr.* 1.2.53–56: *est aliquid, fatoue suo ferroue cadentem | in solida moriens ponere corpus humo, | et mandare suis aliqua et sperare sepulcrum | et non aequoreis piscibus esse cibum.*

[126] Stelten 1990, 292. Cf. Amm. Marc. 31.13.17: *sepulturam (qui supremitatis honor est).*

[127] See Capitani 1980, 179–185. On other possible influences, see Dalmasso 1907, 805–814.

But even this does not prove that Vegetius had actually read the *Iliad*, for he merely mentions that Homer *Tydeum minorem quidem corpore sed fortiorem armis fuisse significat* (*Epit.* 1.5.4).[128] Such information could obviously have been gleaned from a Latin translation, if such a thing *did* exist.[129] Alternatively, it was simply the product of 'common knowledge'. At *Epit.* 4.21.2, there is some evidence that he had read some of the literature pertaining to the 'Seven against Thebes'. Once again, this proves little. Such literature could have been translated a) from the Greek into Latin, or b) had been originally composed in the Roman tongue.[130] Of course, one cannot dismiss the possibility that our author may also have read and noted military information from Greek authors such as Polyaenus or Polybius, even if this does not especially manifest itself in the text. Yet the obvious Latin (i.e., western) slant that permeates the entire *Epitoma* seems to indicate that Vegetius felt far more comfortable with Latin than he did with Greek.

Greek script, however, appears in some manuscripts at *Epit.* 4.40.3, which prompted Lang, Önnerfors and Stelten to include the words προχειμάζειν, χειμάζειν and μεταχειμάζειν[131] in that section of the text where Vegetius discusses astral phenomena that presage stormy weather. As Stelten points out, "it is not clear what Vegetius wrote".[132] It would seem that the confusion is largely due to our author's imperfect understanding of the scientific work(s) written *Graeco uocabulo*. How else to explain, for example, why we read *praecedentes* προχειμάζειν, *nascentes die sollemni* χειμάζειν, *subsequentes* μεταχειμάζειν *Graeco uocabulo nuncuparunt* in Önnerfors' edition?[133] The plural adjectives must obviously be accusative and agree with *tempestates*, a word found in the previous line: *aut enim circa diem statutum aut ante uel postea tempestates fieri compertum est* (*Epit.* 4.40.3). Of course, an element of doubt remains in any textual reconstruction. Reeve, who believes that Vegetius himself probably did not use Greek script in the original text, provides *praecedentes prochimazon, nascentes die sollemni chimazon, subsequentes metachimazon Graeco uocabulo nuncuparunt* for the same *locus*.[134] Still, it is worth noting Reeve's opinion that

[128] See Andersson 1938, 27–28. This is put between brackets by Lang 1885, *ad loc.*

[129] There was a Latin translation of the *Odyssey* (i.e., that of L. Livius Andronicus), so why not one of the *Iliad*, or, at least, some of its books?

[130] A good example of a Latin work relating to the Theban cycle is Statius' *Thebaid*.

[131] The *apparatus criticus* of the various modern editions reveals a variety of orthography for the three Greek words, which, of course, is understandable given Western Europe's general ignorance of Greek in the centuries that followed the barbarization of the West. In any case, many Latin words fare little better in some of the manuscripts and suffer similar levels of corruption.

[132] Stelten 1990, 286. Stelten (1990, 284 n. 'i') provides the suggestion that the *auctorum attestatio*, a phrase which Vegetius writes at *Epit.* 4.40.1 (this chapter treats of the *ortus occasusque siderum*), may refer to "Plin. *N.H.* 18.57, Arist. *Pr.* 26.8, Hdt. 7.191, Xen. *Oec.* 8.16". It is somewhat doubtful, however, that Vegetius would have thought to consult Xenophon for astronomical and meteorological information.

[133] Önnerfors 1995, *ad loc.*

[134] Reeve 2004, *ad loc.* Reeve (2004, xliv) suggests that the use of Greek characters "seems unlikely". On this, see also id. 2000, 248–249.

> The most serious possibilities [for Greek characters] occur in 4.38.6–12,[135] where some descendants of δ use Greek characters, and 4.40.3, where the Latin forms transmitted cannot be converted into any Greek characters that would rescue the syntax.[136]

One might also ask why Vegetius, in those manuscripts that employ Greek script, would have included three Greek infinitives, rather than an etymologically related substantive (i.e., χείμασιν for χειμάζειν)[137] – unless, of course, he had an imperfect understanding of the Hellenic tongue. In view of this, we might assume that Vegetius *did* have access to Greek scientific works, and that he was at least able to locate the desired material. But whether he fully comprehended what he read is a matter for debate. This, however, is a problem beyond the scope of this volume.

Vegetius' 'Latinocentric' attitude is further evinced by the following statement, in which he advertises his work's *raison d'être*:

> Lacedaemonii quidem et Athenienses aliique Graecorum in libros rettulere complura quae tactica uocant, sed nos disciplinam militarem populi Romani debemus inquirere, qui ex paruissimis finibus imperium suum paene solis regionibus et mundi ipsius fine distendit (*Epit.* 1.8.9).

Note the considerable difference in ethos between the above and Frontinus' first-century assertion that it would be almost impossible to examine all the military records written in both classical tongues: *omnia monumenta, quae utraque lingua tradita sunt* (*Strat.* 1 prol. 3). One is reminded of Claudius' witticism on the occasion of a *barbarus* addressing him in both Latin and Greek: "*cum utroque ... sermone nostro sis paratus*" (Suet. *Claud.* 42.1).[138] However, Vegetius' dismissal of Greek works has more to do with cultural ideology than indolence. He insists that *tactica* have little relevance to the restoration of traditional Roman military superiority. According to Vegetius, such works can be dismissed by those seeking to re-establish the *consuetudo antiqua*. He thus writes that "we ought to examine (*debemus inquirere*) the military discipline of the Roman People who extended their empire from the smallest territories almost to the regions of the sun and to the end of the world itself" (*Epit.* 1.8.9).[139]

But why examine the discipline that had been practised by the *populus Romanus* instead of that of the Greeks? The reason is simple: the *Romani*, unlike the Athenians, Spartans, Macedonians and contemporary military writers of the East, are introduced as the ancestors of the present generation of Romans. It would be most appropriate, therefore, for the present generation to emulate the deeds of Scipio, Caesar and Trajan, and not those of a militarily inferior people who had been conquered by Rome. Greek methods, it follows, were for the

---

[135] This section deals with the names of the various winds recognized by the ancients.

[136] Reeve 2004, xliv–xlv.

[137] Stelten (1990, 286) notes that a later printing (1806) of Schwebelius' 1767 edition of the *Epitoma* preserves χείμασιν or "winter weather" or "storms".

[138] Ammianus also uses similar language, for he writes that Musonianus, the Praetorian prefect of the East, was *facundia sermonis utriusque clarus* (15.13.1), and that a certain Antoninus was *utriusque linguae litteras sciens* (18.5.1).

[139] English translation adapted from that of Stelten 1990, *ad loc.*

Greek-speaking world. They had little place in the Latin-speaking West.[140] Vegetius seems to imply that *tactica*, which were written by nameless *alii Graecorum* (presumably men such as Aeneas, Asclepiodotus, Aelian and Arrian),[141] were lightweight works of more literary than practical worth. In Vegetius' opinion, worthwhile military instruction can only be gained from the people who conquered much of the known world, i.e., the Latin-speaking Romans of what was – for the citizen of the Late Empire – relative antiquity.

The above is certainly speculative. Yet it does present a preferable alternative to any theory propounding an eastern origin for Vegetius. Indeed, Vegetius' support of Latin authors and concomitant dismissal of Greek writers suggest that he was raised and educated in the western half of the Empire. He was thus imbued with the patriotic fervour of a descendant of those *milites Romani* who had forged an Empire that, at one stage, stretched from the Persian Gulf to the Atlantic. As Goffart writes,

> Vegetius did not just write Latin; he also worked for an audience that was limited to consulting Latin texts, and he adopted a *kleinrömisch* outlook upon military affairs and the recent past. These traits point to the West as his area of activity.[142]

One should also consider the sources used in Vegetius' *Mulomedicina*. At *Mul.* 1 prol. 2, he names Pelagonius, the author of an *Ars ueterinaria*, as one of his sources.[143] In addition, we find references to Columella (*Mul.* 1 prol. 2), and to Chiron and Apsyrtus (*Mul.* 1 prol. 3). Of these, there seems to be no internal evidence to suggest that he used either Columella or Apsyrtus. His other major source appears to have been the pseudonymous author of the *Mulomedicina Chironis*.[144] It is generally believed that both the work of Pelagonius and that of Chiron may have drawn on common sources.[145] While Fischer points out that Vegetius' section on animal sicknesses (i.e., *Mul.* 1.2–20) incorporates information not found in either Pelagonius or the *Mulomedicina Chironis*,[146] it seems that the work, as Adams suggests, is largely "a compilation of passages from these two writers". Still, it would appear that the text, in general, owes more to Pelagonius' treatise, and, in particular, a version of the text (called *E*) that has only recently become available. It was previously thought that, when Vegetius departed from the text of *R*, he did so in order to correct 'vulgarisms' in Pelagonius' Latin. The present scholarly consensus, however, is that Vegetius had consulted a different version of the text, and not *R*. In addition, Adams notes that Vegetius "constantly agrees with *E* against *R*".[147] But witness the following:

[140] Vegetius, however, does praise the discipline of the Spartans at *Epit.* 3 prol. 1–3. On this, see Wheeler 1983, 1–20.

[141] These works generally dealt with Hellenistic infantry formations and tactics, with some digressions on allied cavalry units, and, in the case of Arrian, a section on Roman cavalry. For further details, see the relevant entries in *RE*.

[142] Goffart 1977, 83.

[143] The definitive text on this author remains Adams 1995.

[144] For a list of correspondences, see Lommatzsch 1903, 339–342.

[145] Hoppe 1927, 203–216; id. 1928, 7–22; id. 1933, 506–507.

[146] Fischer 1991, 364–365.

[147] Adams 1995, 7. Adams writes that "There appears to have been at least two recensions of

> Vegetius acts in ways that point towards a western audience. [Vegetius'] ... book on veterinary medicine is largely a revision in a more elegant Latin of an earlier, coarse translation of a Greek manual; such a revision would have been pointless in a region where the original Greek was easily accessible.[148]

For some reason, Goffart must have believed that Pelagonius' work was no more than a translation of a Greek text (perhaps that of Apsyrtus?), a supposition which may have been influenced by the fact that the *Ars ueterinaria* was translated into the eastern tongue at some time in late antiquity. It is evident that Vegetius' text, as Adams' stemma of provenance shows,[149] was the final product of a generally Latin tradition of veterinary science. Apsyrtus, who was probably consulted by both Pelagonius and the author of the *Mulomedicina Chironis*, represents the most notable exception. Yet, as stated above, there is no evidence whatsoever that Vegetius knew this work, which, like the original form of Pelagonius' text,[150] employs the epistolary convention. Goffart's observation is thus of limited value.[151] Despite this, the same scholar's contention that Vegetius' *Mulomedicina*, a text which is little more than a re-working of earlier Latin material,[152] would have been of little use in the East remains more or less valid. This supposition might be used to exclude Theodosius II from our list of possible recipients of the *Epitoma*.[153]

Apart from references to Rome, as noted above, and the ancient Italian fleets at Ravenna and Misenum (*Epit.* 4.31.4–6, 4.32.1), there are further examples of the decidedly 'western' slant of the *Epitoma*. By far the most important of these is that Vegetius mentions only two military units by name, viz., the *Iouiani* and the *Herculiani* (*Epit.* 1.17.2) – presumably the two *legiones palatinae* of the Western Empire listed in the *Notitia Dignitatum* at *Occ.* 5.2–3 and 145–146.[154] Although *Iouiani iuniores* and *Herculiani iuniores* were stationed in the East (*Or.* 5.3–4,

---

Pelagonius available in late antiquity, that represented by *E* (and Vegetius), and that by *R* (and the Greek translation ...)". The same scholar concludes that "when Vegetius seems to have changed Pelagonius (in passages preserved uniquely in *R*), one must avoid making the automatic assumption that he has 'improved' the Latin of his source. The truth may be that he had a different version from that extant in *R*". See also 171 of the same work.

[148] Goffart 1977, 82.

[149] See Adams 1995, 10.

[150] Adams (1995, 9–11) holds that the "format of the treatise has ... been substantially changed in transmission .... Whereas some epistles seem to be intact ..., others have been either lost or abbreviated. Nevertheless enough remains to allow us to form some idea of Pelagonius' use of the epistolary convention"; see also id. 1992, 494–496. Fischer (1981, 221) contends that the letters addressed to friends and patrons are "fictitious".

[151] On Vegetius and his sources, see Lommatzsch 1903, xxxi–xl.

[152] On this, see von Albrecht 1994, 455 (vol. 1), 1172 (vol. 2).

[153] One cannot entirely exclude the possibility that there may have been some audience, however minute, for a Latin veterinary work of scant originality, particularly in those areas of the Eastern Empire adjoining the West. And who is to say, moreover, that Vegetius, although living in the empire of Constantinople, could not have produced a Latin *Mulomedicina* for a western audience for no other reason than his own scholarly satisfaction, or perhaps because he was requested to do so by a western acquaintance?

[154] On these two units, see Charles 2004a, 109–121.

5.43–44), there appears to be little doubt that Vegetius refers to the much more famous western *seniores*. As I have argued elsewhere, these are the units to which Claudian seems to allude at *Bell. Gild.* 418–419.[155]

Other examples of a 'western' orientation, however, are of a rather more dubious quality. Seeck draws our attention to a reference to the *Urcilliani* (*Epit.* 3.23.1), which he describes as "eines ganz obscuren afrikanischen Stammes, welcher in der gesammten Litteratur [*sic*], so viel ... ich weiß, nur noch einmal erwähnt wird und ihm daher kaum aus Büchern bekannt sein konnte".[156] It is difficult to assess the importance that one should place on Vegetius' references to peoples belonging to the western sphere of the Empire. Did an eastern origin necessarily preclude knowledge of 'western' affairs, even if they were of rather trifling importance? One would think not. As Dorjahn and Born point out, Vegetius may have gained seemingly obscure and western-oriented information simply by word of mouth.[157] And could not Vegetius simply have read about such things? Residence in the East, after all, did not prevent a person from reading books or hearing information about the West.

In a similar fashion, we might ask ourselves whether an eastern author would have made reference to the fact that the *Britanni*[158] describe *exploratoriae*,[159] i.e., scouting vessels with nearly twenty oars on each side, as *picatos* (in some MSS. given as *picatas* or *pictas*[160]) (*Epit.* 4.37.3).[161] While 'western' subject matter was obviously more relevant to a western audience, the appearance of such a statement, like that regarding the *Urcilliani*, adds little to the present discussion.[162] In passing, it should be pointed out that Vegetius' reference to the *Britanni* does not necessarily mean than Vegetius was writing before the official Roman withdrawal from Britain in *c.* 410 (i.e., during the reign of Honorius)[163] –

---

[155] Charles 2004a, 109–121.

[156] Seeck 1876, 63. See Coripp. *Ioh.* 6.389–390: *sed tunc male fida Latinis / Vrceliana manus Romanis addita fatis.*

[157] Dorjahn/Born 1934, 148 n. 3.

[158] Gauld's suggestion (1990, 405) that *Britanni* is "a late Latin form of, or a copyist's error for *Britanniaci*", which could mean "personnel serving in Britain", is completely unwarranted.

[159] Cf. Caes. *B Gall.* 4.26.4: *speculatoria nauigia.*

[160] Dove (1971, 18) believes that the forms *pictas* and *picatas* are preferable to *picatos*. In contrast, Lang (1885, *ad loc.*) preferred either *picatos*, following the ε-class MSS. or *pecatos*, following the early-tenth-century Palatinus 909 (P), which belongs to his π-class. Likewise, Önnerfors (1995, *ad loc.*) and Reeve (2004, *ad loc.*) use *picatos*. The variant *pictas* is found in two MSS. (V., P.) of the twelfth and eleventh centuries (both of which belong to Lang's π-class or Reeve's δ-class). Giuffrida Manmana (1997, *ad loc.*) uses *picati*, as does Müller 1997, *ad loc.*

[161] For a discussion of this passage, see Dove 1971, 17ff.; Chadwick 1958, 163–166; Gauld 1990, 402–406; Tavender 1972, 320–322.

[162] See also *Epit.* 2.11.5, where Vegetius' association of the Bessi (a people of mountainous north-eastern Thrace) with mining activity does not mean that he wrote in the East; on the Bessi, see also Claud. *Cons. Manl. Theod.* 40–41. On the other hand, the *Britanni* were rarely associated with maritime achievement in the ancient world.

[163] See Procop. *Vand.* 3.2.38; Zos. 6.10.2 (on the controversial nature of the latter reference, see Paschoud 1971–1979, 57–60 n. 133 [vol. 3.2]). Cf. Zos. 6.5.3, where we are told that the Britons, in 409, declared themselves independent of Roman rule. See also Bleckmann 1997, 566,

no one, for instance, would suggest that the same author's reference to the
Persians at *Epit.* 3.26.36 means that this nation, at the time of the composition of
the *Epitoma*, was subjected to Roman rule. In any case, the *Britanni* are not invoked as subjects of the Empire. Rather, they are introduced for the sole purpose
of displaying Vegetius' erudition in matters naval.[164] Moreover, as Gauld points
out, there remains the remote possibility that *Britanni* refers not to the inhabitants
of *Britannia*, but to those "of the Pas de Calais" (i.e., the Bretons).[165]

One last point of interest should be raised with respect to Vegetius' discussion of the oared craft of the *Britanni*. In book 4, Vegetius tells us that the sails of
these ships – in addition to the clothes of the sailors – were *colore Veneto* (*Epit.*
4.37.5). Although this has been translated as "sea-green", there is little justification for such a translation.[166] One should recall that Suetonius (*Vit.* 7.1, 14.3)
writes of a *ueneta factio* in the Roman circus. These charioteers were the 'Blues',
who, of course, were opposed to their traditional enemies, viz., the *prasini* or
'Leek-greens'.[167] Gauld, in a discussion of *Epit.* 4.37, was moved to write as
follows:

> Vegetius' use of the word suggests that he got his information from metropolitan Italy,
> probably Misenum, since Naples is near enough Rome to go to the races, or at least know
> about them. Ravenna likewise is not so far away from the district of Venetia at the head of
> the Adriatic, after which the colour was presumably named 'Adriatic' blue. Venetus would
> have no meaning for personnel of the *Classis Britannica*.[168]

This argument for a western orientation, although acceptable to the present thesis,
fails to convince. There is no reason to hold that the use of *uenetus* was restricted
to the racing fraternity, or that it was used exclusively in Italy. Indeed, the word,
as Suetonius attests, had been in use for centuries before the *Epitoma*'s composition. A similar term is also found in the *Historia Augusta* (*Ver.* 6.2: *a uene-*
tianis).[169] It is quite likely, therefore, that the use of *uenetus* for a particular shade
of blue would not, *pace* Gauld, have been entirely unfamiliar to personnel of the
Classis Britannica (or, for that matter, any other Latin-speaking person of northern Gaul or Britain). In any case, one should not assume that the twenty-oared
craft had any special British significance, for the association of these craft with

---

571–574; Stevens 1957, 316–347; Thompson 1956, 163–167. The last Roman troops might not
have been withdrawn until some time later. On the period, see James 1984, 161–186.

   [164] Gauld (1990, 403) writes that the phrase in question "reads like a snippet of information
Vegetius wanted to display".

   [165] Gauld 1990, 404. Chadwick (1958, 164) makes the same point: "The word *Britanni* is
usually understood to have reference in this context to the Britons; but it is of course not
impossible even at this date that the reference is to the Bretons, although this, on the whole,
would seem to be the less probable".

   [166] On this, see Tavender 1972, 321, with the reply of Dove on the same page.

   [167] Dove (in Tavender 1972, 321) points out that Benoit and Goelzer, in their *Nouveau
Dictionnaire Latin-Français*, translate *uenetus* as "azure". Note *HA Ver.* 6.2, and that Magie
(1921–1932, *ad loc.* [vol. 1]) translates *a uenetianis* as "from the 'Blues'".

   [168] Gauld 1990, 404.

   [169] In this volume, references to the *HA* follow Hohl's Teubner text (1997).

the *liburnae* in military operations (*Epit.* 4.37.3) places them in an Empire-wide military context. It would seem, then, that Vegetius' *quas Britanni picatos uocant* is a purely parenthetical piece of information. All he means is that the *Britanni* call the ships that we (i.e., Vegetius and his immediate audience) call *exploratoriae* by a different name, viz., *picati, picatae, pictae*, or whatever.

Other aspects of the text might be used to demonstrate that Vegetius was a westerner, although caveats remain. For example, Vegetius appears to possess considerable knowledge of the western barbarian world, and he even uses a number of possibly Celtic- and Germanic-derived words.[170] Although it is, of course, impossible to presume that a man born in the West could not have written a military treatise for an eastern emperor, the balance of probability would perhaps appear to weigh in favour of a western author addressing his *Epitoma* to a western Augustus.[171] However, this must remain, without concrete evidence, a more or less subjective conclusion.

One might like to consider, too, that the context of Vegetius' work is most closely aligned to the barbarian-besieged West of the late-fourth and fifth centuries. The inhabitants of the eastern half of the Empire, during the period in which Vegetius wrote, seem to have enjoyed a greater level of political and economic stability – in relative terms at least – than their cousins in the West, especially in the years following the disastrous battle of Adrianople in 378.[172] That this was the case is asserted in confident tones by the church historian Sozomen (*H.E.* 9.6.1), who actually lived through this calamitous and uncertain age. The forty-two-year rule of Theodosius II, who reigned from 408, undoubtedly fostered rather more confidence than the tortured political and military atmosphere of the West – and this despite the constant threat of the formidable Sassanian Persians. Procopius (*Pers.* 1.2.8–10) records that Isdigerdes (*regnauit* 399–420), the Persian king at the time of Arcadius' decease, maintained amicable relations with Constantinople until his death.[173] As a consequence, there ensued a long period of relative peace, an era of tranquillity along the Empire's eastern borders marred only by Vararanes' abortive expeditions against the Romans, the first in 421–422,[174] and the second in 441.[175] These factors, however, can only be relevant if

---

[170] That Arrian used words such as πέτρινος (*Tact.* 37.4), ξύνημα (*Tact.* 42.4) and τολού-τεγον (*Tact.* 43.2), which he tells us are Celtic, does not demonstrate, of course, that he lived in the western half of the Empire. On Arrian's use of ξύνημα, see DeVoto 1993, 103 n. 52. DeVoto mistakenly transliterates τολούτεγον as *Tolougeton* in his English translation of Arrian's text.

[171] This, of course, would not have affected the circulation of the *Epitoma* in the East. The *subscriptio* of Flavius Eutropius at Constantinople (which is referred to above) is a clear indication that the *Epitoma* was being read in the capital of the Eastern Empire.

[172] In the Eastern Empire, none of the frontiers could really be described as permanently breached. Despite this, the Danubian region did suffer at the hands of the Goths and Huns.

[173] See also Socrat. *H.E.* 7.18; Sozom. *H.E.* 9.4.1.

[174] Socrates provides an account of Vararanes' hostility towards Rome (*H.E.* 7.18, 7.20) and writes that Theodosius II's conflict with the Persians was concluded in Honorius' thirteenth consulship and Theodosius' tenth, i.e., 422. Of the *chronica*, only that of Marcellinus Comes mentions the Persians (*Chron.* 422.4 [*MGH:AA* 11, *Chron. min.* 2, 75]); see also Theod. *H.E.* 5.38. The sixth-century Evagrius (*H.E.* 1.19) thinks that Socrates may have mistaken the actions

we accept that Vegetius wrote *after* the death of Theodosius the Great. With the above material borne in mind, a western emperor would appear to be a more appropriate candidate for the *Epitoma*.

of Isdigerdes for those of his son. Indeed, he places a Persian incursion in Valentinian II's reign (but does not *directly* link it to his reign) and records that the perpetrator was Isdigerdes – who was dead by the time of Valentinian's accession in 425. It is therefore difficult to determine if Evagrius refers to the first or second conflict. Procopius (*Pers.* 1.2.11–15) seems to describe only the second incursion.

[175] See Procop. *Pers.* 1.2.11–15; Marcell. *Chron.* 441.1 (*MGH:AA* 11, *Chron. min.* 2, 80).

CHAPTER 2

IN THEODOSIUM I:
MISCELLANEOUS REFERENCES

Upon the death of Theodosius the Great, the Empire appears, once more, to be a fully-functioning political and administrative body. While this body had been rocked by internal discord in the latter years of Theodosius' reign, the failure of Eugenius' usurpation meant that the Roman world was now under the control of a middle-aged man of proven ability who, so one might have expected, would have desired to consolidate his sovereign position and work towards deadening the pain of more than twenty years of grim uncertainty and bloody strife. But with the emperor's decease comes a reversal of fortune, consolidation turns to dissipation, and, as this work argues, we witness the spluttering collapse of the old world and the beginning of the new. Save its most mannered forms, continuity is abandoned within the space of little more than a decade. It is now a question, not of keeping the old ways alive, but of restoring them. Thus Vegetius' *Epitoma* is imbued with the desire to entrust the safety of the Empire to 'Roman' troops rather than to its barbarian allies. The text calls for a return to a military system that had not yet collapsed when Theodosius the Great drew his final breath.[1]

In the previous chapter, we examined some of the more oft-occurring arguments in favour of a dating under the emperor Theodosius I. Most of this 'evidence' concerned the identity and provenance of Vegetius and so could be dealt with together. Other arguments, however, embody varied aspects of our theme. Although they lack a common thematic thread, five disparate areas of concern have been grouped together *infra* for convenience's sake. While some of these arguments, particularly those voiced by recognized authorities such as Barnes, Chastagnol, Mazzarino and Sirago, do present certain challenges to anyone attempting to demonstrate that the *Epitoma* was not addressed to Theodosius I, many of the arguments appear relatively groundless. Even the more superficially weighty 'evidence' suggesting a late-fourth-century date poses no insuperable problems to the present thesis. Still, the systematic deconstruction of these arguments provides useful information about Vegetius' world and delivers fur-

---

[1] Williams/Friell (1994, 72) provide a concise description of the Empire at Theodosius' death in 395. Of especial interest is their scepticism regarding thoughts that the Empire's fall was inevitable and that the weakness of Theodosius' imperial system contributed in no small way to its demise. But Cameron (1969b, 270) reminds us that, while Theodosius had left the East "in a peaceful state" in 394, the situation had been "shattered in his absence" owing to problems with the Huns, the Marcomanni and Alaric's failure to remain in the territories assigned to him. Of course, Cameron's point is that Theodosius must have intended to return to the East in order to restore order and reassert his imperial authority.

ther valuable clues with which his milieu might be constructed. It is for this reason that considerable space has been afforded to this task in order that positive results may be achieved from what might otherwise be viewed as an essentially negative exercise.

1. CITIES AND SIEGES

Rome was pillaged and burned by Alaric, king of the Visigoths, on August 24, 410 when someone inside the walls of the city opened the Salarian Gate to the barbarian army outside.[2] Stelten writes that, if Vegetius had written his work during the reign of Valentinian III, he "most certainly would have referred to ... [the sack of Rome]".[3] Such an event had not happened since 387 B.C., the year in which a Gallic host laid siege to Rome and forced its inhabitants to yield a great deal of booty before withdrawing.[4] Stelten's view is shared by Sabbah: "Végèce ne parle pas de la prise de Rome par Alaric".[5]

Yet does the lack of a specific reference to Alaric's conquest necessarily mean that the *Epitoma* was written *before* this date? Of course not. The sack of the *urbs aeterna* by barbarian forces would have caused tremendous embarrassment to any Roman, especially to an antiquarian such as Vegetius. Moreover, that Vegetius mentions "the loss of such great cities" or *tantarum urbium excidia* (*Epit.* 1.20.5) could, with little stretch of the imagination, be taken as an oblique reference to the destructive post-Theodosian campaigning of Alaric, which, of course, included the sack of Rome. Seeck certainly favoured this line of reasoning.[6] Furthermore, Dorjahn and Born contend that "we can postulate that [Vegetius] ... wrote some twenty or twenty-five years [after 410] ... and in that period of chaos felt no cause to single out one example, however striking it may seem to us".[7] Others, however, would view "the loss of such great cities", or, as Milner translates, the "sacking of so many cities" (*tantarum = tot*),[8] as an allusion to the

---

[2] For some descriptions of the siege and the subsequent sack of the city, see Oros. 7.39; Philostorg. *H.E.* 12.3; Socrat. *H.E.* 7.10; Sozom. *H.E.* 9.9. Cf. *Cons. Ital.* 541 (*MGH:AA* 9, *Chron. min.* 1, 300); Marcell. *Chron.* 410 (*MGH:AA* 11, *Chron. min.* 2, 70); Jord. *Rom.* 323 (*MGH:AA* 5.1, 41); Prosp. 1240 (*MGH:AA* 9, *Chron. min.* 1, 466).

[3] Stelten 1990, xv.

[4] See Livy, 5.41.4ff. Livy puts the sack in 390.

[5] Sabbah 1980, 138. See also Förster 1895, 8, where it is held that the *Epitoma* must have been written before 410 since, if the work were written after that date, his words would have offended the "animum imperatoris".

[6] Seeck 1876, 80. Although Giuffrida Manmana (1981, 32) merely paraphrases Seeck's argument, her contention that the *Epitoma* was addressed to Honorius (who must necessarily be freed from any military culpability) suggests that she does not favour the theory that *tantarum urbium* refers to attacks conducted by the Goths under Alaric. See also ead. 1997, 21–22. On the Gothic incapacity to lay siege to the better-protected Thracian *urbes*, see Amm. Marc. 31.6.3–4.

[7] Dorjahn/Born 1934, 150.

[8] Milner (1996, *ad loc.*) translates the phrase in question as "the sacking of so many cities". This derives from his assertion (20 n. 1) that *tantarum*, in late Latin, is equivalent to *tot*. This

Thracian and Balkan cities ravaged by the Goths in 379 and 380.[9] Yet this would mean that the Roman soldiers who were unable to prevent this destruction lacked armour, as is discussed at *Epit.* 1.20.2–5. But, as I have argued elsewhere, this could hardly have been the case.[10] A date after the death of Theodosius I, it follows, seems much more attractive. Moreover, it should be remembered that Alaric's forces, although beaten tactically on a number of occasions by Stilicho, were allowed to ravage the Western Empire for many years. During this time, a number of *tantae urbes* – including Rome itself – fell prey to barbarian depredation.

Milner, however, would object to the reasoning employed above. According to him, "Rome is cited three times, no less, as the example of the inviolate city (4 prol., 4.9, 4.26), whereas this would be in poor taste, surely, after 410".[11] What Milner forgets is that the sack of 410 was the result of an internal betrayal – it did not involve the storming of the city's defences. The walls of Rome, so it seems, had proved quite impregnable to the Gothic host. Note the following passage, which Milner cites as proof of Rome's "inviolability":

> sed dispositionibus uestrae clementiae quantum profecerit murorum elaborata constructio Roma documentum est, quae salutem ciuium Capitolinae arcis defensione seruauit ut gloriosius postea totius orbis possideret imperium (*Epit.* 4 prol. 7).

This passage, which has merited surprisingly little comment, is especially interesting because it initially suggests a connection between Vegetius' honorand to some augmentation of the defences at Rome, a city which was normally the preserve of the western emperor. If the passage is cut off at *documentum est*, the text seems to suggest that *muri*, which were constructed *dispositionibus uestrae clementiae*, had protected the *ciues Capitolinae arcis* from danger. This was the interpretation favoured by Teuffel and Förster.[12] On the other hand, Mazzarino, who finds an unlikely ally in Goffart, contends that the sentence merely pertains to the defence of the Capitol in the distant past.[13] Sirago adds that the incident in question may refer to the Gauls in the age of the dictator Camillus.[14] Vegetius, then, is not referring to any improvement of the walls at Rome – he merely notes that the worth of the emperor's construction of walls elsewhere, which is men-

belief also appears to be shared by Dorjahn and Born (1934, 150), who provide "*excidia tantarum* (= *tot*?) *urbium*". Milner (1996, 20 n. 1) adds that he can see "no reference to the sack of Rome". Note also the translation of Ferrill 1991, 61: "the loss of great cities"; Formisano 2003, *ad loc.*: "la strage di così grandi città"; and Giuffrida Manmana 1997, *ad loc.*: "[la] ... distruzione di così grandi città". Cf. Müller 1997, *ad loc.*: "[die] ... Zerstörung so vieler Städte", which emphasizes the quantity of the cities rather than their quality.

[9] Sabbah 1980, 138 n. 26. Milner (1996, 20 n. 1) holds that "The cities are likely to have been in the Danube-lands, including such famous fortresses as Carnuntum, abandoned between A.D. 375 and *c.* 390". Cf. Amm. Marc. 30.5.2.

[10] See Charles 2003, 127–167.

[11] Milner 1996, xxvii; these thoughts are repeated at 120 n. 5.

[12] Teuffel 1913, 314; Förster 1895, 8.

[13] Mazzarino 1956, 542. Cf. Goffart 1977, 83 and n. 87.

[14] Sirago 1961, 467–468.

tioned in the same *praefatio*, is demonstrated by the way in which the *arx* of the Capitol has protected Roman citizens in the past. In English, Milner's translation comes closest to reflecting Vegetius' intentions:

> But the value added to the dispositions of Your Clemency by the elaborate construction of walls is demonstrated by Rome, who saved the lives of her citizens through the defences of the Capitoline citadel, to the end that she might later win a most glorious Empire of the whole world.

The error of Teuffel's belief that Vegetius referred to a contemporary improvement of the walls at Rome, which protected her citizenry from foreign attack, is thus readily demonstrable from a historical perspective. Any effort on the part of Valentinian III can summarily be ruled out, for Rome was not directly threatened by barbarians between 425 and our *terminus ante quem* of 450. No evidence suggests that Theodosius I conducted the hypothetical defensive work. Moreover, who could have threatened the *ciues Capitolinae* save the forces of Arbogast and Eugenius, men who were, in any case, ultimately successful in gaining control of the city? Valentinian II, a ruler apparently incapable of protecting anyone, may be excluded for similar reasons. The only emperor whom Teuffel's interpretation seems to fit is Honorius.[15] And this is precisely the emperor nominated by Förster.[16]

In the reign of Honorius, the only appropriate date for the execution of the words found in the *praefatio* of book 4 must lie between Alaric's first abortive siege of Rome, in which defensive work initiated by Honorius may have played a part in protecting the populace, and its eventual capture. This represents a window of only one year. Förster attempts to show that the passage in question relates to Honorius by citing inscriptions from 402–403 that allude to *muros, portas ac turres* constructed under the auspices of Stilicho (*ex suggestione ... Stilichonis*), defences which he thinks saved Rome on one occasion before its eventual capture in 410.[17] He concludes that "sequitur ut Vegetius, nisi forte elegantius quam sanius scripsit, Capitolinam arcem volverit defensam esse suis temporibus".[18] This does not convince. If it is assumed that the last three books were presented as a cohesive whole, the words that Vegetius uses in the *praefatio* of book 2 (which would have been, in effect, book 1 of the new compendium) would not seem merely flattering but completely absurd, almost to the point of appearing contemptuous. After all, the latter half of the first decade of the fifth century is hardly renowned for the western emperor's continual *uictoriae ac triumphi*. Any suggestion that this was an age of military achievement, however limited or qualified, could not have been particularly well received by Honorius,

---

[15] Giuffrida Manmana (1981; 1997), who advocates an Honorian date for the *Epitoma*, does not comment on this possibility.

[16] Förster 1895, 8.

[17] *CIL* 6.1188–1190. The relevant part of the inscription reads as follows: *OB INSTAVRATOS VRBI AETERNAE MVROS PORTAS AC TVRRES EGESTIS INMENSIS RVDERIBVS EX SVGGESTIONE ... STILICHONIS.*

[18] Förster 1895, 8.

the man ultimately responsible for the Empire's well-being. Even Claudian, if he had lived past Stilicho's death in 408, would have been hard-pressed to cast the Roman reversals in a positive light. In view of this, the lines in question are of no worth whatsoever to the present argument. Mazzarino's view, formulated in order that it might accord with his promotion of the case for Theodosius I, is thus vindicated.

That the 'Romanocentric' nature of the *praefatio* of book 4 seemingly points to a western Augustus does not in itself preclude a Theodosian dating for the *Epitoma*. Of course, Theodosius I was not the official ruler of the entire Roman world until 394 (he held this position until his death in the following year). Yet it seems clear that Theodosius enjoyed enormous power in the West after his defeat of the usurper Maximus in 388. The emperor's famous edict against pagan sacrifice and temple-worship, issued in February 391, represents considerable proof of this.[19] Valentinian II, the 'legitimate' ruler of the West, was little more than a puppet during Theodosius' well-documented sojourn in Italy during 388–391.[20] Without any firm witnesses to a Theodosian upgrade of the walls of Rome, there is no reason to hold that the passage in question (viz., *Epit.* 4 prol. 7) is proof of anything – especially of Rome's inviolability.

The second passage cited by Milner (*Epit.* 4.9.2–4) proves nothing either. It merely tells us that Roman matrons cut off their hair in order to provide sinews for missile-throwing machines. It is impossible to nominate the siege to which Vegetius refers, yet one suspects an era far distant in time from Vegetius' day. Indeed, the tale is used allegorically and cannot be used as evidence for Rome's inviolability. The last passage cited by Milner (*Epit.* 4.26.5–6) describes an instance when the cackling of geese during a Gallic attack on the Capitoline citadel alerted the besieged citizens to the danger. Once again, there is no specific reference to Rome's inviolability – the example is of military significance and nothing else.

At this point in our discussion, it is worth addressing the debate that has ensued regarding Vegetius' assertion that his addressee was involved in construction projects:

> ideo potentissimae nationes ac principes consecrati nullam maiorem gloriam putauerunt quam aut fundare nouas ciuitates aut ab aliis conditas in nomen suum sub quadam amplificatione transferre. in quo opere clementia serenitatis tuae obtinet palmam. ab illis enim uel paucae uel singulae, a pietate tua innumerabiles urbes ita iugi labore perfectae sunt ut non tam humana manu conditae quam diuino nutu uideantur enatae (*Epit.* 4 prol. 2–3).

That the emperor is described as having built or restored *innumerabiles urbes* has often been used to augment pro-Theodosian arguments. Chastagnol writes that the emperor whom Vegetius addressed had "une solide réputation ... de constructeur et restaurateur de villes", and that this must refer to Theodosius I.[21] Mazzarino and Sirago follow suit.[22] Milner notes that Theodosius I is generally believed

---

[19] *Cod. Theod.* 16.10.10. The law against paganism was addressed to Caeionius Rufius Albinus, the prefect of Rome.

[20] On Theodosius' stay in Italy, see Matthews 1975, 231ff.; Williams/Friell 1994, 71.

[21] Chastagnol 1974, 62.

[22] Mazzarino 1956, 542; Sirago 1961, 468.

to have founded or renamed a number of cities in the East, among them Arcadiop-
olis-Bergula in Thrace, Theodosiana in Arcadia and Aegyptiaca, Theodosiopolis
in Armenia,[23] Theodosiopolis-Resaina in Osrhoene,[24] and "perhaps two other
Theodosiopoleis in Egypt".[25] In addition, John Malalas, whose testimony is very
often of scant value, associates Theodosius I with an extension of the walls at
Antioch in Syria (13.40). He also records that the emperor initiated fortification
work on small Syrian towns such as Gindaros and Lytargon (13.40). Thus the
assumption that *Epit.* 4 prol. 2–3 suits Theodosius I makes a good deal of sense,
at least ostensibly. Still, it should be noted that, of these sites, few of them would
have had their origins in the Theodosian era. What is more, most of the Theodosian building would have taken place upon existing sites. With this in mind,
Goffart uses *Epit.* 4 prol. 2–3 as evidence *against* those who would identify
Vegetius' *imperator inuictus* as Theodosius I.[26]

Architectural achievement had traditionally been one of the means by which
an individual could claim a place in the pantheon of Rome's greatest statesmen.
Augustus was a prolific builder who not only authorized the construction of
magnificent new edifices, but also ordered the repair and refurbishment of
Rome's oldest and most sacred buildings – and encouraged others to do so *pro
facultate quisque* (Suet. *Aug.* 29.4).[27] Indeed, Vitruvius attests that the public
works of Augustus will provide a lasting tribute to the industry of his reign (*De
Arch.* 1 prol. 3). Likewise, Trajan's reputation as a 'good emperor' rests, in part,
on his spectacular monuments, e.g., the Forum Traianum, the Column, and the
arch at Benevento.[28] That building continued to be associated with statesmanship
in the Late Empire is demonstrated by Procopius' *De Aedificiis*, a work generally
devoted to the architectural accomplishments of Justinian I. In similar fashion,
Claudian, in his invective against Eutropius, asks *quid nobile gesset / eunuchus?
… quas condidit urbes?* (*In. Eutrop.* 1.336–337). Again, the cultural context in
which Vegetius wrote must be considered.

Goffart points out that Vegetius' "dismissal of so paltry an achievement as
the founding of a single *urbs*" is at odds with our knowledge of Theodosius'
achievements.[29] The passage in question, according to his argument, would
appear insulting if directed to Theodosius I – an emperor who refounded and
renamed several cities, yet founded only one or two. Still, refurbishment of existing defences clearly took place under Valentinian III.[30] The *Chronicon Paschale*,

---

[23] See Procop. *Aed.* 3.5.2.

[24] Malal. 13.39. According to Malalas, Theodosius made the village formerly known as
Resaina into a city and named it Theodosioupolis.

[25] Milner 1996, 120 n. 2; see also xli: "in fact an impressive number of foundations can be
attributed to Theodosius I".

[26] Goffart 1977, 78.

[27] *RG* 19–21. See also Suet. *Aug.* 29.1–5.

[28] For some ancient opinions on aspects of Trajan's building programme, see Amm. Marc.
16.10.15; Cass. Dio 69.4.1. Cf. Amm. Marc. 27.3.7.

[29] Goffart 1977, 78.

[30] On this, see Schmidt 1953, 87.

although of dubious reliability, informs us that the maritime wall at Constantinople was augmented in 439 (while Theodosius II was emperor of the East),[31] and that the reconstruction of defensive towers and walls at Rome itself was ordered in a decree dating to March 440 (*Nov. Valent.* 5.3). The fortifications at Naples were also apparently improved at this time.[32]

The same scholar holds that, if Vegetius had Theodosiopolis in mind when he wrote the lines introduced above, "he would not have made a deliberate point of outdoing this fact, but would rather have turned it to best advantage".[33] A relatively cogent argument, but what to do with the *innumerabiles urbes*? How can this phraseology be reconciled with a post-Theodosian date? Goffart's solution is that *urbs* need not necessarily refer to a city of the "Hellenistic type" (such as Theodosiopolis, the refounded Resaina) but may refer to "cities of another class", i.e., citadels or hill-forts.[34] This view appears to derive from Seeck, who thought that the *innumerabiles urbes* must refer to a kind of "Festungssystem".[35] Seeck, on account of his now untenable contention that the *urbes* were constructed by the *magister militum* Felix along the Danubian frontier, believes that the text must be dated to 427–430.[36] As Goffart brings to our attention, "no archaeological evidence whatever sustains the idea that Felix refortified the frontier".[37] Moreover, the supposed Roman loss of Valeria, on which Seeck's case rested, is inferred from what appears to be a transcription error in the *Notitia*. This is argued convincingly by A.H.M. Jones,[38] who points out that Italian Valeria should have been deleted from the *Notitia* instead of Valeria in Illyricum, and that this was the result of a clerical equivocation.[39]

Goffart contends that Merobaudes, in a fragment of the first *Panegyricus*,[40] writes that the general Aëtius, when not engaged in defending the Empire, surveyed sites for the establishment of *urbes*, in addition to recording other sites of military significance:

---

[31] See *Chron. Pasch.* 439 = Dindorf, *Chron. Pasch.* 583, lines 3–4. Note that Mango (1985, 25 n. 12) argues that the order for the construction of these walls was never carried out, for sea-walls, at least on the Golden Horn side, appear to have been lacking during the siege of 626.

[32] Fiebiger/Schmidt 1917, no. 33. See also no. 34, with Schmidt 1953, 87 n. 6.

[33] Goffart 1977, 78.

[34] Goffart 1977, 78.

[35] Seeck 1876, 66. It is worth noting that Ammianus (30.9.1), in his list of the *uirtutes* of Valentinian I, writes *oppidorum et limitum conditor tempestiuus*. Cf. Anon. *DRB* 20.

[36] Seeck 1876, 66.

[37] Goffart 1977, 85.

[38] See A.H.M. Jones 1964, 351 (vol. 3, Appendix II: The Notitia Dignitatum).

[39] A.H.M. Jones 1964, 351 (vol. 3). See also Ward 1974, 419. On Valeria and the *Notitia*, cf. Mazzarino 1942, 141–146, 152–155.

[40] This work may be a *gratiarum actio* rather than a *laudatio*; see Clover 1971, 33ff. Niebuhr (1824, 7–12) originally suggested that the fragments were part of a prose preface to *Panegyricus II*. Later, it was supposed that the *panegyricus* in question was written for Aëtius' second consulship in 437. See Vollmer 1904, i–iv, 7–10. According to Clover, Vollmer's view is supported by Olajos 1966, 178–181 (in Hungarian).

> tunc si quid a bellis
> uacat, a]ut situs urbium aut angustias montium
> aut uasta] camporum aut fluminum transitus aut
> uiarum] spatia metiris atque ibi quis pediti, quis
> equiti] accommodatior locus, quis excursui
> aptior, qu]is receptui tutior, quis stationi uberi-
> or, explo]ras (*Pan. I*, frg. IB, 2–8).[41]

Unfortunately, there is no corroborative evidence to suggest that *innumerabiles urbes* were constructed under Valentinian III.[42] After all, there is a considerable difference between surveying the sites for *urbes* and actually building them. Still, the passage in question is useful for the present purpose since it refers to *urbes*, not as urban metropolises, but as a form of military protection. That this is so is demonstrated by line 8 of the same fragment, where we are told that, because of the surveying activities introduced above, *ita ad bellum proficit etiam ipsa in- / tercaped]o bellorum (Pan I*, frg. IB, 8–9).

Like Goffart, Seeck undoubtedly believes that *urbes* means, at *Epit.* 4 prol. 3, a small settlement (of course, Vegetius would have intended the meaning of the word to be suitably ambiguous in order to magnify his honorand's 'achievements'). Although *urbs* is normally used in the sense of a large conurbation, it could be argued that the generic sense of the word is simply that of a walled town, or a fortified location of any size.[43] But, if Vegetius wanted to refer to a series of hill-forts, why did he not use *oppida* (or even *oppidula* or *castellae*) instead of *urbes*? The simple answer is that *urbs* probably held greater prestige than *oppidum*, especially since it suggested a commercial metropolis rather than a military bastion. Vegetius surely would not have considered the use of *oppidula* or *castella* in a laudatory context. What emperor would have wanted to be known as *conditor innumerabilium oppidulorum* or *conditor innumerabilium castellorum*? In any case, it seems that the two terms, viz., *urbs* and *oppidum*, were more or less interchangeable. Although the *OLD* states that the latter term refers "to a town, ... esp[ecially] an Italian town" and was often used in "opp[osition] to *urbs*, i.e. Rome",[44] *oppidum* was even used, on occasion, to refer to Rome, the very *Urbs* itself.[45] One might consider, too, that Vegetius, when discussing siege warfare, refers to the inhabitants of any walled settlement as *oppidani*,[46] yet refers to the

---

[41] Clover (1971, *ad loc.*) does not comment on these lines.

[42] In addition, Goffart (1977, 85–86) gives the example of one Claudius Postumus Dardanus, a Gallo-Roman dignitary and correspondent of Jerome and Augustine, who built a citadel called Theopolis "for everyone's safety". It is difficult to determine precisely how this demonstrates that Valentinian III built "innumerable" numbers of fortified positions. On Dardanus, see Stroheker 1970, 162–163; Matthews 1975, 323–324.

[43] See Lewis & Short, s.v. *urbs*. The *OLD*, however, states that *urbs* refers to "[a] ... city, large town". Eutropius, in his account of Trajan, applies the word to localities *trans Rhenum in Germania* (*Brev.* 8.2.2), and to those in recently conquered Dacia (*Brev.* 8.6.2).

[44] *OLD*, s.v. *oppidum*.

[45] Cf. Livy, 42.36.1: *eos [legatos ab rege Perseo] in oppidum intromitti non placuit*; Mart. 10.30.2: *oppidum Martis*; Varro, *Ling.* 6.14: *per totum oppidum*.

[46] Veg. *Epit.* 4.12.3, 4.18.2, 4.24.3, 4.25.2, 4.28.2. There are no references to *ciues* in chapter 4.

places in which they live as either a *ciuitas*[47] or *urbs*.[48] Although the frequency of *ciuitas* outweighs that of *urbs*, it is evident that the two terms are often used interchangeably within the same chapter. One might well argue that Vegetius, who sought to aggrandize the accomplishments of his emperor, would have insisted on using *urbs* when lauding the emperor's achievements.[49] Thus there is no reason to suppose that the *urbes* to which Vegetius refers are especially large settlements. Goffart's contention, accordingly, is not without merit. Even if his argument fails to prove that Valentinian III was Vegetius' honorand, it does at least show that 4 prol. 2–3 of the text does not necessarily exclude this possibility.

With regard to sieges, it is worth adding some thoughts with respect to the debate surrounding Vegetius' invocation of a twenty-year peace at *Epit.* 1.28.8. The relevant part reads as follows:

> sed longae securitas pacis homines partim ad delectationem otii, partim ad ciuilia transduxit officia. ita cura exercitii militaris primo neglegentius agi, postea dissimulari, ad postremum olim in obliuionem perducta cognoscitur. nec aliquis hoc superiore aetate accidisse miretur, cum post primum Punicum bellum uiginti et quod excurrit annorum pax ita Romanos illos ubique uictores otio et armorum desuetudine eneruauerit ut secundo Punico bello Hannibali pares esse non possent. tot itaque consulibus, tot ducibus, tot exercitibus amissis, tunc demum ad uictoriam peruenerunt cum usum exercitiumque militare condiscere potuerunt (*Epit.* 1.28.6–9).

Goffart uses the above to demonstrate that Vegetius wrote at some time after 410, the year of Alaric's sack of Rome.[50] He reads Vegetius' description of the Carthaginian wars in the following fashion:

> first, a success against Carthage; then, over twenty years of relaxed discipline (our manuals specify 241–218 B.C.); and, in consequence, disasters at the hands of Hannibal. The second passage supplements the first [i.e., 1.20] by supplying a definite term of years. Two decades from Gratian carry us to the early 400s, when another Hannibal in the form of Alaric the Goth began to wreak havoc in Italy.[51]

Unfortunately, Vegetius' language is simply too ambiguous to project such a tight chronology, for he simply envisages a continuing period of military decadence stemming from the reign of Gratian until the date of the text's composition. The *pax longa*, which, as Milner points out, "really means a lengthy period of neglect of the army", is nothing more than a reflection of a traditional literary

[47] Veg. *Epit.* 4 prol. 2, 4.1, 4.3, 4.6–8, 4.10–12, 4.15–17, 4.19–21, 4.24–25, 4.27–28, 4.30. Note that the use of *ciuitas* in the sense of a city, as Lewis & Short, s.v. *ciuitas*, suggest, is "rare and mostly post-Augustus". The *OLD*, s.v. *ciuitas*, provides several instances where the word refers to a "[a] .. state (usu. a city, or city and surrounding city)", or "a town or city".

[48] Veg. *Epit.* 4 prol. 1 (this reference in the *praefatio* is aside from *innumerabiles urbes*, which is found at 4 prol. 3), 4.1–2, 4.5, 4.10, 4.17, 4.19, 4.21, 4.24, 4.28, 4.30.

[49] The primacy of *urbs* over *ciuitas* might be suggested by the fact that the first word that Vegetius employs for 'cities' or 'towns' in chapter 4 is *urbes*, and not *ciuitates* (*Epit.* 4 prol. 1).

[50] Goffart 1977, 82.

[51] Goffart 1977, 82. Goffart supplements his conclusion with the following note (82 n. 79): "The chronology need not be very precise: twenty years from Gratian's death coincides with Alaric's ravaging Greece; the approximation implied by 'over twenty' allows the needed latitude in a book such as this".

topos.[52] Milner invites us to compare Vegetius' language with that of Juvenal at 6.292: *nunc patimur longae pacis mala*. While a *longa pax* could have existed in the latter half of the first century, the same sense of *pax* could hardly have been employed by Vegetius at *any* time from 383 to 450. This adds weight to the present contention that, for Vegetius, the phrase *pax longa* was no more than a euphemism for the relaxation of the *consuetudo antiqua* mentioned at *Epit.* 1.20.2. It therefore has no chronological significance. Only the present emperor, conveniently exonerated from any guilt by the passage of time separating him from the laxity of the late fourth century, can reverse the situation. The references to the First Punic War, a twenty-year peace and the rise of Hannibal are made for rhetorical purposes only.[53] They are used to remind Vegetius' audience that military success should not lead to the relaxation of discipline. The lesson is as follows: the martial apathy that Rome displayed between the First and Second Punic Wars must serve as a lesson to the present generation.

In view of this, *Epit.* 1.20 and 1.28 have no chronological relationship with contemporary military and political affairs. In any case, it is difficult to imagine where Goffart's time-scale begins. Indeed, what would he regard as the fourth-century equivalent to Rome's victory in the First Punic War? According to the time-scale that Goffart projects, twenty years before the beginning of Alaric's post-Theodosian campaigning, i.e., the advent of a second Hannibal, takes us back to the battle of Adrianople. This is the point in time supposedly equivalent to the beginning of the *pax uiginti annorum*. Yet how can one possibly equate the happy conclusion to Rome's first Carthaginian conflict with the biggest military disaster suffered since Cannae or the Teutoburgerwald? Goffart's argument, when seen in this light, is not convincing. Once again, Vegetius' invocation of a legendary era in Roman history seems to bear scant relevance to specific events of the fourth and fifth centuries.

2. THE *PRIMISCRINIUS*

Mazzarino tried to show that the *Epitoma* could not have been written during the reign of Valentinian III by attempting to demonstrate that Vegetius' statement that the *primiscrinius* was the ultimate position *in officio praefectorum praetorio*

---

[52] Milner 1996, 27 n. 7.

[53] Cf. Milner 1996, xxxviii. One might well compare Claud. *Cons. Stil.* 3 prol. 21–22, where Stilicho is the new Scipio, the conqueror of a second Hannibal even more terrible than the first. It would seem, to judge from the African content of the poem (written in order to celebrate Stilicho's consulship of 400), that Claudian refers, on this occasion, to Gildo. Stilicho had yet to achieve his major victory over Alaric at Pollentia in 402. But Prudentius (*c. Symm.* 2.739) makes reference to a *Poenorum dux* – obviously Hannibal – who was destroyed more by *luxus* and *libido* than by Roman arms, whereas *noster Stilicho congressus comminus ipsa | ex acie ferrata uirum dare terga coegit* (2.739–244). This is a reference to Stilicho's victory at Pollentia (on this, see Harries 1984, 76–77). Thus the second Hannibal before Pollentia was Gildo, but, after this engagement, the Carthaginian was likened to Alaric. On the above, see Cesa/Sivan 1990, 361–374.

would be anachronistic after 425.[54] The relevant section of Vegetius reads as follows:

> ideo primi pili centurio, postquam in orbem omnes cohortes per diuersas administrauerit scolas, in prima cohorte ad hanc peruenit palmam in qua ex omni legione infinita commoda consequatur, sicut primiscrinius in officio praefectorum praetorio ad honestum quaestuosumque militiae peruenit finem (*Epit.* 2.21.3).

Vegetius, therefore, holds that the position of *primus pilus* and that of *primiscrinius* were the terminal positions in the respective careers of a centurion and a bureaucrat in the *officium* of a *praefectus praetorianus* (there were four such officials in the late Empire).[55] Mazzarino states that, in Vegetius' day, the most senior official in the prefectorial *officium* was the *primiscrinius*.[56] Yet he points out that, in a) the *Notitia* (*Or.* 2.60–62; *Occ.* 2.44–46), b) a Novel of Theodosius II addressed to Zoilus, Praetorian prefect of the East (*Cod. Iust.* 1.51.11 of 26 February, 444) and c) *Cod. Iust.* 12.52.3 of 444(?),[57] the most senior position in order of rank, to the exclusion of the *princeps* (who was appointed from outside the *officium*),[58] is the *cornicularius*.[59]

The reference to *Cod. Iust.* 1.51.11, however, is somewhat specious, for it merely refers to *consiliarios uirorum illustrium praefectorum tam praetorio quam huius inclitae urbis* [presumably Constantinople] ... *nec non etiam uiri illustris magistri officiorum*. That the *consiliarii* of the prefects may be identified with the *cornicularii* is obviously dependent upon external evidence. Thus the import of *Cod. Iust.* 1.51.11 to Mazzarino's argument appears to be minimal. In any case, the *consiliarius* (*cornicularius*?) is not listed ahead of the *primiscrinius* at *Cod. Iust.* 1.51.11, for this official does not appear at all (!). But, in the remainder of the documentation referred to above, the *cornicularius*, specified by name, is listed ahead of the *primiscrinius* or *adiutor*, the latter term being synonymous with *primiscrinius*. This situation evidently continued into the sixth century.[60] Mazza-

---

[54] See Mazzarino 1956, 542.

[55] Note Stelten's mistaken translation (1990, *ad loc.*) of *sicut primiscrinius in officio praefectorum praetorio ad honestum quaestuosumque militiae peruenit finem* as "in like manner, the chief officer among the officers of the Praetorian Guard comes to that honorable and sought-after goal in the service". Goffart (1977, 72) prefers "just as the *primiscrinius* in the office of the praetorian prefects attains the end of an honorable and lucrative career". Milner's version (1996, *ad loc.*) is of a similar nature. Such a translation is to be preferred since it avoids confusion between the prefect of the Praetorian Guard, the commander of the imperial bodyguard until the time of Constantine the Great, and the various *praefecti praetoriani* of the Dominate, i.e., members of the civil administration. See also Formisano 2003: *ad loc.*; Giuffrida Manmana 1997, *ad loc.*; and Müller 1997, *ad loc.*

[56] Mazzarino (1956, 542) writes that "gli officiali della prefettura al praetorio erano considerati legionarii della *legio I Adiutrix*". It should be noted that *Cod. Iust.* 12.52.3.2 records that such 'officiali' *in legione prima adiutrice nostra militant*.

[57] On this, see Stein 1962, 6.

[58] Goffart 1977, 73.

[59] For a detailed treatment of the position of *cornicularius* leading up to the period in question, see Perea Yébenes 2004, 451–472.

[60] Cassiod. *Var.* 11.17ff. See also *Cod. Iust.* 12.49.12, written during the reign of the Byzantine emperor Anastasius: *cornicularius et primiscrinius*.

rino holds that Vegetius could not have mistaken the *primiscrinius* for the *cornicularius* because he was a bureaucrat himself. According to the same scholar, it follows that Vegetius was writing at a time when the *primiscrinius* – and not the *cornicularius* – was the final post in the praetorian *officium*.

As Mazzarino explains, Stein showed that, during the reign of Gratian, the *primiscrinius* was elevated in rank.[61] The primiscriniate, therefore, supplanted the corniculariate as the ultimate post in one's administrative career. If it is accepted that the final form of the *Notitia* was not reached until perhaps very early in the reign of Valentinian III,[62] it would seem most likely that Vegetius wrote his treatise some time before this emperor's accession in 425, i.e., at a time when the Gratianic elevation of the *primiscrinius* was still maintained.[63]

Mazzarino's argument has been countered by the rather weighty arguments of Goffart.[64] From an inspection of the sources used by this scholar, and the work of John Lydus in particular, there remains little doubt about his conclusion that *Epit.* 2.21.3 cannot be used to define further the era in which Vegetius wrote. Even proponents of a Theodosian date for Vegetius' military treatise have rejected Mazzarino's contention. For example, Chastagnol writes that "l'argument ... doit, me semble-t-il, être rejeté".[65] There is little to add, although it does seem necessary, for the purpose of completeness, to review Goffart's refutation of the *terminus ante quem*[66] that Mazzarino proposes.

Goffart refers to Stein's conclusion that, between 368 and 374, the assistant to the most senior man in the *officium*, viz., the *adiutor* to the *princeps*, became a dignitary rather than the senior member of a *scrinium* overseen by a superior. Yet Stein failed to point out that this resulted in changes in rank at the top of the *officium*. This was especially with respect to the "one-two relationship" between *princeps* and *cornicularius*.[67] Of significance for us is that there is no cause to believe, *pace* Mazzarino, that the *adiutor* (*primiscrinius*) was ever senior to the *cornicularius* and that, subsequent to this, the positions were reversed to the form found in the *Notitia Dignitatum*. The rank of *cornicularius* beneath the *princeps officii* is now accepted as a matter of course, although not every *officium* had a *cornicularius*. What is more, Goffart draws our attention to a "set of western military *officia*" in which the *cornicularius* is in fourth position.[68] Yet even in

---

[61] Stein 1962, 60. Note that Mazzarino would have used the first edition of 1922, published in Vienna by Rikola-Verlag.

[62] A.H.M. Jones (1964, 350–351 [vol. 3]) believes that the Eastern part must be dated before 413, for the *comes Ponticae*, mentioned at *Cod. Theod.* 6.13.1 (413), is not recorded in the *Notitia*. See also Mann 1976, 1–9. Yet Brennan (1998, 35) notes the presence of the *Placidi Valentinianici felices* (*Occ.* 7.36), a military unit which seemingly takes its name from Valentinian III. On this, see also Kubitschek 1925, 1833. The history of the study of the document is conveniently summarized by Clemente 1968, *passim*.

[63] Mazzarino's contention is supported by Sirago 1961, 467.

[64] Goffart 1977, 73. Goffart's refutation of Mazzarino's premises spans 71–75.

[65] Chastagnol 1974, 60.

[66] The other, of course, is the date of the Eutropian recension, viz., 450.

[67] Goffart (1977, 73 n. 40) points out that "The contrary is implied"; see also Stein 1962, 61.

[68] Goffart 1977, 73–74.

such cases, i.e., where the first three positions are external appointments, the *cornicularius* is placed ahead of the *adiutor* or *primiscrinius*.[69] Thus we are presented with no real cause to believe that a) the *primiscrinius* was ever senior to the *cornicularius*, or b) that Vegetius wrote before the compilation of the *Notitia*, a time when – as Mazzarino would have us believe – the *primiscrinius* was head of the *officium*.[70]

Of course, the final problem to be solved is the reason why Vegetius portrays the primiscriniate in the way he does at *Epit.* 2.21.3. Goffart holds that this "happens to be comparatively easy".[71] He points out that we know, from *Cod. Iust.* 12.52.3 and Cassiodorus' *Var.* 11.17–18, that the corniculariate and the primiscriniate were the terminal posts in the careers of those men who held these positions, and that "normal rotation called for these dignitaries to retire together after a year of service".[72] John Lydus appears to be stating the same thing at *De magist.* 3.6.1–2 and 3.9.2 when he writes that, out of a select group (τάγμα) of short-hand writers called *Augustales*, some continue their service until they reach the office of *cornicularius* while others, viz., the short-hand writers who fail to rise to the level of *Augustalis*, continue until they reach the post of *primiscrinius*. John calls both these posts a πλήρωμα (*De magist.* 3.6.2, 3.9.1–2), which certainly suggests that the positions represented terminal stages in one's administrative career. Why Goffart did not make more of this particular point is surprising. As a consequence, it may be seen that a man could not advance from the primiscriniate to the corniculariate.

The key to refuting Mazzarino's premise, as Goffart demonstrates, is to recognize that "both positions in the *officium* were terminal" on account of the fact that "there were distinct ladders of promotion, one leading to each dignity [i.e., to the primiscriniate and to the corniculariate respectively]".[73] Thus the two ladders to these two senior ranks differed markedly. The position of *primiscrinius* was attained by a slow career within the *officium*. On the other hand, the corniculariate was achieved more quickly given that he was appointed out of a subgroup within the *officium* called the *Augustales*.[74] It follows that, when the

---

[69] Goffart directs us to A.H.M. Jones 1964, 565–566 (vol. 1); id. 1960, 167. Goffart also explains his position in a note (1977, 73 n. 42), the text of which reads as follows: "Conspectus in Seeck's edition of the *Notitia Dignitatum*, 335–36; the *officia* where he is in fourth position, *ND Occ.* 26.23–26 to 31.34–37 where the last entries show the foreign source for the officials set ahead of the *cornicularius*. Regardless of whether *cornicularii* are always second to the *principes*, no *adiutor* is ever set ahead of a *cornicularius* in the *Notitia*. John Lydus, *De magist.* 3.3–4, and 22–25, argues at length that the corniculary was always the top man in the ladder of promotion. This is fanciful as regards the *princeps* but not in relation to the *primiscrinius*".

[70] Goffart 1977, 73–74.

[71] Goffart 1977, 74.

[72] Goffart 1977, 74.

[73] Goffart 1977, 74.

[74] Goffart (1977, 74) notes that "John Lydus' circumstantial account of the *Augustales* (*De magist.* 3.6 and 3.9), while open to question because of its late date [i.e., mid-sixth century], offers a highly satisfactory explanation for the joint retirement of these two officials (attested since 444 [i.e. by *Cod. Iust.* 12.52.3])". Cf. Stein 1962, 31–32.

emphasis that Vegetius places upon a lengthy chain of promotion is considered, "his preference for the primiscriniate as the last career step is not surprising".[75]

Goffart adds that Vegetius referred to the primiscriniate rather than the corniculariate at *Epit.* 2.21.3 because the *primiscrinius* may have made more money than the *cornicularius*.[76] He does concede, however, that we have no information regarding the profits of the position until the mid-sixth century. According to John Lydus, himself a *cornicularius*, the corniculariate is a post that no longer brings the same profit to its holder as it once did (*De magist.* 3.23.1–3.25.6).[77] Yet John fails to discuss the relative profitability of the primiscriniate. Despite this, it is clear that the *primiscrinius* had been well placed with respect to making profits.[78] Stein demonstrates that the *primiscrinius* became a distinct dignitary at some time before 386,[79] and that this official was also an assistant to the head of the prefectorial *officium*, viz., the *princeps*. Goffart points out that, once the *princeps* came to be appointed from outside the *officium* (this first began in the fourth century), "his assistant was in the best position of all to intercept gratuities coursing in the *princeps*' direction".[80] *Cod. Theod.* 1.16.7 of 331 tells us that the *adiutores* (i.e., *primiscrinii*) were listed just after the *princeps* as recipients of illegal bribes.[81] In similar fashion, *Nov. Valent.* 28.1 of 449 names the *primiscrinius* as one of the *primores ... officii* who were stripping the *princeps* of the perquisites to which he was entitled. However, that the profitability of the position continued on into the sixth century is affirmed by Cassiodorus (*Var.* 9.6).[82]

To conclude, the reason why Vegetius compares the career of the *centurio primipili* to that of the *primiscrinius* (*adiutor*) should be readily apparent. Even though the position is listed third in the *Notitia*, the *primiscrinius* was, in fact, the

---

[75] Goffart 1977, 74.

[76] Goffart 1977, 74. Goffart admits that "We know very little about the awards of the *cornicularius*". He does point out that, in an inscription relating to the Numidian *ordo salutationis* (360–363), the *cornicularius* is next after the *princeps* as a collector of fees. This inscription, of course, is quite irrelevant to the present discussion, for the *adiutor* (*primiscrinius*) does not appear – he was not yet a dignitary. For the *ordo salutationis in prouincia Numidia*, see Mommsen 1865, 481–482, lines 13–25. Cf. Stein 192, 59. Goffart (1977, 74 n. 45) contends that, although the inscription in question relates to a governor's *officium* rather than that of the *praefectus praetorianus*, "the evidence retains value since *officia* tended to have a standard organisation". On this, see A.H.M. Jones 1964, 565 (vol. 1).

[77] John Lydus writes that a change was effected during the reign of Arcadius, and that Rufinus brought this about (*De magist.* 3.23.1–2).

[78] Goffart 1977, 75.

[79] Stein 1962, 60.

[80] Goffart 1977, 75.

[81] On the means by which the *primiscrinii* could exact illegal bribes, see John Lydus, *De magist.* 3.11.3.

[82] This royal letter (Cassiod. *Var.* 9.6) permits an unnamed *primiscrinius* to enjoy all his perquisites while recuperating from an illness at Baiae. Cassiodorus (*Var.* 9.6.2) relates that the bureaucrat, upon receiving the letter, was relieved of *emolumenticius terror*, which, according to Goffart (1977, 75 n. 48), refers to "the fear of having his long-awaited gains intercepted as a result of his absence".

terminal point of the career of men belonging to one group of public servants. What is clear, as Goffart points out, is that "he attained this position by the longer, and more traditional, of the two ladders of internal promotion, and he very possibly filled the most lucrative senior post in the *officium*".[83] Vegetius' reference to the *primiscrinius*, therefore, cannot be used with any real security to divine the *Epitoma*'s date of composition. For what it is worth, Goffart affirms that the reference to the primiscriniate might suggest "a moment not too distant from 449 – when Valentinian III felt bound to legislate a definite perquisite for the *princeps* – which marked a high point in the secure profits of the *princeps*' onetime assistant, the *primiscrinius*".[84] But one should obviously not make too much of this.

3. *DIVUS GRATIANUS*

Although some of the pro-Theodosian arguments are not without some slight merit, others are to be treated with the utmost caution. A notable example is Schöner's late-nineteenth-century contention (1888) that the appearance of *diuus Gratianus* at *Epit.* 1.20.3 could not have been written later than the reign of Theodosius I.[85] This belief has found some favour in the twentieth century.[86] Neumann, in the relevant volume of Pauly-Wissowa, credits the notion,[87] as does Silhanek. According to Silhanek, "the adjective, *diuus*, in the phrase *ad tempus diui Gratiani*, indicates not only that Gratian is dead, but that he is recently dead" – a 'fact' which he uses as evidence for his belief that the *Epitoma* was composed during the reign of Theodosius I.[88] Schöner's argument has recently found renewed support. Reeve, who ignores Neumann and Silhanek, cites Schöner and states that

> there is an argument for Theodosius I that has not been refuted: as deification is not recorded for Gratian, *divus* can only mean 'the late' and would not have been applied to him beyond the next reign.[89]

[83] Goffart 1977, 75.

[84] Goffart 1977, 75.

[85] Schöner 1888, 36–39. According to this scholar, "Die Bezeichnung des Gratianus als *divus*" (36) serves as a strong indication that the text was written during the reign of Theodosius I: "Es kann somit *divus Gratianus* in der epitoma ... nur heissen: 'der kürzlich verstorbene, der hochselige Gratianus'; und er kann nur so genannt werden unter der Regierung seiner unmittelbaren Nachfolger, nicht aber unter der Valentinians III." (37). Schöner (1888, 37) then adduces Servius' commentary on Verg. *Aen.* 5.45 (*diuos ex hominibus factos, quasi qui diem obierint; unde diuos etiam imperatores uocamus*) before turning to "de Rossi, inscript. Christ. p. X" (*non vidi*): "Caeterum his saeculis (i.e. quarto et quinto) divi vocabulum ita receptum usu erat, ut vix quidquam praeter vita functum principem significaret"; and "p. XXV" (*non vidi*): "neque enim ante Maxentium divi vocabulum, quemadmodum seniore aetate, vita functum principem significabat, sed consecratum ut in divos relatum".

[86] Goffart (1977, 76) holds that Schöner's contention scarcely deserves a footnote.

[87] Neumann 1965, 993: "wie Schöner ... zeigt".

[88] Silhanek 1972, 13–14.

[89] Reeve 2000, 349–350.

Now it would appear that Reeve, when he wrote the above, had not paid a great deal of attention to Goffart's article on Vegetius' date,[90] for this scholar, in only nine lines, goes some way to disarming Schöner's contention.[91] Although they require elaboration, Goffart's basic points nevertheless remain valid. Despite this, it is certainly too much to say that Schöner's arguments provide "impressive documentation for the contrary view that [Theodosius I] ... cannot possibly have been the emperor whom Vegetius addressed".[92] The following material treats of the issue in more detail.[93]

There are three important points to be considered. First, Schöner's argument that *diuus* could not have been used *post* 395 does not preclude the admittedly unlikely possibility that the text was addressed to Valentinian II. The reign of Gratian's younger brother, of course, was more or less contemporaneous with that of Theodosius I. Second, Theodosius I's reign was not "the next reign" after Gratian. Theodosius did not even become the senior Augustus upon the death of Gratian,[94] for Valentinian II had been raised to the imperial position in 375 following the death of his father. Thus Theodosius I cannot be envisaged as Gratian's direct successor – Theodosius the Great, emperor of the East, took great pains to ensure that Valentinian II, Gratian's 'successor' as emperor of the West,[95] maintained his imperial position in the face of Maximus' usurpation. Despite his many apparent faults, even those who sought to denigrate his conduct, namely the pagan historians Eunapius (as least from what we know about this fragmentary historian) and Zosimus (who is thought to have based his account of Theodosius' reign on Eunapius), do not question the emperor's apparent loyalty to the offspring of Valentinian I. Nor should we. Third, there is no reason why *diuus*, if it had come to mean simply 'the late' rather than 'the deified' (as seems likely), would not have the same force under Honorius, Arcadius, Theodosius II, or Valentinian III.

That Symmachus, writing under Valentinian II, regularly applies the adjective *diuus* (and the related *diualis*) to Gratian obviously helps us little.[96] But we

[90] Reeve, strangely enough, does not cite Goffart in his 2003 edition of the *Epitoma*.

[91] Goffart 1977, 76.

[92] Goffart 1977, 75–76.

[93] I have briefly touched upon this theme elsewhere at Charles 2004c.

[94] Note, too, that Arcadius was elevated to the rank of Augustus in the year of the western emperor's death; see Cassiod. *Chron.* 1140 (*MGH:AA* 11, *Chron. min.* 2, 153); *Cons. Constant.* 383.1 (*MGH:AA* 9, *Chron. min.* 1, 244); Marcell. *Chron.* 383.2 (*MGH:AA* 11, *Chron. min.* 2, 61); Prosp. 1179 (*MGH:AA* 9, *Chron. min.* 1, 461); Socrat. *H.E.* 5.10.5; Sozom. *H.E.* 7.12.2. Philostorgius (*H.E.* 10.5) does not give a precise date. Rufinus (*H.E.* 11.34) merely states that Arcadius was Augustus at the time of Theodosius' victory over Eugenius and Arbogast.

[95] Of course, Valentinian II did not 'succeed' his brother in the normal sense. Rather, he became the sole western Augustus.

[96] *diuus*: *Rel.* 3.1: *diuus princeps*; *Rel.* 4.1: *diuus princeps*; *Rel.* 3.20, 13.2, 29.1: *diuus frater*; *Rel.* 34.9, 34.11, 40.4; *Ep.* 9.150.2: *diuus Gratianus*. The adjective *diualis* is associated with his deeds: *Rel.* 29.1: *remedii diualis*; 41.3: *rescripta diualia*. Note that Symmachus (*Rel.* 3.20) describes Valentinian I as follows: *spectat senior ille diuus ex arce siderea*. Likewise, Valentinian and Valens are given divine status at *Rel.* 13.2: *diuis parentibus tuis*. In a letter to

do find *diui parentis nostri Gratiani* in one of the Novels of Valentinian III (*Nov. Val.* 11.1). This Novel is dated to 443. Another Novel (*Nov. Marc.* 5), this time dating to 455, uses *diuae memoriae* in connection with Valentinian I, Valens and Gratian, and in connection with Valentinian II, Theodosius I and Arcadius. Perhaps more relevant is that, at *Cod. Theod.* 16.10.20.1 of 415, we find *secundum diui Gratiani constituta*. Symmachus also associates *diuus* with the Christian emperors Constans (*Rel.* 40.2), Constantius II (*Rel.* 3.4, 3.6, 34.2, 34.4, 34.5; *Ep.* 9.150.1)[97] and even Constantine the Great (*Rel.* 40.2).[98] Julian is described similarly (*Rel.* 40.3).[99] Moreover, the *Codex Iustinianus* (12.49.12) records a directive of Anastasius in which Zeno is described as *diuae memoriae*. What is more, Theodosius I is himself called *diuus* in a famous inscription recording the career of Nicomachus Flavianus sr., which was set up under Theodosius II and Valentinian III (*CIL* 6.1783 = *ILS* 2948). Now, if Theodosius I could be awarded the epithet *diuus* during the reign of Valentinian III, who was obviously not the former emperor's successor, it is not improbable that Vegetius could have written *diuus Gratianus* at some time after 425.

If the adjective, as Schöner supposes, had come to have a non-religious connotation by the late fourth century (and it worth noting that Ambrose naturally prefers the phrase *augustae memoriae* to the more pagan-flavoured *diuus*[100]), the Vegetian references to *diuus Augustus* (*Epit.* 1.27.1), *diuus Vespasianus* (*Epit.* 2.7.3), *diuus Traianus* (*Epit.* 2.3.7) and *diuus Adrianus* (*Epit.* 1.27.1)[101] must all necessarily have the same honorific significance, i.e., 'late' or 'deceased'. Note Schöner's assertion that "*divus* im 4. Jahrhundert entspricht somit ganz den deutschen Ausdrücken: 'verstorben, selig, hochselig'".[102] So, if emperors of the first and second centuries could be called 'late', there remains no reason whatsoever why the same adjective, when applied to Gratian, could not have been employed later than the reign of Theodosius I. Schöner himself demonstrates the absurdity of his argument by quoting de Rossi's conclusion regarding the mean-

---

Stilicho (*Ep.* 4.4.2), Symmachus writes *receptus caelo principum parens* – again, Valentinian I. These instances represent merely a few examples of Symmachus' treatment of the imperial family, and Gratian in particular. See also *AE* 1932.60: *IMP CAES VALENTINIANO PIO FEL AVG DIVI VALENTINIANI AVG FILIO* (lines 5–7).

[97] Vera (1981, 33–34) provides some useful commentary and documentation on "La possibile divinizzazione di Costanzo II".

[98] On Constantine the Great's *consecratio*, see Calderone 1973, 213–261. Useful discussion follows from 262; see especially 248–249, where he deals with coins bearing the legend *diuus Constantinus*.

[99] See also *Cod. Theod.* 14.6.5 of 419.

[100] e.g., *Ep.* 17.5: *augustae memoriae Gratiano* (ablative case introduced by *a fratre clementiae tuae*); *Ep.* 18.32: *Constantius augustae memoriae* (i.e., Constantius II); *Ep.* 21.2: *augustae memoriae pater tuus* (i.e., Valentinian I, for the letter was addressed to his son Valentinian II); *Ep.* 21.15: *sub Constantio augustae memoriae*; *Ep.* 57.5: *Valentiniano augustae memoriae principi* (i.e., Valentinian II).

[101] The actual text reads as follows: *diui Augusti atque Adriani*. One might presume that *diuus* qualifies both substantives, although one cannot obviously be certain.

[102] Schöner 1888, 37. Jähns (1966, 110) also translates the adjective in question as "hochselig".

ing of *diuus* in late antiquity: "Et sane imperatores omnes, qui vita excesserant, divos appellari hac aetate consuevisse leges in Theodosiano codice et in Novellarum libris collectae passim demonstrant".[103]

To settle this aspect of the problem, let us play the devil's advocate and postulate, for argument's sake, that Vegetius may have used *diuus* to mean 'deified' in the case of the earlier emperors, and 'late' in the case of Gratian. If the association of *diuus* with Augustus, Vespasian, Trajan and Hadrian was made in the traditional pagan sense,[104] Vegetius thereby attributes divinity to the four *principes* in question. But would Vegetius, a man ostensibly predisposed to orthodox Christianity, have ever used *diuus* in its traditional sense of *relatus inter diuos*? One would think not. More importantly, how was Vegetius' audience supposed to know that he was using *diuus* in two rather different senses, i.e., 'deified' for the earlier emperors and 'late' for Gratian? Our postulation thus makes no sense at all. It is safe to assume that *diuus*, by the time of the *Epitoma*'s composition, had lost most – if not all – of its earlier religious force.[105] Reeve's point that Gratian was not 'deified' is irrelevant. The adjective *diuus*, clearly enough, could be used for all deceased emperors, regardless of whether or not they achieved an imaginary apotheosis.

In any case, Reeve's contention that "deification is not recorded for Gratian" shows a misunderstanding of the nature of fourth-century *consecrationes*. Christian emperors could not achieve apotheosis like Vespasian or Trajan. Thus Constantine the Great achieved ἀναβίωσις or revivification, but not the traditional ἀποθέωσις or reception among the gods.[106] According to pagan beliefs, the *consecratio* of a Christian emperor could never be considered complete, for the ritual required cremation rather than interment.[107] This is demonstrated by the case of Decius, whose body was unable to be recovered. The last emperor given traditional *honores caelestes* by the Senate was Constantius Chlorus (Constantine the Great's father) in 314.[108] Thereafter, senatorial *consecrationes* had a rather more honorific significance.[109] A devout pagan senator such as Eutropius could no longer write that Constantine the Great *inter Diuos relatus est*. He could only claim that *inter Diuos meruit referri* (*Brev.* 10.8.3), as he also did with Constantius II (*Brev.* 10.15.2).[110] What Eutropius means is that these emperors, owing to

---

[103] Schöner (1888, 37) gives the reference as "de Rossi, inscript. Christ. ... p. 338" and directs his audience to "Heumann, Handlexikon zu den Quellen des römischen Rechts s.v. divus". These works were unable to be consulted.

[104] All four of these emperors were demonstrably accorded this posthumous honour.

[105] This might depend on whether the author was pagan or Christian. That is not to say, of course, that all pagans would have used *diuus* in a truly religious sense.

[106] Eusebius (*V.C.* 4.73) tells us that coins were minted depicting Constantine's ascent to the heavens in a *quadriga*; cf. Euseb. *V.C.* 4.71.

[107] See Koep 1958, 96–104, and especially 95.

[108] On the evidence for this, see Cracco Ruggini 1977, 427 n. 8. Constantius Chlorus died in York in 306; see Prosp. 976 (*MGH:AA* 9, *Chron. min.* 1, 447); Hieron. *Chron.* 306 p. Chr. (*Euseb. Werk.* 7, 228 g).

[109] See Cracco Ruggini 1977, 427ff.

[110] On the significance of Eutropius' use of *merere*, see den Boer 1972, 156–157, and

their meritorious actions, *would* have been deified if they had have adhered to pagan rites, but were unable to achieve apotheosis because of their Christian faith. For the purpose of religious neutrality, Eutropius also uses this expression in connection with the pagan emperor Aurelian (*Brev.* 9.15.2). But the 'apotheosis' of the emperor Decius, even though his body was unable to be cremated according to the prescribed ritual, is nevertheless described in the expected fashion at *Brev.* 9.4: *inter Diuos relati* (the plural participle refers to both emperor and son).

Cracco Ruggini holds that it was the revised form of *consecratio* that enabled later writers to call Gratian *diuus* – and this despite the apparent incongruity of an anti-pagan emperor being treated in a fashion contrary to his religious principles.[111] Yet this should not surprise. In dedicating his *Breuiarium* to Valens, an emperor of great Christian zeal (although an Arian), Eutropius writes *tranquillitatis tuae ... mens diuina*. Adjectives such as *diuus* and *diuinus*, either attributed to the emperor's qualities or person, must have been of a sufficiently uncontroversial nature as to allow their use in connection with Christian rulers. After the death of such emperors, sycophantic pagan senators would even claim that the Augusti had risen *in caelum* (which could conveniently be interpreted as having been received into heaven by the Christian god).[112] Not every pagan was as scrupulous as Eutropius. Aside from his references to *diuus Gratianus*, Symmachus, in suitably ambiguous language, declaims to Valentinian II that his brother was now looking down from above: *nouissime relatus in caelum germanus clementiae tuae* (*Rel.* 34.6). He also writes *receptus in caelum germanus numinis uestri* (*Rel.* 41.1).

Perhaps most significant of all is that Ausonius,[113] in his *Panegyricus ad Gratianum*, includes excerpts from the imperial letter announcing his consulship for 379. Gratian is reported to have said *"palmatam ... tibi misi, in qua diuus Constantius parens noster intextus est"* (*Grat. Act.* 11.53), with Constantius referring to Constantius II. And if the words are not really Gratian's (as seems most probable), one can be sure that his former tutor Ausonius, obviously an intimate of the emperor, would not have chosen language that would displease. The importance of the above is threefold: a) it demonstrates that *diuus* was not exclusively used in the reign of the succeeding emperor – in the West, the reign of Valentinian I separates that of Constantius II and Gratian; b) it shows that *diuus* could be used for an emperor who was not 'deified' in the traditional sense (the

especially n. 133. Eutropius mentions Christianity only once in his *Breuiarium*, viz., in that section of the text where he censures Julian's persecution of the Christians (*Brev.* 10.16.3). Cf. Amm. Marc. 22.10.7, 25.4.20. Eutropius does not refer to Constantine's conversion. Note the lack of any reference to the emperor's deathbed baptism at Aur. Vict. *Caes.* 41.16; Ps.-Aur. Vict. *Epit.* 41.15.

[111] See Cracco Ruggini 1977, 436.

[112] Of course, this does not accord with the contemporary orthodox belief that the souls of the elect would be called up from their corporeal remains on the *dies irae*.

[113] The most recent edition is used throughout the present work (Green 1999). Green's edition uses the same order and subdivisions as found in his previous commentary (1991).

emperor in question was buried rather than cremated); and c) it provides (the authenticity of Gratian's words notwithstanding) reasonable evidence that a devout Christian emperor could use *diuus* to describe mortals without compromising his religious principles.[114] The last point is reinforced by Ausonius' affirmation that Gratian had shown piety by having his father consecrated *diuinis honoribus* (*Grat. Act.* 2.7). Although *consecratio* was a senatorial honour, the author of this deed, at least according to Ausonius, was Valentinian's son.[115]

4. GOTHS, HUNS AND ALANS

The apparent description of the Huns and Alans as a single people (*Epit.* 3.26.36: *Hunnorum Alanorumque natio*) and the simultaneous mention of Goths, Alans and Huns (*Epit.* 1.20.2) cannot be regarded as firm evidence for a Theodosian date as many modern authorities would have us believe. [116] Although the cited sections of the *Epitoma* (3.26.36, and especially 1.20.2) may arguably have had more contemporary relevance during the reign of Theodosius I than in the following century,[117] one should refrain from holding these factors as proof-positive of a Theodosian date. Pacatus, declaiming a speech under Theodosius the Great, may have said *Gothus ille et Chunus et Halanus respondebat ad nomen et alternabat excubia* (*Pan.* 32.4), but there is no reason to suppose that the names of these three peoples could not be found in close proximity to each other at some time in the next century.

Vegetius' mention of the Goths, Alans and Huns at *Epit.* 1.20.2 (witness *exemplo Gothorum et Alanorum Hunnorumque, equitum arma profecerint*) can readily be explained.[118] The "collocation", as Barnes describes,[119] of these three

---

[114] Ausonius writes elsewhere that *nullum tu umquam diem ab adulescentia tua nisi adorato dei numine et reus uoti et ilico absolutus egisti, lautis manibus, mente pura, inmaculabili conscientia et, quod in paucis est, cogitatione sincera* (*Grat. Act.* 14.63). In another passage, Ausonius quotes the imperial epistle that announced his impending consulship. The letter reads as follows: *"cum de consulibus in annum creandis solus mecum uolutarem, ut me nosti atque ut facere debui et uelle te sciui, consilium meum ad deum rettuli. eius auctoritati obsecutus te consulem designaui et declaraui et priorem nuncapaui"* (*Grat. Act.* 9.43). This moves Ausonius to exclaim as follows: *quae comitia pleniora umquam fuerunt quam quibus praestitit deus consilium, imperator obsequium?* (*Grat. Act.* 9.44). So, it would seem that Gratian's decision to have his father consecrated must also have been in accord with the design of the Christian god! Indeed, in his discussion of Gratian's use of the words *eius auctoritati obsecutus*, Ausonius writes *scilicet ut in consecrando patre ... fecisti* (*Grat. Act.* 10.48).

[115] Note also Ausonius' reference to *diuinitas tua* (*Grat. Act.* 10.45).

[116] e.g., Barnes 1979, 256; Chastagnol 1974, 62; Milner 1996, xl; Richardot 1998, 142; Sirago 1961, 468ff. Giuffrida Manmana (1997, 24 n. 38) makes no comment other than that Barnes' contention "non esclude ... la datazione sotto il regno di Onorio".

[117] Barnes 1979, 256. Sirago (1961, 469) would strongly agree with this.

[118] Such a tradition would have been undoubtedly fostered by Amm. Marc. 31.16.3, where the historian writes of the *Gothi Hunis Halanisque permixti*. The latter two peoples were drawn to the Goths by Fritigern, who promised them a share in the spoils of Constantinople, a city which they mistakenly thought they could sack. Ammianus tells us that a *Halanorum manus* was

barbarian races seems to have been made for no other reason than to demonstrate a specific military point. Nothing more, nothing less. Indeed, there is no need to suppose that Vegetius' statement (*Epit.* 1.20.2)[120] is related to his following remarks regarding the disappearance of infantry armour, or to the subsequent description of the defeat of unprotected Roman infantry by the Goths and the concomitant loss of *tantae urbes*. In view of this, one should not immediately assume that Vegetius is invoking the names of the Goths, Alans and Huns as enemies. Thus Richardot's statement that "Végèce évoque ... les Goths, les Alains et les Huns comme des ennemis" appears to lack foundation.[121]

The real point that Vegetius makes at *Epit.* 1.20.2 is that Roman cavalrymen, like those of the three peoples previously mentioned, were equipped with armour. Of course, that Vegetius writes that the Romans did this after the fashion of the Goths, Alans and Huns is hardly accurate – imperial cavalry had worn armour for centuries. Why Vegetius wrote what he did is difficult to explain. Still, it may be that our author was referring to Theodosius' supposed use of the Goths, Alans and Huns in the contest against the usurper Maximus,[122] a historical event which would still have had some relevance in the following decades. In any case, it matters not that a large body of Alans had allied themselves with the Vandals by 406,[123] and that the Huns remained settled in Pannonia until 427.[124] It is equally irrelevant to adduce that "any Alans who remained north of the lower Danube after 378 were absorbed and assimilated by the Huns within twenty or thirty years",[125] and that these once-formidable people were no longer of any singular importance by the reign of Valentinian III.[126]

Likewise, Vegetius' apparent description of the Huns and Alans as one nation, witness *Hunnorum Alanorumque natio* (*Epit.* 3.26.36), is also very much a red herring for the unsuspecting reader. Milner believes that Vegetius is "alluding to an event noticed by Ammianus Marcellinus", i.e., 31.3.1 of the *Res Gestae*, where we read the following: *Huni peruasis Halanorum regionibus ... interfectisque multis et spoliatis, reliquos sibi concordandi fide pacta iunxerunt.*[127]

---

present at Adrianople with Fritigern's host (31.12.17). Claudian describes the Alans (*stridor uenientis Alani*) and Huns (*uaga Chunorum feritas*) sequentially at *Cons. Stil.* 1.109–110, but as two distinct groups.

[119] Barnes 1979, 256.

[120] On Veg. *Epit.* 1.20.2, see Bachrach 1973, 36.

[121] Richardot 1998, 142.

[122] Cf. Pacat. *Pan.* 32.4: *Gothus ille et Chunus et Halanus respondebat ad nomen.*

[123] See Isid. *Hist. Goth.* 71–72 (*MGH:AA* 11, *Chron. min.* 2, 295); Oros. 7.40.3–5.

[124] Milner 1996, xl. That the Huns remained in Pannonia until 427 is suggested by the chronicler Marcellinus Comes (*Chron.* 427.1 [*MGH:AA* 11, *Chron. min.* 2, 76]: *Pannoniae, quae per quinquaginta annos ab Hunnis retinebantur, a Romanis receptae sunt.*

[125] Barnes 1979, 256.

[126] This is the thesis of Sirago 1961, 469.

[127] Milner 1996, xl. Marcellinus Comes (*Chron.* 379.2 [*MGH:AA* 11, *Chron. min.* 2, 60]), in reference to the conflict of 379, writes that *Halanos, Hunnos, Gothos, gentes Scythicas magnis multisque proeliis uicit*. One might well presume that the subject of *uicit* is Theodosius. Note also *Cons. Const.* 379.3 (*MGH:AA* 9, *Chron. min.* 1, 243) of 379: *deinde uictoriae nuntiatae sunt*

Yet, as even a reasonably cursory inspection of the *Epitoma* will show, Vegetius does not refrain from invoking the names of groups that were no longer distinct political or ethnic entities when he wants to provide his audience with a military example; or, alternatively, when he makes a comparison between ancient practices and those of the present.

For example, the Athenians, Lacedaemonians and Macedonians, mentioned together at *Epit.* 3 prol. 1, might reasonably be held to have assimilated themselves with the Romans in much the same way as Barnes points out that the Alans, by Valentinian III's reign, had assimilated themselves with the Huns. Indeed, Vegetius may even have thought that the Romans, that glorious conquering race, were not *really* the same people as those who called themselves *Romani* in the Late Empire. As Rowell notes, "All inhabitants [of the Late Empire] were ... *Romani*, regardless of origin, and formed a single group or nation in contradistinction to the barbarian tribes beyond the frontiers".[128] Thus any subject of the Augusti was a *Romanus*. But such a definition, in Vegetius' mind, would have been an insult to the *ciues Romani* of the past. For example, in his discussion of ancient swordsmanship, Vegetius writes *ideoque ad dimicandum hoc praecipue genere usos constat esse Romanos (Epit.* 1.12.4).[129] To Vegetius, the 'real' *Romani* belong to an earlier age – they are not necessarily identical to the present so-called 'Romans'.[130].

In view of the above, Gordon presents what he believes to be a minor piece of evidence against a fourth-century date for the *Epitoma*. He points out that the *Epitoma* mentions the Huns on two occasions.[131] First, the Huns, along with the Goths and Alans, had demonstrated the benefits of cavalry armour (*Epit.* 1.20.2). Second, Vegetius, in an example of the most abject flattery, states that not even the Huns or Alans can match the emperor's horsemanship (*Epit.* 3.26.36). The second reference, of course, proves nothing – there is no reason to believe that the Romans were not aware of the Huns' outstanding horsemanship before any significant military engagements with them. The first reference, however, deserves closer attention. Gordon adduces the fact that the Huns are mentioned only seven or eight times in the (extant) literary record before 405, and that the Huns presented no real threat to Roman interests until the accession of Attila in the early 430s: "references to a very dangerous enemy would be more likely at this

---

aduersus Gothos, Alanos atque Hunos die XV k. Dec. See also Oros. 7.34.5, where we find language almost identical to that employed in the chronicles: *[Theodosius] ... Alanos, Hunos et Gothos ... magnis multisque proeliis uicit.*

[128] Rowell 1967, 290.

[129] *hoc genere* refers to the type of sword-thrust (in this case, *punctim,* "with the point of the blade", as opposed to *caesim,* "with the edge of the blade" – i.e., a thrust versus a slash)

[130] It may be a minor point, but this sort of attitude is not really displayed in the literature of Theodosius' reign. Theodosian writers are still most certainly 'Romans', i.e., they still view themselves as the direct heirs of the classical tradition. But this is subjective analysis and some readers might feel otherwise. For *Romani* and *populus Romanus,* see also *Epit.* 1.1.2, 1.12.1, 2.2.3, 2.2.12 (*magnitudo Romana*), 3 prol. 3, 3 prol. 5, 4.31.2.

[131] Gordon 1974, 26. Cf. Barnes 1979, 256.

later period than under Theodosius I".[132] Still, this is hardly conclusive evidence
for a non-Theodosian dating, especially since a) Hunnic tribes drove the Goths
into the Empire, an event which most definitely occurred *before* the reign of
Theodosius I; b) the Huns are mentioned by Pacatus as one of the foreign enemies
subdued by Theodosius (*Pan.* 11.4);[133] c) Orosius remarks that Theodosius
defeated the *Alanos Hunos et Gothos* in many great battles (7.34.5); and d) a later
chronicle records that a victory was effected over these three peoples in 379:
*uictoriae nuntiatae sunt aduersus Gothos, Alanos atque Hunos die XV kal. Dec
[Ausonio et Olibrio]* (*Cons. Constant.* 379.3).[134] Themistius, in a speech cele-
brating the consulship of Saturninus in 383,[135] writes that the Scythian (= Gothic)
αὐθάδεια, the τόλμα of the Alans and the ἀπόνοια of the Massagetae (= Huns)
yielded to Rome in accordance with divine will (*Orat.* 16.207c). This certainly
suggests the three peoples in question. Ambrose, too, mentions *Hunnos atque
Alanos* in a letter to Valentinian II dating to 386 (*Ep.* 24.8).[136]

More significant, perhaps, is Vegetius' reference to the superiority of Hunnic
horses in the *Mulomedicina*. The following demonstrates the author's intimacy
with Hunnic horse-breeding, knowledge which would have been hard to come by
in times of constant conflict:

> Huniscis grande et aduncum caput, extantes oculi, angustae nares, latae maxillae, robusta
> ceruix et rigida, iubae ultra genua pendentes, maiores costae, incurua spina, cauda siluosa,
> ualidissimae tibiae, paruae bases, plenae ac diffusae ungulae, ilia cauata totumque corpus
> angulosum, nulla in clunibus aruina, nulli in musculis tori, in longitudine magis quam in
> altitudine statura propensior, uenter exhaustus, ossa grandia, macies grata et quibus pulchri-
> tudinem praestet ipsa deformitas: animus moderatus et prudens et uulnerum patiens (*Mul.*
> 3.6.5.)

Furthermore, Vegetius notes that *ad bellum Huniscorum longe prima docetur
utilitas patientiae, laboris, frigoris, famis* (*Mul.* 3.6.2) and that, *de temporibus
uitae* (the title of this particular chapter), *aetas longaeua Persis, Huniscis, Epiro-
tis ac Siculis, breuior Hispanis ac Numidis* (*Mul.* 3.7.1). Such detailed information may point to an era of greater inter-relationship between Roman and Hun,

---

[132] Gordon 1974, 26. Of the "seven or eight times" before 405, Ausonius (*Precationes
Variae* 1.8 [Green 1999] = *Epigr.* 26.8 [White 1919–1921]) provides one: *arma inter Chunosque
truces.* Socrates, although he obviously wrote after 405, mentions that the Praetorian prefect
Rufinus was suspected of having invited the Huns into the Empire (*H.E.* 6.1.6). But Marcellinus
Comes (*Chron.* 395.4–5 [*MGH:AA* 11, *Chron. min.* 2, 64]) and Zosimus (5.5.4) write that it was
the Goths, not the Huns, whom Rufinus invited into Roman territories. Cf. Sozom. *H.E.* 8.1.2.

[133] Cf. Pacat. *Pan.* 32.4.

[134] = *MGH:AA* 9, *Chron. min.* 1, 243. Richardot (1998, 141–142) notes "à laquelle [chro-
nique] on peut ajouter une autre date, ... l'année 380, qui voit de nouvelles «victoires des deux
empereurs» *uictorias amborum Augustorum*" (i.e., *Cons. Constant.* 380.1 [*MGH:AA* 9, *Chron.
min.* 1, 243]: *Gratiano Aug. V et Theodosio Aug. his conss. uictoriae nuntiatae sunt amborum
Augustorum*), and that Philostorgius (*H.E.* 9.19) writes of "[une] ... annonce des succès au cours
de l'année 380".

[135] On this, see Heather/Moncur 2001, 255.

[136] The same passage also contains the following: *et ideo aduersus Iuthungum Hunnus
adscitus est* (*Ep.* 24.8).

i.e., the fifth century, a time when the continual exchange of hostages (such as Aëtius and his son Gaudentius) would have resulted in greater familiarity with Hunnic preferences.[137] The Huns and their habits are thus no longer the stuff of pseudo-myth, as they are in the pages of Ammianus and Jerome. Instead, they represent a verifiable reality. For Vegetius, the Huns are a 'real' people from whom things can be learned (and even admired), rather than simply the horse-borne bogeymen of earlier writers. Notable, too, is Vegetius' assertion that the *mulomedicinae ars* has fallen into a state of decline owing to avarice and apathy (*Mul.* 2 prol. 1). He goes on to state that

> nuper uero exemplo Hunnorum siue gentium aliarum artis ipsius etiam usus intercidit, dum homines, refugientes expensas, barbarorum consuetudinem imitari uelle se simulant et incurata animalia hibernis pascuis et negligentiae casibus dedunt (*Mul.* 2 prol. 1).

Of course, the implication is that the Hunnic horses are much hardier than those of the Romans, and that the latter cannot suffer the same degree of neglect (*Mul.* 2 prol. 2–3). The above could imply that the Romans had been under the influence of the Huns for some period of time before attempting to emulate their example. We cannot, of course, be sure. Once again, this situation is more comprehensible in the fifth century (and especially in the age of Aëtius) than towards the end of the fourth.

5. VEGETIUS AND THE *HISTORIA AUGUSTA*

Chastagnol wrote a paper entitled "Végèce et l'Histoire Auguste", in which he argued that the author of the *Historia Augusta* (henceforth referred to as the *HA*) had access to Vegetius' *Epitoma*. In all, Chastagnol believes that the author of the *HA*, "the most enigmatic work that Antiquity has transmitted",[138] used the *Epitoma* on no less than fifty-five occasions, and that he used the same author's *Mulomedicina* on a further four. The full list of Chastagnol's correspondences is found in a footnote below.[139] Chastagnol claims that information gleaned from

---

[137] See Mezzabotta 2000, 52–64. Although she thinks that Vegetius wrote his veterinary text "in the last years of the fourth century A.D." (53), Mezzabotta pays particular attention to the author's knowledge of the Huns and their horses (57–64).

[138] Syme 1971b, 1.

[139] Chastagnol 1974, 79–80 (Chastagnol's numbers have been placed between parentheses in order to provide greater clarity): "(1). Ant. Pius. 7, 5. – Veg. , De re milit., 1, 7. (2). Marc., 4, 9. – I, 7. (3). Av. Cass., 5, 3. – III, 3. (4). Av. Cass., 6, 2. – III, 4. (5). Av. Cass., 6, 3–4. – II, 23–24 et III, 4. (6). Pert., 14, 2. – De Mulomed., II, 16, 5. (7). Pesc. Nig., 3, 6. – De re milit., III, 3. (8). Pesc. Nig., 10, 3–4. – III, 3. (9). Pesc. Nig., 11, 1. – I, 3. (10). Hel., 4, 4. – De Mulomed., II, 59, 1–2. (11). Hel., 27, 3. – De re milit., I, 7 et II, 11. (12). Alex. Sev., 14, 6. – II, prol. (13). Alex. Sev., 16, 3. – II, prol. (14). Alex. Sev., 37, 1. – II, 24. (15). Alex. Sev., 45, 1–4. – III, 6 et 8. (16). Alex. Sev. 47, 1. – II, 19 et III, 8. (17). Maxim., 2, 6–7. – I, 10. (18). Maxim., 3, 3. – I, 9. (19). Maxim., 3, 5. – I, 10 et II, 7. (20). Maxim., 4, 3. – I, 10 et II, 7. (21). Maxim., 6, 1. – I. 9. (22). Maxim., 6, 2. – I, 15; II, 15–16 et 23; III, 4. (23). Maxim., 6.8–9. – I, 6. (24). Maxim., 10, 4. – III, 2 et 4. (25). Maxim., 27, 2. – I, 5. (26). Maxim., 29, 8–9. – II, 15–16. (27). Gord., 28, 2. – III, 3. (28). Gord., 28, 3. – III, 4. (29). Max. et Balb., 5, 1. – I, 7. (30). Max. and Balb., 17, 1. – II, prol.

Vegetius' work (including the *Mulomedicina*) can be found in the lives of Antoninus Pius, Marcus Aurelius, Avidius Cassius, Pertinax, Pescennius Niger, Elagabalus, Severus Alexander, Maximinus Thrax (*Maximini duo*), Gordian, Claudius Gothicus, Aurelian and Probus. Of the lives of the so-called 'tyrants', Vegetian influence can be found in the lives of Marius and the oddly named Ballista.

E. Birley was impressed with Chastagnol's argument, which he describes as "important and fascinating"; moreover, he writes that he found the latter scholar's reasoning "decisive, as far as the indebtedness of the *HA* to Vegetius is concerned".[140] Likewise, Lindsay, in a review of Milner's translation of Vegetius, expresses wholehearted approval: "it is clear that the author of the Historia Augusta used Vegetius".[141] Despite these positive comments, not much else, as far as I am aware, appears to have been written on the theme. Still, Birley's revised belief (largely prompted by Goffart's paper) that the *Epitoma* was written under Valentinian III encouraged him to conclude his brief study of the text's date in the following fashion:

> And if we may accept the case which Chastagnol has stated so convincingly for the Historia Augusta having drawn on Vegetius in so many passages, that ought to imply that Seeck and Lang – and Goffart too – were justified in dating Vegetius to the reign of Valentinian III. How much later the Historia Augusta itself could be dated, in that case, must be a matter for consideration at a later time, and by other people.[142]

While Birley's assignation of the *Epitoma* to the reign of Valentinian III is in line with this volume's general contention, the task of demonstrating that the *HA* was written, for example, in the late fifth century (which is certainly not the accepted view) obviously lies beyond the scope of the present discussion.[143] Still, it would be well to offer a few brief thoughts on the matter. Volumes have been written on the authorship of the *HA*, specifically with regard to whether the collection was the product of several authors, as the manuscript tradition would have us believe, or the work of a single writer who chose to cloak his identity behind a series of

---

(31). Gall., 8, 6. – I, 23. (32). Gall., 8, 7. – III, 16 et 19. (33). Trig. tyr., 8. – I, 6 et 7. (34). Trig. tyr., 18, 4–9. – III, 3. (35). Claud., 7, 5. – II, 15. (36). Claud., 8, 5. – II, 16. (37). Claud., 13, 5–6. – I, 6. (38). Claud., 14, 3. – I, 13 et III, 3. (39). Claud., 14, 5. – I, 20 et II, 25. (40). Claud., 14, 10. – II, 11. (41). Claud., 14, 11. – I, 7. (42). Claud., 14, 14. – III, 3. (43). Claud., 16, 2. – I, 14–16. (44). Aur., 4, 1. – I, 15; II, 23; III, 4. (45). Aur., 6, 1. – I, 6. (46). Aur., 7, 5. – III, 3. (47). Aur., 9, 3. – III, 8. (48). Aur., 9, 6–7. – III, 3. (49). Aur., 11, 3. – I, 14–16. (50). Aur., 11, 5–6. – III, 8. (51). Aur., 31, 7. – II, 7 et 13. (52). Tac., 11, 1–3. – De Mulomed., I, 2, 4 et 38, 10–11. (53). Prob., 4, 6. – De re milit., III, 3. (54). Prob., 10, 4. – III, prol. (55). Prob., 19, 2. – III, 16 et 19. (56). Prob., 20, 4. – III, prol. (57). Prob., 20, 6. – De Mulomed., III, prol. (58). Prob., 21, 4. – De re milit. II, prol. (59). Quadr. tyr., 4, 1–2. – I, 6".

[140] E. Birley 1988, 58.

[141] Lindsay 1993, 41.

[142] E. Birley 1988, 68.

[143] Bertrand-Dagenbach (1990, 6) points out that, "De la fin du IIIe siècle au début du VIe, une quinzaine au moins de datations … ont été proposées pour situer chronologiquement l'*Histoire Auguste*". For a convenient summary on the authorship question, see Johne 1976, ch. 1 (who seems to favour a *terminus post quem* of 405).

obscure names. This aspect of the problem is irrelevant for our purpose. Thus we will assume that the collection was penned by one person at an indeterminate point of time, but quite possibly towards the end of the fourth century.[144] First suggested by Dessau,[145] this thesis has received renewed impetus since the publication of several disquisitions on the topic by Syme,[146] and a good deal of work by Paschoud. Although not indisputable, it certainly seems the most meritorious of the convictions offered. Note that Cameron, although he "readily concede[s]" that the *HA* was written in the "late fourth century", holds that the work is "*pre*-Theodosian".[147] This scholar, writing after the publication of Chastagnol's article, cannot agree (or so it would appear) with the French scholar's postulate regarding Vegetius and the *HA*.

Chastagnol's argument, as E. Birley and Lindsay have pointed out, is ostensibly convincing. Indeed, it provides – at first glance at least – a significant stumbling block to a post-Theodosian dating. By the same token, so many other factors, as the present work contends, point to a different honorand. But Chastagnol's surmises, of course, are contingent upon a thesis that is impossible to prove beyond question – the *HA* will always remain something of an enigma. The overly confident tone of the article is also somewhat disquieting, particularly since the author endeavours to solve a complex problem by means of one avenue alone. Likewise, the *rapprochements* that Chastagnol discerns between the *HA* and the *Epitoma*, no matter how compelling they may seem, need not necessarily signify that the biographer borrowed slavishly from Vegetius.[148] Indeed, could it not be that Vegetius, writing in the fifth century, borrowed material from the *HA*, rather than the other way around? This possibility will be discussed in detail further below.

It is relevant to note that Barnes, though he believes that the *Epitoma* was addressed to Theodosius I, does not, in his 1978 discussion of the *HA*'s sources, raise the issue that the playful author of the collection of imperial lives may have borrowed from Vegetius. He is "convinced" that there were only six main sources (viz., the *Ignotus*,[149] Marius Maximus, Herodian, Dexippus, the lost *Kaiserge-*

---

[144] *OCD*³, 713: "There is ... general agreement that the author is a single person working in or very close to the last decade of the 4th cent.". Likewise, Paschoud 2000a, 174: "Aujourd'hui, la très grande majorité des spécialistes de l'*Histore Auguste* s'est ralliée au point de vue de Dessau".

[145] Dessau 1889, 337–392; id. 1892, 561–605.

[146] The following studies reiterate and reinforce Dessau's contention: Syme 1968; id. 1971b; id. 1983.

[147] Cameron 1977, 9–10.

[148] Ambrose (*Ep.* 18.5 [dated to 394]) and Vegetius (*Epit.* 4.26.5–6) both mention the cackling of the sacred geese that alerted the Romans to a Celtic attack, but nobody would ever suggest that one had borrowed from the other in this instance.

[149] The existence of the *Ignotus*, supposedly the basic source of the *HA* as far as 217, was conceived by Syme (enounced in a variety of works, e.g., 1968; 1971a; 1972) and later supported by Chastagnol (1970, 6–8). Indeed, chapter three of Syme 1971a is called "*Ignotus*, the good biographer". Others, however, have cast doubt on his existence. For example, A.R. Birley (forthcoming) writes that the *Ignotus* was "conjured up by Syme"; see also id. 1971, Appendix 2. In

schichte and Eunapius), in addition to Aurelius Victor and Eutropius ("clearly ... used in several passages"), and "perhaps" Festus and Ammianus.[150] Barnes showed himself to be aware of the discussion in which Chastagnol's argument is contained, and, while he does not mention the latter scholar's treatment of Vegetius, he describes one element of Chastagnol's study (on Eutropius and Aurelius Victor) as "not ... in the least convincing".[151] Barnes modified his view slightly in a work dating to 1992. He admitted that "The identification of Eunapius as the Greek source after 270 was over-confident", and that he "would now admit Victor and Eutropius as sources on the same level as the lost *Kaisergeschichte*".[152] But, once again, Vegetius does not enter Barnes' list of sources for the *HA*.

Now, I do not deny that certain Vegetian passages *do* bear a resemblance of sorts to elements found in certain sections of the *HA*, as Chastagnol contends. Still, some of the rapprochements do not seem to prove anything. Let us take one example cited by Chastagnol. That *Prob.* 21.4 gives us *uictor omnium gentium barbararum* and *Epit.* 2. prol. 4 provides us with *domitori omnium gentium barbararum* would appear to prove nothing, for expressions such as these were probably widespread in a variety of media.[153] I cannot see how this could possibly be used to show a relationship between the two texts in question. This topic receives a detailed treatment in a later section of the present volume.

Of more import, perhaps, is that Chastagnol cites four passages in which Vegetius discusses "les armes offensives et défensives des soldats". At *Epit.* 1.16.2, he writes that soldiers need to be protected *cassidibus catafractis loricisque*; at *Epit.* 1.20.3, we find references to *catafractae* and *galeae*, and that the soldiers cast their armour aside on account of their negligence: *primo catafractas, deinde cassides se refundere* (*Epit.* 1.20.4). One also finds *quid enim pedes sagittarius sine catafracta, sine galea, qui cum arcu scutum tenere non potest, faciat?* (*Epit.* 1.20.6), in addition to mention of *draconarii atque signiferi: quid ipsi draconarii atque signiferi, qui sinistra manu hastas gubernant, in proelio facient, quorum et capita nuda constat et pectora?* (*Epit.* 1.20.7). At *Epit.* 2.15.4, we read that the *principes* wore *cassides, catafractas* and *ocreas*, carried *scuta*,

---

his review of Syme's *Ammianus and the Historia Augusta*, Cameron (1971, 262–257) is also rather critical: "Syme's case is ... surprisingly weak" (262). See also Paschoud 2001, xii ff.; id. 1991, 217–269.

[150] Barnes 1978, 125.

[151] See Barnes 1978, 93 n. 19: "A. Chastagnol, *BHAC 1971* (1974), 55 f., wishes to explain the similarities between the two writers as due to Eutropius' copying of Victor. He asserts that 'Eutrope a lu Aurélius Victor', but I do not find the sole example which he adduces in the least convincing (Victor, *Caes.* 33.12; Eutropius, *Breu*, IX.9.2)". Likewise, Barnes (1978, 18 n. 19) finds Chastagnol's attempt to deduce a precise date for the *HA* from Claudian's verse to be "not ... persuasive" (see Chastagnol 1970, 444–463). Chastagnol (1970, 463) concludes that "Les vies d'Élagabal et de Probus appartiennent certainement à l'année 398; celles d'Alexandre Sévère et des Gordiens datent de la fin de 398 et du début de 399, de même que le Quadrige des tyrans; la Vie de Carus et de ses fils clôt enfin l'oeuvre entière dans le premier semestre de 399".

[152] Barnes 1995, 1–34.

[153] Paschoud (2001, 152) notes this, but does not make much of it.

gladios maiores, quos spathas uocant, in addition to two sorts of javelin, one bigger (*pilum ... nunc spiculum dicitur*), and one smaller (*uerriculum, nunc uerrutum dicitur*: *Epit.* 2.15.5). Lastly, at *Epit.* 2.16.2, we read that the *signiferi* of the *triarii* wore helmets covered with bearskins (*galeas ... ursinis pellibus tectas*) and that their centurions (at *Epit.* 2.16.3) wore iron helmets with silver transverse crests (*galeas ferreas, ... transuersis et argentatis cristis*).

Chastagnol makes much of these references to armour. Indeed, he writes that "ces listes on indubitablement influencé plusieurs passages de l'H. A.".[154] At *Maxim.* 6.2, we read that Maximinus was accustomed to review the weapons and armour of his troops on a daily basis: *gladios, {lanceas}, loricas, galeas, scuta, tunicas et omnia arma illorum cotidie circumspicere*. According to Chastagnol, the author of the *HA* would have been incapable of compiling such a list without having consulted Vegetius' *Epitoma*.[155] Moreover, the armour of Maximus' adolescent son, as described by the *HA*, was also apparently influenced by the passages discussed above:

> usus autem e<s>t idem adulescens et aurea lorica exemplo Ptolem<a>eorum, usus est et argentea, usus et clypeo gemmato inaurato et hasta inaurata. fecit et spatas argenteas, fecit etiam aureas et omnino quicquid eius pulchritudinem posset iuuare, fecit et galeas gemmatas, fecit et bucculas (*Maxim.* 29.8–9).

How this could possibly have been derived exclusively from Vegetius is puzzling. Yes, Vegetius does write that the crests of centurions' helmets were silver (*Epit.* 2.16.3). But the passage of the *HA* in question is notable mainly for the preponderance of references to gilt armour rather than silver (in fact, a ratio of 2:1); witness the use of *aurea, inaurato, inaurata* and *aureas* versus *argentea* and *argenteas*. Of significance, too, is that no reference to golden cuirasses worn by Ptolemaic princes is found in the *Epitoma*.[156] The use of gemstones in armour (mentioned twice, witness *gemmato* and *gemmatas*) is also clearly not Vegetian. In fact, Vegetius nowhere describes the armour of high-ranking officers. Furthermore, one could hardly imagine the emperor's son being dressed like a mere centurion. So why look for references to imperial armour in Vegetius? And, if *Maxim.* 29.8–9 *was* derived, at least in part, from *Epit.* 2.16.3, it would not be unreasonable to expect a reference, perhaps, to a transverse crest after the fashion of Roman centurions.

[154] Chastagnol 1974, 69.

[155] Chastagnol (1974, 69) also notes that Maximianus "exerçait ses soldats à la course" (*accepta igitur legione statim eam exercere coepit. quinta quaque die iubebat milites decurrere, in<ter> se simulacra bellorum agere*; *Maxim.* 6.1), which is a reprise, in his view, of *Epit.* 1.9. This conclusion seems rather tendentious. Equally surprising is the view (Chastagnol 1974, 70) that "La revue des armes est signalée en outré en Av. Cass., 6, 2 et en Gord., 28, 3; elle s'inspire directement de Veg., III, 4: *inspectionemque armorum adsidue faciant*".

[156] But references to a golden cuirass worn by Neoptolemus (Achilles' son, also known as Pyrrhus) is found in Vergil (*Aen.* 3.467: *loricam consertam hamis auroque trilicem*; see Charles 2004, 131). Could this have been a source of confusion for the writer of the *HA*? It is clearly impossible to tell.

Likewise, that the *locus* in the *HA* mentions *spathae* need not mean that the author had consulted *Epit.* 2.15.4, as Chastagnol contends: "la présence des *spathae*, qui nous rappellent Veg., II, 15".[157] Are we meant to believe that the *HA*'s author had to turn to Vegetius in order to acquaint himself with the existence of the *spatha*, the type of sword with which most regular cavalry and infantry were equipped in the Late Empire (and, indeed, in earlier times)?[158] It is worth noting that Chastagnol even mentions that *spathae* are found at "Tacite, Ann. XII, 35, 5".[159] This is probably the *locus classicus*, although *spathae* are mentioned on innumerable occasions in a variety of disparate texts (including Greek ones).

Chastagnol also finds elements of the Vegetian passages on armour in the life of Claudius Gothicus: "La Vita Claudii est plus probante encore sur le point de sa dépendance à l'égard de Végèce".[160] At *Claud.* 8.5 is found a reference to rivers and riverbanks that, after the emperor's battle against the Goths, were covered with shields, swords (again *spathae*) and small lances: *tecta sunt flumina scutis, spatis et lanceolis omnia litora operiuntur.* Chastagnol holds that "on retrouve donc les *spathae*, et le mot *tecta*, normal en pareille circonstance, rappelle en même temps la couverture des casques en Veg., II, 16.".[161] This makes for a rather free interpretation of *galeas ad terrorem hostium ursinis pellibus tectas.* If this was indeed a "jeu de mots", the point seems rather obscure – I, for one, cannot see any relationship between the two *loci* in question other than the highly circumstantial appearance of *tecta/tectae*. It hardly seems to represent firm evidence that the *HA* borrowed from Vegetius. No further comment is required on this point.

Finally, on weapons and armour in the *HA* and Vegetius, Chastagnol draws our attention to *Claud.* 14.5, where Claudius receives *cassidem inauratam unam, scuta c<h>rysografata duo, loricam unam, quam refundat.* According to Chastagnol, this excerpt is of signal import. More than any other *rapprochement*, it supposedly demonstrates that the *HA*'s author *must* have consulted the *Epitoma*:

> Le calembour implique par conséquent, si je ne me trompe, une date postérieure à Gratien en même temps qu'une référence parodique à Végèce lui-même, sans possibilité de recours à une source commune.[162]

Of course, this assertion rests on the veracity of the problematic statement, made at *Epit.* 1.20.2–3, that Roman infantry ceased to wear protective armour from some point in Gratian's reign. As seems patently obvious, Vegetius' claim is nonsense and few scholars today give it any credence at all. We shall briefly look at

---

[157] Chastagnol 1974, 70.

[158] Especially after the classic legionary stabbing sword, i.e., the shorter but still lethal *gladius hispanicus* (or *hispaniensis*), fell into disuse.

[159] Chastagnol 1974, 70 n. 36; the Tacitean *locus* (Chastagnol presumably used the Budé edition) is equivalent to *Ann.* 12.35.3 in the Teubner version of the text.

[160] Chastagnol 1974, 70.

[161] Chastagnol 1974, 70.

[162] Chastagnol 1974, 70.

this problem in a later chapter.[163] Furthermore, it does not necessarily follow that, because both authors used *refundere* in close proximity to armour, that one author had copied from the other. Indeed, manuscripts variants of *Epit.* 1.20.4 are certainly found. Reeve's latest OCT version prefers *primo catafractas, deinde cassides se refundere*.[164] Stelten provides *primo catafractas, deinde cassides se debere fundere* ("they ought to shed first …").[165] This possibility is listed in Reeve's *apparatus*.[166] Önnerfors gives *primo catafractas, deinde cassides se deponere*,[167] which is not unexpectedly followed by Müller, especially given that his edition (and translation) is based on Önnerfors' text.[168] Whatever the case may be, what *is* clear is that the exact reading of the passage in question is open to debate, something which should hardly allow us to draw any detailed conclusions from the text. To put it simply, *refundere* – the verb found in the problematic section of the *HA* – represents just *one* of the possibilities. This is not made clear by Chastagnol, who would seem to prefer that his readers remain unaware of the manuscript problems.

It also behoves us to look at the excerpt from the *HA* (found in an apocryphal letter from the emperor Valerian to a mysterious Zosimio, supposedly a *procuratorem Syriae*) in its correct context.[169] The letter records items that were given by Valerian to Claudius, who was, at that time, *tribunum Martiae quintae legioni* (*Claud.* 14.2). Let us look at the military items:

> tunicas russas militares annuas <*duas*>, sagoclamydes annuas duas, fibulas argenteas in-auratas duas, fibulam auream cum acu[m] Cyprea[m] unam. balteum argenteum inauratum unum, anulum bigemm<*em*> unum uncialem, brachialem unam unciarum septem, torquem libralem unum, cassidem inauratam unam, scuta c<*h*>rysografata duo, loricam unam, quam refundat. lanceas Herculianas duas, aclydes duas, falces duas, falces fenarias quattuor. cocum, quem refundat, unum, mulionem, quem refundat, unum. mulieres speciosas ex captiuis duas. albam subsericam unam cum purpura Girbitana, subarmalem unum cum purpura Maura. notarium, quem refundat, unum, structorem, quem refundat, unum. accubital-ium Cypriorum paria duo, i<*n*>terulas puras duas, {fascias uiriles duas}, togam, quam refundat, unam, latum clauum, quem refundat, unum (*Claud.* 14.5–10).

---

[163] In addition, see especially Charles 2003, 127–167.

[164] Reeve 2003, *ad loc.*

[165] Stelten 1990, *ad loc.* Note *apparatus*: "LangAFM, c. se deponere: HJPQ". Cf. Milner (1996, *ad loc.*): "they should hand in …" Milner (1996, 19 n. 6) writes that he follows Otto: "*se de<be>re refundere*".

[166] Reeve 2003, *ad loc.*

[167] Önnerfors 1995, *ad loc.*: "locum desperauit Lang". Önnerfors also notes, *inter alia*, the presence of *se debere fundere* and *sedere fundere* in some MSS.

[168] Müller 1997, *ad loc.* Müller generally follows the Teubner text. Giuffrida Manmana (1997, *ad loc.*) uses the verb "deporre", which suggests a preference for *deponere* in place of *refundere*, likewise Formisano 2003, *ad loc.*

[169] On the nature of such documentation, see Syme 1971b, 1: "a mass of fabrications, notably forged documents"; at 112, the author of the *HA* is described as "a rogue scholar"; see also 1971a, 283: "a plethora of faked documents". For comments on the controversy surrounding false documents in the *HA*, see Paschoud 2001, viii–xii. Paschoud emphasizes that "l'historien ancient fait tout d'abord oeuvre d'art, de rhétorique" (xi), and that "il était normal de recourir à la fiction pour être plus eloquent" (xii). This, of course, is taken to extremes in the *HA*.

When viewed in this context, the reference to a cuirass that had to be returned (*loricam unam, quam refundat*) pales into relative insignificance. As far as I am aware, Vegetius nowhere in the *Epitoma* mentions soldiers (let alone high-ranking officers) returning a cook (*cocum*), a muleteer (*mulionem*), a secretary (*notarium*), a table servant (*structorem*), a toga (*togam*) or a broad-striped tunic (*latum clauum*) at any stage in the Empire's history. All these words appear with *quam*/*quem refundat*, just like *loricam unam*. When viewed in context, the 'Vegetian' *rapprochement* looks far less convincing than it does in Chastagnol's article. The same might be said of the vast majority of the *rapprochements* that he signals, which are generally found in isolation from the context and presented with considerable emendation and truncation.

Indeed, I find far more similarity between the passage introduced above and *Maxim.* 29.8–9 than I do between *Claud.* 14.5 and *Epit.* 1.20.4.[170] For example, both *Maxim.* 29.8–9 and *Claud.* 14.5 list elaborate forms of armour worn by officers. Moreover, both passages use words such as *inauratus, aureus, argenteus* and *gemmatus/bigemmen* (in their appropriate forms). Vegetius does not mention bejewelled officer's equipment, although Ammianus does.[171] If a source for the two passages were to be divined other than Vegetius, it would seem most likely that the *HA*'s author had come upon a list of officer's equipment. Such lists of equipment would have been very much prevalent at the time (one might also adduce lists of military equipment found on recovered papyri or other media). In any case, could not the author have invented the officer's equipment from his own general knowledge? We know that the author was not lacking with respect to verbal creativity. So why is a source absolutely necessary on this occasion? Given that the *Maximini Duo* and *Claudius* were supposedly written by separate authors (Julius Capitolinus and Trebellus Pollio respectively), the above should give further credence to the notion that the *HA*, as a whole, was composed by one hand. One might also note references to decorative military equipment found at *Hadr.* 10.5, where we read as follows: *sine auro balteum sumeret, sine gemmis fibula <sagum> stringeret[ur], capulo uix eburneo spatham clauderet*. Thus it seems, once again, that the author already had material relating to officer's equipment at his fingertips. It is hardly needs to be pointed out that there is no corresponding section in the *Epitoma* whence the above language might have came.

At the risk of labouring the point, let us compare one further significant passage of the *HA* that Chastagnol believes was derived from the *Epitoma*. The similarity of these two passages is less forced. First, the Vegetian *locus* (the capitalization, text[172] and omissions are those of Chastagnol):

---

[170] I have mentioned these two passages elsewhere in passing but did not make a connection (Charles 2004, 129 n. 5).

[171] See Amm. 27.10.11, where the *galeam* of Valentinian I is described as *auro lapillisque distinctam*, which is obviously a reference to a golden helmet studded with precious stones. If it is accepted that the heroes in Latin epic are modelled on contemporary officer figures (see Charles 2004, 127–148), it might well be noted that poets such as Vergil and Silius Italicus also wrote of golden armour of various sorts (especially gilt mail and scale cuirasses).

[172] Önnerfors (1995, *ad loc.*) has *pabuli* in place of *pabulo*; *maximum* for *magnum*; and

Ordo postulat, ut de commeatu pabulo frumentisque dicatur ... Pabulatio et annona in necessitate remedium non habent ... In omni expeditione unum est et magnum telum, ut tibi sufficiat victus ... De copiis expensisque sollers debet esse tractatus, ut pabula, frumentum ceteraeque annonariae species, quas a provincialibus consuetudo deposcit, maturius exigantur et in oportunis ad rem gerendam ac munitissimis locis amplior semper modus, quam sufficit, adgregetur ... Praeterea quidquid in pecore vel quacumque fruge vinoque hostis inferens bellum ad victum suum poterit occupare, non solum admonitis per edicta possessoribus sed etiam coactis per electos prosecutores ad castella idonea ... Sed fidelis horreorum custodia et erogatio moderata consuevit sufficere pro copia ... Hieme lignorum et pabuli, aestate aquarum vitanda est difficultas. Frumenti vero et aceti vel vini nec non etiam salis omni tempore necessitas declinanda (*Epit.* 3.3).

Now for the *HA* (again, the capitalization, text and omissions are those of Chastagnol):

Fuit (Ballista) ... eruditus ad gerendam rem p. ... in expeditionibus clarus, in provisione annonaria singularis ... ["] Si quid in te bonae frugis est, ... dispositiones tu Ballistae persequere. His rem p. informa. Videsne ut ille provinciales non gravet, ut illic equos contineat ubi sunt pabula, illic annonas militum mandet ubi sunt frumenta, non provincialem, non possessorem cogat illic frumenta ubi non habet dare, illic equum ubi non potest pascere? Nec est ulla alia provisio melior quam ut in locis suis erogentur quae nascuntur ... Illic pedites conlocentur, quamquam in Thracia etiam equites sine noxa provincialium hiemare possint. Multum enim ex campis faeni colligitur. Iam vinum, laridum, iam ceterae species in his dandae sunt locis, in quibus adfatim redundant ["] (*Trig. Tyr.* 18.4–9).

It must be admitted that some rather superficial similarities – at least in terms of subject matter – *are* found in these two passages. But, upon closer inspection, the similarities seem to relate most closely to a handful of substantives. The section of the *HA* is taken from what one must regard as an unquestionably spurious letter written by Valerian and addressed to a fictitious *praefectus Illyrici et Galliarum* called Ragonius Clarus (*Trig. Tyr.* 18.5).[173] In the letter, Valerian advises that Ragonius should copy the supply methods of Ballista. The Vegetian passage, though it employs similar words (e.g., *annona, frumentum, uinum,* etc.), deals with sieges and the stockpiling of supplies in case of wartime. One also wonders why Vegetius wrote about oil and salt, whereas the *HA*'s author did not (however, the latter does include bacon, which is not mentioned by Vegetius). The Vegetian passage also asserts that the enemy must be deprived of supplies – a reference, it would seem, to Fabian tactics.

It is interesting to note that the Vegetian references to siege-warfare are conveniently extirpated from the passage by Chastagnol, which does not surprise given that the passage from the *HA* nowhere mentions siege warfare. In fact, if the two passages are compared in detail, it emerges that the very broad central theme of army supply is the only thing that binds them together. Once again, Chastagnol has elided, in the case of the *HA*, elements of the text that would be essential to

---

executores for *prosecutores*; Reeve (2004, *ad loc.*) has *maximum* in place of *magnum*; *quicquid* for *quidquid*; and *executores* for *prosecutores*.

[173] Of course, it need not necessarily follow that all the otherwise unknown addressees and recipients of letters named in the *HA* are fictitious persons (though it is obviously convenient – and perhaps not entirely inaccurate – to do so).

anyone bent on identifying the provenance of the passage. In this case, the Teubner edition preserves *Galatia frumenti<s> abundat, referta est T<h>rac[h]ia, plenum est [inh]Illyricum (Trig. Tyr.* 18.8). This cannot come from Vegetius and is a telling omission in Chastagnol's excerpts. In short, the more one looks at the information contained within the two passages, the more one doubts that one text was derived from the other, although this possibility remains at a somewhat remote level.

Still, let us assume, for argument's sake, that the passage referred to above *does* show some relationship to the *Epitoma*. This seems necessary given that some readers, despite the contrary arguments established above, may still wish to adhere to the belief that Chastagnol's article demonstrates a definite relationship between the two texts. In order to explain the hypothetical similarities, three possibilities present themselves: a) the *HA* borrowed from Vegetius, which would probably mean that Vegetius was writing during the reign of Theodosius I; b) that Vegetius borrowed from the *HA*, which would probably mean that *HA* was written in the fifth century rather than the very late fourth century; and c) that both the *HA* and Vegetius borrowed from another work (or indeed works). Of these possibilities, it will be argued that the third possibility, if we need to explain away supposed verbal similarities, is the more likely.

That the *HA* borrowed from Vegetius presupposes that the *Epitoma* was freely available at some point late in the fourth century. The question must be asked: need we assume that the *Epitoma*, if directed to Theodosius I, would have been disseminated so widely that the author of the *HA* would have been able to gain access to it with such alacrity?[174] Chastagnol evidently thinks so. In any case, it remains a mystery that the *Epitoma*, apparently composed for the attention of a single man and apparently not written with an eye for popular consumption (as far as one can tell), should have enjoyed such popularity at all. If we adhere to the widely-held and generally compelling belief that the *HA* contains passages of immediate relevance to the political situation at the end of the fourth century, and that Vegetius completed the four books of the *Epitoma* at some time after 383 and before mid-395, we are not left with much room to manoeuvre. The window narrows even further if we adhere to the view that the last book of the *Epitoma* was presented to Theodosius in 391, as Chastagnol has proposed in the same article.[175] Finally, with respect to possibility no. 1, why would the author of the *HA*, even if he knew that the *Epitoma* existed, have bothered to consult this work whilst writing imperial biography (even if it is biography of the most spurious and problematic kind)? Unless he knew of the work's contents, it does not necessarily follow that the title would have attracted him.

Now for possibility no. 2. It obviously suits the present thesis to postulate that Vegetius borrowed from the *HA*. This would explain the supposed verbal similarities between the two texts and would mean that Vegetius must have been writing

---

[174] In this context, one might well note that the *HA*'s author hardly appears to have been of the Theodosian party or that of his heirs, especially given his clear pro-pagan bias.

[175] Chastagnol 1974, 62.

in the fifth century, or, at the very least, after the death of Theodosius I. But this seems unduly facile. Now, this line of thought (which, despite our obvious reservations, is not completely beyond the realms of possibility) was not even raised by Chastagnol, such is the thoroughly embedded belief that Vegetius' sources must nearly all be of the calibre of Cato the Elder, Celsus, Frontinus, Paternus, etc.[176] It is far easier to imagine that a work such as the *HA*, the content of which (especially in the later lives) seems little more than the ancient equivalent of tabloid fodder, or else a grand joke on the author's part (albeit with a reasonably demonstrable political or satirical message), should achieve greater popularity and thus greater circulation.[177] That Vegetius, writing after Theodosius I's demise, may have read the *HA* and used some of the material contained therein is thus not entirely improbable. Despite this, it is difficult to give this theory much credence. Although the *Epitoma* certainly has a contemporary polemical flavour, it was the author's desire to resurrect wisdom from the *distant past* so that it could be put to good use in the present. This is a highly simplistic summation of Vegetius' research methodology. Still, it is one that closely reflects the general perception of his *modus operandi*. Thus Vegetius primarily – if not almost exclusively – looked to written sources hailing from the most glorious epoch of Rome's history. Anything written after the second century A.D. would therefore have been dismissed as largely irrelevant.

Let us now look at possibility no. 3, viz., that both the *HA* and Vegetius contain similar passages because the authors used identical, or at least similar, source material. That the majority of the passages in question pertain to imperial lives of the third century matters little. Indeed, these lives are among the more spurious works handed down to us by antiquity. What is clear is that, if these lives are more or less fantasy on the part of the *HA*'s author, the fabricated historical information contained within these lives could have been derived from any number of now-lost sources.[178] If Vegetius also used these now-lost sources for a more legitimate purpose, i.e., in order to compile the *Epitoma*, it is little wonder that *rapprochements* may be found (if, of course, these *rapprochements* are identified as such). What seems likely is that, if the majority of the material contained within the lives of the *HA* is of almost negligible historical reliability for the periods in question, the rest of the material contained within these lives was probably adapted from other sources to suit the occasion. Paschoud has recently calculated that, in the *Probus*, only 16.8% of the information encompasses serious historical information.[179] In the *Quattuor Tyranni*, this figure falls

---

[176] Cato the Elder is mentioned at *Epit.* 1.8.10, 1.13.6, 1.15.4, 2.3.6; Cornelius Celsus at *Epit.* 1.8.11; Frontinus at *Epit.* 1.8.11, 2.3.7; Sallust at *Epit.* 1.4.4, 1.9.8; Tarruntenus Paternus at *Epit.* 1.8.11; Varro at *Epit.* 4.41.6; the *constitutio* of Augustus at *Epit.* 1.8.11, 1.27.1, that of Trajan at *Epit.* 1.8.11, and that of Hadrian at *Epit.* 1.8.11, 1.27.1.

[177] Honoré (1987, 156) contends that the *HA* was meant to represent different things to different audiences, from vulgar humour to serious political commentary.

[178] One might also suggest that not a little of the author's own imagination went into the composition of the various lives, although it is obviously impossible to give any precise proportion.

[179] Paschoud 2001, 301.

to 0%! The life of Aurelian contains 26.6% of useful information, the life of Tacitus 16.8%, and the life of Carus, Carinus and Numerianus 17.2%.[180] A.R. Birley has also calculated various percentages for other lives. The highest figure does not reach more than 33.3%.[181]

Space does not permit a more detailed discussion of Chastagnol's controversial article on Vegetius and the *HA*. In view of this, some concluding remarks are warranted. We have seen that a good many of the supposed *rapprochements* pointed out by Chastagnol, when a discerning eye is cast over them, are not particularly strong. But, in the case of the more troublesome *rapprochements*, could it not be that both were derived from the same *locus*? We know that authors who wrote during this era were familiar with the full gamut of 'classical' Latin material. Indeed, it is often suggested that the era of Gratian through to the battle of the River Frigidus constituted a sort of western classical Renaissance (although this, strongly supported by Syme and others but confidently rejected by Cameron,[182] certainly seems to be a vast overstatement). If the author of the *HA*, as has been generally accepted, *did* write at this time, what prevented him from gleaning this information from earlier sources? Of relevance, too, is that the material presented by Chastagnol is thoroughly abridged in order to accord better with his central thesis. For example, in one of the Vegetian passages quoted above (viz., *Epit.* 3.3), a good many words have been elided, something which obviously makes the two *loci* appear more similar than they might otherwise appear to a more uncritical reader.

In effect, Chastagnol's contention that the *HA* borrowed from Vegetius is little more than a *possibly* valid hypothesis. But his hypothesis, to my mind, seems far too mechanistic when certain historiographical nuances are taken into consideration. On matters of *Quellenforschung*, Cameron has advised us to "distinguish between facts and hypothesis".[183] Even if it is more or less 'factual' that both works contain passages that are, at the very least, superficially similar, it is also more or less 'factual' that both would have had access to the same types of sources. Thus it would not be surprising to find that other works from the same period, now lost, contained passages similar to both Vegetius' text *and* the *HA*. In sum, Chastagnol's study, after some reflection, need not represent such a 'stumbling block' after all.

[180] Paschoud 2001, 301.

[181] See A.R. Birley, forthcoming.

[182] Cameron 2004, 504: "it is a myth. There never was any such classical revival". For the classic treatment of the traditional view, cf. Bloch 1945, 199–244.

[183] Cameron 1977, 8.

CHAPTER 3

TITULATURE AND PRAISE:
THE AUGUSTUS IN THE LATE EMPIRE

Luis de Camões, a man often referred to as the Portuguese Shakespeare, provides suitable testimony of Trajan's posthumous military reputation when he wrote the following lines in his epic tale of Lusitanian conquest and discovery: "Calle-se de Alexandro e de Trajano | A fama das victorias que tiveram".[1] Camões' juxtaposition of Alexander and Trajan should not surprise. It is curious, though, that a Macedonian should represent the epitome of 'Greek' military achievement, and that Trajan, whose *patria* was distant Spanish Italica,[2] should become the embodiment of Rome's martial prowess. But for reasons that may have more to do with his *locus felix* in history than any inherent excellence or outstanding talent, Trajan became, for subsequent generations of Latin-speaking people – including the multi-lingual Camões – the Roman conqueror-statesman *par excellence*. He easily surpasses Augustus in estimations of general worth. It is also worth noting the Eutropian standard: *felicior Augusto, melior Traiano* (8.5.3). As will be seen, the greatest praise for an emperor in the later stages of the Roman Empire was to have his martial abilities equated with those of Trajan.[3] Ammianus writes that Valentinian I, if he had allowed his virtues to conquer his vices, would have matched the excellence of Trajan and Marcus Aurelius: *ad quos si reliqua temperasset, uixerat ut Traianus et Marcus* (30.9.1). With regard to these lines, Syme writes that "Those two names epitomize the good ruler: the warrior and the sage".[4] We need deal only with the warrior.[5]

Theodosius I, by virtue of geographic coincidence and sound martial lineage, was hailed as the new Trajan, the new warrior-emperor. That this was so is attested by a generation of poets, prose-writers and orators. The problem for us is that Vegetius treats his emperor, not as a man who shares the physical hardships

---

[1] *Os Lusiadas*, canto I, stanza 3 (Pierce 1973, 1): "Speak no more of Alexander and Trajan | and the fame of the victories they gained" (my translation).

[2] Since Trajan's father was a senator and thus obliged to reside at Rome when not serving abroad, it seems most likely that the future emperor was born in Rome. Perhaps the *ultima origo* of his family was Tuder in Umbria; cf. Syme 1958, 786, on Ps.-Aur. Vict. *Epit.* 13.1 (*Vlpius Traianus, ex urbe Tudertina*): "The fellow may be right".

[3] Syme entitled a chapter "The Fame of Trajan" in 1971a, 89–112. See also Bennett 1997, xvi–xvii; Mazzarino 1942, 234.

[4] Syme 1971a, 92.

[5] The *HA* provides a spurious letter from Valerian to Aurelian, in which the latter is urged to follow the military example of Trajan: *ego de te tantum ... spero, quantum de Traiano, si uiueret, posset sperare res p.* (*Aurel.* 11.7).

of his *commilitones*, i.e., a Trajan or a Theodosius, but as a secluded figure, a man protected from any contact with enemy steel by the high walls of his citadel. If Vegetius had Theodosius I in mind when he composed the *Epitoma*, one would naturally expect that he would have employed the same type of flattery used by those who wrote during the years 379–395. Yet, in the *Epitoma*, we find no especially convincing evidence of this. In fact, an objective interpretation of the material at hand, in as much as this is possible, appears to demonstrate the contrary supposition, i.e., that Vegetius was writing at a time when military power had passed from the emperor to the *magister militum*.

That Theodosius, that great champion of orthodox Catholicism, should be likened to Trajan, a pagan and apparent sexual libertine, may seem somewhat odd. Although both had a connection to the Iberian Peninsula, were possessed of fathers of a military background, and were of a similar age upon their accession, the two men were diametrically opposed from an ideological perspective. Still, it should be remembered that Trajan was among the few pagans allowed into paradise. Dante Alighieri, in *La commedia divina*, places Trajan in heaven – though he does not name him specifically – from line 43 of *Paradiso* canto 20, and again from line 100. From line 106, the poet alludes to Pope Gregory's prayers (previously referred to at *Purg.* 10.75 as "la sua gran vittoria"),[6] which caused Trajan's soul to be raised up from hell, reunited with his corporeal form so that its owner might embrace Christianity, and then transferred to paradise.[7] Obviously, certain aspects of Trajan's reign and behaviour were conveniently ignored by those who sought to promote his Christian *apotheosis*. His sexual proclivities can hardly have been described as saintly, nor his drinking habits.[8] One should not forget, too, a letter of Pliny the Younger (*Ep.* 10.96) in which the writer describes the stern punishments – including death – meted out to unrepentant Christians. In his reply (*Ep.* 10.97), Trajan approves of Pliny's actions and, although he writes that Christians should not be hunted actively, he does recommend that, if uncovered, their 'crimes' must be punished in full accordance with the law. But all this seems to have been forgotten by Theodosius' flatterers, who

---

[6] Trajan is named specifically at *Purg.* 10.76: "Traiano imperadore". At *Purg.* 10.73–96, Dante recounts the story of the way in which Trajan, as he was setting off for war, was stopped by a widow seeking redress for the death of her son. In the end, she managed to persuade Trajan that her petition was just. For details of this medieval tale, see especially Toynbee 1968, s.v. "Traiano". See also Grandgent 1972, 401 n. 74–75, 806 n. 45.

[7] See Sisson 1993, 593; Singleton 1975, 334.

[8] Cassius Dio (68.7.4) refers to his penchant for μειράκια καὶ ... οἶνον. According to LSJ, s.v. μειράκιον, this word refers to a "lad" or "stripling". Chantraine (1984, s.v. μεῖραξ) holds that the diminutive of μεῖραξ should be translated as "homme jeune". Fronto, in a letter to Marcus Aurelius, notes that Trajan used to amuse himself with both *histriones* (the reflexive use of *delectare* has a decidedly sexual connotation) and drink. See *De Fer. Als.* 3.5 (Teubner edn.)/ 3.4 (Loeb edn.): *proauus uester summus bellator tamen histrionibus interdum sese delectauit et praeterea potauit satis strenue* (Teubner text). The *HA* asserts that Trajan was said to have had relationships with *pueri* (*Hadr.* 2.7). Note, too, the statement about Hadrian and Trajan (*Hadr.* 2.7): *fuitque in amore Traiani*. But this, of course, need not necessarily mean *amor* of a sexual nature. On this theme, see Charles 2002, 37–38.

focused, instead, on the martial reputation of the dead emperor. As a consequence, the same qualities that Pliny the Younger saw in Trajan were found to be
clearly manifest in Theodosius the Great. Of course, the interest for us is Vegetius' apparent departure from the norms customarily employed to address, or
posthumously laud, Theodosius I. The public portrayal of Theodosius, then, is the
control to which we must compare the qualities of Vegetius' honorand.

1. THE RÔLE OF THE EMPEROR

The emperor to whom Vegetius' dedicated his military treatise was not a martial
figure, a man capable of leading troops on his own initiative. He was not even an
armchair general. Rather, he was an untouchable imperial figure who, in his
palace, was far removed from the sweat, blood and clamour of the battlefield.
This contention is clearly demonstrated by an inspection of late-Latin literature
pertaining to the military rôle of the emperor. It is true that, at *Epit.* 3.26.38,
Vegetius writes that his addressee holds the *imperatoris officium ... et militis*. But
one cannot make a great deal of this, for each and every emperor was, by
definition, an *imperator*, and, as such, had to be regarded as the first *miles* of the
Empire. Of course, it mattered not that the emperor might never have participated
in military action. It was equally irrelevant that his victories were attained
through the skill of his generals rather than through his own personal intervention. Even figures as unmilitary as Gaius (Caligula) and Antoninus Pius would
have been officially styled *milites*, such was the nature of their imperial *officium*.
In addition, it is notable that, in a military text of four books, this is the only direct
reference to the emperor as warrior. One should not be surprised, too, that a
military treatise should be addressed to a man such as Valentinian III. Vegetius'
work, in any case, was not simply an exegesis on military works of antiquity, as it
would be regarded in the centuries that followed. Rather, it was a work of
immediate political significance.

    In order to assess perceptions of the military rôle of the emperor in the late
fourth century, we must familiarize ourselves with the opinions of those who
wrote in the age of Theodosius I. Let us begin with Ammianus Marcellinus. It is
obvious that Ammianus, himself a military man of sorts, believed that the
emperor must assume the rôle of *imperator*. To Ammianus, the emperor is the
first soldier of the Empire. It is he who must personally lead his troops to victory.
Ammianus lived through the age of Julian, Jovian, Valentinian I, Valens, Gratian,
and, of course, Theodosius I. While the generalship exhibited by some of these
soldier-emperors – Julian and Valens in particular – was not always first-rate,
Ammianus, nevertheless, would rather praise a general who suffered reverses on
the battlefield (such as his ostensible hero Julian) than laud one whose victories
were won through the agency of his generals. Ammianus notes with approval
actions that show contemporary emperors equalling the hardiness displayed by
the great Republican *duces*. He is especially concerned with praising emperors
who were prepared to comport themselves like common soldiers. For example,

Julian was *munificis militis uili et fortuito cibo contentus* (Amm. Marc. 16.5.3)
and was seen to partake of the *cibum breuem uilemque* (Amm. Marc. 25.4.4).[9]
Ammianus takes especial pleasure, too, in describing the emperor's courage in
the face of battle, to the extent that he turns Julian's slaughter of a single Persian
into a matter of great moment (24.4.4).[10] Moreover, Ammianus' belief in the
soldier-emperor concept readily accords with the image that Theodosius I attempted to promote, i.e., that of an omnipotent military leader.

Upon Valentinian I's elevation of the nine-year-old Gratian to the rank of
Augustus in 367, the emperor called an assembly of his troops. After justifying
his decision to elevate his son, the emperor is moved to discuss the qualities of
character that will serve Gratian in his imperial capacity:

> "librabit suffragiis puris merita recte secusue factorum: faciet, ut sciant se boni intellegi: in
> pulchra facinora procursabit, signis militaribus et aquilis adhaesurus: solem niuesque et
> pruinas et sitim perferet et uigilias: castris (si necessitas adegerit aliquotiens) propugnabit:
> salutem pro periculorum sociis obiectabit: et quod pietatis summum primumque munus est,
> rem publicam ut domum paternam diligere poterit, et auitam" (Amm. Marc. 27.6.9).

Valentinian's speech is greeted with rapturous applause, and the emperor, seizing
the moment, crowns his son (Amm. Marc. 27.6.11). The rest of Valentinian's
speech, save for his final words, is addressed to the new Augustus:

> "en ... habes, mi Gratiane, amictus, ut sperauimus omnes, augustos, meo commilitonumque
> nostrorum arbitrio, delatos ominibus faustis. accingere igitur pro rerum urgentium pondere,
> ut patris patruique collega, et assuesce impauidus penetrare cum agminibus peditum gelu
> peruios Histrum et Rhenum, armatis tuis proximus stare, sanguinem spiritumque consider-
> ate pro his impendere quos regis, nihil alienum putare, quod ad Romani imperii pertinet
> statum. haec pro tempore praecepisse sufficiet, cetera monere non desinam. nunc reliqui
> uos estis, rerum maximi defensores, quos rogo et obtestor, ut accrescentem imperatorem
> fidei uestrae commissum, seruetis affectione fundata" (Amm. Marc. 27.6.12–13).

These words clearly express, and with far more authority and accuracy than those
of any modern scholar, Ammianus' thoughts on the relationship between the

---

[9] On Julian, see also Amm. Marc. 16.5.5, 17.1.2 and 25.2.2, where we again find a reference
to the emperor's meagre diet. Valentinian I is also applauded at Amm. Marc. 29.4.5 for
eschewing luxury in the field. Such remarks, by the fourth century, had enjoyed a long history in
Latin literature. Tacitus praises Vespasian's habits on campaign, where he ate whatever came to
hand and marched at the head of his troops. According to Tacitus (*Hist.* 2.5.1), this emperor, save
his *auaritia*, was *antiquis ducibus par*. Tacitus (*Ann.* 14.24.1) uses very similar language when
he describes Domitius Corbulo. See also Sall. *Iug.* 85.33–34, where Marius enunciates a
general's duties; and also Suet. *Iul.* 57, 62. Cf. also Hdn. 4.7.1–7 (on Caracalla).

[10] On Julian's bravery, see Amm. Marc. 24.2.14–15 and also 25.3.5, where he tells us that
Julian was *inter prima discrimina proeliorum*. At Amm. Marc. 25.4.10, we are told that Julian
fought *inter primos*. Julian died of wounds sustained in battle, and his bravery is attested by
accounts that he neglected to wear a cuirass in the fatal encounter. Zonaras (13.13.17) says that
he had taken off his θώραξ on account of its weight and the stifling weather, while Ammianus
(25.3.3) merely writes that the emperor was *oblitus loricae*. Socrates (*H.E.* 3.21.11–12) holds
that Julian spurned armour because of over-confidence; see also the testimony of Libanius
(18.268). Ammianus (25.3.4) relates that he acted *sine respectu periculi sui*, i.e., he put the
safety of the Empire before his own security.

princeps and his *commilitones*.[11] Above all, Valentinian's speech stresses the bond between emperor and soldier, a bond which, if both parties fulfil their obligations, should enable Rome to flourish and resist her enemies.

Claudian, too, promotes the idea of an emperor leading his forces into battle. He should not be a silent recluse but a man who, like Theodosius I and many of his imperial predecessors, does not shirk from the field. After all, this is the way to engender the love and respect of the troops. And even if he does not raise his sword in the van (Alexandrian heroics were no longer expected), he must nevertheless be somewhere in the rear, ever-present in the rôle of encourager, admonisher and witness to the bravery of his men. Although Stilicho was attempting to fill the vacuum of martial leadership, Claudian perhaps still nurtured hopes that the young Honorius, upon coming of age, would follow the example of his father and grandparent.[12] It is impossible to be sure. Even if Claudian himself did not particularly care about Honorius' imperial duties, it is difficult not to view him as a spokesman for sections of the Roman élite who, even if they had conceded that Honorius was incapable of personal military endeavour, at least wanted the public (or at least the section that mattered) to maintain faith in Stilicho's regency and the possibility of a martial *princeps*. That a similar school of thought existed in the East is demonstrated by Synesius of Cyrene, who encourages the young Arcadius to be a true αὐτοκράτωρ, "a military leader with absolute power" (*De Regno* 19C).[13] Like Claudian's Honorius, Synesius' Arcadius must eventually take the field.

In view of the above, doubts remain about the validity of "the military policy of Claudian" as a useful historical notion, for he may merely be reiterating the viewpoint of Stilicho and his party.[14] Still, a military policy, or at least a semblance of an ideal, can be gleaned from his writings. The *De Quarto Consulatu Honorii* of 398 provides one of the more interesting sources for Claudian's martial idealism. His repeated reference to Trajan, as Paschoud points out, must surely be significant.[15] Trajan is the model on which Honorius must base his rule. Paschoud attributes Claudian's predilection for Trajan to the fact that the latter was "un conquérant victorieux qui étendit les frontières de l'Empire".[16] This is certainly an important consideration, but, as we shall see, there are other – and perhaps more subtle – reasons why the *exempla* of Trajan should serve as models for Honorius.

[11] Often found as *commilites*; see Rowell 1967, 296–297.

[12] Cameron, Long and Sherry (1993, 4) briefly explore this possibility.

[13] Translation of Cameron/Long/Sherry 1993, 119. We are told that philosophy demands that the ruler spend most of his time in the camps rather than in the palace (Synes. *De Regno* 21C–D).

[14] Cameron (1970, *passim*) argues that Claudian was little more than Stilicho's literary puppet and that the majority of his 'official' *opera* was composed for the primary reason of lauding the regent's 'achievements'. This view is also expressed by Christiansen 1966, 45–54; Sebesta 1978, 72–75. *CIL* 6.1710 (= *ILS* 2949) tells us that Claudian had become a sort of 'poet laureate', i.e., the mouth-piece of Stilicho, the *de facto* ruler of the West.

[15] Paschoud 1967, 150.

[16] Paschoud 1967, 150.

In the *De Quarto Consulatu Honorii*, Theodosius delivers a speech to his son in which he instructs him in the art of statesmanship. Would Theodosius have approved of Claudian's choice of an imperial *exemplum*, viz., the emperor Trajan? Given Trajan's reputation, there is certainly no reason why he would not have, and it may very well be that Theodosius himself had modelled his career on that of his fellow 'Spaniard'.[17] As we have seen, Pacatus equated the two Spaniards when he sought the emperor's approbation, and Claudian, it may well be argued, does not follow suit for any idle reason. That Theodosius was "said to have addressed [his son] in these terms"[18] may be as close to actuality as any event that occurs in the panegyric. According to Theodosius, *annales ueterum delicta loquuntur*, while the *portenta* of the Caesars will stand condemned through the ages (*IV. Cons. Hon.* 311–313). From the context, 'Caesars' is not used in a general sense but in a very specific one, i.e., to describe the Julio-Claudians, including the Dictator himself: *Romani ... qui nec Tarquinii fastus nec iura tulere Caesaris* (*IV. Cons. Hon.* 309–310). This conclusion is reinforced by the following:

> quem dira Neronis
> funera, quem rupes Caprearum taetra latebit
> incesto possessa seni? (*IV. Cons. Hon.* 313–315)[19]

On the other hand, the *gloria Traiani* will never die, not just because of his conquest of Dacia and Parthia, but because *patriae ... mitis erat* (*IV. Cons. Hon.* 315–320). Thus Trajan provides a most suitable model of leadership for any emperor: *ne desine tales, / nate, sequi* (*IV. Cons. Hon.* 319–320).[20]

But why are the Julio-Claudians summarily dismissed as malignant despots one and all? Surely there must be some more profound significance to Claudian's fixation with Trajan. And perhaps there is. For Claudian, Spain remains a bastion of virtue, a fitting cradle for the greatest of Rome's soldier-emperors.[21] From this land came Theodosius, the grandfather of the young Honorius and the father of Theodosius the Great.[22] His martial deeds are recounted from line 26 of the

[17] The similarity between Trajan and Theodosius I is taken to such an extent by Pseudo-Aurelius Victor that he writes *fuit autem Theodosius moribus et corpore Traiano similis* (*Epit.* 48.8). He then lists all the personal characteristics that Theodosius shared with Trajan.

[18] This is part of Platnauer's Loeb translation (1922, *ad loc.*) of *ut domus excepit reduces, ibi talia tecum / pro rerum stabili fertur dicione locutus* (*IV. Cons. Hon.* 212–213).

[19] Although Domitian was posthumously ranked among the most evil of the Roman emperors, the Flavians do not rate a mention.

[20] Cf. Pliny, *Pan.* 24.1: *solum ... te commendat augetque temporis spatium*.

[21] See especially Claud. *IV. Cons. Hon.* 18–23. Note, too, Claud. *Nupt. Hon. et Mar.* 2.21–25.

[22] Pseudo-Aurelius Victor also remarks on the provenance of the two emperors: *Theodosius ... genere Hispanus, originem a Traiano principe trahens* (*Epit.* 48.1). Pacatus (*Pan.* 4.2–5) limits himself to saying that Theodosius was a compatriot of the two great 'Spanish' emperors. Themistius also developed the theme of Ulpian ancestry (see *Orat.* 16.205a of 383; *Orat.* 19.229c of 386). Part of this tradition was followed by Marcellinus Comes, who asserts that Theodosius was born at Italica (379.1 [*MGH:AA* 11, *Chron. min.* 2, 60]). Jordanes writes similarly (*Rom.* 315 [*MGH:AA* 5.1, 40]). Cf. Oros. 7.34.2–3, who points out that Trajan was a

panegyric. We are told that Honorius' *auus* had wreaked havoc on the enemy in the north. Saxons, Picts and Scots alike had fallen in vast numbers. The deserts of Africa had also provided victories for him. Although the Moors had proved a valiant foe, they were no match for his armies. Yet these feats of arms pale before the achievements of the elder Theodosius' imperial progeny: *sed laudes genitor longe transgressus auitas* (*IV. Cons. Hon.* 41).[23]

Theodosius the Great was the new Trajan, the second *optimus princeps*. Like the empire of the founder of the *Hibera domus* (*IV. Cons. Hon.* 20), Theodosius ruled from Gades to the Tigris, and all that lay between the Tanais and the Nile (*IV. Cons. Hon.* 43–44). Like Trajan, Theodosius had gained this empire *non generis dono, non ambitione* (*IV. Cons. Hon.* 46). Rather, Theodosius was elevated through merit alone (*IV. Cons. Hon.* 47). What Claudian seems to neglect, at this stage at least, is that Theodosius was only initially designated emperor of the East. It was through force of arms and his desire to avenge the murdered Valentinian II that Theodosius became master of both East and West.[24] But this matters little, and Claudian does at least admit – some twenty-five lines later – that it was the East and not the whole Empire that was initially entrusted to him (*IV. Cons. Hon.* 69–70). As always, Claudian is happy to neglect details in order to present us with the grand truth, which, on this occasion, is that Theodosius was always meant to rule the entire Roman world. For Claudian, all that matters is that Theodosius was there to take the helm of the ship of state and guide it through tempestuous waters (*IV. Cons. Hon.* 59–62). Although a cliché to modern eyes, the metaphor of a tireless *gubernator* steering his vessel through perilous straits was the very image of an ideal leader in the ancient world.[25] A somewhat less elaborate instance can be seen in Pliny's *Panegyricus* at 6.2. Like Trajan, like Theodosius – or so it would seem.

Further allusions to Trajan are found from *IV. Cons. Hon.* 337. Here, Theodosius describes the manner in which a *princeps* should behave on the march, and in battle. Similarities to Pliny's description of Trajan on campaign are immediately obvious. Trajan, so Pliny tells us, shared both the hunger and thirst of his

persecutor, while Theodosius was a *propagator Ecclesiae* (7.34.3). Neither Socrates (*H.E.* 5.2.2) nor Sozomen (*H.E.* 7.2.1) make any direct connection between Trajan and Theodosius. Theodoret (*H.E.* 5.5) says much the same thing, while Rufinus (*H.E.* 11.14) does not even name Theodosius' place of birth.

[23] As Malosse (1997, 519) points out, according to the epideictic genre, "the father had to be praised so that the sons could be praised too". Of course, this is doubly significant in the case of the *De Quarto Consulatu Honorii* – Honorius' grandfather *and* father (at least according to Claudian) were manifestly worthy of praise.

[24] See Claud. *IV. Cons. Hon.* 93ff.

[25] Other examples are found at Eumenius, *Pan.* 14, which quotes Fronto with regard to Antoninus Pius' conduct of the war in Britain; Amm. Marc. 25.5.7, 25.9.7, 26.1.5; *HA Claud.* 1.3, 5.1, 9.2; *Car.* 2.5; Sid. Apoll. *Carm.* 2.15; Claud. *In Eutrop.* 1.424–427; *Bell. Goth.* 271–277. On Claudian's use of this commonplace, see Born 1934, 29. Prudentius uses similar imagery in the preface to book 1 of his *Contra Orationem Symmachi* (45–66), where Wisdom and the Church are both compared to a ship (*ratis ... Sapientiae* [46]; and *catholicam ... puppem* [59–60]).

men on manoeuvres and was not afraid to mingle his *sudor* with their own (*Pan.* 13.1). In battle, he was afraid of no man – he even rejoiced in deadly hand-to-hand combat (*Pan.* 13.1). As a commander, he regularly ensured that his soldiers' weapons (*tela*) were of optimum weight (*Pan.* 13.2), inspected his comrades' tents before retiring to his own, and remained alert if others were needed on duty (*Pan.* 13.3). Like the great generals of old, Trajan led by personal example (*Pan.* 13.4). During his journey from Spain to Germany, we are told that Domitian's legate forsook his mount. Instead, he preferred to walk with his legionary infantry (*Pan.* 14.3). Trajan's actions in the field, such as those described at *Pan.* 19.2–3, caused him to be loved by all. According to Pliny, the commander (*imperator*) and the common soldier (*commilito*) were so combined in Trajan that he could simultaneously fire men's zeal and endurance with his very supervision, whilst mollifying their hardships by sharing in their toil (*Pan.* 19.3). Claudian could easily have written the same about Theodosius I.

With the above borne in mind, it is important to review the works of Merobaudes, the only extant author of any real relevance to hail from the era of Valentinian III, the emperor under whom the *Epitoma* may have been written. The verse of this poet and the writings of Ammianus and Claudian are in need of juxtaposition, and much can be gained from a comparative evaluation. In the *panegyrici* and *carmina* of Merobaudes, there is no reference whatsoever to a martial emperor. No hope is entertained that the emperor himself will descend from his lofty palace in order to smite the foe. Instead, that task falls to men such as Aëtius. The second *panegyricus* takes the form of a *laudatio* devoted entirely to the valiant conduct of the imperial champion. Still, it is notable that, unlike Claudian's *laudationes* on the general Stilicho, the emperor is a figure of no real military importance.

In *Carmen I*,[26] we read about the opulence of the imperial court, a place of constant feasting and unimaginable luxury: *aeternas*[27] *ubi festa dapes conuiuia gestant / purpureisque nitent regia fulcra toris* (*Carm. I*, 3–4). The emperor is a secluded and god-like figure, munificent but untouchable. He is not a man to mingle with the troops or endure the hardship of a forced march. Rather, he is the axis around which the heavens revolve:

> ipse micans tecti medium cum coniuge princ[eps
> lucida ceu s[u]mmi possidet astra poli,
> terrarum ueneranda salus (*Carm. I*, 5–7).

---

[26] Clover (1971, 17) thinks that this poem must date to some time after the second treaty between Rome and the Vandals, which occurred in 442. Vollmer (1904, 1), however, writes that "carmina I et II non possunt esse anni prioris quam p. Chr. 439, cum agatur de baptismo Placidiae secundae Valentiniani filiae; duxit autem uxorem imperator anno 437".

[27] Testi Rasponi (1926, 45) believes that the "l'eterno cibo" (his translation of Merobaudes' *dapes aeternas* [see line 3]) "è sicuramente allusivo alla eucarista". This interpretation, as Clover (1971, 17 n. 16) suggests, should be rejected. There is no need to find Christian allegory in a poem of this nature.

In *Carmen II*, which forms a companion piece to *Carmen I*, we again find the image of a purple-clad emperor shining light upon his subjects.[28] Merobaudes even writes that *celsa*[29] *tenet socia cum coniuge princeps* (*Carm. II*, 9).

It is generally agreed that both *Carmina* represent examples of *ekphrasis*, which literary genre had its origins in the Hellenistic world.[30] In this case, it would appear that the description treats of a work of art (perhaps a mosaic) depicting members of the imperial household.[31] Witness the very first line preserved: *incumbit foribus pictae Concordia mensae* (*Carm. I*, 1). The artwork must have portrayed members of Valentinian III's family rather than that of any previous ruler – a contrary belief would make little sense. This is the interpretation favoured by critics of the *Carmina*.[32] Certainly, the scene of an emperor and his spouse 'on high' is one that should be immediately recognizable to students of late-Roman/Byzantine art.[33] But this does not detract from the worth of these two poems for the present argument, for the dissociation of the emperor from martial and indeed any secular affairs demonstrates the changing rôle of the Augustus in late antiquity (which paved the way for the ritualized and increasingly oriental court-ceremonial that characterized the Byzantine empire).

It is notable that, in fragment IB of the first of Merobaudes' *panegyrici*, Aëtius is given the same attributes as an emperor. Aside from his *Mar[tias laud]es* (*Pan. I*, frg. IB, 9–10), Merobaudes asks who might exhibit

> tanta in consiliis alacritas, in
> iudici]is seueritas, in conloquiis mansuetu-
> do, in uult]u aequalitas, in ira breuitas, in amore
> diuturn]itas? (*Pan. I*, frg. 1B, 10–13)

One can imagine Trajan being lauded in a similar fashion.

We have now seen that, in the space of less than half a century, the expected rôle of the Augustus had changed beyond all recognition. Indeed, it seems that the imperial *officium*, from the rise of the first Augustus to Valentinian III, had turned full-circle. Upon accepting the epithet of Augustus, the first of Rome's emperors effectively distanced himself from the troops, the very men who had

---

[28] *[i]psaque primaeuo lumine tecta nitent,* / *[qu]ae Phoebi flammata rotis et principis ostro* / *aetheris ac terrae sidera mixta tenent* (Merob. *Carm. II*, 2–4).

[29] Of the noun that this adjective qualifies, only *]mina* remains extant.

[30] Catull. 64.50–266 gives the poet's reflections on an embroidered tapestry.

[31] See Bury 1919, 7–8; Clover 1971, 16; Heimsoeth 1843, 532; Olajos 1966, 175–176; Oost 1965, 4–7; id. 1983, 264; Sirago 1961, 355–357, and especially 356; Testi Rasponi 1926, 43–47.

[32] e.g., Bury 1919, 7–8; Clover 1971, 16ff.; Heimsoeth 1843, 532; Oost 1965, 4–7; Vollmer 1904, 1–2; Sirago 1961, 356; Testi Rasponi 1926, 44–46. Debate has ensued over the identification of some of the figures in the two *Carmina*. Still, the *princeps* to whom the poet refers in both works is generally described as Valentinian III.

[33] Oost (1965, 5) draws our attention to the mosaics depicting Justinian and Theodora in the church of San Vitale at Ravenna, and the reliefs at the base of Theodosius I's obelisk at Constantinople. For the Ravennan mosaic, see Rice 1959, monochrome pl. 58. For the reliefs of the obelisk, see Rice 1959, monochrome pl. 5, and the illustrations accompanying Wace/Traquair 1909, 60–69. One might also note diptychs of the consuls, often accompanied by women and children or allegorical figures, who preside over games or other festive scenes.

been, and still would be, a significant element of his power. Of course, Augustus did this largely for political reasons, viz., to disguise the true nature of his position and to allay senatorial discomfort. Happily for Rome, his action had few negative repercussions. The universal desire for peace after generations of internal conflict allowed this separation of emperor and soldiery to be effected without the indignation or alienation of the men whom he had once called *commilitones* (Suet. *Aug.* 25.1). Once again, in the mid-fifth century, the emperor had chosen to distance himself from the mire of the battlefield, and his Drusus and Tiberius, the agents of Augustus' will, would be Aëtius and the barbarian chiefs who had sworn their allegiance to the emperor. Like Augustus, Valentinian III was a figure of court, a wielder of the stylus rather than the sword. Let us now see how the recipient of Vegetius' *Epitoma* fits into this picture.

2. *IMPERATOR ORBIS TERRARUM*

After Theodosius the Great's death in 395, the Empire was divided between his two sons, both of whom had already been raised to the rank of Augustus. Arcadius, the elder son, gained the East and Honorius, the younger son, became ruler of the West. That the division between East and West was militarily significant is attested by the division of the contemporary *Notitia Dignitatum* into oriental and occidental sections.

Yet nowhere in the *Epitoma* do we find a reference to any division between Constantinople and Rome (or Ravenna). This, perhaps understandably, has fostered notions that the text was written under Theodosius I, the last emperor to rule both sections of the Empire. Indeed, several scholars have argued that certain tracts of the *Epitoma* can only mean that the emperor to whom the work was addressed was the ruler of both East and West. In order to show that the emperor need not rely on foreigners to fill the ranks, Vegetius names a series of war-like peoples who have long been subjects of the Roman Empire:

> neque enim degenerauit in hominibus Martius calor nec effetae sunt terrae quae Lacedaemonios, quae Athenienses, quae Marsos, quae Samnites, quae Paelignos, quae ipsos progenuere Romanos. nonne Epiri armis plurimum aliquando ualuerunt? nonne Macedones ac Thessali superatis Persis usque ad Indiam bellando penetrarunt? Dacos autem et Moesos et Thracas in tantum bellicosos semper fuisse manifestum est ut ipsum Martem fabulae apud eos natum esse confirment (*Epit.* 1.28.2–4).

This list includes not only westerners, such as the Marsi, Samnites and the Romans themselves, but also the subjects of Constantinople, *inter alios*, the Spartans, Dacians, Macedonians and Thracians. Several scholars have used the above to advance their own particular imperial choice. The most unusual conclusion is that of Zuckerman. He holds that *Epit.* 1.28.2–4 can be used to show that the Augustus to whom the *Epitoma* was dedicated was "un jeune empereur qui règne sur l'Italie et les Balkans".[34] Zuckerman's argument fails to convince.

---

[34] Zuckerman 1994, 73. See also preceding pages of the same article (70–72).

More significant, at least in terms of its influence on subsequent writers, is Mazzarino's conclusion.[35] The inference that he draws from *Epit.* 1.28.2–4 is that the unnamed emperor must have ruled both East and West – given our *termini* of 383 and 450, this could only have been Theodosius I.[36] According to Mazzarino, that Vegetius mentions peoples who lived in the eastern half of the Empire precludes the possibility that the work was addressed to either Honorius or Valentinian III. Witness, too, the following argument of Chastagnol:

> Il ressort de l'ensemble du traité militaire de Végèce que l'empereur destinaire semble régner à la fois sur l'Orient et l'Occident .... c'est sans conteste le règne de Théodose Ier qui convient plus particulièrement, entre 383 et 395, et surtout, dans ce laps de temps, le moment où Théodose a séjourné en Italie et dirige l'ensemble du monde romain, après la defaite de Maxime, de 388 à 391.[37]

Such an interpretation, however, should be regarded as groundless, especially since the list at *Epit.* 1.28.2–4 is not meant to be merely a list of potential recruits. As Goffart first proposed,[38] its main purpose is to group together, in quasi-chronological and geographical order, valiant peoples of a "notoriously glorious military ... [past]" whose descendants live within the boundaries of the Empire. The Dacians represent the only exception.[39] To return to Vegetius' "ensemble de peuple", the Athenians and Spartans, the main combatants of the Peloponnesian War, are grouped together.[40] The Marsi, Samnites, Paeligni and Romani, all of whom were involved in Italian struggles, are treated in a similar fashion. Next, there is an allusion to Epirus (i.e., the kingdom of Pyrrhus) and the might of Alexander's Macedonians and allied Thessalians. Finally, Vegetius alludes to Roman encounters with the Dacians, most probably those that occurred during the reigns of Domitian and Trajan. For reasons of geographic unity, it is at this point that our author invokes the Moesians and the Thracians.

The list at *Epit.* 1.28.2–4, therefore, has a purely rhetorical import. Its real purpose is to point out that Rome need not rely on Germanic mercenaries. Despite

---

[35] Mazzarino 1956, 542. In his argument against a Honorian date, Mazzarino writes that "Vegezio non sembra rivolgersi ad un imperatore che governi solo una delle due *partes*: il suo imperatore non è soltanto *domitor omnium gentium barbarorum*, ma anche *dominus et princeps generis humani*". In addition: "Vegezio, quando vuole rassicurare il suo imperatore sulla capacità guerriera dei suoi uomini (I 28), cita gli antichi italiani e greci, ma anche Macedoni, Tessali, Daci, Mesi, Traci; che significato avrebbe avuto quest'ultima citazione (specie quella dei Traci) per rassicurare un imperatore come Onorio che governava la *pars* occidentale?" Sirago (1961, 468) endorses and largely reiterates Mazzarino's argument.

[36] Mazzarino 1956, 542.

[37] Chastagnol 1974, 62. Cf. Richardot 2003, 537: "Végèce écrit son traité ... entre 386 et 388".

[38] Goffart 1977, 77.

[39] Still, Vegetius might have imagined that it was not the descendants of Roman colonists who were withdrawn from Dacia when the province lapsed into barbarian control during the reign of Aurelian, but the descendants of Decebalus. Roman colonists were moved south of the Danube to Moesia, and to the province of Dacia Aureliani. This probably occurred in 271; see *HA Aurel.* 39.7.

[40] Note Merobaudes' references to these two peoples at *Pan. I*, frg. IA, 11–13.

this, some modern scholars have taken Vegetius' words at face-value, and, in particular, his assertion that *longum est si uniuersarum prouinciarum uires enumerare contendam, cum omnes in Romani imperii dicione consistant* (*Epit.* 1.28.5).[41] Indeed, such authorities ignore the political realities and cultural context in which the *Epitoma* was written, i.e., that one was expected to praise, sometimes in outlandish fashion, the incumbent ruler. As Goffart points out, "the same reading of a panegyric by Sidonius would turn Majorian into the ruler of the entire Empire".[42] The ineffectual Majorian, emperor of the West during the twilight years of the occidental Empire, was hardly in control of such places as Corinth, Epirus, Pontus and Sparta, let alone the lands of the Assyrians, India and distant China (*Ser*) (*Carm.* 5.40–50).

In similar fashion, Gratian is described by Ausonius in his *Gratiarum Actio* as the ruler of the whole Empire, even though, when the speech was declaimed (the second half of 379),[43] he was only emperor of the West – a position which he maintained in association with his half-brother Valentinian II.[44] Ausonius writes that, while the cities of Rome, Constantinople, Antioch, Carthage, Alexandria and Trèves are far apart, *uota consentiunt* (*Grat. Act.* 7.35). According to the orator, *unus in ore omnium* – and the name of that man is *Gratianus* (*Grat. Act.* 7.35). That Theodosius I was master of Constantinople, Antioch and Alexandria is ignored. To Ausonius (who largely ignores Valentinian II), there is only one emperor regnant. Elsewhere, this obvious falsehood is expanded upon, to such an extent that Gratian is credited with having avenged the death of his uncle Valens at the hand of the Goths (*Grat. Act.* 2.7),[45] and having conquered the Sarmatae (*Grat. Act.* 2.9). Yet these feats were presumably accomplished by Theodosius.[46] Gratian is even credited with restoring order to the eastern half of the Empire, a claim which, though not entirely unwarranted before Theodosius' accession on 19 January 379, is certainly specious after that date.[47] Lastly, Ausonius expresses

---

[41] On the other hand, Giuffrida Manmana (1997, 25) correctly identifies the nature of the passage in question – and its irrelevance to the problem at hand.

[42] Goffart 1977, 77.

[43] Green (1991, 537), after considering the available evidence, holds that "a date in August is possible" and that "the speech was probably, but not certainly" delivered before December.

[44] See Auson. *Grat. Act.* 2.7, where brief mention is made of Valentinian II. Ausonius writes that there is ample evidence to demonstrate the dutiful nature of Gratian, among which is *instar filii ad imperium frater ascitus* (*Grat. Act.* 2.7). At *Grat. Act.* 10.48, we are told that Gratian obeyed divine will *in cooptando fratre*. The four-year-old Valentinian II was raised to the purple by the army in 375; see Amm. Marc. 30.10.1–6; Zos. 4.19.1. Cf. Philostorg. *H.E.* 9.16.

[45] At *Grat. Act.* 10.48, Ausonius writes that Gratian acted in accordance with the will of God *in ulciscendo patruo*.

[46] Of course, these campaigns had begun while Theodosius was merely a subordinate of Gratian. In view of this, Gratian could legitimately claim any victories before January 19 as 'his'. Theodosius also had success against the Sarmatians after Gratian's death. See Symm. *Rel.* 47.1, where a victory over the Sarmatae is attributed to Valentinian II, Theodosius and Arcadius. Barrow (1973, 229 n. 1) thinks that the victory "must have occurred recently, perhaps in 383, and by an army of Theodosius". The campaign was carried out by an unnamed general (*felicem ... belli istius ducem*) (*Rel.* 47.2).

[47] Theodosius' pre-imperial victories, of course, can be assigned quite satisfactorily to his commander-in-chief.

his *gratiae* to a man whom he describes as *consultissimus* (*Grat. Act.* 2.7). In order to demonstrate this quality, he writes that *probat hoc tali principe oriens ordinatus* (*Grat. Act.* 2.7). Once again, no mention of Theodosius is to be found.[48] While Sivan thinks it "surprising" that "Theodosius is altogether absent from this record",[49] silence with regard to Gratian's imperial colleague in the East was a thoroughly acceptable convention. Conversely, it should hardly surprise us to find that Themistius, delivering a speech in Theodosius' presence (*Orat.* 16.200c, 16.201a), should give the eastern emperor sole credit for the peace that was established with the Goths, to the detriment of his western colleague Gratian (*Orat.* 16.207b).[50] Note that Themistius, at *Orat.* 16.203d, calls Theodosius "the ruler of all things" (τῷ κρατοῦντι τῶν ὅλων).[51]

The emperor of either the East *or* the West, so it seems, was still the sole Roman emperor, the *dominus ac princeps generis humani*, when referred to in any literature of a laudatory nature.[52] For instance, an eastern courtier would hardly have referred to his imperial master as 'emperor of the East'. Likewise, a western courtier would not have addressed his sovereign as 'emperor of the West'.[53] Zuckerman is of a similar opinion. Although he promotes the case for Valentinian II, he acknowledges that it is preposterous to believe that an emperor would ever be given "le titre de maître d'une moité du monde".[54] Inscriptions dating to after 443 reinforce this. These inscriptions record that Valentinian III, the emperor of an ever-dwindling Western Empire, was saluted as *dominus rerum humanarum*.[55] This title is also conferred on Gratian by Ausonius (*Grat. Act.* 18.80). Such a salutation, which hardly corresponds to the actual power of Valentinian III, is obviously of similar value to *dominus ac princeps generis*

---

[48] The Teubner text has been used here. Green (1991, 541) does read *participe* for *principe* at *Grat. Act.* 2.7 ("[*principe*] ... make[s] a strangely oblique tribute to Gratian"), but all other editors have opted for the latter reading. Green retains *participe* in the 1999 Oxford edition.

[49] Sivan 1996, 205.

[50] As Heather and Moncur (2001, 275 n. 230) write, the orator "unambiguously gave Theodosius all the credit .... This may have been true, but he was carefully downplaying Gratian's role".

[51] Translation of Heather/Moncur 2001, *ad loc*. Cf. Prudent. *c. Symm.* 1.9, where Theodosius I is called *moderator ... orbis*. Presented as a reply to Symmachus' petition of 384, the work is generally believed to date to several years after Theodosius' death. Note, too, *c. Symm.* 1.35–36: *contigit ecce hominum generi gentique togatae / dux sapiens*; *c. Symm.* 1.427–429.

[52] The author of the fourth-century *De Rebus Bellicis* addressed his work to *sacratissimi principes* (prol. 1) and *clementissimi principes* (prol. 8), perhaps emperors of both the East and West. Yet, in the body of the text, he refers to a single recipient (*DRB* 2.6–7, 18.7, 21.1).

[53] For example, Ambrose writes that Theodosius I, present in Italy at the time, ought to cultivate the *domini ... clementiam* for the *imperium Romanum* (*Ep.* 40.31), i.e., the whole Empire. The letter dates to December 388, a time when Valentinian II was still nominally in control of the West.

[54] Zuckerman 1994, 74. See also Goffart 1977, 77 n. 57.

[55] *CIL* 6.1197–1198 (= *ILS* 807–808). Cf. *CIL* 6.1140 (= *ILS* 692), which ascribes the title *restitutor humani generis* to Constantine the Great in 314/315, i.e., ten or so years before he became ruler of the whole Empire. Note that Constantine was also addressed as *triumphator* (*CIL* 6.1141 of 334, 6.1144 [no date]) and *uictor* (*CIL* 6.1144). See also Chastagnol 1974, 61.

humani. Moreover, records such as those discussed above clearly demonstrate that the application of nonsensical titles continued while the Empire crumbled. There should be no real reason, then, to use the references mentioned by scholars such as Chastagnol and Mazzarino to confirm a Theodosian date for the *Epitoma*. The matter of titulature will be discussed in greater detail below.

A further relevant point is that Sozomen, in the dedicatory section of his ecclesiastical history, provides a prospectus of the contents of his work. Sozomen, who dedicated his volume to Theodosius II (*Ded.* 3), writes that the ninth book will cover events of the current emperor's reign (*Ded.* 21). No mention of Valentinian III here. Moreover, this emperor is mentioned only once in the entire history (viz., *H.E.* 9.16.2).[56] That Sozomen fails to refer to Valentinian III in the dedication, but does so in the body of the text, should clearly demonstrate the gulf that existed between panegyric and history. Still, Sozomen, in the dedication, does not refrain from making reference to the collegiate nature of imperial rule before Honorius' death. He notes that the Empire was ruled simultaneously by Valentinian I and Valens (*Ded.* 19); then by Gratian, Valentinian II and Theodosius I (*Ded.* 20); and that, afterwards, the purple was shared by Arcadius and Honorius (*Ded.* 20). From the chronology that Sozomen employs, it would appear that Theodosius II became emperor of the East after his father's death in 408, and sole emperor after the death of his uncle in 423.[57]

If one assumes that Vegetius dedicated his work to Valentinian III, a ruler whom he would have addressed anachronistically as emperor of East *and* West, Sozomen provides a contemporary eastern parallel to the epitomator's approach. Like the *praefationes* of Vegetius' *Epitoma*, the dedicatory section of the *Historia Ecclesiastica* is of a panegyrical nature. Thus it may be seen that, in the West, one addressed one's work to Valentinian III and that, in the East, one did so to Theodosius II. While the collegiate reality of the Empire continued to be acknowledged in official documentation (such as *leges nouellae*), those who sought to flatter their imperial patron could dispense with the truth in order to magnify the glory of their immediate Augustus.

Although Pacatus does mention that his honorand Theodosius I was given the helm of the Empire in order to guard the youth of one emperor (i.e., Valentinian II) and assist another (i.e., Gratian) (*Pan.* 3.5),[58] the panegyrist writes as if both these historical figures no longer existed when he declaimed his speech – and indeed Gratian had been murdered in 383. A reference to Arcadius, already an Augustus by this date, is made by the spirit of the Republic in the context of an exhortation to accept Gratian's offer of imperial rule (*Pan.* 11.4). By means of this chronological artifice, Pacatus avoids having to make reference to a further imperial colleague. Instead, the Republic merely warns the future emperor that

---

[56] Cf. the ecclesiastical history of Socrates, who tells us that Theodosius II, under whom he wrote, nominated his young cousin Valentinian as emperor of the West after the death of Honorius (*H.E.* 7.24.2). See also Socrat. *H.E.* 7.44.1.

[57] Note, too, that one finds no mention of Constantius III in the dedication.

[58] See also Pacat. *Pan.* 11.5, where it is asserted that the elder of the two young *principes* is unequal to the task of governing the whole Empire, while the other is still a child.

his descendants (an oblique reference to both Arcadius *and* Honorius) may suffer if the barbarian masses are not tamed by him: *nescis me tibi tuisque decrescere?* (*Pan.* 11.4). In any case, Pacatus' references to Valentinian I's imperial progeny are only made in order to demonstrate the legitimacy of Theodosius' accession, i.e., to rebuff any suspicion that Gratian's hand had been forced.[59] As Pacatus states twice, Theodosius had been made emperor *inuitus* (*Pan.* 12.1–2).[60] Throughout Pacatus' panegyric, there is only one emperor in real control of the Empire, and that man is Theodosius.

3. QUALITIES OF THE *PRINCEPS*

Even more dubious grounds for nominating Theodosius (or Valentinian II) are provided by Wisman. She points out that it is unlikely that the *Epitoma* was directed towards Valentinian III because this emperor "était un homme faible et dissolu".[61] After naming some of his faults, including his jealousy of Aëtius and his supposed predilection for violating beautiful women, Wisman offers that "Il semble que les mots d'éloge de Végèce à l'empereur ne peuvent guère s'appliquer à Valentinien III".[62] In order to demonstrate this point, Wisman draws our attention to the following:

> cunctos imperatores felicitate moderatione castimonia, exemplis indulgentiae, studiorum amore praecedis. regni animique tui bona cernimus et tenemus, quae anticipare et superior optauit aetas et extendi in perpetuum uentura desiderat (*Epit.* 4 prol. 4–5).

Wisman seems to hold that Vegetius' "mots d'éloge" do not accord with the general perception of Valentinian III, and that this emperor, as a consequence, need not be considered as Vegetius' recipient. This represents a rather strange interpretation. What living emperor was not supposed to promote *felicitas* or possess *moderatio, castimonia, indulgentia,* and embrace a love of study? Those seeking to court the imperial ear habitually refer to such qualities. Moreover, they represent the inverse of the character faults displayed by 'bad' emperors.[63] As Lang initially observed, such eulogistic compliments, in addition to other words of praise and titles that will be dealt with below, could be addressed to any emperor.[64] Does Wisman expect that Vegetius, if he were writing under Valentinian III, would mention the emperor's *debilitas, libido* and *inuidia*? Would he write of *miseria* instead of *felicitas*? Of course not. In literature, the present age was generally a happy age. Tacitus, in the earlier Principate, writes thus on three

[59] On this, see Sivan 1996, 198–211.

[60] See also Pacat. *Pan.* 11.1–7.

[61] Wisman 1979, 14.

[62] Wisman 1979, 14. Wisman seems to have based her assessment of Valentinian III on that of Procopius (see especially *Vand.* 3.3.10–11).

[63] On 'good' and 'bad' emperors, see Dunkle 1971, 12–20. In this article, Dunkle traces the development of the rhetorical tyrant in Roman literature. See also Wallace-Hadrill 1995, 142ff.

[64] Lang 1867, n. 67. As Goffart (1977, 79 n. 69) points out, "he went on to argue from them nevertheless" (!).

occasions.[65] And, as we see from more contemporary works (e.g., those of Ausonius, Claudian, and even the late-fifth-century Sidonius Apollinaris), this tradition was alive and flourishing in the last century of the Western Empire. With this
in mind, there remains no conceivable reason why Vegetius' words at *Epit.* 4
prol. 4–5 could not have been directed towards Valentinian III.

The tone with which Vegetius addresses his honorand is also significant. To
my mind, the tone is one of somewhat ill-disguised condescension. Witness the
following:

> digesta sunt, imperator inuicte, quae nobilissimi auctores diuersis probata temporibus per
> experimentorum fidem memoriae prodiderunt, ut ad peritiam sagittandi, quam in serenitate
> tua Persa miratur, ad equitandi scientiam uel decorem, quae Hunnorum Alanorumque natio
> uelit imitari si possit, ad currendi uelocitatem, quam Saracenus Indusque non aequat, ad
> armaturae exercitationem, cuius campidoctores uel pro parte exempla intellexisse se gaud-
> ent, regula proeliandi, immo uincendi artificium iungeretur, quatenus uirtute pariter ac
> dispositione mirabilis rei publicae tuae et imperatoris officium exhiberes et militis (*Epit.*
> 3.26.35–38).

Such a tone would hardly have been suitable for addressing an experienced
general and military commander such as Theodosius I. That the Augustus was
(supposedly) skilled in archery, a fine horseman, a swifter runner than the Indians
and Saracens, and a master at *armatura*, points to a young emperor such as
Valentinian III. Sirago, however, wonders how the admiration of the Persians,
"che ormai non avevano più alcun rapporto con la pars Occidentale", could
possibly be attributed to Valentinian III. Once again, Sirago fails to take into
account the panegyrical nature of Vegetius' language. The *Persae*, be they 'native' Persians or their Parthian overlords, were famed in antiquity for their skill
with the bow.[66] In view of this, to have one's ability with the bow compared to
that of the *Persae* constituted an especially high form of praise. Perhaps Sirago
has forgotten that Honorius, who, like Valentinian III, was a western emperor,
also had his archery skills compared to those of a Persian people, in this case the
Parthians.[67] Furthermore, at line seven of Merobaudes' *Carmen III*, which was
certainly written during the reign of Valentinian III, we find another reference to
Persian marksmanship, albeit a fragmentary one: *nec Achaemeniae possent pene-
trare sagittae*.[68]

Milner, like Mazzarino and Sirago,[69] also sees the passage in question as an
indication that the emperor was Theodosius:

> The presence of these barbarians [i.e., those found at *Epit.* 3.26.35–38] in the context of
> feats of arms ... may suggest tournaments, i.e. friendly competition. In any event, the

---

[65] According to Tacitus (*Agr.* 44.5), it was unfortunate that his father-in-law Agricola was
not permitted *durare in hanc beatissimi saeculi lucem ac principem Traianum uidere*. See also
Tac. *Agr.* 3.1; *Hist.* 1.1.4.

[66] Claudian describes the Parthian (i.e., Persian) masses as a *plebs pharetrata* (*Cons. Stil.*
1.55).

[67] See Claud. *IV. Cons. Hon.* 530–531; *Nupt. Hon. et Mar.* 1.1–2.

[68] That which cannot be pierced is a *buxus amoena* (Merob. *Carm. III*, 6).

[69] Mazzarino 1956, 542; Sirago 1961, 468.

particular combination of names best suits the reign of Theodosius I, who concluded peace-treaties with the king of Persia, and with the Saracens and people called 'Indians' ... as well as with the Huns and Alans ... in the A.D. 380s. [70]

No evidence whatsoever exists to support the notion of friendly games between Rome and her erstwhile enemies during the Theodosian period.[71] Moreover, the various skills that Vegetius introduces are meant to be personal qualities of the emperor – there is no other reason for their inclusion in the *Epitoma*. Despite Milner's rather fanciful digression, one can hardly imagine that a forty-year-old general, a man who had apparently proved a successful *dux* in Moesia as early as 374,[72] would have been particularly impressed by the rejoicing of the *campidoctores* (*Epit.* 3.26.37), especially when his real military achievements were left unmentioned. Indeed, this very same passage forced Seeck to conclude that:

> Von dem man solche Leibesübungen zu erwarten berechtigt war; einen mehr als vierzigjährigen Mann aber, der immer zu Ruhe und Wohlleben neigte und zuletzt an der Wassersucht starb, wegen seiner Schnellläuferkünste rühmen, das hätte wie Hohn geklungen.[73]

That Vegetius' emperor was a young man, rather than a dropsical individual of over forty, makes a good deal of sense. Förster, though he disagrees with Seeck's overall conclusion, writes that "Cum laudes, quibus Vegetius imperatorem suum ornat, communes ac tritas esse recte Seeck moneat".[74] Pacatus, in his panegyric of 389 (the time when some believe that the *Epitoma* was presented to Theodosius), wrote of the emperor's brief retirement from public life. Of course, this 'retirement' to the family estates in Spain was the result of his father's execution in 376. The panegyrist holds that this period of relative inactivity was the work of Fortuna (*Pan.* 9.1), who wanted the future emperor to rest, since he had already developed a complete mastery of the martial arts: *quia iam ad plenum bellicis artibus abundabas* (*Pan.* 9.2). Pacatus thus asserts that Theodosius had completed his military training well before his first foray into the Italian peninsula. Vegetius' praise for his emperor's athletic ability, consequently, seems to be at odds with the above. Indeed, Giuffrida Manmana holds that the passage in question intimates that that the emperor, though supposedly an expert in the practice of arms, still needed a guide to help perfect his developing skills.[75] The same cannot be said for Theodosius the Great. One is reminded of Sozomen' assertion that Pulcheria, Theodosius II's elder sister, saw to her brother's instruc-

---

[70] Milner 1996, 119 n. 6. Cf. Pacat. *Pan.* 22.2–5. Socrates (*H.E.* 5.12.2) records that the Persians sent an embassy to Theodosius while preparations were being made for the war against Maximus.

[71] It is certainly difficult to imagine Theodosius I instituting his own version of the 'Goodwill Games' in order to foster amicable relations between the Empire and its former enemies.

[72] On this victory, see Amm. Marc. 29.6.15; Zos. 4.16.6. Note, too, Hieron. *Chron.* 375 p. Chr. (*Euseb. Werk.* 7, 247 g): *quia superiore anno Sarmatae Pannonias uastauerant, idem consules permansere.* The events that occurred *superiore anno* are presumably those referred to by Ammianus and Zosimus.

[73] Seeck 1876, 64.

[74] Förster 1895, 7.

tion in horsemanship (ἱππική) and the use of arms (ἐν τοῖς ὅπλοις) – and this in addition to more intellectual instruction in the liberal arts ([ἐν] ... τοῖς λόγοις: *H.E.* 9.1.6). According to this sober ecclesiastical account, martial instruction is largely a boyhood activity. The Latin panegyrists, as will be seen directly below, provide further evidence of this.[76]

Claudian's *De Quarto Consulatu Honorii*, composed *c.* 398, makes especial mention of the athletic abilities of the young emperor, who, despite the poet's assertions to the contrary in a previous panegyric,[77] had never witnessed combat before his father's death. Nor would he do so at any time in his twenty-eight-year reign. Whether Honorius really excelled in the various martial fields is quite immaterial.[78] All that matters is that the exercise of these skills is the preserve, in late-Latin literature, of a young, palace-bound emperor. Such a figure is clearly divorced from the rigour of campaigning. Rather, he is a perpetual youth who, although capable of shooting arrows at a body of straw, has never loosed a shaft into a man's living flesh. Claudian makes mention of what may very well be Vegetius' *armatura*, i.e., fencing with helmet and golden armour (*IV. Cons. Hon.* 523–524). Furthermore, he is moved to comment that *promittitur ingens / dextra rudimentis Romanaque uota moratur* (*IV. Cons. Hon.* 521–522). We then find reference to Honorius' proficiency with missile weapons – in this case, arrows and a type of late-Roman javelin called the *spiculum*.[79] In particular, note the reference to the skill of the Parthians, which recalls *Epit* 3.26.36:

> quae uires iaculis uel, cum Gortynia tendis
> spicula, quam felix arcus certique petitor
> uulneris et iussum mentiri nescius ictum!
> scis, quo more Cydon, qua dirigat arte sagittas
> Armenius, refugo quae sit fiducia Partho (*IV. Cons. Hon.* 527–531).

Next, Claudian praises the young emperor's equestrian skills. The following represents merely a sample of the twenty-six lines (*IV. Cons. Hon.* 539–564) that he devotes to the topic: *non te Massagetae, non gens exercita campo / Thessala, non ipsi poterunt aequare bimembres* (*IV. Cons. Hon.* 542–543). So, Claudian's

---

[75] Giuffrida Manmana (1997, 18) writes that Vegetius' emperor "è esperto in tutte le attività pratiche, ma sembra abbia bisogno di una guida".

[76] It is worth noting that Prudentius (*c. Symm.* 2.7) calls Arcadius and Honorius *armorum dominos uernantes flore iuuentae*.

[77] Claudian (*III. Cons. Hon.* 93–98) credits Honorius with summoning the divine wind (*turbo*) at the Frigidus. More reliable accounts place the young prince at Constantinople (see Socrat. *H.E.* 5.26.2; Sozom. *H.E.* 7.24.1, 7.29.4).

[78] Literary critics dealing with verse written in the first century A.D. have paid increasing attention to what they consider to be the ironical and ambiguous content incorporated in material ostensibly meant to praise the emperor. On *figurae*, see Quint. *Inst.* 9.2.65ff., and especially 9.2.67–68; see also Suet. *Dom.* 10.1. Despite this, Claudian's laudatory treatment of the supposed martial abilities of Honorius is to be read as outrageous flattery (rather than subtle criticism of his non-martial character).

[79] Vegetius (*Epit.* 2.15.5) describes the *spiculum* as the 'modern-day' equivalent of the *pilum*.

reference to the athletic and sporting abilities of Honorius, an emperor who never commanded his troops in person, closely reflects *Epit.* 3.26.35–38.[80]

But what of those emperors who were most definitely *duces*? Did they not also have the same physical qualities? Of course they did. As will be seen, all the emperors for whom material of a panegyrical nature remains[81] are described in the fashion employed by Vegetius at *Epit.* 3.26.35–38. However, these qualities are exhibited in youth, and are almost always a precursor to actual military achievement. Thus Ausonius' *Gratiarum Actio*, directed towards Gratian, and Sidonius Apollinaris' *panegyrici* on the emperors Avitus (*Carm.* 7), Majorian (*Carm.* 5) and Anthemius (*Carm.* 2) – all of whom were military leaders before their respective accessions – provide a telling contrast to the Vegetian passage cited above, and the relevant section of the *De Quarto Consulatu Honorii*.[82]

Ausonius' prose *Panegyricus ad Gratianum* effectively illustrates the contemporary belief that personal ability in war-like pursuits presages a successful military career. After remarks on his subject's Christian piety, Ausonius informs us that the emperor excels at running, wrestling, leaping and hurling missile weapons:

> in exercendo corpore quis cursum tam perniciter incitauit? quis palaestram tam lubricus expediuit? quis saltum in tam sublime collegit? nemo adductius iacula contorsit, nemo spicula crebrius iecit aut certius destinata percussit (*Grat. Act.* 14.64).

Ausonius devotes further space to Gratian's equestrian skills, which recall those of the Numidians at 4.41 of Vergil's *Aeneid* (*Numidae infreni*):

> mirabamur poetam, qui infrenos dixerat Numidas, et alterum, qui ita collegerat ut diceret in equitando uerbera et praecepta esse fugae et praecepta sistendi. obscurum hoc nobis legentibus erat; intelleximus te uidentes, cum idem arcum intenderes et habenas remitteres aut equum segnius euntem uerbere concitares uel eodem uerbere intemperantiam coerceres (*Grat. Act.* 14.65).[83]

Ausonius adds that those who were supposed to provide the emperor with martial instruction now take advice from the student. Note the brief reference to archery

---

[80] In the *Epithalamium* (5–6), Claudian records that Honorius no longer cares for hunting, horses and javelins (witness the use of *spicula* and *iaculum*), such is his passion for Maria. See also Claud. *Nupt. Hon. et Mar.* 1.1–3, 10–15. Eucherius, Stilicho's son and *primae signatus flore iuuentae*, also hunts stags *iaculis* and *arcu* (Claud. *Cons. Stil.* 2.350–354). Even Stilicho is supposed to have amazed the Persians with his horsemanship and archery whenever he took part in a hunting expedition (Claud. *Cons. Stil.* 1.67–68). The difference here, of course, is that the corpus of Claudian's poetry is replete with information pertaining to Stilicho's military successes.

[81] For reasons of space, I have excluded material contained in panegyrics addressed to members of the Tetrarchy. What is more, although replete with specific military detail, these works are perhaps not as suited to direct comparison with Vegetius' text owing to their earlier date.

[82] See also the thoroughly panegyrical *HA Aurel.* 4.1, which deals with Aurelian's youth. Throughout the rest of the life, we are given examples of 'real' military achievement, including the claim that he slew forty-eight Sarmatians *manu sua* in a single day, and over 950 *diuersis diebus* (*Aurel.* 6.4).

[83] The exemplary horsemanship of Gratian is further praised at Auson. *Grat. Act.* 18.81.

in the above passage: *cum idem arcum intenderes*. Whether the emperor was as precocious as Ausonius implies is immaterial. In any case, it is not especially clear if these feats of arms were boyhood activities, or whether they continued into the period of Gratian's principate. It is relevant to note that Ausonius addresses the emperor as *Auguste iuuenis* at *Grat. Act.* 4.20. Fit and in good health, Gratian was still physically capable of such vigorous activities at the time of the speech.

Elsewhere we read of Gratian's military successes. His pacification of the Danubian and Rhenish frontiers *uno ... anno* are remarked upon (*Grat. Act.* 2.7). Furthermore, Ausonius writes that he could legitimately address the honorand as Germanicus *deditione gentilium*, Alamannicus, *traductione captorum*, and Sarmaticus *uincendo et ignoscendo* (*Grat. Act.* 2.9). As discussed elsewhere, the last of these three successes seems to belong properly to Theodosius I, although the future emperor, if this assertion is correct, would have been acting under Gratian's orders shortly before his accession in January 379. But this is controversial. Gratian's close relationship with the generals and the imperial soldiery is also emphasized (*Grat. Act.* 2, 4, 16–17),[84] as is his ability to endure privations and physical exertion (*Grat. Act.* 17–18). The panegyrist also salutes Gratian's military ability elsewhere.[85]

The *panegyrici* of Sidonius Apollinaris exhibit similar traits. The emperor Avitus was a keen sportsman and had demonstrated a good aim since his early boyhood.[86] Later, we are told that he revelled in the hunt (*Carm.* 7.187–197).[87] Avitus was also an expert in falconry (*Carm.* 7.202–206). Like Vegetius' addressee, Avitus' athletic qualities are compared to those of foreign peoples:

> uincitur ...
> cursu Herulus, Chunus[88] iaculis Francusque natatu,
> Sauromata clipeo, Salius pede, falce Gelonus (*Carm.* 7.235–237).

Apart from these skills, Sidonius lauds the emperor's achievements as a soldier and military commander: *ducis hinc pugnas et foedera regum / pandere, Roma, libet* (*Carm.* 7.214–215). From line 215, we read of Avitus' hold over the Visigoths, a bond which would later prove invaluable when fighting the Huns.[89]

---

[84] Like Trajan, Gratian took especial interest in his wounded comrades (Auson. *Grat. Act.* 17.76). Ausonius even asserts that Gratian was superior to Trajan in this regard, for the latter emperor merely visited the wounded, while the former actually took pains to nurse them back to health.

[85] See Auson. *Precationes Variae* 1 (Green 1999) = *Epigr.* 26 (White 1919–1921).

[86] We are told that Avitus, when he had scarcely emerged from infancy into boyhood, slew a she-wolf with a stone; see Sid. *Carm.* 7.177ff.

[87] In this, he resembles men of the calibre of Trajan (Pliny, *Pan.* 81.1–3), and also lesser figures such as Valentinian II (Philostorg. *H.E.* 11.1). The beginning of the latter reference is no longer extant, but the subject of the initial remaining sentence, i.e., the man who hunted bears and lions (witness ἄρκτων καὶ λεόντων), was surely Valentinian II, for it is stated that he lost both his life and the purple in his twentieth year.

[88] *Chunus = Hunus.*

[89] See Sid. *Carm.* 7.336ff. In addition, note the content of lines 547–549.

Sidonius relates that Avitus was a partner in many of Aëtius' victorious campaigns in northern Gaul, and, after the victory of the latter against the Iuthungi, Noricans and Vindelicians, aided him in protecting the Belgians from the rapacious Burgundians (*Carm.* 7.233–235).[90] Indeed, Sidonius writes as follows: *[Aëtius] ... quamquam celsus in armis, / nil sine te gessit, cum plurima tute sine illo* (*Carm.* 7.231–232). For his conduct, Avitus was given the title *inlustris* (*Carm.* 7.241).[91] Next, we read of his *gesta uiri* (*Carm.* 7.295), the success of his operations against the forces of the Hunnic leader Litorius, and his alleged single combat with a 'Scythian' champion (*Carm.* 7.246–294). Afterwards, he was named prefect of Gaul (*Carm.* 7.296). A *priuatus* at the time of the campaign against Attila (*Carm.* 7.353), he was named *magister peditumque equitum* and sent to fight the Saxons, Franks and the Alamanni (*Carm.* 7.375–378). Avitus' military reputation was such that Rome's enemies immediately sued for peace (*Carm.* 7.388–391) and the Visigoths, who had once again demonstrated a hostile intent, were cowed into submission by his very presence.[92] It can be seen, therefore, that Avitus, apart from his supposed athletic and sporting qualities, enjoyed real military success.

Now for Majorian. Although he later earns Sidonius' praise for his valour in battle, we are told first, in the words of Aëtius' wife,[93] that Majorian presaged his own accession by his skill in archery (*Carm.* 5.151–160), his mastery of boxing (*Carm.* 5.160–163), his speed in running (*Carm.* 5.164–176), his unsurpassed horsemanship (*Carm.* 5.177–181), the power of his sword-thrust, and the venom with which he hurled his javelin (*Carm.* 5.185–197). These skills, which recall those of Gratian and Honorius, are those perfected by the youthful nobility. Once again, one doubts that they would have been practised by a forty-year-old general in a decidedly poor state of health. It may legitimately be argued that the physical condition of the practitioner matters little in a panegyrical context, but, once again, the distinct lack of what we expect to see directed at a seasoned military campaigner remains disquieting.

[90] *nam post Iuthungos et Norica bella subacto / uictor Vindelico Belgam, Burgundio quem trux / presserat, absoluit iunctus tibi* (the unspecified subject of *presserat* and *absoluit* is Aëtius). See Anderson 1936–1965, 138 n. 3 (vol. 1): "authorities infer from this passage that Avitus took part in the campaign against the Iuthungi and their neighbours, but Sidonius does not say so". He is quite correct, for the poet does not actually mention Avitus' participation in the military events of 430. Indeed, Avitus seems to have taken no part in this campaign and only lent his support to Aëtius in the struggle against the Burgundians (Sid. *Carm.* 7.233–235). While the lines that immediately precede the passage in question (viz., *[Aëtius] ... quamquam celsus in armis, / nil sine te gessit, cum plurima tute sine illo* [Sid. *Carm.* 7.231–232]) give the impression that Avitus had always accompanied the senior general, this, in all probability, is precisely the effect that Sidonius sought to achieve.

[91] For commentary, see Anderson 1936–1965, 139 n. 6 (vol. 1). Anderson writes that "one is tempted to suspect that Sidonius has antedated the conferment of the title". Avitus, of course, would have received the title of *inlustris* after becoming *praefectus* of Gaul.

[92] See especially Sid. *Carm.* 7.411–416.

[93] Aëtius' wife fears that she is nursing a viper and warns her husband of the danger posed by the young man's brilliance. On this problematic theme, see Oost 1964, 23–29.

Sidonius clearly relegates the exercise of what he calls *ludus* (*Carm.* 5.151) to the idle hours of youth while martial achievement, the true test of a leader's worth, is held to be of much greater importance. Moreover, it is this aspect of Majorian's character that threatens Aëtius' position. The hunting of boar and the slaying of deer, no matter how expertly these activities are prosecuted, do not win empires. As Aëtius' wife says after describing Majorian's mastery of the skills noted above, *"parua loquor"* (*Carm.* 5.198). Thus the evocation of his battlefield prowess, which follows the previous *locus*, constitutes the highest form of praise. Upon Majorian's return to military life, we find that the promising young soldier has matured into an unconquerable general. Sidonius later makes detailed mention of Majorian's victorious campaign, as *magister militum*, against the Alamanni (*Carm.* 5.373ff.), in addition to the campaign that he waged against the Vandals in the first year of his brief reign (*Carm.* 5.385ff.).

The panegyric composed for Anthemius reveals similar traits. We are told of the manifold sporting activities that the emperor pursued as a boy. Like Avitus, he was an expert huntsman (*Carm.* 2.144–155). Moreover, he was an archer *sans pareil*:

> non principe nostro
> spicula direxit melius Pythona superstans
> Paean[94] (*Carm.* 2.152–154).

As a boy, the future emperor was strong enough to string a man's bow and hurl a javelin, as Sidonius informs us (*Carm.* 2.138–141). Like Majorian, the young Anthemius prosecuted all the activities, including equestrian sports (*Carm.* 2.142–143), that noble youths were accustomed to practise. But, unlike Vegetius' honorand and Claudian's Honorius, Anthemius pursued a successful military career before his accession. A *comes rei militaris*, he examined and solidified the frontiers (*Carm.* 2.199–201). Later, we are told that he was awarded a *magisterium militum* (*Carm.* 2.205–206), while his youthful military exploits allowed the panegyrist to describe him as *iuuenis ueteranus* (*Carm.* 2.209). We also read of his *triumphi* over the forces of Walamir, one of the three Ostrogothic kings (*Carm.* 2.223–226).[95] These events took place before Anthemius' accession. Sidonius then relates his achievement against the Huns: *hanc tu directus per Dacica rura uagantem / contra is, aggrederis, superas, includis* (*Carm.* 2.272–273).[96] Anthemius appears as a martial emperor. And, in anticipation of the impending contest with the Vandal foe, the poet writes as follows:

> uos ..., Castalides,[97] paucis,[98] quo numine nobis
> uenerit Anthemius gemini cum foedere regni,
> pandite: pax rerum misit qui bella gubernet (*Carm.* 2.314–316).

---

[94] *Paean* = an epithet of Apollo. Sidonius also employs this epithet at *Carm.* 2.307.

[95] See also Sid. Apoll. *Carm.* 2.232–235.

[96] The Hunnic episode begins at line 235 and includes a description of the appearance and customs of the 'Scythian' raider.

[97] i.e., the Muses.

[98] *uerbis* is understood.

When the above is considered, it is clear that comparisons are warranted between, on the one hand, Ausonius' treatment of Gratian and Sidonius' treatment of Anthemius, Majorian and Avitus, and, on the other, Vegetius' treatment of the *imperator ignotus*. In addition, Merobaudes, in his second *Panegyricus* (delivered in 446), tells us that Aëtius' childhood precocity at arms presaged his future ability as a general (*Pan. II*, 121–126).[99] He adds that, while a hostage with the Huns, Aëtius continued to develop his martial skills (*Pan. II*, 127–143). After a lacuna in the text, Merobaudes describes the manner in which the mature Aëtius, now a Roman general, destroyed a Teutonic foe (*Teutonicum ... hostem*) with Roman arms (*Latiis ... [armis]*) (*Pan. II*, 144) and successfully continued the struggle in Gaul over a period of *bis quinos ... [annos]* (*Pan. II*, 147).

Thus the lack of any reference in the *Epitoma* to Theodosius' victories remains highly conspicuous. One notes Merobaudes' assertion that *[semper] bella sonant, semper memorabitur hostis* (*Pan. II*, 188). While Vegetius may have written of war, *non hostis memorauit*. As has been seen, the highest form of praise that a panegyrist can deliver is that which lauds the honorand's martial valour. It seems strange, therefore, that Vegetius, obviously seeking to ingratiate himself with the imperial court, did not describe the military successes of the emperor. This omission, however, is not so strange if one holds that the emperor to whom the work was addressed is someone like Valentinian III, a palace-bound *imperator* condemned as a *semiuir amens* by Sidonius (*Carm.* 7.359), and an emperor who left the control of his armies to men such as Aëtius. True, an emperor could claim a victory *in absentia*,[100] but the turbulent nature of Valentinian III's reign was such that very few victories of note were achieved until the early 450s. The first major success did not come about until the defeat of Attila at Châlons-sur-Marne in 451.[101] Therefore, it is not unreasonable to argue that the *Epitoma*, if addressed to Valentinian III, was probably composed some time before this decade.

Moreover, Aëtius' victories, even those achieved in Gaul in the 440s against various foes, were effected more through the dextrous manipulation of barbarian allies than by the might of Roman arms – Theodoric I's Visigoths were as responsible for the victory over the Huns as Aëtius' generalship.[102] In any case, Vegetius would have found little joy in Aëtius' 'victories'. Indeed, he wished to do away with the barbarian-filled armies that Aëtius was accustomed to employ in his Gallic campaigns. This will be discussed in some detail in the following

---

[99] Merob. *Pan. II*, 121–126: *ut uix prona nouis erexit gressibus ora | primaque reptatis niuibus uestigia fixit, | mox iaculum petiere manus lusitque gelatis | imbribus et siccis imitatus missile lymphis | temptauit pugnas tenerosque ad proelia ludos | imbuit et ueras iam tunc respexit ad hastas.*

[100] This had been the norm since the very beginning of the Principate.

[101] Cassiod. *Chron.* 1253 (*MGH:AA* 11, *Chron. min.* 2, 157); Isid. *Hist. Goth.* 25 (*MGH:AA* 11, *Chron. min.* 2, 277); Prosp. 1364 (*MGH:AA* 9, *Chron. min.* 1, 481–482).

[102] See note above and cf. *Chronicorum Caesaraugustanorum Reliquiae, ad. a. 450* (*MGH:AA* 11, *Chron. min.* 2, 222), which not only ignores Aëtius' contribution, but also gives an incorrect date.

chapter. On the other hand, Theodosius I had experienced *real* military successes upon which our author could make specific comment. Praise for the emperor's generalship in the various campaigns in which he fought – such as his victory over the so-called 'Free Sarmatians' as *dux Moesiae*,[103] his victory over various barbarians (including Sarmatians again?) immediately before and after his accession,[104] and his crushing defeat of the usurper Maximus, a recurring theme in Pacatus' panegyric and a feat found throughout Claudian's verse[105] – would have obviously been preferable to the nebulous statements witnessed throughout the *Epitoma*.[106] Finally, a victory over the Sarmatae *c.* 383 by one of Theodosius' generals could also have been introduced. Symmachus certainly did not refrain from doing so (*Rel.* 47.1–2).[107] Even Ambrose makes reference to Theodosius' military exploits in a letter to the same emperor. The bishop makes Christ himself comment on the emperor's victories over the Goths: *ego tibi subieci nationes barbaras* (*Ep.* 40.22). A detailed account is then presented of Theodosius' victory over Maximus, who is first referred to by Christ as the *usurpatorem*

---

[103] Amm. Marc. 29.6.15; see also Zos. 4.16.6.

[104] Victories over 'barbarians': *Cons. Constant.* 379.3 (*MGH:AA* 9, *Chron. min.* 1, 243) of late 379: *deinde uictoriae nuntiatae sunt aduersus Gothos, Alanos atque Hunos die XV k. Dec.*; and *Cons. Constant.* 380.1 (*MGH:AA* 9, *Chron. min.* 1, 243): *his conss. [Gratiano Aug. V et Theodosio Aug.] uictoriae nuntiatae sunt amborum Augustorum*; see also Philostorg. *H.E.* 9.19; Sozom. *H.E.* 7.4.2 (the barbarians are not named here, but Sozomen does state that the enemy hailed from around the banks of the Danube [ἀμφὶ τὸν Ἴστρον]). Note, too, Claud. *III. Cons. Hon.* 22–28. Theodoret (*H.E.* 5.5) mentions a victory in Thrace over unspecified barbarians and that this occurred *before* Theodosius had been proclaimed emperor. Errington (1996, 438–453) assumes that these barbarians are "Goths" (he invites his readers to note the concluding remarks of *H.E.* 5.4). But Themistius informs us that they were Sarmatians (*Orat.* 14.182c of 379). It seems highly unlikely that Themistius confused this event with the victory of 374 since he was a contemporary of Theodosius I. Despite this, Kaufmann (1872, 475) believes that it is "schwer zu entscheiden, ob Themistius den sieg von 374 oder, wenn er kein fabel ist, den andern von 378 im sinne hat" (see also 476 of the same article). Still, Themistius delivered his panegyric in front of an imperial audience, and the authenticity of his claim, therefore, is difficult to deny, more so since Pacatus (also a contemporary) makes reference to a victory over the Sarmatians immediately after the emperor's return to military life (*Pan.* 10.2). On this, see Errington 1996, 439–440; Kaufmann 1872, 473–480; Sivan 1996, 199 n. 7. Errington (1996, 439) concludes that Theodoret's apparent reference to the Goths is a mistake, if not a deliberate invention. If so, the victories recorded in the *chronica* mentioned above should not be connected to the incident described by Themistius. In this context, consider, too, Auson. *Grat. Act.* 2.9, where a Sarmatian victory is ascribed to Gratian instead of Theodosius. If Theodosius' first victory after Adrianople did in fact occur before he became emperor, as Theodoret supposes, Ausonius' claim would theoretically be legitimate, for Gratian would have been Theodosius' commander-in-chief. On Theodosius' early imperial victories, see also Errington 1996, 1–27.

[105] Victory over Maximus: *Cons. Constant.* 388.2 (*MGH:AA* 9, *Chron. min.* 1, 245); Philostorg. *H.E.* 10.8; Socrat. *H.E.* 5.14.3–7; Sozom. *H.E.* 7.14.6–7. Claudian often introduces the theme of usurpers and civil war in his verse, e.g., at *Cons. Olyb. et Prob.* 108, 138 (written while Theodosius was still alive); *In Rufin.* 2.389; *IV. Cons. Hon.* 71–97.

[106] The battle of the River Frigidus would have occurred far too late for commentary.

[107] See Barrow 1973, 229 n. 1; Vera 1981, 338–342. In relation to the unnamed general, Vera (1981, 341) writes that "si tratta di Flavius Bauto" and provides an account of Bauto's career, which he uses to bolster his argument.

imperii (*Ep.* 40.22), and then by Ambrose in the following way: *Maximus destitutus est* (*Ep.* 40.23). That Theodosius defeated a Roman usurper instead of a foreign power did not prevent Ambrose from remarking upon it at length, so it is difficult to suggest any reason why Vegetius would have failed to do likewise. It is worth adding that, even if Valentinian III were to be excluded from our list, other non-military emperors (such as Valentinian II, Honorius, Arcadius or Theodosius II) would, on the basis of what has been argued above, make far better choices than Theodosius I.

One should consider, too, the laudatory language employed by Pliny the Younger in his *Panegyricus* addressed to the emperor Trajan – a general whose military ability, as I have previously intimated, is not incomparable to that of Theodosius I. Although Vegetius' *Epitoma* and Pliny's *Panegyricus* would not normally lend themselves to comparison (the two works were written some three hundred years apart and, in the main, are examples of different genres), an examination of the *Panegyricus* proves instructive. Pliny not only makes the usual comments about the martial skills of the emperor and his peerless ability to handle military weapons (*Pan.* 10.3, 13.1–2), but also makes mention of various specific examples of Trajan's martial leadership. We are told of his successful forays against the Parthians[108] during his military tribunate (*Pan.* 14.1), his part in the suppression of the would-be usurper Saturninus (*Pan.* 14.5), and, of course, his victory, as emperor, over the formidable forces of the Dacians (*Pan.* 12.1–4, 16.2–5). If the recipient of the *Epitoma* were also a successful general, as some scholars would have us believe, why did Vegetius not use the same programme of flattery employed by Pliny? The answer may very well be that Vegetius' imperial patron, whoever he was, had no military successes worth mentioning – an inference which would support our conviction that the *Epitoma* was not addressed to Theodosius I.

Similar conclusions can be draw from the beginning of book 6 of Polyaenus' *Strategemata*. Like the preceding five books, and those that follow, the sixth was addressed to Marcus Aurelius and his co-emperor, Lucius Verus (*Strat.* 6 prol.). Published on the eve of Verus' Parthian expedition,[109] the prologue of book 6 begins, after an assertion that the martial ability of the two emperors outshines that of previous generals, with a brief résumé of the military successes of the Augusti and their father. Polyaenus writes that "By skill you prevailed in many wars against many barbarians, after planning well with your father [i.e., the emperor Antoninus Pius]: the Maurusii are conquered (Μαυρουσίων ἁλόντων),[110] the Britanni are being conquered (Βρεττανῶν ἁλισκομένων),[111] the Ge-

---

[108] Trajan was a military tribune in one of the Syrian legions (Pliny, *Pan.* 14.1). These units were under the overall command of his natural father – a man whom we shall refer to as Ulpius Traianus in order to distinguish him from his imperial son.

[109] i.e., the summer of 162. Cf. the *praefatio* of book 1, in which it is asserted that his work will prove invaluable in the war κατὰ Περσῶν καὶ Παρθυαίων. On Verus' conduct of the war, see *HA Ver.* 4.4–6, 6.7, 7.1ff.; *Marc.* 8.9ff.

[110] This refers to the suppression of an uprising in Mauretania Tingitana during Pius' reign (*HA Ant. Pius* 5.4; *CIL* 3.5211–5215, 6.1208), rather than to the victory over the Mauri in Spain effected by Marcus' *legati* in 172–173 (*HA Marc.* 21.1; *Sev.* 2.4).

tae have fallen (Γετῶν πεπτωκότων)".[112] In this, the author combines traditional flattery (especially given that much of the above activity occurred in the reign of Antoninus Pius) with actual examples of military success.

Moreover, it would seem, as Gordon points out, "somewhat presumptuous to address a military text to an emperor who had already proved himself a consummate general".[113] Zuckerman goes one step further: "affirmer que l'empereur, élevé sur le trône pour son expérience militaire, devait apprendre son métier de général dans un manuel serait une impertinence intolérable".[114] Theodosius, already a successful military leader, could hardly have approved of being bombarded with trite maxims such as *amplius iuuat uirtus quam multitudo* (*Epit.* 3.26.10), *amplius prodest locus saepe quam uirtus* (*Epit.* 3.26.11), and *subita conterrent hostes, usitata uilescunt* (*Epit.* 3.26.15). Would anyone have dared to proffer such maxims to generals of the ability of Trajan, Diocletian or Valentinian I? One would think not. We must conclude that our author was either the most gauche individual who ever served in the imperial administration, or that his addressee was completely bereft of military experience. The implication of what Vegetius writes is that the emperor, although supposedly a tamer of barbarian nations, *needs* his advice.[115] This hardly supports a Theodosian dating.[116]

That Vegetius praises the triumphs and victories of the emperor demonstrates nothing either. Despite this, Silhanek is adamant that the language of Vegetius 'proves' that his addressee was a "strong emperor who had has ruled for a number of years" – i.e., Theodosius I.[117] Silhanek's contention smacks of some naïveté. As Gordon points out, one need only "glance at the sycophantic panegyrics of Claudian, directed to the hapless Honorius", in order to see that Vegetius' praise, mainly found in the four *praefationes*, should count for little.[118] Likewise, Giuffrida Manmana believes that the flattery of the *praefationes* must be distinguished from the bitter aspects of reality that are none too cleverly disguised by Vegetius' formulaic praise.[119] Vegetius' laudatory language, therefore, cannot be

---

[111] See HA *Marc.* 8.7–8. Command of this war was entrusted to Calpurnius Agricola. There had also been successful campaigning in Britain under Pius; see *HA Ant. Pius* 5.4.

[112] Translation of Krentz/Wheeler 1994, *ad loc.* This refers to success against the free Dacians under Pius (*HA Ant. Pius* 5.4), either to a victory early in his reign, or to that achieved by M. Statius Priscus in 158–159 (*CIL* 3.1416; cf. Arist. *Or.* 26.70 of 144). It is unlikely that the *locus* refers to activity against the Chatti during Marcus' reign (see *HA Marc.* 8.7–8, with 3.8), for these people could hardly have been called Getae.

[113] Gordon 1974, 36.

[114] Zuckerman 1994, 70.

[115] Goffart 1977, 79–80.

[116] Such a reflection has altered Dove's opinion. He originally supported the Theodosian case (1971, 17), but was later moved to write as follows: "can Vegetius really have written with a view to educating ... Theodosius? In places his book reads like the proverbial Idiot's Guide, and one often wonders whether what looks like clarifactory detail is not mere reiterative gabble" (Dove in Tavender 1972, 322).

[117] Silhanek 1972, 15–16; see also 15 n. 27 of the same work.

[118] Gordon 1974, 36.

[119] Guiffrida Manmana 1981, 30.

used as evidence to support the Theodosian case even though he, to be sure, enjoyed rather more success in warfare than the young and inexperienced Valentinian III (at least at the time of the latter's accession). In any case, Vegetius preserves a hint that all was not well with respect to military success. Indeed, he appears to comfort the emperor by suggesting that ultimate victory often follows lost battles: *si quis hunc casum ultimum putat, cogitet euentus omnium proeliorum inter initia contra illos magis fuisse quibus uictoria debebatur* (*Epit.* 3.25.13). One might note, too, the statement that *cum barbaris nationibus agitur terrestre certamen* (*Epit.* 4.31.1). Such language, *pace* Barnes,[120] would appear out of place during Theodosius' successful stewardship of the Empire (especially after the first few troubled years of his reign)[121] and would properly belong to the years either preceding or following his reign. Since the phrase *diuus Gratianus* (*Epit.* 1.20.3) immediately discounts the first possibility, the latter suggestion remains the only plausible alternative.

It is generally accepted that Theodosius I was a known admirer of the *duces* of the middle Republic and specifically those of the second century B.C., a view primarily derived from Claudian's *De Quarto Consulatu Honorii* and Pseudo-Aurelius Victor's brief biography.[122] Barnes, with the above borne in mind, holds that the "antiquarianism which pervades Vegetius' handbook admirably suits Theodosius [I] as its addressee, for he had an especial interest in Republican history".[123] 'Evidence' such as this, however, is merely circumstantial. Pseudo-Aurelius Victor and Claudian reinforce Theodosius' reputation as a 'good' emperor, a reputation facilitated by the peaceful transition of the imperial power to his two sons, and through his two sons to Valentinian III in the West (after John's abortive usurpation[124]) and Theodosius II in the East.

Now, a 'good' emperor, apart from the usual attributes of *clementia, uirtus*, etc., was also well read. Works from the first two centuries of the Principate abound in which the 'good' emperor is praised for his devotion to the *acta* of the *maiores*. More relevant is Sidonius' late-fifth-century panegyric (*Carm.* 2) on

---

[120] Barnes (1979, 257) argues that the *Epitoma* "finds its most appropriate historical niche as part of the debate which the disaster of 378 initiated".

[121] See introduction, where it is proposed that the text's *terminus post quem* may be *c.* 388. This is because a possible reference to Theophilus' development of a paschal calendar suggests that the work could not have been written in the very early years of Theodosius' reign.

[122] Claud. *IV. Con. Hon.* 399ff. Cf. Ps.-Aur. Vict. *Epit.* 48.11–12: *litteris, si nimium perfectos contemplemur, mediocriter doctus; sagax plane multumque diligens ad noscenda maiorum gesta. e quibus non desinebat exsecrari quorum facta superba, crudelia libertatique infesta legerat, ut Cinnam, Marium Syllamque atque uniuersos dominantium, praecipue tamen perfidos et ingratos.* Festy (1999, 234 n. 17) points out that references to Cinna, Marius and Sulla resemble references made to them in two fourth-century *panegyrici*, viz., *Pan. Lat.* 12(9).20.3–21.1 (313) and Pacat. *Pan.* 46.1 (389), the latter of which texts was actually addressed to Theodosius I. Cf. August. *De civ. Dei.* 5.26.

[123] Barnes 1979, 256. See also Milner 1996, xli.

[124] See Cassiod. *Chron.* 1211 (*MGH:AA* 11, *Chron. min.* 2, 155); Jord. *Rom.* 327–328 (*MGH:AA* 5.1, 42); Prosp. 1282, 1288–1289 (*MGH:AA* 9, *Chron. min.* 1, 470–471); Socrat. *H.E.* 7.23–24.

Anthemius, who was appointed to the position of Augustus by Leo, emperor of the East, in 467.[125] While lines 156–181 celebrate Anthemius' devotion to the works of the *ueteres sophistae*, i.e., the tomes of the learned men of the Greek-speaking world, from the next line we are told that *praeterea quicquid Latialibus indere libris / prisca aetas studuit, totum percurrere suetus* (*Carm.* 2.182–183). Among these Latin works,[126] and indeed those written in Greek, would have been accounts of battles and stratagems – works fit for the eyes of a future emperor. Even more pertinent is Sidonius' earlier panegyric on Avitus (*Carm.* 7), Valentinian III's successor after the fleeting reign of Petronius Maximus.[127] Sidonius places especial emphasis on the future emperor's childhood study of military history, almost as if it were by means of this very study that Avitus rose from relative obscurity to the highest of stations:

> surgentes animi Musis formantur et illo
> quo Cicerone tonas; didicit quoque facta tuorum
> ante ducum; didicit pugnas libroque relegit,
> quae gereret campo (*Carm.* 7.174–177).

Theodosius, so it seems, was not the only emperor in late antiquity who valued the *sapientia* and *mores* of the *ueteres*.[128]

4. *DOMINUS* AND *DOMITOR*

Barnes contends that the fact that Vegetius salutes his emperor as *domitor omnium gentium barbararum* (*Epit.* 2 prol. 4) is of especial significance and believes that this salutation may be used to support the case for Theodosius I.[129] In addition, Barnes holds that Vegetius' assertion that the emperor is enjoying "continual victories and triumphs [*Epit.* 2 prol. 1: *continuis … uictoriis ac triumphis*] presupposes that he has himself defeated barbarians in the field of

---

[125] After the usurper Severus' death in November 465, there was no western Augustus until April 467 – a period of seventeen months. The Augustus Leo, as Anderson (1936–1965, xxvi [vol. 1]), points out, "had legally been the sole Roman Emperor since the death of Majorian". See *Cons. Ital.* 588–598 (*MGH:AA* 9, *Chron. min.* 1, 305); Jord. *Get.* 45.236 (*MGH:AA* 5.1, 118); id. *Rom.* 335–336 (*MGH:AA* 5.1, 43); Marcell. *Chron.* 465.2–467.1 (*MGH:AA* 11, *Chron. min.* 2, 89).

[126] Sidonius alludes to Vergil's *Aeneid* (*Carm.* 2.184–185), the works of Cicero (*Carm.* 2.186–188), and Livy's *Ab Vrbe Condita* (*Carm.* 2.188–189). From line 190, he mentions by name Crispus, Varro, Plautus, Quintilian and Tacitus, *numquam sine laude loquendus* (*Carm.* 2.192).

[127] Petronius Maximus 'ruled' for scarcely two months before he was murdered by an angry Roman mob; see Cassiod. *Chron.* 1262 (*MGH:AA* 11, *Chron. min.* 2, 157); Marcell. *Chron.* 455.1–2 (*MGH:AA* 11, *Chron. min.* 2, 86); Prosp. 1375 (*MGH:AA* 9, *Chron. min.* 1, 483–484); Vict. *Chron.* 455 (*MGH:AA* 11, *Chron. min.* 2, 186).

[128] Cf. Val. Fl. 4.621–622: *sed te non animis nec solis uiribus aequum / credere; saepe acri potior prudentia dextra.* It is notable that Ambrose, when he addressed Gratian, calls the emperor *ueteris imitator historiae* (*De Fide* 1 prol. 1).

[129] Barnes 1979, 255.

battle".[130] According to Barnes, the word *domitor* "is surely more than the conventional attribution of titles such as *uictor* and *triumphator*[131] to an emperor who may never have commanded troops in person". To support this, he cites *ILS* 794–798 and points out that emperors who had never set foot upon a battlefield, such as Arcadius, Honorius and even the infant Theodosius II, were addressed as *uictores* and *triumphatores*, titles which he evidently believes had no real meaning.[132] Honorius even calls himself *perpetuus triumphator* in a letter addressed to his Spanish soldiers.[133] On the other hand, emperors who most definitely commanded troops in person, such as Constantine the Great, Valentinian I, Valens and Gratian, were often called *trumphatores* and *uictores*.[134] Even Theodosius I, in company with Valentinian II and Arcadius, is saluted by Symmachus in like fashion: *ddd. imppp. Valentiniane Theodosi et Arcadi inclyti uictores ac triumphatores semper Augusti* (*Rel.* 46.1, 47.1). Ambrose, in a letter to Symmachus, follows suit (*Ep.* 17a.1). Barnes continues his case by claiming that the noun *domitor* has "a strong and vivid meaning, where the verbal force is never lost".[135] He mentions, in a footnote, that the word is "conspicuously rare among epigraphical examples of imperial titles and honours".[136] Unfortunately, the only pre-Theodosian example that he provides is *CIL* 8.2387, an inscription from Numidia on which the mid-fourth-century emperor Julian is saluted as *domitor hostium*.[137]

---

[130] Barnes 1979, 255.

[131] Sometimes found as *triumfator*.

[132] Valentinian II is often addressed as *uictor* and *triumphator* in Symmachus' *Relationes*, e.g., *Rel.* 43.1. In similar fashion, Honorius and Arcadius are accorded these epithets on inscriptions (e.g., *CIL* 6.1188–1190).

[133] *Epistula Honorii* (codex of Roda, 190 recto), lines 4–5 of Sivan 1985, 274. See also Lacarra 1945, 268.

[134] Barnes 1979, 255. Dedicatory building inscriptions from Jordan give Constantine the Great the titles of *triumfator* and *uictor*: (i) 326–333: *[SALVO] CONSTANTINO MAXI | [MO VICTO]RE TRIVMFATORE SE | MP(ER) AVG.*, reconstruction of Zuckerman 1994, 84; (ii) 333: *[PROVIDENTIA ...] CONSTANTI | MAXIMI [TRIVM]FATORIS SEMP(ER) AVG.*, reconstruction of Kennedy 2000, 56; (iii) 323–333: *SALVO D. N. CON[STANTINO MAXIMO ...] | AC TRIVMFATOR[E SEMP(ER) AVG.*, reconstruction of Kennedy/MacAdam 1985, 98. Likewise, Valentinian I, Valens and Gratian: (iv) 367–375: *SALVIS AC VICTORIBUS D(OMINIS) N(OSTRIS) VALENTINIANO ET VALENTE ET GRATIANO AETERNIS TRIVNFATORIBVS SENPER* [sic] *AVGVSTIS, PES* III.A.2: 127–128 no. 229; (v) 371: *SALVIS D(OMINIS) N(OSTRIS) VALENTINIANO, VALENTE ET GRATIANO | VICTORIOSISSIMIS, SEMPER AVG(VSTIS), PES* III.A.3: 132 no. 233 = *ILS* 773; (vi) 367–375: *SALVIS D(OMINIS) N(OSTRIS) VALENTINIANO, | VALENTE ET GRATIANO, VICTORIOSIS | SIMIS*, published by Gatier 1998, 381 no. 64.

[135] Barnes 1979, 255.

[136] Barnes 1979, 255 n. 13.

[137] Cf. a dedication to Julian from Ephesus (*AE* 1924.71): *OMNIum barbararum | GENTIVM debellatori* (lines 7–8). Note, too, legends on Constantine's coins: *VICTOR OMNIVM GENTIVM* (*RIC* VI, 222 no. 818); *EXVPERATOR OM–NIVM GENTIVM* (*RIC* VII, 331 no. 296; Gnecchi 1912, 133 n. 1 [vol. 2]); *DEBELLATORI GENTIVM BARBARARVM* (Gnecchi 1912, 15, no. 6 [vol. 1]); and of Maxentius: *VICTOR OMNI–VM GENTIVM AVG N* (*RIC* VI, 401 no. 6); *VICTOR OMNI–VM G–ENTIVM AVG N* (*RIC* VI, 405 no. 55). Diocletian and the other tetrarchs were called *parentes ... generis humani* in 301; see Diocletian's *De Pretiis, Praef.* 7 (I 10–11), ed. Lauffer 1971, 92. Cf. the contemporaneous *CIL* 3.133 (= 6661): *PROPAGATORES GENERIS HVMANI.*

Zuckerman, however, holds that the appearance of *domitor omnium gentium barbararum* is not of especial significance and claims that the monetary legend *triumfator gent(ium) barb(ararum)*, found on coins of not only Theodosius but also Valentinian II and even the infant Arcadius,[138] is commensurate with the Vegetian formula.[139] The *Historia Augusta*, generally of dubious reliability, tells us that *uictor omnium gentium barbararum, uictor etiam tyrannorum* was the epitaph found on the tomb of the late-third-century emperor Probus (*Prob.* 21.4). A similar expression is found on an inscription of 315–317 bearing the names of Constantine and Licinius: *edomitis ubique barbararum gentium populis* (*ILS* 8938).[140] A clear precedent had been established for claiming that the emperor held sway over all barbarian nations.[141] This prompted Chastagnol, who never-theless believes that the *Epitoma* was addressed to Theodosius I, to hold that "On ne saurait malheureusement rien tirer de précis et assuré de l'usage de ces titres".[142] To demonstrate this, he provides instances where similar titles have been accorded to emperors both before *and* after Theodosius I, some of which have already been introduced.[143] Likewise, Sirago is forced to admit that the formula *domitor omnium gentium barbararum* is "un'espressione che potrebbe sembrare dettata dall'enfasi retorica".[144]

In any case, one cannot argue a great deal from the 'fact' that the word *do-mitor* occurs rarely in imperial nomenclature. Examples of inscriptions contain-ing this word may still lie uncovered. How are we to believe, then, that Valentin-ian III could not have been accorded a title such as *domitor*? Even though one incumbent Augustus was usually thought to be 'senior' to the other incumbent Augustus – consider Valentinian II's seniority to Theodosius I (375 vs. 379)[145]

---

[138] *RIC* IX, 123 no. 32: *DN VALENTINIANVS PF AVG*); 129 no. 52a: *DN THEODO–SIVS PF AVG*; no. 52b: *DN ARCADI–VS PF AVG*. See also Gnecchi 1912, 81 no. 7 (vol. 1) (coin of Theodosius I), 82 nos. 4–11 (coins of Honorius), 83–84 nos. 3–4 (coins of Arcadius).

[139] Zuckerman 1994, 74. The legend *TRIVMFATOR GENT(IVM) BARB(ARARVM)* also appears on coins of Constantine the Great (Gnecchi 1912, 27 no. 11 [vol. 1]), Constans (Gnecchi 1912, 63 nos. 18–21 [vol. 1]), Constantius II (Gnecchi 1912, 67–68 nos. 46–53 [vol. 1]), the usurper Magnentius (Gnecchi 1912, 70 no. 5 [vol. 1]), Valentinian I (Gnecchi 1912, 74 no. 11 [vol. 1]) and Valens (Gnecchi 1912, 76 no. 11 [vol. 1]). Note, once again, that *triumfator* is sometimes written as *triumpfator*.

[140] *DD NN FL VAL CONSTANTINO ET V[AL LICINIANO LICINIO]*.

[141] This sort of language continues in Latin works through to the late sixth century. For example, in the *praefatio* of Corippus' *In laudem Iustini Augusti minoris*, which celebrates the accession of Justin II on 14 November 565, is found the following: *deus omnia regna / sub pedibus dedit esse tuis* (1–2).

[142] Chastagnol 1974, 61–62.

[143] See Chastagnol 1974, 61–62.

[144] Sirago 1961, 468.

[145] This is reflected in most literature, but note the bronze *missorium* found in 1847 near Mérida and now in the Museo Arqueológico, Madrid, showing Theodosius the Great enthroned between his co-rulers Arcadius and Valentinian II. Theodosius is much larger than any of the accompanying figures. The inscription dates the work to 388: *DN THEODOSIVS PERPET AVG OB DIEM FELICISSIMVM X*. For a clear reproduction, see Feugère 2002, 194; Gregory 2005, 83.

and that of Theodosius II to Valentinian III (402 vs. 425) – it is difficult to believe that there was a hierarchy of titles between the Augusti past and present. Therefore, if Theodosius – or any other emperor for that matter – had been (hypothetically) hailed as *domitor omnium gentium barbararum*, there should be little doubt that his successors and imperial descendants would have expected similar salutations.[146] Finally, on this theme, two inscriptions dedicated to Valentinian III hail the Augustus as *dominus rerum humanarum*.[147] This, of course, neglects his co-emperor Theodosius II. As can be seen, less evidence of the collegiate nature of the Empire is found *after* the death of Theodosius the Great than before his decease. This, of course, makes it quite possible that Vegetius used the language that he did to address an emperor who ruled part of the divided post-Theodosian empire.

From the literary and epigraphic *exempla* presented above, it would seem that Barnes, like Chastagnol, Mazzarino and Wisman, is guilty of merely accepting the words of Vegetius without linking them to the cultural context in which they were written. Once again, it must be asked: why not specify, to some degree at least, the emperor's military successes?

5. EMPEROR AND DYNASTY

Richardot, using lines 320–351 of the *De Quarto Consulatu Honorii* of 398 as evidence, holds that the *Epitoma* was prepared for the instruction of Theodosius' sons – and Honorius in particular, which prince was supposedly being groomed to rule the western half of the Empire (an assumption which presupposes that either Valentinian II was dead, or that Theodosius eventually sought to do away with him).[148] Richardot notes that lines 320–351, which constitute military advice that Theodosius I gives to his youngest son, demonstrate that the emperor was familiar with Vegetius' military *praecepta* and that the *Epitoma* had an immediate impact on its audience:

> Les parallèles nombreux entre Végèce et Claudien dans ce panégyrique daté de 398 permettent de déceler l'influence presque immédiate du *De Re Militari* [*sic*]. Théodose souhaitait probablement que Végèce composât un traité d'éducation militaire à l'intention de ses fils, en particulier Honorius.[149]

---

[146] Gone were the days when an emperor would hesitate to be called *imperator* until he had achieved success on the battlefield (witness Suet. *Claud.* 12.1), or when a young emperor would not want to be called *pater patriae* until he had reached a certain age (witness Suet. *Ner.* 8).

[147] *CIL* 6.1197*a* (= *ILS* 807/8): DOMINO RERVM HVMANARVM VALENTI[NIANO PP AVGVS] (443); and *CIL* 6.1198 (= *ILS* 807/8): DOMINO RERVM HVMANARVM VALETINI-ANO [*sic*] AVGVSTO (443–455). Cf. *CIL* 6.1140 (= *ILS* 692) from the reign of Constantine: DN RESTITVTORI HVMANI GENERIS PROPAGATORI IMPERII ... FL VAL CONSTANTINO (314–315).

[148] Richardot 1998, 144–146.

[149] Richardot 1998, 146.

Such conjecture belongs firmly in the realm of historical romance. Richardot equates many of the points that Theodosius is made to raise with comparable sections of the *Epitoma*. For the reader's convenience, the passage in question is juxtaposed with Richardot's Vegetian selections in a note below.[150] While it is interesting to note the similarities between what Claudian writes and the corresponding parts of Vegetius' treatise – indeed, the similarity of some of the *praecepta* is quite startling on occasion – there is no reason whatsoever to believe that Claudian based Theodosius' speech on information extracted from any part of the *Epitoma*. To do so is to underestimate seriously the erudition of the poet, a man of demonstrably encyclopaedic knowledge, a man who, like Vegetius, had all the works of classical antiquity at his disposal but possessed the added advantage of being fluent in both Latin and his native Greek. We have previously dealt with a

---

[150] As an aid to intelligibility, Claudian's verse and Richardot's commentary = Roman characters; Vegetius' prose from the *Epitoma Rei Militaris* = *italics*: "Si bella canant, prius agmina duris | exerce studiis et saeuo praestrue Marti. | non brumae requies, non hibernacula segnes | eneruent torpore manus (Sur les exercices pendant l'hiver, 2.3: *De exercitatione militum*, où Végèce suggère de s'entraîner dans des *basiliques* pour rester à l'abri du froid; 3.2: *Quemadmodum sanitas gubernetur exercitus*; L'exercise permet de lutter contre l'oisiveté, cause de sédition, 3.4: *Quemadmodum oporteat prouideri, ne seditionem milites faciant*; Végèce a pour principe, 3.26: *Exercitus labore proficit, otio consenescit*). ponenda salubri | castra loco (Le choix d'un emplacement salubre est développé, 1.22: *De munitione castrorum*; 3.8: *Quemadmodum castra debeant ordinari*); praebenda uigil custodia uallo (4.26: *Quae sit adhibenda cautela, ne hostes furtim occupent murum*). | disce, ubi denseri cuneos, ubi cornua tendi | aequius aut iterum flecti (3.20: *Quot generibus pugna publica committatur et quomodo etiam qui inferior numero et uiribus est ualeat obtinere*); quae montibus aptae, | quae campis acies (3.9: *Quae et quanta consideranda sint, ut intellegatur, utrum superuentibus et insidiis an publico debeat Marte confligi*), quae fraudi commoda uallis, | quae uia difficilis (3.6: *Quanta sit seruanda cautela, cum uicinis hostibus mouetur exercitus*). fidit si moenibus hostis, | tum tibi murali libretur machina pulsu (4.22: *De ballistis onagris scorpionibus arcuballistis fustibalis fundis, per quae tormenta defenditur murus*); | saxa rota; praeceps aries protectaque portas | testudo feriat (4.14: *De ariete falce testitudine*); ruat emersura iuuentus | effossi per operta soli (4.20: *Quo pacto suffodiatur terra, ut machina nocere nihil possit*). si longa moretur | obsidio, tum uota caue secura remittas | inclusumue putes (4.26: *Quae sit adhibenda cautela, ne hostes furtim occupent murum*); multis damnosa fuere | gaudia; dispersi (3.26, *Regulae bellorum generales*: *Qui dispersis suis inconsulte sequitur, quam ipse acceperat, aduersario uult dare uictoriam*) pereunt somnoue soluti; | saepius incautae nocuit uictoria turbae. | neu tibi regificis tentoria larga redundent | deliciis, neue imbelles ad signa ministros | luxuries armata trahat (Végèce est hostile au luxe qui affaiblit l'esprit guerrier, 1.3: *Vtrum ex agris an ex urbibus utiliores sint tirones*, où il fait cette terrible remarque: *Minus mortem timet qui minus deliciarum nouit in uita*; Les armes sont plus dissuasives et utiles que d'ostentatoires richesses, 1.13: *Armaturum docendos tirones*). neu flantibus Austris | neu pluuiis cedas, neu defensura calorem | aurea summoueant rapidos umbracula soles. | inuentis utere cibis. solabere partes | aequali sudore tuas: si collis iniquus, | primus ini; siluam si caedere prouocat usus, | sumpta ne pudeat quercum strauisse bipenni. | calcatur si pigra palus, tuus ante profundum | pertemptet sonipes. fluuios tu protere cursu | haerentes glacie, liquidos tu scinde natatu. | nunc eques in medias equitum te consere turmas; | nunc pedes adsistas pediti. tum promptius ibunt | te socio, tum conspicuus gratusque gereritur | sub te teste labor (Chez Végèce, l'empereur est un exemple, parfait général et parfait soldat, 3.26: ... *quatenus uirtute ac dispositione mirabilis reipublicae tuae et imperatoris officium exhiberes et militis*)".

similar theme, i.e., the supposed connection between the *Epitoma* and the *Historia Augusta*. The same sentiments hold true here. Besides, there is nothing especially arcane or noteworthy about the information that Theodosius is made to relate in the *De Quarto Consulatu Honorii*.

Most of Theodosius' imagined *praecepta* appear to be the product of common sense, especially to a man as well read as Claudian. It must be asked: do we really need to nominate specific sources for what he writes from line 320? And, if a source-based solution to Richardot's 'problem' must be found, it is conceivable that both poet and epitomator could have arrived at similar turns of phrase through their familiarity with the same source material. Claudian and Vegetius, after all, would hardly have hesitated to paraphrase their sources when the occasion warranted it. Plagiarism, or its near equivalent (literary mimesis), was not a sin to the ancients. Rather, it was the means by which a writer or rhetorician could display his familiarity with the works of his peers and predecessors. Thus it is enough to say that the poet and epitomator were practitioners of the antiquarianism that pervades Latin literature of the last century of the Western Empire.

Especially significant is that Richardot does not fail to find similarities between the *Epitoma* and *IV. Cons. Hon.* 320–339. Yet he struggles to find any convincing similarities between the same treatise and *IV. Cons. Hon.* 339–352. With regard to the emphasis that Theodosius places on the need for a general to share the hardships of his men, Richardot is only able to summon the following: "Chez Végèce, l'empereur est un exemple, parfait général et parfait soldat".[151] He then invites the reader to inspect *Epit.* 3.26.38: *quatenus uirtute pariter ac dispositione mirabilis rei publicae tuae et imperatoris officium exhiberes et militis*. This is supposed to have inspired Claudian to state that the imperial general should not shield himself against the raging storm and the burning sun; that he should eat a soldier's diet; that he should be the first to scale a hill, fell a tree or cross a marsh; and that he should ride with the cavalry and stand foot-to-foot with his infantry in battle. These thoughts remind one of sections of Pliny's *Panegyricus*, or Valentinian's speech to Gratian in Ammianus' *Res Gestae*. And these are merely the *loci* most familiar to me. Moreover, the sentiments discussed above have no immediate equivalent in Vegetius' military treatise. Indeed, Vegetius, as has been discussed *supra*, hardly envisages the emperor as a battlefield commander. He is an armchair general who, if he must be present in the field, need not expose himself to excessive danger or actively participate. Richardot, it would appear, has argued against himself. If he had wanted to convince his audience that part of the *panegyricus* in question was inspired by the *Epitoma*, he should have terminated his discussion of the cited tract at line 339, for the remaining lines of Theodosius' speech (*IV. Cons. Hon.* 339–352)[152] clearly expose the tenuous nature of his argument.[153]

---

[151] Richardot 1998, 146.

[152] Indeed, from the second half of line 339: *neu flantibus Austris ...*

[153] It is interesting to note that the same scholar (1998, 141) writes that "[l'attribution du texte à Valentinien III] ... repose davantage sur l'intime conviction de ses défenseurs que sur des arguments solides". This is a surprising statement, especially given that Richardot's attempt to

One final thought on Richardot's 'evidence': why does Vegetius, if he addressed his treatise to Theodosius I, not mention or allude to the emperor's two sons? After all, Pacatus saw fit to mention Arcadius and the emperor's 'descendants' – who surely must include Honorius – in his panegyric to Theodosius I (*Pan.* 11.5). Likewise, Ambrose offers the following wish upon concluding a letter to the same emperor: *beatissimus et florentissimus cum sanctis pignoribus fruaris tranquillitate perpetua, imperator auguste* (*Ep.* 51.17).[154] Note, too, that the same writer, in a letter dating to September 394, calls Theodosius *parentem principum* (*Ep.* 61.5). If Vegetius' text was supposed to be "un traité d'éducation militaire à l'intention de ses fils", as Richardot proposes, the absence of any reference to the young princes is difficult to explain. It is readily apparent from reading any literature – negative or otherwise – pertaining to Theodosius I that he valued family and domestic tranquillity above almost all things. Claudian, for one, emphasizes this tradition and stresses, on innumerable occasions, the emperor's dynastic ambitions. Theodosius' obsession with family is also displayed by the fashion in which the historian Ammianus deals with the emperor's father. Theodosius the Elder, a man disgraced and executed just after Valentinian I's death, appears in a rather different light in the *Res Gestae*; and it is especially notable that his death is not mentioned at all, let alone the exact circumstances. The reason for this treatment should be obvious and will be dealt with in somewhat greater detail in the following chapter. In addition, Pacatus was not silent in praising the achievements of Theodosius père (*Pan.* 5.1–4). He even asserts, at *Pan.* 6.2, that the father of the *princeps* should have been a *princeps* himself!

While nothing solid or irrefutable may be gained from Vegetius' silence on the emperor's family circumstances, an emperor with no (male) heirs fits either Honorius, Theodosius II, Valentinian II or Valentinian III,[155] but hardly corresponds to the situation of Theodosius I in the early 390s, the time when the *Epitoma*, if one believes the pro-Theodosian party, was supposedly composed. By this decade, of course, Arcadius had been made Augustus (he was raised to this position in 383) and was being groomed, like his younger brother, to take part in the affairs of the Empire.

As has been seen in Ausonius' *Gratiarum Actio ad Gratianum* and even Pacatus' *Panegyricus*, the conventions of the late-Latin panegyric (be it an *actio gratiarum* or a *laudatio*) demanded that the author generally keep silent about the existence of a divided empire.[156] While it was acceptable to acknowledge briefly the existence of a lesser imperial colleague (e.g., Valentinian II in Ausonius' case), there need be no mention of an emperor of the East or an emperor of the West. Thus Ausonius, in the second half of 379, could write of Gratian as ruler of the whole Empire, in association with his junior colleague, without any reference

---

divine a Vegetian influence in Claudian's verse hardly represents 'un argument solide' and is based on what appears to be little more than 'une conviction intime'.

[154] The *sancta pignora*, of course, need not necessarily refer to just Arcadius and Honorius.

[155] Arcadius, of course, had a son, viz., the future Theodosius II.

[156] This is especially true after the tetrarchic period.

whatsoever to Theodosius I. On the other hand, literature that fell outside the category of panegyric incorporated different features. The *praefationes* and concluding remarks of the four books of Vegetius' *Epitoma* are widely recognized as panegyrical in nature, but the work, as a whole, was not conceived as *laudatio*. In fact, it almost takes the form of an imperial petition, for it recommends a radical departure from the military policy of the day. Obviously, no definite rules existed, and the reader will recall that Polyaenus' military text, viz., the *Strategemata*, was addressed to Marcus Aurelius *and* his co-emperor Verus. Yet this should hardly surprise, for Marcus and Verus were both Augusti of the whole empire rather than rulers of the East or the West. What makes Vegetius' form of address difficult to reconcile with Theodosius I is that he always refers to *imperator* in the singular.[157]

One might also take into account the *Relationes* of Symmachus, which hail from the reign of Theodosius I. Of the forty-nine extant, only a quarter have titles, and some of these titles do not make specific reference to their addressee. Symmachus wrote these epistles in the capacity of Urban Prefect, a post which he held in 384, the year after Gratian's death. It is incontestable that almost all these letters were meant for the eyes of the western emperor and his advisers, i.e., Valentinian II and his court. Despite this, and the fact that only Valentinian is mentioned in some of the titles, Symmachus frequently makes reference in his epistles to plural emperors, e.g., *domini imperatores* (e.g., *Rel.* 1.1, 6.1, 11). Barrow notes that "sometimes the title does not always agree with the abbreviated form 'd. n.' or 'dd. nn.'".[158] For the present purpose, it is especially notable that only four titles record an address to Theodosius alone (*Rel.* 2–5). Even in these letters, one still finds *ddd. nnn. imperatores* and *domini imperatores* at least once. From the epistles' subject matter, it is clear that these letters pertain to western affairs. The *ddd. nnn. imperatores* found at *Rel.* 2.1 indicates that Symmachus was referring to Valentinian II, Theodosius I and Arcadius, the three *imperatores* of the day. Barrow holds that only two of the *Relationes* were meant for Theodosius, viz., 9 and 42, and that the rest "were written for the attention of Valentinian II".[159] An analysis of the subject matter of these forty-seven epistles demonstrates the accuracy of this conclusion, although I must confess some confusion with regard to why *Rel.* 42 need necessarily be associated with Theodosius I.[160] Of the two *Relationes* apparently meant for an eastern emperor's attention, 42 has

[157] It is also worth noting that Ausonius (*Epigr.* 3.3 in Green 1999 = *Epigr.* 28.3 in White 1919–1921) writes *saluere Augustos iubeo natumque patremque.* This represents an obvious reference to Valentinian I and Gratian.

[158] Barrow 1973, 15.

[159] Barrow 1973, 15.

[160] This letter, the text of which names all three Augusti (viz., Valentinian II, Theodosius I and Arcadius), concerns the award of a *testimonium ... castrensis industriae* to a *cornicularius* by the name of Petronianus. Barrow (1973, 217 n. 1) writes that the reference to the *cohortes urbanae* (Petronianus is styled a *urbanarum ... cohortium miles*) is an allusion to the time "before the urban cohorts were converted into civil servants serving in government departments, especially the *officium urbanum*"; see also Vera 1981, 311–116.

no title, while that of 9 reads as follows: *DD. NN. Theodosio et Arcadio Semper Augg. Symmachus V. C. Praefectus Vrbis*. The name of Arcadius is found in many of the titles (e.g., *Rel*. 6–10, 12) and also in the text (e.g., *Rel*. 42, 46.1, 47.1). Conversely, *Ep*. 17 and 18 of Ambrose, which are addressed to Valentinian II[161] and concern the restoration of the altar of Victory (i.e., western affairs), sometimes mention a plurality of Augusti in the text: *imperatoribus terrarum atque principibus* (*Ep*. 17.1), *imperatores* (*Ep*. 18.22, 18.32), and *fidelissimi principes* (*Ep*. 18.22) – and this despite the numerous occasions where only the boy-emperor Valentinian II is addressed.[162] Once again, let us reflect on the fact that Vegetius' military text, supposedly written during the reign of Theodosius I – a man eager to preserve the fiction that Valentinian II was his imperial partner and a father willing to share power with his two young sons – makes no mention of a plurality of Augusti. Nor does Vegetius give any hint that the honorand had any male offspring who were *capaces imperii*.

The obvious conclusion to be drawn from the material presented in this chapter is that the least likely of the five main imperial candidates to whom Vegetius could have addressed his *Epitoma* is Theodosius I. While the language employed by the epitomator does not, of course, immediately dismiss this emperor from our list of candidates, juxtaposition of Vegetius' form of address and praise with that found in works demonstrably addressed to Theodosius I presents disquieting results. Theodosius I was a martial emperor who had enjoyed real military success, and the lack of any acknowledgement of these capabilities leads one to imagine that Vegetius' honorand was of a somewhat less bellicose disposition. The emperors Honorius and Arcadius obviously fit into this category, but an inspection of Claudian's verse, written while these emperors (especially the former) were still young, certainly suggests that this purveyor of imperial propa-

---

[161] *beatissimo principi et Christianissimo Imperatori Valentiniano* (*Ep*. 17); *beatissimo principi et clementissimo Imperatori Valentiniano Augusto* (*Ep*. 18).

[162] e.g., Ambros. *Ep*. 17.3: *imperator Christianissime*; *Ep*. 17.15: *quid respondebis his uerbis? puerum esse te lapsum?*; *Ep*. 18.1: *et tu, imperator*; *Ep*. 18.39: *fratris statuta* (i.e., of Gratian). Perhaps the most surprising example of collegiality is presented by a letter addressed to the usurper Eugenius, where we find *uobis imperatoribus* (*Ep*. 57.1). In this letter, Ambrose also mentions two letters sent to a plurality of emperors (*dedi libellos imperatoribus duos* [*Ep*. 57.2]), a clear reference to missives addressed to Valentinian II in which he advised the youthful emperor against restoring the altar of Victory (viz., *Ep*. 17, 18). See also the synodal letters *Ep*. 10–12 (addressed to Gratian, Valentinian II and Theodosius I, but with some references to emperor in the singular, e.g., at *Ep*. 10.2: *clementissime principum Gratiane*). The synodal letter *Ep*. 13 is addressed to Theodosius but does mention Gratian (*a beatissimo principe fratre tuae pietatis* [*Ep*. 13.8]), while the essentially similar *Ep*. 14 is notable because it makes no mention of any emperor other than the addressee. This is unusual. Of course, Claudian repeatedly refers to two emperors, but this, it seems, owes much to his claim that both halves of the Empire were supposedly entrusted to the stewardship of Stilicho upon Theodosius' death in 395. Stilicho, therefore, is portrayed as guardian of both Honorius *and* Arcadius, e.g., at Claud. *In Rufin*. 1 prol. 15–18, *In Eutrop*. 2.546–547. Yet, when it suited Claudian's purpose, he could imagine Honorius as ruler of the whole Empire, e.g., in the *Epithalamium*, where Venus addresses Maria, Honorius' intended wife, in the following way: *"i, digno nectenda uiro tantique per orbem | consors imperii!"* (276–277); and, furthermore: *"toto pariter donabere mundo"* (281).

ganda still offered the hope that these Augusti might eventually take up the sword and don the cuirass like their sire and grandfather. As a consequence, we are left with the Valentiniani and Theodosius II. With regard to Valentinian II, it seems difficult to believe that Vegetius would have addressed his work solely to this young man, especially since he only seems to be addressed in company with the Augusti Theodosius I and Arcadius, as the material presented in this chapter has demonstrated. Theodosius II, being an emperor of the East, also seems an unlikely recipient. Still, he cannot be excluded from our list according to the postulates of this chapter, for he, like his western colleague, was not a particularly martial ruler. A better choice, though still admittedly a subjective one, is the son of Galla Placidia, a man who eminently fits our criterion of a palace-bound western *princeps* who was never expected to take his place on the battlefield in defence of his crumbling *res publica*.

CHAPTER 4

MILITARY I:
VEGETIUS AND 'BARBARIZATION'

For Vegetius, the words of the Romans not only reflect prior greatness, but also provide the catalyst for the revival of a state that was, as Ammianus wrote in the reign of Theodosius I, *uergens in senium* (14.6.4).[1] In retrospect, the end seems inevitable, but our relative omniscience blinds us to the small rays of hope that lie in much of the *Res Gestae*. Ammianus believed that Adrianople might be regarded as another Cannae (31.13.19), a manifestation of a virulent but curable disease, and not that of a terminal cancer.[2] Ammianus' approval of the massacre of the Goths by the *magister* Julius reminds his audience that Rome's fate lies in the hands of those who protect her (31.16.8). The essential difference between Ammianus' 'philosophy' and that of Vegetius is that, for the historian, the tomes of antiquity form part of a received linguistic, historical and ideological *patrimonium*, the intrinsic worth of which lies in itself, timeless and insular and with very little relationship to the present. But, for Vegetius, the tomb of the past is a cradle for the future. Of course, the folly of such thoughts in the last century of the Western Empire is readily apparent, but retrospection is an inherent characteristic of late-Roman political and literary sentiment.

At the close of the fourth century, Rome's now-fragmented Empire had long been assailed by various Germanic hordes. By Theodosius I's reign, some of these groups had already forced Rome to accommodate them within her borders as *foederati*. Roman prestige had suffered an enormous blow. In addition, the Empire was regularly attacked by rather more sophisticated enemies, such as the formidable Sassanian Persians and their horse-borne allies. According to traditional estimates, the legions, being poorly trained, ill equipped and drastically attenuated, were reduced to a shadow of their former glory. Moreover, the heavy infantryman of yesteryear had given way to a more general-purpose type of soldier, one who, unlike the 'classic' legionary, merely served as a support for the ever-expanding cavalry arm of the Empire. This cavalry force was to become the most important arm of the Roman *exercitus* by the fifth century.

---

[1] It is notable that Ammianus (14.6.3) foreshadows this sentiment by stating that *uictura dum erunt homines Roma*. So, does the historian envisage that Rome, *iam uergens in senium*, would last forever? Old age must come to an end. While the city itself lives on, her Empire, at least in the West, lasted not even a century after Ammianus wrote these words. Still, Barnes (1998, 174) sees this passage as "pessimistic" in tone. On this passage, cf. Matthews 1986, 20.

[2] Elbern 1987, 106: "Für Ammian ist die Katastrophe von Adrianopel nicht der Endpunkt der römischen Geschichte".

In accordance with his belief that the continued existence of the Empire lay in the resurrection of the old ways, Vegetius advocated a return to the military formations and institutions that had served Rome so well in the past. In particular, it is his advocacy of the *antiqua legio* that has attracted particular attention from several generations of military scholars.[3] Yet, before we continue, it is interesting to note Wisman's belief that the text could not have been written under Valentinian III because "le système militaire à l'époque du dernier Valentinien était tombé si bas qu'il semble peu probable que Végèce en ait pu faire l'éloge."[4] As a consequence, she argues that it can only have been written "sous le règne de Théodose Ier [and, by extension, that of Valentinian II]".[5] As is evident from even a cursory perusal of the *Epitoma*, Vegetius most certainly does not praise the contemporary "système militaire". While he does mention, at *Epit.* 2 prol. 1, that the emperor is enjoying continual *uictoriae ac triumphi* (something for which he may have had some small justification), one of the main purposes, if not *the* most important purpose, of the *Epitoma* was to improve the Roman infantry, an arm which had fallen into neglect through mismanagement and ill-discipline. But this, according to Vegetius, could only be achieved by resurrecting the disciplined legions of Caesar and Trajan, and by filling their ranks with rugged country folk. Vegetius, therefore, proposed a Roman legionary army to fight for Rome. Although the legions had become very much weakened by Vegetius' day, that the very word *legio*, in the Late Empire, still evoked Rome's glorious military heritage is further attested by the bishop Ambrose, who wrote that *uictoria*, rather than a goddess, was simply the product of the legions (*legionum gratia*: *Ep.* 18.30).

1. BARBARIAN VS. BARBARIAN

In a previous article, I have discussed at length Vegetius' claim that the infantry of his day no longer wore armour.[6] It will be well to reiterate, albeit very briefly, my findings on this topic. At *Epit.* 1.20.3, Vegetius writes that *ab urbe enim condita usque ad tempus diui Gratiani et catafractis et galeis muniebatur pedestris exercitus* (*Epit.* 1.20.3). This has generally been taken to mean that some kind of change took place in Gratian's reign, i.e., that defensive armour was worn from Rome's foundation until some time between the years 375–383. Vegetius goes on to assert that, *cum campestris exercitatio interueniente neglegentia desidiaque cessaret*, protective armour fell into disuse (*Epit.* 1.20.3). The soldiers' *cataphracta*

---

[3] Vegetius appears to propose a return, not to any recognizable legion of the Republic, Principate or early Dominate, but to what he considers the ideal legionary formation. It is clear that Vegetius' *antiqua legio* was, in many respects, an imaginary concatenation of various sources hailing from various points in time. As Gordon (1974, 49) puts it, "all of [Vegetius'] ... ideas are assigned to some nebulous golden age of the far past".

[4] Wisman 1979, 14.

[5] Wisman 1979, 14.

[6] Charles 2003, 127–167.

and *galeae*, or so the story goes, were found to be too heavy for their liking and, as a result, *antiqua penitus consuetudo deleta est* (*Epit.* 1.20.2). According to Vegetius, the soldiers' *neglegentia* was to prove disastrous, for he adds that a large number of unprotected Roman troops regularly (*saepe*) fell to Gothic arrows in an unspecified conflict, which some have attempted to show refers specifically to Adrianople: *sic detectis pectoribus et capitibus congressi contra Gothos milites nostri multitudine sagittariorum saepe deleti sunt* (*Epit.* 1.20.4).[7] Even more disastrous was that *tantae urbes* were apparently sacked by this implacable enemy (*Epit.* 1.20.5).

A great deal of controversy surrounds the 'facts' related by Vegetius at *Epit.* 1.20. Moreover, a sufficient body of evidence exists to cast doubts on the notion that Roman troops did not wear armour under Theodosius I, or his immediate successor in the West. Certainly, Ammianus describes Roman troops wearing defensive armour at the battle of Adrianople, i.e., when Gratian was still emperor. Indeed, Ammianus (31.13.7) informs us that the Roman soldiers (*Romani*) were burdened *armorum grauantibus sarcinis* – a *locus* which represents "a clear allusion to *arma* that are worn as well as carried".[8] We also read that *mutuis securium ictibus galeae perfringebantur atque loricae* (Amm. Marc. 31.13.3).[9] As for Theodosius' reign, Zosimus (4.25.2) tells us that Modares, in an operation of 379, ordered his soldiers to take off their heavy armour in order to mount a stealthy attack on inebriated barbarians.[10] Themistius also makes mention of Theodosius' soldiers wearing breastplates (ἐν θώραξι), though perhaps in a rhetorical sense, at *Orat.* 16.207c.[11]

My overall conclusion was that *Epit.* 1.20.2–5 should not be used to support a Theodosian date for the work, or even a date during the disastrous reign of Honorius. The *tantae urbes* sacked at *Epit.* 1.20.5, and especially the use of *saepe* (*Epit.* 1.20.4), might well be used to demonstrate that, for Vegetius, "all of the disasters suffered since the *tempus Gratiani* [were] ... a collective slab of Roman history, the culmination of which was the Visigothic sack of Rome".[12] Of course, the *tantae urbes* need not necessarily refer to Gothic depredation immediately after Adrianople,[13] as some have thought.[14] In particular, I have suggested pre-

---

[7] Mazzarino (1956, 488) seems to suggest that Vegetius was writing in the near aftermath of Adrianople; see also Lenski 1997, 147–148, 162.

[8] Charles 2003, 140.

[9] A detailed examination of sources that undercut the notion that Vegetius referred specifically to Adrianople at *Epit.* 1.20.5 can be found in my previous discussion of the *locus* in question, in addition to *loci* suggesting that armour continued to be worn by Roman soldiers into Honorius' reign; see especially Charles 2003, 155–160. Although the references to armour in Claudian's verse may not pertain entirely to infantry, the general nature of the references appears to indicate that the poet, in several of the *loci* discussed, was indeed thinking of the equipment of *pedites*.

[10] For discussion, see Charles 2003, 146.

[11] See Charles 2003, 144–145.

[12] Charles 2003, 166.

[13] Giuffrida Manmana (1997, 22) perspicaciously notes that the *locus* need not have "un valore specifico".

viously that the reference to unarmoured 'Roman' troops (*milites nostri*) has a polemical quality, i.e., that it criticizes, and not always with great subtlety, the growing reliance on non-Roman (read federate) troops. One needs to comprehend the historical circumstances that caused Vegetius to write what he did. And it is these circumstances, more than anything else, that enable us to assign a degree of credibility to statements that, taken out of context, would seem to be grossly exaggerated, if not misleading or entirely untruthful. A portion of the Roman infantry remained armoured throughout the era of which this discussion treats. So much seems clear. But an increasing number of the men who fought on Rome's behalf may not have been so well protected. Thus it is these men, i.e., the barbarian *foederati*, whom Vegetius sought to replace. From our perspective, the real problem, of course, is that this was a policy diametrically opposed to that of Theodosius I.

In view of the above, the veracity of Vegetius' statement that *antiqua penitus consuetudo deleta est* and that *pedites constat esse nudatos* (*Epit.* 1.20.2) remains highly doubtful. The real import of Vegetius' call for a return to armoured infantry is not simply that such troops are less vulnerable than their unarmoured counterparts. Rather, Vegetius advocates the return of the *lorica* (which he calls a *cataphracta*) because this was the protection worn by the members of his *antiqua legio* – the type of military unit, traditionally composed of *ciues Romani*, which had served Rome so well in the past. One should also note that, while Vegetius mentions that barbarian cavalry wore armour, he does not tell us whether the barbarian infantry of his day normally wore similar protection. It is generally accepted that Ostrogothic and Visigothic infantry fought bareheaded and without cuirass and were thus, as Ferrill suggests, "light and mobile".[15] Armour was generally the preserve of the mounted component of their forces, and this cavalry arm was, at least to a reasonable extent, constituted by members of the aristocracy.[16] This situation was probably more the result of a lack of manufacturing capacity rather than design.[17] Vegetius' premise, then, is that Roman tactical superiority can be restored by reverting to the situation of the distant past, i.e., an era when Roman armoured heavy infantry would invariably defeat their unarmoured barbarian counterparts.

Vegetius, so it seems, laments that Rome, by employing *pedites* of more or less the same quality as her enemies, has lost her tactical man-for-man advantage over the infantry of the Germanic hordes. His concern may be summarized as

[14] See especially Sabbah 1980, 142: "Végèce avait toujours en vue les événements tragiques qui marquèrent les longues «guerres gothiques» de 376 à 382". This may only partially be true.

[15] Ferrill 1986, 145. See also Gabriel/Boose 1994, 449; Maenchen-Helfen 1973, 241–251. Of interest is Constantius II's statement, recorded by Ammianus (21.13.13), that his imperial opponent Julian had waged war *cum Germanis ... semermibus*. This, of course, relates to the Alamanni and the Franks, whom he campaigned against during the years 356–359.

[16] Ferrill 1986, 144–145 (see also id. 1991, 61–62). For example, Ammianus (16.12.24) writes that a German chief was *armorum nitore conspicuus ante alios*.

[17] Of course, there is no need to assume that non-federate barbarian infantry, despite their apparent shortcomings in protection, operated as anything other than heavy infantry when fighting in the centre of the field in a pitched battle. Cf. the naked, sword-wielding Celts of the Republican era; see Diod. 5.30.3; Polyb. 2.29.7–2.30.3 (the Gaesatae); 3.114.4 (Celts in Spain).

follows: if barbarian infantry in the pay of Rome are used to fight barbarian infantry of the enemy, the favourable issue of any battle can no longer be assured.

By Vegetius' time, the use of foreign troops was a long-established norm.[18] During the reign of Constantine and his immediate successors, many Germanic tribesmen were enrolled into the army, in addition to Irish, Scottish, Sarmatian and Armenian soldiers.[19] These men were thus all of an extra-Roman origin. Even Constantine's imperial bodyguards, the *scholae palatinae*, were generally composed of troops born outside the Empire.[20] A precedent of sorts may be found in the Julio-Claudian *Germani*,[21] or even the non-citizen *equites singulares Augusti* that Trajan apparently brought with him to Rome in order to offset the power and influence of the Praetorian Guard.[2] Although the *Bataui*, unlike most of the guard troops employed by fourth-century emperors, were born on the periphery rather than outside the Empire, the principle behind their recruitment remained the same. Of course, most of the élite foreign troops in the later Roman army were volunteers. But others, viz., the *dediticii* (literally, 'the surrendered ones'), were prisoners of war impressed into Roman military service.[23]

Still, the recruitment of 'foreign' troops did not directly contravene the precepts of Vegetius, who, as will be discussed below, was not entirely opposed to the employment of non-Romans. The real danger began in the second half of the fourth century, a time when those who settled on Roman territory were compelled to serve the emperors according to the terms of a *foedus*. These men were the first of the *foederati*, i.e., barbarian *milites* serving under their own chieftains in their traditional formations and not directly commanded by imperial generals. Rome issued block sums to the commanders of these forces, who paid their own troops in the manner in which they saw fit. As a consequence, the troops' loyalty was not to Rome but to their own native leadership. It is debatable whether Theodosius was foolish to allow the Visigoths to settle as a federate state within the Roman Empire, yet Gordon's view that this settlement "was the culmination of a long-standing trend" is probably close to the mark.[24] In view of this, it is fair to say that large portions of the Western Empire in the early fifth century were under the *de facto* control of various Germanic warlords who owed

---

[18] On the 'barbarization' of the Roman army, see Sander 1939, 1–34; Schenk von Stauffenberg 1947, 107ff.

[19] See Frank 1969, 63–64.

[20] Cf. Amm. Marc. 20.8.13 (a letter sent by Julian to Constantius II in 360). For a discussion of the recruitment of the *scholae palatinae*, see Frank 1969, ch. 4. Cameron, Long and Sherry (1993, 207) note that 18A of Synesius' *De Regno* clearly demonstrates that Arcadius' *scholae palatinae* were composed of "tall, blond and long-haired guards".

[21] Often simply called *Bataui*, their actual title was probably *Germani corporis custodes*; see Speidel 1994, 18–31; Coulston 2000, 78.

[22] The definitive work on the *equites singulares Augusti* remains Speidel 1965. See also id. 1987, 375–379 = id. 1992, 379–384.

[23] The differences between *dediticii* and *foederati* are explained by Gigli 1947, 284–285; Mazzarino 1942, 185–186, and especially 186 n. 1. On the rise of foreign units in Roman service, see especially Speidel 1975, 202–231.

[24] Gordon 1974, 39.

little, if any, allegiance to the government at Ravenna.[25] This was the situation that Vegetius presumably sought to change.

Thus it seems evident that Vegetius' criticism of the Roman infantry at *Epit.* 1.20 was not directed solely at so-called 'Roman' troops, but rather at the federate (i.e., 'barbarian') soldiers employed by the emperor. For the purposes of the present argument, 'Roman' troops will refer to soldiers who were members of Roman-style military units. These soldiers need not have been born within the confines of the Empire – the requisite is simply membership of the types of units found in the pages of the *Notitia Dignitatum*. On the other hand, 'federate' or 'barbarian' soldiers refers to troops who served under their own hereditary or elected leaders in recognizably non-Roman military formations. As will be demonstrated, the supposed relaxation of traditional military discipline, which demanded that the line infantry wear armour in battle, was not simply "[une] ... mesure d'économie",[26] nor an outward manifestation of the soldiers' "effeminate luxury".[27] Rather, it was brought about, in the main, by the political environment of the age and the demographic situation, which seems to have precluded the recruitment of sufficient numbers of non-barbarian infantry.[28] Barbarian infantry, though called upon to fight for Rome, would have generally been equipped in the fashion in which they had penetrated the *limites* of the Empire. This meant that they retained, for the most part, their traditional equipment, which suggests that many of these soldiers may have served the emperors without cuirass and helmet. More than anything else, this probably accounts for the dearth of archaeological evidence for body-armour pertaining to post-Gratianic military contexts.

Couissin provides a sensible reflection on the situation: "la disparition de ... [la cuirasse], fut, vraisemblablement, comme celle du casque, un effet de l'incorporation en masse de Barbares, et spécialement de Germains, inaccoutumés à la cuirasse".[29] As the number of 'Roman' infantry units (which normally wore armour) was reduced, an ever-increasing number of federate infantry (which normally *did not* wear armour) were enlisted in their stead. The result was that the number of infantrymen wearing armour declined while the number who fought unprotected rose: "on voit cependant ... que l'usage ... [du casque et de la cuirasse] devint de moins en moins fréquent".[30] Vegetius, if he were indeed writing under Valentinian III, probably lived at a time when most of the armoured infantry would have belonged to élite imperial units. Like Napoleon's Old Guard infantry, these units were probably deemed too valuable to risk in battle. Most of the fighting, one might reasonably suggest, was left to the *foederati*.

[25] Gordon 1974, 43.

[26] Harmand 1986, 199. According to Coulston (1990, 149), "ill-equipped infantry in the aftermath of Hadrianopolis are quite understandable .... Replacement of lost troops required increased recruitment and equipment production".

[27] Gibbon 1994, 439.

[28] On this, see Boak 1974, *passim,* and especially 86–129.

[29] Couissin 1926, 513; see also 509–510: "Accoutumés à combattre sans armure, ils refusèrent, sans doute, bien souvent, d'en accepter une, et le pouvoir impérial, en Occident du moins, n'avait plus la force de la leur imposer".

[30] Couissin 1926, 513.

At this stage, the reader might be forgiven for thinking that any attempt to demonstrate, by citing evidence of armour-equipped Roman infantry from the reigns of Theodosius and Honorius, that the *Epitoma* was not written between Adrianople and the sack of Rome does not follow. While it is evident that Theodosius' army became increasingly barbarized, it seems that the federate corps of the Theodosian *exercitus*, although a useful and often significant element (witness the use of some 10,000 Goths at the Frigidus),[31] did not yet outnumber the Roman or non-federate troops. The same might be said for the earlier part of Honorius' reign, especially at the time of the Gildonic war. Yet Claudian does mention that Stilicho made good use of allied troops, which he inaccurately describes as *auxilia*, in the later struggle against Alaric during Honorius' reign. It might initially appear that these troops, in terms of their employ and combat-function, were still roughly equivalent to the *auxilia* described in the *Notitia Dignitatum*, i.e., 'Roman-style' military units. But the context in which these troops are introduced indicates that they were not regular infantry. Rather, they were ethnic units led by their own leaders – if not actually *foederati* in the term's strictest sense, then common mercenaries lured by the promise of federate status in the future, and other rewards. Claudian, therefore, uses the word *auxilia* in a very literal sense.

The best example of the manner in which Stilicho used these allied troops is found in the *De Sexto Consulatu Honorii*. From line 218, Claudian describes the general's campaign against Alaric. The poet writes that *si deficit agmine miles* (we must naturally assume that these troops were *milites Romani*), Stilicho was prepared to expend the lives of his 'auxiliaries': *utitur auxiliis damni securus* (*VI. Cons. Hon.* 219). This was done not for mere tactical gain. Claudian assures us that it was Stilicho's intent to weaken the savage peoples of the Danube by opposing one group of barbarians against another (*VI. Cons. Hon.* 219–222).[32] The Romans hoped that the barbarian tribes might destroy each other, a wish also espoused by Ambrose in a letter dating to 384 (*Epist.* 24.8). The true *Notitia*-style *auxilia* of the Late Empire would not have been treated in this fashion.[33]

If one maintains the proposition that *Epit.* 1.20 hints at the inefficiency of Rome's federate troops, which constituted the bulk of the available infantry by the latter half of Honorius' reign, it is clear that such criticism does not suit a

---

[31] Oros. 7.35.19: *decem milibus Gothorum*. See also Socrat. *H.E.* 5.25.11–13; Sozom. *H.E.* 7.24.1; Zos. 4.58.2–3. Heather (1991, 199, 223) believes that Theodosius may have deliberately exposed his Gothic allies to the brunt of the fighting.

[32] [Stilicho] ... *astu | debilitat saeuum cognatis uiribus Histrum | et duplici lucro committens proelia uertit | in se barbariem nobis utrimque cadentem* (*VI. Cons. Hon.* 219–222). He adds that Alaric himself would have been captured *ni calor incauti male festinatus Alani | dispositum turbasset opus [Stilichonis]* (*VI. Cons. Hon.* 224–225).

[33] In this context, it is worth noting Claud. *In Eutrop.* 1.382–383: *bellorum alios transcribit in usus, | militet ut nostris detonsa Sygambria signis*. According to Claudian, these barbarians will serve in Roman units (*militet ut nostris ... signis*) rather than as *foederati*. But cf. Claud. *Cons. Stil.* 1.233–334: *quotiens sociare cateruas | orauit iungique tuis Alamannia signis!* This seems to refer to a request for federate status (witness the use of *cateruas*), something which was refused (Claud. *Cons. Stil.* 1.235–236).

fourth-century context. As Nicasie points out, "[Germanic] ... influence on the Roman army during most of the fourth century should not be overestimated".[34] So, the situation described by Vegetius refers more to the lamentable state of the Roman army (and the western army, in particular) after the successive military disasters experienced in the first quarter of the fifth century. The three imperial *panegyrici* of Sidonius (*Carm.* 2, 5, 7) provide sufficient witness to this contention. Thus it is possible to view Vegetius' criticism of the contemporary 'Roman' practice of allowing the infantry to fight without *cataphracta* and *galeae* – and thus *nudatos* – as a criticism of a Roman state that has decayed to the point of allowing foreign troops to fight its battles.[35]

Vegetius' bid to return Rome's armies to a legionary-based force implies that the use of barbarian mercenaries should be limited. One might recall Lucan's admonition regarding the danger of placing too much faith in foreign troops: *ciuilia bella | non bene barbaricis umquam commissa cateruis* (7.526–527).[36] For Vegetius, the auxiliary should be as his very name implies, a 'help' or *auxilium* to the legions. Therefore, units comprised of non-Romans should not constitute the most fundamental elements of the imperial army. This honour should be the preserve of the Roman legionary. Vegetius, then, was not against the idea of non-Roman auxiliaries *per se*. Rather, he was opposed to the widespread employment of barbarian *foederati* as front-line and indispensable military units. Indeed,

---

[34] Nicasie 1998, 188.

[35] By Vegetius' day, the age-old Roman *clamor* took the form of the *barritus* (*Epit.* 3.18.9), a Germanic feature in Tacitus (*Germ.* 3.1) and Ammianus (16.12.43), where it is associated with the *Cornuti*; see Alföldi 1959, 174. One might feel tempted to use this as further proof of greater barbarization in Vegetius' era. Still, Ammianus, writing under Theodosius I, uses *barritus* in a puzzling way. While Vegetius (*Epit.* 3.18.9) seems to imply that the *barritus* was the traditional shout given by Roman troops (*clamor autem quem barritum uocant prius non debet attolli quam acies utraque se iunxerit*), one cannot draw the same inference from one of Ammianus' references. It is true that, at 21.13.15, Constantius II says that Julian's army will not be able to endure *barritus ... sonum ... primum*. Likewise, at 31.7.11, we are told that *Romani* gave the *barritus* before charging into combat. But, on this occasion, Ammianus qualifies his description with *quam gentilitate appellant barritum*. What does *gentilitate* mean? In an earlier tract, Ammianus (26.7.17), when he describes the proclamation of the usurper Procopius, writes that *ad eum, et pro terrifico fremitu, quem barbari dicunt barritum, nuncupatum imperatorem*. So, if *gentilitate* is translated as "in the national name" (Rolfe 1950–1952, *ad loc* ([vol. 3]), this, at first glance, seems to be at odds with what Ammianus says at 26.7.17. It is likely, however, that Ammianus implies that the *barritus* is not 'Roman' on both occasions. Thus *gentilitas*, in this context, may refer to people from the Empire's periphery. What is clear from Ammianus is that both eastern and western troops used the *barritus* in the late fourth century. Still, the explanation that the historian provides in order to qualify the *barritus* may suggest that a) it was still a more or less novel feature of Roman warfare; and b) that it would have been unfamiliar to elements of his Latin-speaking audience. But cf. Nicasie 1998, 110, who holds that "Our scant evidence does not seem to warrant the conclusion ... that the *barritus* originated with the supposedly Germanic *auxilia* and then spread to the Roman army in general" (on the traditional assumption, see Grosse 1920, 250). Given the controversy, it seems unwise to make too much of Vegetius' reference to the *barritus*.

[36] On this occasion, Lucan refers to the *cateruae* of Pompey (i.e., cavalry) that quit the field at Pharsalus.

Vegetius mentions, at *Epit.* 3.1.3, that auxiliary units should be an important element of the Roman army: *exercitus dicitur tam legionum quam etiam auxiliorum nec non etiam equitum ad gerendum bellum multitudo collecta.*

Let us first review what Vegetius says about the function of auxiliary troops in the past. In the following passage, he explains the difference between the legions and the auxiliaries:

> auxiliares cum ducuntur ad proelium, ex diuersis locis, ex diuersis numeris uenientes nec disciplina inter se nec notitia nec affectione consentiunt; alia instituta, alius inter eos est usus armorum (*Epit.* 2.2.5–6).

According to Vegetius, the auxiliaries were recruited from different locations around the Empire and used the traditional weapon of the region whence they were recruited. For example, men from the Balearic Islands became *funditores* (*Epit.* 1.16.1). Thus it seems that the auxiliaries, in general, performed a light infantry combat-function, something which the heavy infantry of the legions could not provide. This is reinforced by Vegetius' contention that *legionibus semper auxilia tamquam leuis armatura in acie iungebantur, ut in his proeliandi magis adminiculum esset quam principale subsidium* (*Epit.* 2.2.9). As is often the case, Vegetius is a slave to his sources – and his statements regarding the traditional use of legionaries generally seem to relate to the Republic and the very early Principate. Although there were, of course, specialist light infantry units composed of *sagittarii* and *funditores*, in addition to more general-purpose cohorts, sufficient evidence exists to suggest that a substantial part of Rome's auxiliary forces, especially by Flavian times, provided a function almost identical to that of the legions. Certainly, it appears that Vegetius had neglected at least one important *locus*, for Tacitus' account of Agricola's victory at Mons Graupius demonstrates that auxiliaries could, if properly equipped, supplant Roman legionaries in the line of battle (*Agr.* 35–36).[37] Trajan's Column also depicts auxiliaries fighting pitched battles without legionary aid.[38] Of course, these two sources date from the height of the Principate. Augustus radically departed from Republican practice (which is what Vegetius appears to describe) and regularized the majority of Rome's auxiliary forces.[39] Suetonius (*Aug.* 49.2) writes as follows:

> quidquid ... ubique militum esset [including, presumably, the auxiliary cohorts], ad certam stipendiorum praemiorumque formulam adstrixit definitis pro gradu cuiusque et temporibus militiae et commodis missionum.

Given the nature of these vast changes, it seems inappropriate to assume that all auxiliaries in the Principate continued to operate in the same fashion as their Republican predecessors.

---

[37] On the battle, see Charles 2004b, 129–140.

[38] Rossi (1971, 118–119) writes that there are "about twenty" major military engagements on Trajan's Column and that "the auxiliaries take part in nineteen of them, the legionaries and/or Praetorians are to be found in seven, while *auxilia* and *symmachiarii* fight alone in twelve". When auxiliaries fought without legionary support, it is difficult to believe that they fought solely as light infantry.

[39] See also Webster 1985, 142.

It is uncertain whether Vegetius would have approved of Agricola or Trajan's use of auxiliaries as front-line troops. Indeed, he fails to mention whether a general should risk Roman lives when there is no need to do so. Yet there is an obvious distinction between the widespread use of traditional auxiliary units (many – if not the majority – of which were organized into recognizably Roman-style military entities) and the use of *foederati*, most of whom fought and were equipped in 'barbarian' fashion. The auxiliaries who fought as line-of-battle troops in the Flavio-Trajanic period appear to have been highly disciplined and not markedly dissimilar to the legionaries in terms of military ethos and pay.[40] Perhaps citizenship was the most important difference between such men and their legionary comrades. By the time of the Severan dynasty, however, even this distinction had become more or less academic. Vegetius' thoughts on the unsuitability of foreign troops, therefore, need not be regarded as diametrically opposed to the tactics employed by Agricola and his contemporaries. The auxiliary co-horts of the Principate, commanded by Roman equestrians, were spread through-out the Empire. With no common bond other than the desire of their constituent members for Roman citizenship, they could never have evolved into the type of force that Vegetius feared. As suggested above, Vegetius wrote at a time when sufficient Roman forces no longer remained to counter the armies of the German-ic leaders. It was an era when Roman military objectives were often pursued by means of dexterous diplomacy rather than by force of imperial arms. This suggests a date after the wars against Alaric, an age when the grim consequences of Theodosius I's policy of barbarian accommodation had fully manifested themselves.

The Vegetian theme of a general decline among the 'Roman' infantry units is also demonstrated by the epitomator's description of the legions as mere shadows of their former selves. The question, of course, is whether this description fits a Theodosian context, or one in the fifth century – and specifically under Valentin-ian III. Vegetius writes that *legionum nomen in exercitu permanet hodieque, sed per neglegentiam superiorum temporum robur infractum est* (*Epit.* 2.3.1). Veter-ans who have left the service after the requisite amount of years are not replaced, desertion is rife, and sickness has taken its toll.[41] In addition, we find *attenuatae sint legiones* (*Epit.* 2.3.4), which is translated by Stelten as "the legions are decreasing in number".[42] Yet this interpretation does not really suit a Theodosian date, for the *Notitia Dignitatum* (the *terminus post quem* for which must be Theodosius' death in 395) includes a large number of units styled *legiones* – in

---

[40] Alston (1994, 113–123) even argues that the rate of pay for legionaries and auxiliaries was identical. But the suggestion that auxiliaries received approximately five-sixths of a legion-ary's pay seems somewhat more likely. On this, see M.A. Speidel 1992, 87–106; M.P. Speidel 1973, 141–147.

[41] Veg. *Epit.* 2.3.2–3: *deinde contubernalibus completis stipendiis per testimoniales ex more dimissis non sunt alii substituti. praeterea necesse est aliquantos morbo debilitari atque dimitti, aliquantos deserere uel diuersis casibus interire, ut nisi annis singulis, immo singulis paene mensibus, in recedentium locum iuniorum turba succedat, quamuis copiosus exhauriatur exercitus.*

[42] Stelten 1990, *ad loc.*

fact, more than Vespasian or Trajan would have ever commanded. But, for the era of Valentinian III, in whose reign this document is believed to have reached its final form, the *Notitia* hardly seems a reliable guide. I have already argued at length elsewhere that two of the *legiones palatinae* listed in the western *Notitia*, viz., the élite *Iouiani seniores* (*Occ.* 5.2, 5.145) and *Herculiani seniores* (*Occ.* 5.3, 5.146), had possibly disappeared by Vegetius' day.[43] This was originally suggested, in passing, by Seeck.[44]

Important to us is that the *Iouiani* and *Herculiani* are described by Vegetius (*Epit.* 1.17.1–4) as if they no longer existed at the time of writing, an inference which can be drawn from the verbal tenses that Vegetius employs. Witness, for example, the following:

> nam in Illyrico dudum duae legiones fuerunt quae sena milia militum habuerunt quae quod his telis [i.e., plumbatae] scienter utebantur et fortiter Mattiobarbuli[45] uocabantur (*Epit.* 1.17.1).

The use of *dudum* and the presence of verbs in the imperfect and perfect tenses (viz., *uocabantur, fuerunt, habuerunt*, etc.) might be regarded as especially significant. One should also consider the following:

> quinos autem mattiobarbulos insertos scutis portare consuerunt, quos si oportune milites iactent prope sagittariorum scutati imitari uidentur officium. nam hostes equosque consauciant priusquam non modo ad manum sed ad ictum missibilium potuerit perueniri (*Epit.* 1.17.3-4).

These lines, and especially the appearance of *portare consuerent* (note the tense), suggest that the infantrymen once known as *Mattiobarbuli* did not simply exchange their *plumbatae* for other equipment. Rather, the implication is that the *Iouiani* and *Herculiani* had ceased to exist and that, after their demise, *plumbatae* were no longer used by élite regular infantry units in combat.[46] As a consequence, the case of the *Iouiani* and *Herculiani* presents us with further cause to believe that the *Epitoma* was compiled at some time in the fifth century, especially after the *Notitia* had reached its final form (i.e., *c.* 425, or some time shortly thereafter). Despite this, an inspection of Vegetius' language shows that it is not necessarily the number of legions that is being reduced (although this, too, was presumably occurring) – it is the strength and thus quality of these units that is falling away. With this in mind, Milner prefers "the legions have become attenuated",[47] a translation which hints at a general decline. Legion size is irrelevant

---

[43] Charles 2004a, 109–121.

[44] Seeck 1876, 82.

[45] This is the orthography of Önnerfors 1995, *ad loc.*; Reeve 2003, *ad loc.* Some authors refer to *martiobarbuli*, e.g., Bennett 1991, 60; Elton 1996, 108. The etymology is uncertain; on this, see Bishop/Coulston 1993, 162; Lammert 1930, 2323.

[46] Despite this, archaeological evidence suggests that these weapons continued to be used throughout the period in question, especially in provincial zones; see Charles 2004a, 113.

[47] Silhanek's translation (1972, *ad loc.*) is neither one thing nor the other: "our legions have been spread thin". Cf. Formisano 2003, *ad loc.*: "le legioni si sono impoverite"; Giuffrida Manmana 1997, *ad loc.*: "le legioni si sono indebolite"; Müller 1997, *ad loc.*: "die Legionen [sind] geschwächt".

since it is generally believed that these units were composed of *c.* 1,000 troops throughout the entire period in question,[48] although it should not automatically be assumed that all *legiones* were of the same size.[49]

In light of the above, Vegetius' lament that the *legiones* are *attenuatae* (*Epit.* 2.3.4) can hardly be used with confidence to date the *Epitoma*. One might just as easily suggest that Vegetius, with his assertion regarding the decline of the legions, is merely using a stock *topos* in order to maximize the impact of his call for a return to the military dispositions of yesteryear. But, if one were to nominate the most probable context in which these words might have been written, one would surely hesitate to put forward the reign of Theodosius I, an era when 'regular' Roman infantry formations still had an important rôle to play. The same might be said about the early part of Honorius' reign, and, by extension, that of his brother Arcadius. It seems difficult to accept that Vegetius specifically meant that the number of *legiones* had decreased (although a reduction does seem likely). Rather, he introduces a universal decline in its broadest possible sense, almost as if these units were no longer deemed sufficiently important to justify any great amount of imperial attention or – what is more important – expenditure.

Thus we find ourselves in an era when the great bulk of Rome's infantry manpower was derived, not from 'Roman' formations like the *legiones* and *auxilia*, but from the federate armies that had agreed to fight on Rome's behalf. In view of this, the thoughts expressed at *Epit.* 2.3 are very much in line with Vegetius' concern with respect to the restoration of infantry armour, his belief that the best soldiers are Roman *pagani* organized into well-trained units, and his disquiet regarding the current lack of field-craft skills, both of which themes will be dealt with below. When all this is considered together, a clearer picture of Vegetius' world emerges, and it is one of a fragmented Empire, defended, in the main, not by 'Roman' soldiers, but by federate armies of a Germanic or Gothic origin. It is a fifth-century world that would have been quite familiar to Valentinian III – if he had dared to leave his sheltered Italian bastions in order to tour what remained of his shattered provinces.

2. QUALITY OVER QUANTITY

Although Vegetius' advocacy of the *antiqua legio* is sufficient for us to draw the conclusion that he believed that the ordinary Roman soldier was the key to military success, he does not hesitate to add further incentives for a return to the *consuetudo antiqua*. First, Vegetius points out that it is cheaper to train one's own soldiers than to pay for a foreign army: *uilius enim constat erudire armis suos quam alienos mercede conducere* (*Epit.* 1.28.10).[50] He also states that Rome's present domain covers lands that gave – and still give – birth to such famous

---

[48] MacMullen 1980, 457: "In the early fifth century, the palatine army legions were barely over 1,000".

[49] Tomlin 2000, 169.

[50] On this, see Planck 1977, 57.

fighting peoples as the Lacedaemonians, Athenians, Marsi, Samnites, Paeligni, Epirotes, Macedonians, Thessalians, Dacians, Moesians and Thracians, in addition to the 'Romans' themselves (*Epit.* 1.28.2–4). What need, then, was there to hire foreigners for military service? While Vegetius was obviously opposed to the widespread use of Germanic mercenaries, it might initially seem puzzling that he advocates the recruitment of troops from among the *septentrionales populi* at *Epit.* 1.2.4.[51] Yet before we condemn Vegetius for what appears to be a glaring contradiction, let us not forget that his later advocacy of the *antiqua legio*, for which he prepares us at *Epit.* 1.1, means that he favoured the use of men from the Gauls, in addition to the Italian and Iberian peninsulas, i.e., the regions whence the legionaries of the past were generally recruited. Indeed, the concluding sentence of chapter 2 coheres more readily with the author's general thesis, for he writes that *tirones ... de temperatioribus legendi sunt plagis* (*Epit.* 1.2.5). The regions mentioned above, together with those stated by Vegetius at *Epit.* 1.28.2–4, can be broadly categorized as temperate zones (*plagae temperatiores*: *Epit.* 1.2.5). So, it seems that one should not pay too much attention to this part of the text, which, as Vegetius himself admits, is the fruits of the research conducted and approved *a doctissimis hominibus* rather than the experience of the author himself (*Epit.* 1.2.2).[52]

Vegetius' claim regarding the economy of employing Roman soldiers does not appear to have been a particularly novel idea. For example, the Anonymus' *De Rebus Bellicis*, while it does not explicitly state that Roman troops might be more cost-effective than allied military contingents, is generally devoted to providing solutions for what appears to have been an economic crisis caused by excessive (or perhaps ill-controlled) military expenditure.[53] Similar sentiments are found in Ammianus' *Res Gestae*. During Constantius II's eastern campaign, the state-treasurer Ursulus, upon seeing the ruins of Amida after it had been destroyed by the Persians, is purported to have uttered the following pearl of sarcasm: *"en quibus animis urbes a milite defenduntur, cui ut abundare stipendium possit, imperii opes iam fatiscunt!"* (Amm. Marc. 20.11.5). Like Ursulus, the Anonymus, who probably wrote at a time reasonably close to the Persian campaigns of the mid-fourth century, evidently believed that the greatest cause of burden to the tax-payer was military expenditure.[54] From the above, two things

---

[51] It was believed that people from regions nearer to the sun have less blood, a factor, says Vegetius, which reduces their *constantia* and *fiducia* and means, moreover, that they fear wounds more readily than do people from more temperate areas (*Epit.* 1.2.3).

[52] It might be noted that Vegetius is responsible for one of the most racially tolerant maxims of late antiquity: *constat quidem in omnibus locis et ignauos et strenuos nasci* (*Epit.* 1.2.2).

[53] The text used is that of Ireland (1984). See *DRB* 5.1: *ad enormia militum alimenta ratione non incongrua prohibenda ueniamus, quorum causa totius tributariae functionis laborat illatio.* Of course, the use of federate troops, at the time when the Anonymus was writing, does not yet appear to be of especial significance.

[54] This opinion was evidently shared by the author of the *HA*. The biography of Probus records the emperor's alleged statement that he wished to dispense with the army altogether (*Prob.* 22.4). See also Zos. 4.16.1, which *locus* refers to the reign of Valentinian I. Zosimus

might be concluded: a) that a reduction in military spending was highly desirable in the last century-and-a-half of the Western Empire; and b) that Vegetius undoubtedly thought that his schemes would prove far more palatable to his audience if there were a financial incentive attached to them. It is difficult to imagine, in any case, that an antiquarian reactionary like Vegetius would have placed economic concerns above the maintenance and restoration of Roman military power. For Vegetius, the salvation of the Empire was a matter in which bookkeeping was of little import.

What is more, Vegetius explains that large armies, an obvious allusion to the contemporary situation, are a danger unto themselves: *euidenter apparet nimium copiosos exercitus magis propria multitudine quam hostium uirtute depressos* (*Epit.* 3.1.4). In the same section of the text, he relates the memorable examples of Xerxes, Darius and Mithridates, *[reges] … qui innumerabiles armauerant populos* (*Epit.* 3.1.4). Vegetius' reasoning is not without merit. He notes that a large army is slower on the march owing to its cumbersome baggage train, is vulnerable to the attacks of more mobile units when traversing difficult terrain, and is difficult to feed and water (*Epit.* 3.1.5–7). Vegetius then describes the size of the ancient Roman armies (*Epit.* 3.1.8–12). It is notable that the information that he provides relates to the Republic rather than to the Principate, with the inclusion of the phrase *tamquam comes maior* (*Epit.* 3.1.10) looking suspiciously like an attempt on Vegetius' part to 'update' the material. He writes that, *in leuioribus bellis*, one legion *mixtis auxiliis*,[55] all of which was commanded by a praetor – or also, presumably, a general with pro-praetorian *imperium* – was deemed sufficient to deal with the problem (*Epit.* 3.1.9). This force was made up of 10,000 foot soldiers and 2,000 cavalrymen (*Epit.* 3.1.9). However, *quod si magnae hostium copiae dicerentur*, a general with *consularis potestas* would be dispatched,[56] along with 20,000 foot soldiers and 4,000 cavalrymen (*Epit.* 3.1.10). And, if the danger to the *res publica* were sufficiently great, two consuls would be sent out with two armies: a total of perhaps 48,000 men (?) (*Epit.* 3.1.11).

Vegetius then makes a general comment regarding the size of the old Roman armies (*Epit.* 3.1.12). He states that, although the Romans were accustomed to fight wars almost every year *in diuersis regionibus contra diuersos hostes*, the supply of soldiers was sufficient *quia utilius iudicabant non tam grandes exercitus habere quam plures*. From the above, it might be assumed that Vegetius means that the ancients deemed it better to maintain several small yet well-trained armies rather than a large and unwieldy conglomeration of rabble. This supposition gains credence in light of the following: *ueteres … qui remedia difficultatum experimentis didicerant non tam numerosos quam eruditos armis*

---

writes that Valentinian's taxation policy was oppressive and that he exceeded the usual exactions. On the economic concerns of the Anonymus, see Brandt 1988, 103–118; Foraboschi 1987, 111–127.

[55] The phrase *mixtis auxiliis* presumably refers to an auxiliary contingent composed of both infantry and cavalry.

[56] This general could also have had proconsular *imperium* (or *potestas*, as Vegetius would have preferred to write).

exercitus habere uoluerunt (*Epit.* 3.1.8). A similar belief is espoused at *Epit.*
3.20.28, where Vegetius, in his discussion of battlefield tactics, writes that *uictoria ... per paucos fieri consueuit*. It must be admitted that Vegetius is merely
making the point that a swift victory may be obtained by means of *exercitatissi-
mos ... bellatores*, men who are often able to break through the line of the enemy
if deployed in a *cuneus* formation (*Epit.* 3.20.27). Yet Vegetius, once again,
emphasizes that martial skill, which can only be developed through rigorous
training, is far more important than number. He stresses, too, that a small force of
well-trained soldiers is often decisive in a pitched battle. This sound advice may
also have a contemporary significance, i.e., that it was becoming increasingly
difficult to find 'Roman' men to fill the ranks.

Although Vegetius, in his advocacy of a smaller and better-trained army in
place of a *rudis et indocta multitudo* (*Epit.* 1.1.8), seems to intimate that the pool
of suitable men had evaporated to some extent in the course of the last century or
so, it is interesting to note that he maintains that restrictions on origin (*Epit.* 1.2–
3), age (*Epit.* 1.4.1–5), size (*Epit.* 1.5), previous occupations (*Epit.* 1.7.1–2), and
even character (*Epit.* 1.7.3–6) should be enforced rigorously.[57] In all, Vegetius
devotes no less than seven chapters (viz., 2–8) of book 1 to recruitment. His
general contention in these chapters is that the potential recruit must be chosen
with care. Would this have been feasible in the immediate aftermath of Adrianople? One would think not. And that selective recruitment was not possible, even
towards the end of Theodosius' reign, is perhaps demonstrated by the emperor's
need to use large numbers of Gothic troops at the River Frigidus in 394 (Oros.
7.35.19; Zos. 4.58.2–3) – unless, of course, he was attempting to expend them in
battle. Theodosius, so it seems, was unwilling to spend the time that would have
been needed to train Roman soldiers in the traditional manner. E. Birley and
Goffart make the not unreasonable point that Vegetius' advocacy of selective
recruitment suits the reign of Valentinian III far better than it does that of
Theodosius the Great.

Vegetius implies, at several points in the text, that the emperor is actually
putting into practice what he is writing.[58] For example:

> quid enim audacius quam domino ac principi generis humani, domitori omnium gentium
> barbararum, aliquid de usu ac disciplina insinuare bellorum, nisi forte quod ipse iussisset
> fieri, quod ipse gessisset? (*Epit.* 2 prol. 4).

And, in addition:

> nec moueat quod olim est consuetudo mutata quae uiguit; sed huius felicitatis ac prouisionis
> est perennitas tua ut pro salute rei publicae et noua excogitet et antiqua restituat (*Epit.*
> 2.18.6).[59]

---

[57] For a general survey of recruitment policy in the Late Empire, see Gigli 1947, 268–289.
Of particular interest is his treatment of the hereditary nature of the soldierly profession (268–
272).

[58] E. Birley 1988, 66–68; Goffart 1977, 98–99.

[59] Consider, too, that books 2–4 were apparently commissioned by the emperor, which does
not necessarily mean, of course, that it was the emperor himself who authorized the composition
of the last three books.

Such words, of course, may be hollow and designed to deflect imperial criticism if, perchance, the contents of the work were found to be displeasing. Alternatively, they may provide some reflection of reality, however exaggerated. That this may be so is suggested by certain *leges nouellae* of the Late Empire. Issued under the auspices of Valentinian III and his senior colleague in the East (viz., Theodosius II), these Novels appear to be of a similar nature to the recruitment reforms – or rather return to the ancient recruitment procedures – proposed by Vegetius. Várady, in his study on late Roman military organization, cites several of the *nouellae*. He holds that the following, issued by Theodosius II, reflects an increase "in the strictness in the training taking effect in the East Roman Empire":[60]

> eos [duces] igitur ... in ipsis plerumque limitibus commorari et milites ad antiquum redigere numerum, inminentibus magisteriis potestatibus diurnisque eorum exercitationibus inhaerere praecipimus. castrorum quin etiam ipsis lusoriarumque pro antiqua dispositione curam refectionemque mandamus (*Nov. Theod.* 24.1 of 443).[61]

In his commentary on Várady's paper, E. Birley forgets to point out that the above Novel hails from the East of Theodosius II (witness *Constantinopoli*) rather than the West of Valentinian III. As a consequence, he includes it with "several of the Novels of Valentinian III, within the period 440–445".[62] Birley's 'error' is also noted by Milner.[63] Despite this, one should not forget that a closer working relationship had been forged between East and West during the respective reigns of the two emperors in question.[64] Indeed, this feature of the 440s is especially evinced by Theodosius' participation in the campaign against the Vandals.[65] While it was usual to begin a *lex* with the names of the two (or more) reigning *Augusti* (witness, in this case, *impp. Theod[osius] et Valent[inianus]*), this was generally done so in order to promote the fiction that the Empire remained a unified political entity.[66] Yet how can one prove that the 'empty' formula, on this occasion, had no more than its usual symbolic meaning? How can it be demonstrated that the *nouella* in question, although issued by the 'senior' *Augustus*, was not a joint prescription in fact as well as in name? It is clearly impossible to do so.

That *nouellae* of a similar tone and character were issued more or less contemporaneously in the West certainly adds some weight to the highly tentative theory that *Nov. Theod.* 24 reflects an Empire-wide move towards military reform. Thus it is possible that Birley was not entirely mistaken when he connect-

---

[60] Várady 1961, 343 and n. 26.

[61] Várady 1961, 343 n. 26. With regard to this *nouella*, E. Birley (1988, 67) holds that we should compare 1.7 of the *Epitoma* ("for the levying of recruits having hitherto been resulting *per gratiam aut dissimulationem* in the enrolment of unsatisfactory men").

[62] E. Birley 1988, 67.

[63] Milner 1996, xxxviii.

[64] See Goffart 1977, 99 and n. 166.

[65] On this, see Isid. *Hist. Goth.* 76 (*MGH:AA* 11, *Chron. min.* 2, 297); Prosp. 1344 (*MGH:AA* 9, *Chron. min.* 1, 478).

[66] Of course, the name of the 'senior' emperor would normally appear first. For an example, see *Nov. Valent.* 1.1 (*Rauennae*): *impp. Theod(osius) et Valent(inianus)*.

ed the recruitment policy outlined in this eastern *nouella* with 1.7 of the *Epitoma*. To return to the matter at hand, the same scholar, who treats of the *leges nouellae* of the last Valentinian and their relationship to the material contained within Vegetius' text, also claims that "three further Novels [6.3, 6.2, 15] deserve to be taken into account". These three decrees, in addition to other important *nouellae*, will be discussed below. First, special attention is devoted to *Nov. Valent.* 6.2 of 25 May 443:

> quid enim magis professis est desideriis expetendum, quam ut adiectis uiribus per dilectum roboris militaris Romanus augeatur exercitus .... auersum quippe animum a communi defensionis studio iure talis seueritas insequitur .... quia, quisquis in hac parte cessauerit, sese quodammodo confitetur non esse Romanum.

In the same Novel is a reference to the necessity of finding adequate men: *sine ulla tam necessariae rei dissimulatione* (*Nov. Valent.* 6.2.1). Várady claims that, in *Nov. Valent.* 6.2, "the increase of «Roman» military elements was in question", and that this represented an attempt to divorce the emperor from the necessity of having to rely on "the allied ... forces of the barbarians".[67] This largely corresponds to what Vegetius says at *Epit.* 1.28. Furthermore, *Nov. Valent.* 6.3 of 14 July 444 makes especial provision for securing extra financial resources for the required intake and training of recruits, the necessity of which is explained in the following terms: *paruo etenim unusquisque contempto sperare debet securitatem futuri*. In similar fashion, *Nov. Valent.* 15, issued some time between 11 September 444 and 18 January 445,[68] discusses, in considerable detail, the means by which a special sales tax should be levied in order to pay for the formation of a large army. This *exercitus* was to include existing personnel, in addition to new recruits:

> ipso experimento non modo his, qui nouis sacramentis obligantur, sed ne ueteri quidem exercitui quae ab exhaustis aegerrime conferentur ad uictum uel ad uestitum posse praeberi (*Nov. Valent.* 15).

Again, the reason for the policy is explained by the emperor: *nihil tam necessarium cura serenitatis nostrae perspicit, ... quam ut defessis rebus adflictoque publico statu robur numerosi exercitus praeparetur* (*Nov. Valent.* 15). Note that records of such a nature were not issued during the reign of Theodosius I.[69] Despite this, Milner contends that "there was no military revival under Valentin-

---

[67] Várady 1961, 342–343.

[68] E. Birley 1988, 68.

[69] There does exist, however, *Cod. Theod.* 7.13.10 (381), which demands that a landowner supply *duos mutilos iuniores pro uno integro*. Hitherto, peasant men had often amputated their right thumb in order to exempt themselves from military service. See also the post-Theodosian *Cod. Theod.* 7.13.12 of 397, which calls for the utilization of the total strength of the imperial household; and *Cod. Theod.* 7.20.12 of 400, which calls for a re-examination of military discharges and the re-enlistment of men who had left before the completion of their service. Cf. Amm. Marc. 26.7.1 and 31.12.1 for the use of *ueterani* in the fourth century; and Amm. Marc. 26.5.3 (Serenianus) and 26.7.4 (Gomoarius and Agilo) for the recall of officers from retirement. On the recalling of deserters in Britain without penalty, see Amm. Marc. 27.8.10 (368).

ian III".[70] This is true enough. Valentinian III's military successes were, as Milner points out, almost entirely "due to Aëtius' ability to hire ... mercenaries".[71] However, although such a policy would have been "anathema" to Vegetius,[72] the *nouellae* cited above, in addition to those which will be cited below, at least show a *trend* towards the re-establishment of a 'Roman' army. Such a trend was not especially evident during the reign of Theodosius I. It was this particular emperor's desire, after all, to take full advantage of the fighting abilities of the barbarians, and to play off one tribal group against another. This policy, according to Claudian's *De Sexto Consulatu Honorii* (219–222), was continued by Stilicho, with disastrous implications for the West. That Aëtius, contrary to the thoughts of Milner, largely fought his battles with allied mercenaries (for want of a better term) was not the result of a determined policy to maximize barbarian military potential – it was the result of pure necessity. Vegetius' attempt to promote the *antiqua legio* was a lost cause, just as Valentinian III's attempt to recruit a 'Roman' army was doomed to failure for a number of reasons, not the least of which was the reluctance of the Gallic and Italian *possessores* to part with their valuable tenants.

As noted above, it is of particular interest that many of Valentinian III's *nouellae* emphasize that it is the landowners' responsibility to recruit *coloni* and tenants. In addition, landowners were required to furnish three men for one in cases where deserters where found hidden on their property. Várady notes that

> This is the first legal force which particularly and definitely refers to the *coloni, conductores* and *actores*, in other words to the indirect military service of the entire agrarian proletariat and announces the renewal of the army by them (*reparandi feliciter exercitus cura* [*conferre debere tirones possessorem censuimus*]).[73]

Could these measures possibly be a reflection of what Vegetius urged in the first book of his *Epitoma*? It is worth noting that Milner contends that the *Epitoma* most properly belongs to the time of Theodosius I, for, in the *Epitoma*, "it was still normal for *coloni* to be recruited ..., whereas this was banned after pressure from senatorial landowners in the early fifth century".[74] He refers to *Epit.*

---

[70] Milner 1996, xxxix.

[71] Milner 1996, xxxix.

[72] Milner 1996, xxxix.

[73] Várady 1961, 342.

[74] Milner 1996, xl. Milner refers to "Jones, 619" (e.g., A.H.M. Jones 1964 [vol. 3]; see also 184 of same work [vol. 2]). Milner's thoughts are repeated at 1996, 8 n. 4, where he writes that the recruitment of *coloni* was "banned in the early fifth century" and that "V. must have been writing before this ban". It is not entirely clear why Milner cites A.H.M. Jones, for the latter merely points out that the *possessores* were now allowed to commute recruits for gold (1964, 619 [vol. 3]; for evidence, see 1964, 186 n. 24 [vol. 2]; note especially *Cod. Theod.* 7.13.13–14 of 397, where we read that senators were allowed to pay 25 *solidi* for each recruit exempted). A.H.M. Jones writes that "a law of Honorius dated to 403 seems to imply an annual levy" and mentions "Two novels of Valentinian III, dated 440 and 443 [viz., *Nov. Valent.* 6.1, 6.2]" (1964, 619 [vol. 3]). He also notes that, "In the East the last laws which allude to conscription are dated 396, but the absence of *constitutiones* may merely mean that the routine was operating smoothly" (1964, 619 [vol. 3]; see *Cod. Theod.* 11.23.3–4 of 396).

"I.7".[75] However, it appears abundantly clear, from the information provided by the *nouellae* mentioned above, that the practice was certainly in force during the reign of Valentinian III, and that of his eastern equivalent. The relevant part of *Epit.* 1.7 is worth reviewing:

> et quantum usu experimentisque cognouimus, hinc tot ubique ab hostibus inlatae sunt clades, dum longa pax militem incuriosius legit, dum honestiores quique ciuilia sectantur officia, dum indicti possessoribus tirones per gratiam aut dissimulationem probantium tales sociantur armis quales domini habere fastidiunt (*Epit.* 1.7.8–9).

First, one is provided with no cause to assume necessarily that the *possessores* were still providing unsuitable tenants (i.e., *coloni*) to the army in Vegetius' day. The present passive verbal forms *sectantur* and *sociantur*, and the present indicative *fastidiunt*, being governed by *dum*, clearly refer to past action. Note Stelten's translation: "those who were more upright sought civilian duties"; "recruits who were levied"; and "their masters were loathe [*sic*] to have them".[76] Second, the *tot ... clades*, which came after a time of relative peace (witness *longa pax*), are quite likely to be those defeats suffered from the time of Adrianople onwards, and possibly up until the sack of Rome in 410. The phrase is thus reminiscent of – if not equivalent to – the sort of language found at *Epit.* 1.20.4–5, especially *tantarum urbium excidia*. This interpretation of *Epit.* 1.7, *pace* Milner, seems consonant with a date under Valentinian III.

Whatever the case, it does seem certain that Vegetius advocated the practice of recruiting soldiers from the rural peasantry. At *Epit.* 1.3.1, he writes as follows: *numquam credo potuisse dubitari aptiorem armis rusticam plebem.* According to Vegetius (who is probably drawing on the opinions of moralizing sources such as Cato the Elder and Sallust),[77] the rustic lad who has grown up in the open air possesses all the soldierly attributes. He has strengthened his body with hard work, is capable of bearing the sun's heat, and is unfamiliar with luxury (*Epit.* 1.3.1). In addition, the *rusticus*, being from the countryside and familiar with agriculture, has the ability to use iron implements, dig ditches and carry heavy burdens (*Epit.* 1.3.1). These last three skills were certainly requisite qualities. Vegetius, however, notes that *interdum tamen necessitas exigit etiam urbanos ad arma compelli* (*Epit.* 1.3.2) and that, when this occurs, the urban youths must quickly be taught to act in the same fashion as their rustic cousins by means of strenuous exercise, discipline and physical privation (*Epit.* 1.3.2–3). Vegetius also writes that certain men are unsuited to military service on account of their occupations – the Roman *exercitus* is thus no place for *piscatores au-*

---

[75] Milner 1996, xl.

[76] Cf. Milner 1996, *ad loc.*: "all those of decent birth have been pursuing civilian careers"; "recruits levied from landowners"; and "the sort their lords disdained to keep".

[77] For the elder Cato, see *Epit.* 1.8.10, 1.13.6, 1.15.4, 2.3.6. For Sallust, see *Epit.* 1.4.4, 1.9.8. As far as I can tell, sources for Veg. *Epit.* 1.3 have not been analysed in the multifarious *Quellenforschung* articles of scholars such as Lammert, Sander and Schanz, all of whom have sought to establish the sources for various sections of the text in a series of short but well-detailed articles (see bibliography for details).

*cupes dulciarios linteones omnesque qui aliquid tractasse uidebuntur ad gynae-
cea pertinens* (*Epit.* 1.7.1).[78]

Apart from farmers and country labourers, Vegetius holds that the following
make suitable recruits: *fabros ferrarios carpentarios macellarios et ceruorum
aprorumque uenatores* (*Epit.* 1.7.2). The point that Vegetius makes, therefore, is
that those who regularly engage in 'masculine' activity (preferably in the country
rather than in the city) require far less training than their urban counterparts,
which, of course, equates to less expenditure – a consideration which tallies with
the fiscal matters raised in the *nouellae* of Valentinian III. It is also partially
reminiscent of the opinions expressed in the *De Rebus Bellicis*. Moreover, in
times of war, the country recruit can be prepared for battle in much less time than
the supposedly effeminate city-dweller. In sum, Vegetius concludes that *ex agris
ergo supplendum robur praecipue uidetur exercitus. nescioquomodo enim minus
mortem timet qui minus deliciarum nouit in uita* (*Epit.* 1.3.5).

Despite recruitment problems and the difficulty of parting *rustici* from the
possessores, Vegetius seems to have held that small numbers of such men, if
given the requisite drillmaster's polish, would be infinitely preferable to large
numbers of untrustworthy *foederati*. Finally, he explains that the following rule
was always respected by those responsible for military recruitment and the order
of battle: *ne umquam amplior multitudo socialium auxiliarium esset in castris
quam ciuium Romanorum* (*Epit.* 3.1.12). By using these words, Vegetius clearly
evinces his concern about the rising numbers of *foederati*. This concern, undoubtedly shared by a good number of his contemporaries, was not merely inspired by
military expediency. Rather, it was a sober reflection of distrust, a deep-seated
animosity towards the 'barbarian' elements of the post-Theodosian *exercitus*
which had been fostered by numerous – and not always unprovoked – instances
of deception and betrayal.[79]

3. FREE SPEECH AND THEODOSIUS I

Vegetius' apparent contempt for 'foreign' troops, if considered alone, aids us
little in our attempt to date the *Epitoma*, yet one thing remains clear: the words
uilius enim constat erudire armis suos quam alienos mercede conducere (*Epit.*
1.28.10) would not have been especially pleasing to Theodosius I, an emperor
often criticized by modern scholars for his ostensible philobarbarism. Paschoud,
on the other hand, is of the opinion that Vegetius was merely recapitulating the

---

[78] Although *piscatores* is translated by Nicasie (1998, 86 n. 16), Silhanek (1972, *ad loc.*)
and Stelten (1990, *ad loc.*) as "fishermen", and not surprising as "pescatori" by Formisano
(2003, *ad loc.*) and Giuffrida Manmana (1997, *ad loc.*), Müller suggests "Fischhändler" (1997,
ad loc.).

[79] Richardot 1998, 142: "Végèce signale que l'emploi de mercenaires «étrangers» est plus
coûteux que le recrutement des «siens», il fait probablement allusion aux fédérés barbares ....
Végèce se méfie des auxiliaires et donc des mercenaires étrangers, sans cohésion et prompts à se
mutiner". For manifestations of the Roman distrust of barbarians, see Amm. Marc. 31.16.8.

initiatives that Theodosius (his preferred recipient of the *Epitoma*) was already putting into effect.[80] Admittedly, Vegetius does claim something of the sort in the *praefationes* of books 1 and 2. Yet this, perhaps, is merely tactfulness on the part of the author. One might also note that, in these *praefationes*, we are not presented with any indication that the emperor was actually reducing the number of federate troops. Indeed, the statements found in the two above-mentioned *praefationes* might reasonably be used as further proof of the general military ignorance of Vegetius' honorand. Once again, the tone is one of mannered condescension rather than genuine acknowledgement of the emperor's military sapience. If one accepts Paschoud's interpretation of the language contained within these two *praefationes*, as does Barnes,[81] Vegetius' central thesis becomes more or less redundant. Why address a book to an emperor who is already carrying out the author's proposed reforms? In any case, there is no real evidence to suggest that Theodosius (or any other emperor, eastern *or* western) carried out *any* of the changes that Vegetius recommended – far from it. As we know, Vegetius was a proponent of the citizen-infantryman and a clear opponent of the 'barbarization' of the Roman army. Theodosius' reign witnessed a greater use of 'federate' troops than ever before. This emperor's military policy, therefore, was the exact antithesis to that proposed by Vegetius.[82] And this is something that Paschoud also concedes when he mentions "la crainte de suggérer un remède qui va à l'encontre de la politique de Théodose".[83]

On the other hand, Giuffrida Manmana shrewdly points out that the *Epitoma*, because it affirms that the Empire should not be militarily dependent on non-Roman troops, must belong to a post-Theodosian context.[84] Yet Vegetius does not appear to have been alone in his veiled criticism of the prevailing imperial policy. Ammianus, writing under Theodosius I, praises the conduct of Julius, the *magister militiae trans Taurum* who supposedly dealt with the Goths in a brutal fashion shortly after Adrianople (31.16.8).[85] According to Ammianus' account (which appears to be chronologically misleading – other evidence points to a date in early 379),[86] Julius ordered the deaths of all *Gothi* previously admitted into the Roman army. It appears that he acted on his own initiative.[87] Using the terminol-

---

[80] Paschoud 1967, 111, see also 122.

[81] Barnes 1979, 255–256.

[82] Synesius, in his *De Regno*, also contends that the Roman army must be composed of Romans rather than barbarians (22–23). He warns that the shepherd (i.e., the emperor) must not mix wolves (i.e., the Goths) with his dogs (i.e., his 'Roman' troops), for the wolves, given the slightest opportunity, "will attack them, flock, shepherd, and all" (22A) (translation of Cameron/Long/Sherry 1993, 110). This was addressed to Arcadius and could possibly have been delivered in his presence, although one might well remain sceptical about such assertions.

[83] Paschoud 1967, 114.

[84] Giuffrida Manmana 1981, 36.

[85] See Elbern 1987, 99–106.

[86] The date is a source of contention. While Ammianus places the massacre directly after Adrianople (followed by Buck 1988, 39), Zosimus (4.26.2–9) assigns it to the first months of Theodosius' reign. Despite this, Paschoud (1971–1979, 389 [vol. 2.2]) casts doubts on Zosimus' chronology. Cf. Ehrhardt 1964, 10; Zuckerman 1991, 481–486.

[87] That the Goths were Roman soldiers, as is intimated at Amm. Marc. 31.16.8, is refuted by

ogy of Straub,[88] Giuffrida Manmana writes that the «Vernichtung» dei Barbari e ... [il] ritorno alla «altrömische Disziplin»"[89] were

> i punti essenziali su cui si basava la politica tradizionale, espressa chiaramente in Amm. XVI.8 [*sic*], eran l'annientamento dei Barbari, il sacrificio di tutti gli strati sociali, il ritorno all'antica disciplina romana.[90]

How Giuffrida Manmana arrived at this conclusion from Ammianus 31.16.8 is somewhat puzzling, although it might well be noted that Barnes also believes that this particular vignette demonstrates that "Ammianus recommended massacre as politically expedient – and even, if necessary, genocide".[91] Of course, Ammianus approved of Julius' action and describes the general's *efficacia* as *salutaris et uelox*. Furthermore, Ammianus states that, by means of Julius' brutal yet supposedly prudent plan, *orientales prouinciae discriminibus ereptae sunt magnis*.[92] Yet he does not necessarily condemn, here, the policy of allowing *barbari* into the army. Of course, Ammianus was no friend of the barbarian.[93] But the main reason for his support of Julius' conduct was his belief that, in the confused aftermath of Adrianople, all potentially traitorous elements within the eastern army should be removed (if it is indeed true that Julius' victims were soldiers rather than teenage hostages, as the tradition of Eunapius/Zosimus would have us believe).

Ammianus 31.16.8, therefore, does not really constitute a defence of the "altrömische Disziplin", for the Roman *exercitus* had always maintained foreign troops – i.e., *auxilia* and irregular *symmachiarii* – in its midst. The only real difference, at the time and in the location to which Ammianus refers, is that the *Gothi* in question were cousins of the men who had recently defeated the might of the East, and were now at large on the Thracian plains. Quite obviously, this particular situation seemed to demand that Goths already under Roman command should not be allowed to turn on their masters. Julius' decision – at least as Ammianus narrates it – was based more on expediency and distrust than any immediate desire to enforce the "altrömische Disziplin".[94] The employment of non-Roman troops, in one way or another, had been a necessary evil throughout Roman history. If it is indeed true that Ammianus' version of the massacre was distorted, as Zuckerman has argued,[95] and deliberately placed in a context imme-

---

Zuckerman (1991, 485), who uses Zos. 4.26.2–9 and Eunap. frg. 42 in order to demonstrate that the Gothic 'soldiers' were merely rioting teenage hostages. This view is supported by Barnes 1998, 185.

[88] Straub 1943, 261.

[89] Giuffrida Manmana 1981, 35.

[90] Giuffrida Manmana 1981, 35 n. 33.

[91] Barnes 1998, 186. See also Bonanni 1981, 125; Mackail 1920, 116; Matthews 1986, 23.

[92] On the incident, see Camus 1967, 119–120.

[93] It is of interest that Ammianus, in describing the *magister equitum* Victor, writes that this man was *Sarmata sed cunctator et cautus* (31.12.6), something which suggests that one should be very surprised to find these qualities in a barbarian.

[94] See Ladner 1976, 1–26.

[95] Zuckerman 1991, 481–486.

diately after Adrianople rather than in early 379, the historian probably does so in order to hide the true motive for his inclusion of the event. As will be seen below, Ammianus was unwilling to comment directly on Theodosius' policy towards the Goths, or indeed any part of the emperor's reign. So, by shifting Julius' massacre to the months before the new emperor's accession, Ammianus gives himself the freedom to praise an action that ran contrary to the policy pursued by Theodosius I at the time of the *Res Gestae*'s composition.

Despite the present interpretation of 31.16.8, Ammianus certainly did not approve of the widespread use of barbarian troops. He would have held that, while barbarian troops *did* have their place in the army, Rome should not be wholly dependent on allied forces. Camus holds that "L'historien nous fait part à plusieurs reprises du ressentiment qu'il nourrit à l'égard de ces corps étrangers à l'empire".[96] He also notes instances where Ammianus describes the fickle nature of barbarian units. In 354, Constantius II planned a foray into the territory of the Alamanni. The enterprise failed because officers of the same nation serving in the Roman army sent word of the impending danger to their countrymen (14.10.7–8). According to Ammianus, infantry units composed of *Bracchiati* or *Cornuti* would generally offer their services to the highest bidder (15.5.30), and the loyalty of the Gallic *cohortes* was always dubious (30.10.1). When describing the siege of Amida, Ammianus deplores the insubordination and lack of discipline of the two units from Gaul (19.5.2–3, 19.6.3).[97] Gallic troops, although *fortes* and *pernices* (Amm. Marc. 19.5.2), were not suited to the cramped conditions of siege-warfare. This is not simply criticism of non-Roman troops – it is censure of the way in which such troops are employed.

Ammianus was equally critical of the policy of allowing barbarians to attain honours traditionally reserved for the old aristocracy. He quotes Julian's criticism of Constantine for such an action: *eum aperte incusans [sc. Iulianus], quod barbaros omnium primus ad usque fasces auxerat et trabeas consulares* (21.10.8). But Ammianus then criticizes Julian himself for doing the same by awarding a consulship to the Goth Nevitta, a man whom he describes as *inconsummatus*, *subagrestis* and *crudelis* (21.10.8).[98] The above merely represents Ammianus' attitude to barbarian troops organized into Roman-style units, and barbarians who had been given military commands. In view of this, it is not difficult to imagine his reaction to the federate armies of Theodosius' reign, military units which bore no resemblance, either in appearance *or* discipline, to those considered 'Roman'.

Like Vegetius, Ammianus would have welcomed a return to certain aspects of the *consuetudo antiqua*. Although he may have raised an eyebrow at the

---

[96] Camus 1967, 118.

[97] For Ammianus on the Franks, see 15.5.11; and, on the Celts, see 22.12.6.

[98] The consulship was for 362; see Cassiod. *Chron.* 1101 (*MGH:AA* 11, *Chron. min.* 2, 152); *Cons. Constant.* 362 (*MGH:AA* 9, *Chron. min.* 1, 240); *Cons. Ital.* 474 (*MGH:AA* 9, *Chron. min.* 1, 294); Prosp. 1118 (*MGH:AA* 9, *Chron. min.* 1, 457). It is worth noting that Barnes (1998, 219 n. 2) has argued convincingly that Ammianus misunderstood Julian's criticism of Constantine, for, to Julian, the 'barbarians' awarded the consulship by Constantine were Christians, the opposite of Julian's beloved Hellenes (i.e., pagans).

epitomator's belief that Rome's salvation lay in the resurrection of the *antiqua legio*, he would certainly have approved of restoring the traditional discipline and *esprit de corps*. Is it significant, then, that he finishes his history with the events of 378 (the Julius episode aside), and fails to continue his narrative into the reign of Theodosius I? Would Ammianus' account of the early part of Theodosius' reign, in which a settlement with the Goths was agreed upon, have been unfavourable to the new emperor? It is impossible to be sure, but one should consider the words of Tacitus, written some two and a half centuries beforehand:

> si uita suppeditet, principatum diui Neruae et imperium Traiani, uberiorem securioremque materiam, senectuti seposui, rara temporum felicitate, ubi sentire quae uelis et quae sentias dicere licet (*Hist.* 1.1.4).

As far as we know, Tacitus never wrote a history of Nerva's *principatus* or Trajan's *imperium* – and this despite his assertion that Domitian's death had restored literary freedom to the Roman world. Tacitus probably had good reason to end his *Historiae* with the last of the Flavians. Notable, too, is that Suetonius, writing under Hadrian, did not write a biography of Nerva or Trajan (Hadrian's adoptive grandfather and father) – and he was hardly about to deal with the activities of the incumbent *princeps*. It must have been a perilous task to undertake contemporary history,[99] and we have no reason to assume that the situation would have been vastly different in the late fourth century (although some scholars argue that Nicomachus Flavianus' *Annales* may have contained material hostile to the Christian emperors, a contention not beyond question). Indeed, Ammianus himself alludes to the dangers of such activity upon concluding his *Res Gestae*:

> haec ut miles quondam et Graecus, a principatu Caesaris Neruae exorsus, ad usque Valentis interitum, pro uirium explicaui mensura: opus ueritatem professum numquam (ut arbitror) sciens silentio ausus corrumpere, uel mendacio. scribant reliqua potiores, aetate et doctrinis florentes. quos id (si libuerit) aggressuros, procudere linguas ad maiores moneo stilos (31.16.9).

The suitably ambiguous neuter case of *reliqua* undoubtedly refers to the period of history after the death of Valens, viz., from the beginning of the reign of Theodosius I. The verb *monere* is surprisingly strong, yet carries a nuance that is difficult to misinterpret: write of Theodosius' reign at your peril. Of the *stilus maior* to which Ammianus alludes, this may refer to the panegyrical style of composition, something which was, of course, expected when one discussed the actions of the present Augustus. Although the last sentence of Ammianus' history seems rather explicit, the historian, if challenged, could have claimed that the glorious endeavours of Theodosius should not be treated of by a mere *miles quondam* – this should only be attempted by one whose literary skills are consonant with the exalted nature of the task. Rulers of the Late Empire, as is clear

---

[99] However, it does seem possible to denigrate aspects of 'good' emperors – as long as they belonged to a preceding dynasty. For example, Tacitus provides a slight censure of Augustus at *Ann.* 12.6.2. Suetonius, of course, provides unflattering details of the *diui principes* (such as Augustus and Claudius, and even Vespasian and Titus) on many occasions.

from Ammianus and lesser historians like Zosimus, were as mindful of sedition as ever and were always ready to crush the slightest inkling of disaffection. How Eunapius, whose fragmentary history is peppered with anti-Theodosian material, published the final version of his work under Theodosius' successors – and survived – remains something of a mystery.[100] Perhaps a certain level of literary freedom or, what is more likely, apathy had crept in by the early fifth century. Or perhaps censorship was forced to take a back seat as the Empire was rocked by further military catastrophe. Certainly, Synesius of Cyrene's *De Regno* and *De Prouidentia* (both written during his embassy at Constantinople) contain material that could hardly have been flattering to Arcadius, to whom the *De Regno* was actually directed.[101] Despite this, literature relating to the conduct of the incumbent emperor was generally panegyrical in nature (witness the *panegyrici* of Ausonius, Pacatus, Claudian and Sidonius). The objective historian would thus have to compromise his principles if he sought to describe the *acta* of the reigning Augustus.[102] Ammianus' failure to continue the *Res Gestae* past the death of Valens seems to suggest that he did not feel free to relate, with any degree of accuracy, the details of contemporary history. Like Tacitus, he must have realized the dangers of commenting upon the actions of the incumbent régime.[103]

That Ammianus was mindful of these problems appears to be demonstrated by the manner in which he composed the last six books of his history (books 26–31).[104] Much debate has ensued regarding the date of these books, yet it has been traditionally held that they were written in the early 390s.[105] Certain features of the text in the last six books suggest that they were a) published together, and b) at a later date compared to the first twenty-five books of the history. A year or two either side of 390 matters little for the present argument, for Theodosius' anti-pagan policy, though it did not properly manifest itself until the promulgation of *Cod. Theod.* 16.10.10 (February 391), must have already been partly visible after Maximus' defeat in 388. In comparison with books 1–25, considerable changes in the author's *modus operandi* are evident. This seems to be indicative of Theodosius' growing intolerance of opposition, be it intellectual, philosophical or reli-

---

[100] Of course, the chronology of the work is difficult to establish. Matthews (1986, 19) writes that "I think ... that Eunapius' history had appeared (in its first edition) by the time that Ammianus wrote" – i.e., while Theodosius I was still alive.

[101] For commentary on these two works, see Cameron/Long/Sherry 1993, chs. 4–6. It is suggested (110) that the *De Regno* "cannot be later than the first half of 398", which means that it must predate Gaïnas' revolt.

[102] Tacitus (*Hist.* 1.1.1–2) insinuates that historians writing under the Julio-Claudians and the Flavians wrote history in a fashion that compromised the truth. It would seem that Tacitus had no wish to do the same by writing a history of the reigns of Nerva and Trajan.

[103] On this question, cf. Paschoud 2005, 103–118; see also Thompson 1966, 147.

[104] According to Rowell (1967, 280), "it is perfectly clear from the beginning of Book XXVI that Books XXVI through XXXI were written as a separate section of the *History*".

[105] On the date, see Blockley 1975, 15–16, 177ff.; Fornara 1992, 328–344; Hartke 1951, 66–67; Maenchen-Helfen 1955, 384–399; Rowell 1967, 288–289; Seeck 1894a, 1847–1848; Straub 1952, 140; Syme 1968, 10–11, 17–22; Thompson 1947, 18. Apart from Naudé (1984, 70ff.), Cameron (1971, 262) and Matthews (1983, 40 n. 11) prefer a date before the 390s.

gious. Clearly, this was not the time to attack the emperor's philobarbarism. That
the last books of the *Res Gestae* could have been published while Eugenius was
still in power (392–394) matters little. Ammianus, if he were writing at that time,
may have recognized the tenuous nature of the usurper's position, something
which would effectively explain the more 'neutral' tone of the historian towards
politically sensitive issues such as religion and philosophy in books 26–31.

Thompson points out that "no hero" like Julian or Ammianus' old general
Ursicinus dominates the last six books, and that almost all the major historical
figures are criticized to some extent.[106] Only the father of Theodosius I escapes
unscathed. Yet the praise that Ammianus reserves for this figure is "stiff and
formal".[107] Furthermore, Thompson holds that it is "not likely to be a coincidence
that the Western narrative comes down to the eve of the trial and execution of the
elder Theodosius, and stops short without any discussion of the event or its
aftermath".[108] The implication is that the circumstances surrounding his mysterious execution were best forgotten. Indeed, it was Theodosius I's policy to restore
the name of Theodosius the Elder. The gilt equestrian statues dedicated to the
executed general clearly emphasize this.[109] It was this policy, too, that would
result in the rather ironic consecration of the elder Theodosius in 384.[110] Ammianus' failure to address fully the issue of the general's execution suggests that he
was forced to sacrifice the truth. Pacatus, who delivered a panegyric in honour of
Theodosius in 389, is also tellingly silent on the topic.

Even more significant is the manner in which Ammianus' religious attitudes
appear to change in the last six books.[111] Before 391/392, Theodosius generally
dealt with pagans in a relatively liberal-minded fashion, although von Campenhausen thought that he was perhaps attempting to ingratiate himself with the
western pagan aristocracy in order to facilitate the replacement of Valentinian II
with his own son Honorius.[112] Theodosius' initial tolerance with regard to paganism is evidenced by the *Codex Theodosianus*, which records that a *templum* under
the jurisdiction of the *dux Osdroenae* (of Osrhoene) should remain open (*Cod.*

---

[106] Thompson 1966, 148; supported by Syme 1968, 14.

[107] Thompson 1966, 148. The epithets are highly formulaic; see, for example, Amm. Marc.
28.3.1, 29.5.45.

[108] Thompson 1966, 149; cf. Syme 1968, 14. Most of our information comes from a variant
of St. Jerome's *Chronicle* in which the execution is blamed on the machinations of Maximinus
and his cohorts; see Mommsen, *MGH:AA* 9, *Chron. min.* 1, 631; cf. Hieron. *Chron.* 376 p. Chr.
(*Euseb. Werk.* 7, 248 c). Whether the order for his death was issued by Gratian or Valens
(suggested by Jord. *Rom.* 312 [*MGH:AA* 5.1, 40] and glosses on Oros. 7.33.6–7) is the subject of
debate; on this, see A.R. Birley 1983, 22 n. 62; Demandt 1969, 598–626; Errington 1996a, 443–
447; Gasparini 1972, 180–197; Hoepffner 1936, 119–129.

[109] According to Naudé (1984, 76), these statues were erected in places such as Antioch,
Stobi, Ephesus and Rome. See also Egger 1929, 27–32.

[110] Symm. *Rel.* 9.4, with Vera 1981, 82–97. See especially Cracco Ruggini 1977, 425–489
(discussion of an ivory diptych depicting the ceremony), with Naudé 1984, 76–77.

[111] Angliviel de la Beaumelle 1984, 15–23; Ensslin 1923, *passim*; Camus 1967, 133–264.

[112] Von Campenhausen 1929, 222–243, see especially 226–227. This cannot be proved.

Theod. 16.10.8). While this law *does* proscribe ritual sacrifice in the temple, it represents a policy that, while working away at paganism, did not yet ban all aspects of its practice. Non-Christians were promoted to positions of prominence. Pacatus, generally regarded as a pagan,[113] received the prestigious proconsulate of Africa;[114] Nicomachus Flavianus sr., the *praefectus praetorio Italiae*, returned to court after a short retirement;[115] and Tatianus became *praefectus praetorio Orientis* in 388 and held that post until 392.[116] In 390, two prominent pagans (viz., Symmachus and Tatianus) were appointed consuls for the following year.[117] After Gratian's death, the urban prefecture at Rome was generally held by pagans until 391.[118] Chastagnol holds that, of Gratian's twelve urban prefects, only the first, viz., Tarracius Bassus, was pagan.[119] But, after Valentinian's restoration, Theodosius gave the office to pagan men, viz., Sex. Aurelius Victor (388–389) and Caeionius Rufius Albinus (389–391).[120]

That pagans enjoyed Theodosius' favour before 391 is evident. Thus, in the first twenty-five books, Ammianus must have felt relatively free to express his thoughts on religious questions. According to Syme and Thompson, this changed in 392.[121] Rosen, however, rejects the notion that the change in religious policy forced Ammianus to keep quiet about certain issues.[122] Thompson does slightly overdraw his picture of Ammianus' reaction to the increasing religious intolerance, yet a change in approach between books 1–25 and books 26–31 is discernible. In the earlier books, we witness the folly of Constantius II, the Christian ruler who went to extraordinary lengths to suppress fortune-telling (21.16.18) –

---

[113] Galletier (1955, 50–51) uses *Pan.* 4.5, 6.3–4, 10.1, 22.5 and 29 in order to demonstrate that Pacatus was not a Christian, but Nixon (1987, 5) expresses some disquiet.

[114] *Cod. Theod.* 9.2.4 of Feb. 4, 390. A Drepanius was made *comes rei priuatarum* in 393 (*Cod. Theod.* 9.42.13 of June 12, 393; *Cod. Iust.* 11.67.1). Lippold (1968, 228 and n. 6) casts doubt on whether this Drepanius can be identified with the panegyrist, but others find it plausible; see Hanslik 1942, 2058; Matthews 1971, 1079–1082; Nixon 1987, 13 n. 16; Seeck 1883, cxciii; Stroheker 1970, 197.

[115] On this, Hartke (1938, 430–436) should be consulted; on Nicomachus Flavianus, see also *PLRE* I, Flavianus 15, with Bleckmann 1995, 83–99; Hartke 1951, 329–334; Paschoud 1975, 150–168; id. 1994, 71–82; id. 2001, xii–xix; Schlumberger 1974, 305–329; id. 1985, 305–329.

[116] e.g., *Cod. Theod.* 1.5.9 (389), 5.11.12 (388–392 [date lost]), 8.4.16 (389), 8.11.5 (389), 10.22.2 (388), 11.16.18 (390), 11.16.19 (391), 12.1.119 (388), 12.1.120 (389), 12.1.121–122 (390), 12.1.123 (391), 12.1.127 (392), 13.5.19 (390). On Tatianus' removal, see Barnes 1984, 228.

[117] See e.g., *Cons. Constant.* 391 (*MGH:AA* 9, *Chron. min.* 1, 245); *Cons. Ital.* 515 (*MGH: AA* 9, *Chron. min.* 1, 298).

[118] See Chastagnol 1960, 436–442, and especially the tables on 436, 440.

[119] Chastagnol 1960, 436. Gratian's ninth prefect, viz., L. Valerius Septimus Bassus of "Fin 380?", is described as "Chrétien?". For further details, see 438 of the same work.

[120] Chastagnol 1960, 442. Note the respective faiths of the "Préfets de Valentinien II" – Sallustius Aventius (384): "Païen?"; Q. Aurelius Symmachus (384–385): "Païen"; and Valerius Pinianus (385–387): "Chrétien".

[121] Syme 1968, 14; Thompson 1966, 150.

[122] Rosen 1982, 32.

although it must be admitted that Constantius' Arian faith would not have endeared him greatly to the orthodox Theodosius.[123] Ammianus even makes Julian call Constantine the Great a *nouator turbatorque priscarum legum* (21.10.8).[124] This would not have pleased Theodosius after *Cod Theod.* 16.10.10, for it would imply that he, too, was a *turbator priscarum legum*.

In the last books, Ammianus had to resort to far subtler means. For example, at 30.9.5, he praises Valentinian I's religious tolerance, which appears as the antithesis of Theodosius' Christian bigotry.[125] Yet, even if Ammianus had dared to write an account of the early part of Theodosius' reign, he could not have adopted this approach in order to criticize the emperor's use of *foederati*. For Ammianus to have praised a general's exclusive use of citizen troops, he would have had to reach far back into the annals for suitable *exempla*. Such a contrived artifice, of course, would surely have appeared as measured criticism. Valentinian's comparative religious tolerance could be invoked without any real hint of literary contrivance. This is because, upon an emperor's decease in the narrative, Ammianus routinely provides a brief synthesis of the subject's *uirtutes* and *uitia*. It is only in this context that Ammianus found the freedom to express, by the most oblique of methods, his disapproval of contemporary bigotry.

Theodosius, perhaps pressured by Ambrose,[126] moved towards a policy of open anti-paganism in early 391.[127] This policy reversal may have been prompted by a desire to weaken further the influence of the old pagan aristocracy, which had already shown its disloyalty to Valentinian II by favouring Maximus (and this despite the latter's ultra-orthodoxy). Perhaps the most symbolic manifestation of this change was the destruction of the Serapeum in Alexandria by the bishop Theophilus. Whether this was prompted by the emperor himself is debatable, and the ecclesiastical historians do not concur.[128] The famous decree of February 391, addressed to the *praefectus praetorianus* Caeionius Rufius Albinus,[129] ordered that *nemo se hostiis polluat, nemo insontem uictimam caedat, nemo delubra adeat, templa perlustret et mortali opere formata simulacra suspi-*

---

[123] On this, see Camus 1967, 249. On Ammianus' attitude to Christianity, see Cameron 1964, 316–328; Selem 1964, 224–261.

[124] Further criticism of Constantine is found at Amm. Marc. 25.4.23, where the historian, seeking to exculpate Julian from the odium of the Persian disaster, blames Constantine for having kindled the *ardores Parthicos*; see also Amm. Marc. 21.10.8.

[125] This is pointed out by Rosen 1982, 148; Urbainczyk 1998, 300.

[126] See von Campenhausen 1929, ch. 3; Camus 1967, 247; Williams/Friell 1994, 69–70.

[127] One can detect a move towards militant Christianity as early as December 388. In a letter to Theodosius (*Ep.* 40.6–33), Ambrose defends the action of an eastern bishop who allegedly instigated the burning of a synagogue at Callinicum. For further details, see Ambros. *Ep.* 41.

[128] See Ruf. *H.E.* 11.22–30; Socrat. *H.E.* 5.16–17; Sozom. *H.E.* 7.15; Theod. *H.E.* 5.23. Sozomen (*H.E.* 7.15.11–15) also records a near-contemporaneous event that occurred in Aulone, where the bishop Marcellus was burnt alive after commanding the destruction of pagan temples in both Apamea and the neighbouring villages; see also Theod. *H.E.* 5.22.

[129] Note that *Cod. Theod.* 16.7.4–5 are addressed to a new Praetorian prefect, viz., the notable pagan paladin Nicomachus Flavianus sr. (on his career, see *PLRE* I, Flavianus 15). Both decrees can be dated to May 11 (June 9), 391.

ciat (*Cod. Theod.* 16.10.10). It effectively put an end to public worship of the old gods.[130] Worse, however, was to follow. Indeed, a decree of November 392 (*Cod. Theod.* 16.10.12) banned completely the private practice of any pagan ritual. Sozomen records that the penalty was death and the confiscation of the perpetrator's property (*H.E.* 7.20.2). Likewise, the consultation of entrails, previously proscribed by *Cod. Theod.* 16.10.9 (May 385), was now deemed tantamount to *maiestas* (*Cod. Theod.* 16.10.12.1). All persons were subject to the new law. From 392, high-ranking pagans were dismissed from positions of power. In particular, Tatianus was replaced by the Christian Rufinus as *praefectus praetorio Orientis*.

Theodosius, in his attempt to crush the western aristocracy that had supported the usurper Maximus, aimed at intimidating this small yet influential section of Italian society.[131] Ammianus, writing at Rome, bears sufficient witness to this. Thompson notes that, if only the last six books of the *Res Gestae* had survived, i.e., those written after 392, "it would not be easy to prove that Ammianus was a pagan".[132] Thompson also draws our attention to the following: a) the plural of words such as *deus* and *numen* (which would have offended the prevailing orthodox monotheism) is no longer used; b) references to the pagan arts of divination and soothsaying are not written with the expected enthusiasm; and c) there is no longer any discussion of the Neoplatonic philosophers, much less the eulogistic material found in the first twenty-five books.[133]

If the postulation above has any merit, we are presented with even further cause to believe that Vegetius, a man firmly opposed to the trends of the time, would not have dared to write what he did in an era when philobarbarism, in the sycophantic fashion of Themistius, was the order of the day. Quite evidently, Ammianus, a man who, as Bonanni writes, "è realmente convinto che la penetrazione gotica nell'Impero rappresenti un grave pericolo",[134] was generally forced to keep his peace. One might reasonably expect that Vegetius, if he had been writing during this period of imperial absolutism (arguably the last in the Western Empire), would have been forced to follow suit. It is significant that Synesius did not address his *De Regno*, which includes a long section criticizing

---

[130] Cf. *Cod. Theod.* 16.10.11 (June 16, 391), addressed to Evagrius (Augustal Prefect) and Romanus (*comes* of Egypt). Although State subsidies for pagan rites (specifically those associated with the altar of Victory) had been removed by Gratian (see Ambros. *Ep.* 17.5; Symm. *Rel.* 3), Eugenius restored them (Paulin. *Vit. Amb.* 26). Thus the pagan cults did not die out completely – they subsequently relied on private contributions; see especially *CIL* 6.2158 = *ILS* 4944; Anon. *Contra Paganos* (*Carmen aduersus Flauianum* = Cod. Par. 8084) 112–114; and an Ostian inscription discussed by Bloch (1945, 199–241).

[131] On this, see Frend 1984, 744; Williams/Friell 1994, 70. Theodosius' approach would temporarily backfire in the form of Eugenius. Whatever his nominal faith (he had at least ostensibly espoused Christianity), Eugenius was sympathetic to the pagan cause. On his faith, see Ambros. *Ep.* 57.6–7; Paulin. *Vit. Amb.* 28, 31; Philostorg. *H.E.* 11.2; Sozom. *H.E.* 7.22.4.

[132] Thompson 1966, 151. But cf. Rosen 1982, 16; see also id. 1982, 74; Momigliano 1977, 97; Tränkle 196, 32; Samberger 1969, 370ff.

[133] Thompson 1966, 151.

[134] Bonanni 1981, 136.

the Empire's widespread use of 'Scythian' (i.e., Gothic) troops (22A–26C), to Theodosius I. Instead, he addressed it to his son Arcadius, who is encouraged to be a warrior-emperor. One doubts whether Synesius would have declaimed similar material during the lifetime of Theodosius the Great. Ammianus, like Vegetius (and indeed Synesius), would have found no sympathy for his cause in the emperor Theodosius, a ruler whom Giuffrida Manmana succinctly describes as φιλάνθρωπος βασιλεύς.[135] Yet, while the *Epitoma* may be "[una] ... polemica contro la barbarizzazione", it certainly does not reach the level of advocating "epurazioni" of the barbarian elements of the army.[136] Both Ammianus and Vegetius, therefore, might be said to have favoured a broadly similar military policy, i.e., that of recognizing the benefits of quality – and loyalty – over quantity. That Ammianus was forced to restrain himself from voicing his opinions on the ostensible philobarbarism of the Theodosian régime suggests that it would have been unwise to provoke the emperor's wrath. If Vegetius had been a *comes* of Theodosius, as has been contended by some scholars, it seems unlikely that he would have been asked to compose a further three books of insulting material. Rather, he would have been instructed to keep silent in order that he might avoid the consequences of his *contumacia*, his unashamed persistence in error.[137]

---

[135] Giuffrida Manmana 1981, 35 n. 33.

[136] Giuffrida Manmana 1981, 36.

[137] Only Ambrose, it seems, was capable of simultaneously questioning the emperor's actions and retaining his favour – and this was only possible on account of Theodosius' undoubted concern for the safety of his immortal soul. Still, Ambrose always couched his censure in a way that suggests that his (sometimes stern) criticism was merely a manifestation of his love for the emperor (see especially Ambros. *Ep.* 51 *passim*).

CHAPTER 5

MILITARY II:
OTHER MILITARY CONSIDERATIONS

Once again, 'repetition' must be the theme of this chapter. Vegetius' desire to bring back the old ways provides further contemporary information about the epitomator and his milieu. In the previous chapter, we noted that Vegetius' advocacy of the *antiqua legio* need not necessarily be taken at face value. Rather, the real import of his call was probably to reduce the number of barbarian *foederati* and conversely augment the number of 'Roman' troops. In a similar fashion, we saw that Vegetius' description of unarmoured Roman soldiers falling in great numbers to Gothic arrows need not necessarily be considered a specific reference to Adrianople (where the Roman infantry almost certainly *did* wear cuirass and helmet), but an indication of the sort of defeat suffered by Roman troops from this battle onwards, and into the early fifth century. A reference to the post-Theodosian conflict with Alaric may also be adduced. These factors hardly seem to point to a date for the *Epitoma* during the reign of Theodosius I. In this chapter, further military references that do not seem appropriate for the reign of Theodosius the Great (or, for that matter, that of his western counterpart Valentinian II) will be investigated. Once again, none of the pieces of 'evidence' presented below can be called conclusive, but it will be shown once again that further contemporary military data gleaned from the *Epitoma* correspond more to a fifth-century environment than to the world of the late fourth century. If this is the case, the suggestion that the work was possibly addressed to Valentinian III gains even greater weight.

1. CASTRAMENTATION AND DISCIPLINE

As noted above, Vegetius provides further military clues that may be used to widen the gap between credibility and the case for Theodosius I. Our author places especial emphasis on castramentation in the *Epitoma*. In all, he devotes five chapters to the topic in book 1 (*Epit.* 1.21–25). He also provides a further exegesis on the matter entitled *quemadmodum castra debeant ordinari* in book 3 (*Epit.* 3.8). Of particular note is the following *de munitione castrorum*:

> castrorum quoque munitionem debet tiro condiscere. nihil enim neque tam salutare neque tam necessarium inuenitur in bello; quippe, si recte constituta sunt castra, ita intra uallum securi milites dies noctesque peragunt, etiam si hostis obsideat, quasi muratam ciuitatem uideantur secum ubique portare. sed huius rei scientia prorsus intercidit; nemo enim iam diu ductis fossis praefixisque sudibus castra constituit (*Epit.* 1.21.1–3).

The present laxity with regard to building defensible camps may again be a reference to the increased use of *foederati*, something which, of course, is more consonant with a post-Theodosian date for the *Epitoma* than one before 395. Vegetius laments the failure to maintain the engineering skills that once characterized the citizen troops of old. Of importance, too, is a further passage from the same chapter containing language that, in a way, is broadly similar to that expressed at *Epit.* 1.20.[1] Just as 'Roman' soldiers no longer wear armour, and thus suffered at the hands of the Goths, so too do 'Roman' soldiers no longer fortify their own encampments as they did during the apogee of the Empire. This negligence also led to their destruction in an encounter with barbarian forces. Indeed, the nature of the text is such that it suggests recent action rather than a neat summary of broader historical experience:

> sic diurno uel nocturno superuentu equitum barbarorum multos exercitus scimus frequenter afflictos. non solum autem considentes sine castris ista patiuntur, sed cum in acie casu aliquo coeperint cedere munimenta castrorum quo se recipiant non habent et more animalium inulti cadunt, nec prius moriundi finis fit quam hostibus uoluntas defuerit persequendi (*Epit.* 1.21.4–5).[2]

That these sections of the *Epitoma* could be used to disprove a Theodosian dating was first suggested by Grosse in an invaluable article on late-Roman and Byzantine castramentation.[3] Grosse held that the massive influx of barbarians in the reign of Theodosius I paved the way for a significant reduction in field-craft ability during the early fifth century:

> Unter Theodosios hat ein massenhaftes Einströmen von Barbaren in die römische Armee stattgefunden, und unter dem schlaffen Regiment eines Honorius und Arkadios kam dann die lange vorbereitete Entwicklung zum Abschluß.[4]

This makes a good deal of sense. Moreover, it is consonant with the thoughts expressed previously in this volume, i.e., that Vegetius alludes more to the increased reliance on federate armies than to any profound change in the abilities of the remaining 'Roman' soldiers. What we must do is determine the period of time when Vegetius' comments would have had the most profound contemporary relevance.

Grosse did not credit the notion that "[der] … Verfall uralter Institutionen" could have reached such a great extent under Theodosius I that his soldiers were no longer able to construct fortifications.[5] He draws our attention to Ammianus' description of a fully-functioning Roman army under Julian – the engineering

---

[1] This *locus* has already been commented upon in the previous chapter and in further detail elsewhere; see Charles 2003, 127–167.

[2] Cf. Tac. *Ann.* 14.32.2, where Boudicca's forces rout the Romans because they were protected neither by fosse, nor by rampart (*neque fossam aut uallum*). In his criticism of the lack of discipline in the Roman army in Numidia, Sallust notes that *neque [castra] … muniebantur* (*Iug.* 44.5).

[3] Grosse 1913, 96.

[4] Grosse 1913, 96.

[5] Grosse 1913, 96.

skills of which would have probably impressed Julius Caesar – and notes that any "Verfall uralter Institutionen" could not have occurred "unter Soldaten wie Valentinian [I und] ... Gratian".[6] Grosse's conjecture, to which he devotes only two brief paragraphs, deserves to be discussed in detail. As will be seen, Roman soldiers of both the East and the West were quite capable of constructing fortifications up until the very eve of Adrianople. What is more, this ability seems to have continued into the reign of Theodosius I.

Ammianus' *Res Gestae* presents useful evidence that the Roman soldiers of his day possessed traditional Roman military skills – unlike the soldiers described by Vegetius. Tomlin, upon reading Ammianus' history, felt moved to write that "one is struck by [the] ... *esprit de corps* [of the soldiers] and the survival of old skills. They still entrenched themselves in marching camps with palisades and built permanent forts in stone".[7] While this discussion will not deal with the construction of permanent edifices (these, of course, could still be fabricated in Vegetius' day, as the appearance of *innumerabiles urbes* at *Epit.* 4 prol. 3 would appear to indicate), Ammianus' evidence for temporary military fortifications is of especial interest. Ammianus describes Valens' encampment in the vicinity of Adrianople in the following fashion: *agmine quadrato incedens, prope suburbanum Hadrianupoleos [sic] uenit, ubi uallo sudibus fossaque firmato* (31.12.4). Admittedly, Ammianus does not describe the type of camp that was built upon the completion of each day's march. Yet what the above *does* demonstrate is that Roman soldiers, in the year 378, were still entirely capable of constructing their own fortifications in a relatively short space of time.

In 377, the Goths, after a bloody battle with the Romans, shut themselves within their traditional wagon-circle at a location near Salices. The imperial forces, taking advantage of this respite, attempted to trap *immensas alias barbarorum cateruas* by barricading the nearby mountain passes (*aggerum obiectu celsorum*: Amm. Marc. 31.8.1). In the same year, Gratian's general Frigeridus, who had been ordered to return to Thrace, constructed a fortification near Beroea (*uallo metato*: Amm. Marc. 31.9.1).[8] Frigeridus was once again forced to engage his men in fortifying activity in 378, this time in order to protect the *septentrionales prouincias* from enemy raiders: *munireque properanti Succorum angustias* (Amm. Marc. 31.10.21).[9] The speed that the operation required is introduced by *properanti*, which agrees with *Frigerido*. It is also salutary to note that Valentinian I, in a campaign against the Alamanni in the year 372, ordered his soldiers to span the Rhine by means of a *pons* (Amm. Marc. 29.4.2). Later on, Ammianus (29.4.5) points out that this particular military enterprise called for especial haste:

---

[6] Grosse 1913, 96.

[7] Tomlin 2000, 241. Tomlin maintains these thoughts, in identical form, at id. 1990, 117. See also Crump 1975, 75, 132; Gabriel/Boose 1994, 444: "The important point to understand about the Roman army on the eve of ... Adrianople was that it was *not* an army on the verge of collapse. Quite the contrary".

[8] The town was later called Irenopolis and is now known by the name of Verria.

[9] Rolfe (1950–1952, 134 n. 1 [vol. 2]) writes that this was "a narrow pass and a town of the same name in the defiles of Mt. Haemus"; see also Amm. Marc. 21.10.2, 26.7.12.

urgente procinctu pergebant ulterius.[10] We can be sure that a stern and uncompromising general such as Valentinian would not have tolerated tardiness on the part of his soldiers. Indeed, Ammianus tells us that Valentinian punished poor discipline in the ranks *indeflexa saeuitia* (27.9.4). It might well be noted that his troops are elsewhere described as obedient (*morigeri militis labor*: Amm. Marc. 28.2.4).[11] The bridge, therefore, was presumably constructed within a short space of time.[12]

Ammianus provides further evidence of the continuation of traditional Roman military field-craft under Valentinian I. At the very beginning of Valentinian's reign, Aequitius, in order to cut off the usurper Procopius from Illyricum, blockaded three narrow passes leading to the north (Amm. Marc. 26.7.12). In his summary of Valentinian's deeds, Ammianus writes that *utrubique Rhenum celsioribus castris muniuit atque castellis* (30.7.6), a feature of his campaigning also related at 30.5.15. This section of the text describes incidents at the very end of the emperor's reign: *unde hoc,*[13] *etiam si magni intererat, paulisper sequestrato, impigre motus, peragrata fluminis ripa, castrisque praesidio competenti munitis atque castellis, Bregitionem peruenit.* Unfortunately, it is difficult to discern, on those occasions where Ammianus refers to pitching camp, the exact nature of the *castra*. Despite this, it seems natural to assume that Roman troops continued to build the traditional *Marschlager* during the period of which the *Res Gestae* treats.[14]

So now to Vegetius. Did he *really* write about Theodosian times when he decried the supposedly lost art of castramentation? Zosimus (probably deriving his material from Eunapius, himself perhaps reliant on a hypothetical pro-pagan Latin source continuing on from Nicomachus Flavianus)[15] appears to reflect

---

[10] The need for celerity is reinforced by the following: *castrisque ad tempus breuissimum fixis, quia nec sarcinale iumentum quisquam nec tabernaculum habuit* (Amm. Marc. 29.4.5).

[11] On Valentinian's wrath, see Amm. Marc. 27.7.4, 30.6.3 (cf. with Zos. 4.17.2), 30.8.2; Hieron. *Chron.* 365 p. Chr. (*Euseb. Werk.* 7, 244 a); Ps.-Aur. Vict. *Epit.* 45.5. One important case of indiscipline is ascribed to Valentinian's troops, for Ammianus (29.4.6) writes that the emperor was robbed of the *gloria* of capturing Macrianus, the king of the Alamanni, *nec sua culpa nec ducum, sed intemperantia militis, quae dispendiis grauibus saepe rem Romanam afflixit.*

[12] See also Amm. Marc. 27.2.5: *et uallo opportune metato.* This was carried out by Jovinus (*magister equitum per Gallias*) in 365–356 during operations against the Alamanni. Castramentation was also a feature of the campaigns of Constantius II and Julian (see Amm. Marc. 18.2.11, 20.11.6, 24.5.12).

[13] *hoc* refers to the selection of winter-quarters.

[14] On the other hand, we find references to pitching camp, yet the language does not allow us to reconstruct the exact nature of the *castra*, or whether these camps were indeed fortified. Witness the following: *barbari ... oppidum petiuere nomine Dibaltum, ubi tribunum scutariorum Barzimeren inuentum cum suis Cornutisque et aliis peditum numeris castra ponentem assiliunt, eruditum puluere militari rectorem* (Amm. Marc. 31.8.9.). Likewise, a statement such as *Richomeres Profuturo sociatur et Traiano, tendentibus prope oppidum Salices* (Amm. Marc. 31.7.5) is of little use. It is impossible to tell whether the soldiers, as they slept in their tents, were protected by any sort of fortification.

[15] For a résumé of Zosimus' reliance on Eunapius, see Paschoud 2000b, lxix–lxxi, with n.

Vegetius' commentary on the relaxation of camp discipline when he discusses an incident that occurred during the reign of Theodosius I. Although this seems to contradict the present argument, especially since it ostensibly adds credence to the view that Vegetius was discussing the late fourth century, a close investigation of the relevant passage reveals the tenuous nature of his allegations. Zosimus writes of an incident that occurred in late 391 after Theodosius' return from the West. A large contingent of barbarians, who had based themselves in the marshes near Thessalonica, had repeatedly plundered Macedonia and Thessaly during the emperor's absence (Zos. 4.48.1). Theodosius took charge of the campaign, entered the swamps, and killed a great number of the enemy (Zos. 4.48.7). After this had been achieved, the *magister* Timasius induced the emperor to let the men retreat from the swamp in order to eat and rest (Zos. 4.49.1). When the surviving barbarians perceived this, they fell upon the fatigued and drunken soldiers and killed a great many before Theodosius was able to take his vengeance (Zos. 4.49.2). From Zosimus' tale,[16] it would seem that the Romans had merely camped in the open air without adequately fortifying their position (as Vegetius describes at *Epit.* 1.21.4–5). Moreover, all the sentries had fallen asleep.

How can this episode be explained? It will not do to say that Zosimus, because castramentation in the sixth-century Eastern Empire was a forgotten art, did not make the assumption that the emperor's camp would be protected in traditional Roman fashion. There is sufficient evidence to suggest that the army of Zosimus' day (i.e., that of generals such as Belisarius) was entirely capable of avoiding the situation in which Theodosius' troops found themselves. According to Grosse, who conducted an extensive survey of Byzantine sources for the survival of the Roman *Marschlager*,

> [Der] ... Anonymus[17] liefert den Beweis, daß sich dagegen in der byzantinischen Armee die Traditionen römischer Lagerbefestigung erhalten haben. Das Marschlager des 6. Jahrhs. ist mindestens in seinen Grundzügen das jenige Hygins, nur der auf äußerster Selbstbeschränkung beruhende Geist alter Lagerdisziplin ist von den Soldtruppen der Zeit Justinians gewichen.[18]

Paschoud shrewdly suggests that Zosimus writes of an unprotected camp because he wished to highlight the emperor's military laxity.[19] The *topos* of military negligence is a recurring theme in accounts that are unfavourable to any important public figure.[20] With this in mind, he writes that "Ce qu'on peut légitime-

---

169 (where the possible existence "d'une sorte de Nicomaque Flavien *continuatus*, allant de 383 à au moins 410" is briefly discussed, with id. 1975, 147–169, 182–183; Baldini 1999, 15–33); on book 4 in particular, see Paschoud 2000b, lxv.

[16] Schmidt (1969, 424 n. 2) suggests that chs. 48 and 49 of book 4 refer to an event that is also described by Claudian (*VI. Cons. Hon.* 105–107; *Bell. Goth.* 524). On the passage, see also the differing opinions of Piganiol (1972, 286) and Paschoud (1971–1979, 447 n. 196 [vol. 2.2]).

[17] This particular 'Anonymus', who must not be confused with the unnamed author of the fourth-century *De Rebus Bellicis* (also called 'the Anonymus'), lived in Justinian's day.

[18] Grosse 1913, 102. Grosse's main points are recapitulated at id. 1920, 225–229.

[19] Cf. Paschoud 1971–1979, 447 n. 196 (vol. 2.2).

[20] For example, cf. Claud. *In Eutrop.* 2.432ff., where a drunken eastern army led by Leo is

ment se demander, c'est si l'épisode n'est pas déformé avec malveillance par
Eunape-Zosime".[21] For Paschoud, the episode demonstrates, on the one hand,
"l'insouciance et les excès de Théodose laissé à lui-même", and, on the other, "le
caractère quasi miraculeux du sauvetage dû à l'intervention de l'excellent Promotus".[22] Certainly, it is Promotus, arriving with reinforcements, who punishes
the barbarians for their temerity.[23] That a whole Roman army would be allowed
to lie about in a drunken stupor with the enemy close by does seem unlikely –
more so when their commander was an experienced general like Theodosius, a
man who, despite Zosimus' assertions to the contrary, seems to have maintained
a reasonably high standard of discipline throughout his reign. What, then, are we
to do with Zosimus' account? Paschoud notes that Zosimus (presumably following Eunapius) is our only source for the events related in chapters 48 and 49 of
book 4. He therefore assigns only a slight degree of credibility to some of the
material contained within these two chapters. Indeed, he holds that chapters 48
and 49 resemble "un roman d'aventures aux péripéties conventionnelles".[24]

Thus while an uncritical reading of Zosimus might suggest that castramentation was not enforced by Theodosius I and that Vegetius, if he were writing under
this emperor, would have had justification for claiming that the art had been lost,
one should take the *Epitoma*'s nature into account. If castramentation had been
abandoned under Theodosius, Vegetius would hardly have wanted to blame his
addressee for this relaxation of traditional discipline. Zosimus (writing long after
Theodosius' death) could resort to the employment of rhetorical exaggeration and
nonsensical *topoi* in order to demonstrate Theodosius' supposed decadence – as
seems also to have been the case for Eunapius, Zosimus' main source for the
period. But Vegetius, it seems, would have been reluctant to take this path.
Instead, Vegetius writes as if, by his day, the refusal to built temporary *castra*
was so thoroughly ingrained that the emperor regnant would have been absolved
of all guilt by the passage of time. If, *pace* Zosimus, it cannot be demonstrated
that castramentation was no longer carried out in the late fourth century, a date
much later than the death of Theodosius the Great follows.

Of especial interest to our theme is that Theodosius' conduct in the campaign
that Zosimus describes at 4.49.1–2 directly contravenes one of the precepts of the

massacred by Tarbigilus' barbarians. This invective is directed against Eutropius, whose de-
praved nature, according to Claudian, is responsible for the decadence of the soldiers.

[21] Paschoud 1971–1979, 447 n. 196 (vol. 2.2).

[22] Paschoud 1971–1979, 447 n. 196 (vol. 2.2).

[23] Yet Zosimus does not criticize Theodosius in so many words – and this despite the fact
that the emperor was ultimately responsible for the safety of his troops. Indeed, ch. 48, which
precedes the narration of the barbarian attack, notes Theodosius' cunning with respect to his
manner of ascertaining military intelligence and, moreover, records a significant victory in the
swamps. In addition, Timasius, at Zos. 4.49.1, is made to reflect on "the bravery of the emperor"
(τοῦ βασιλέως ... τὴν ἀνδρείαν).

[24] Paschoud 1971–1979, 447 n. 196 (vol. 2.2). Paschoud finds it difficult to believe the tale
(Zos. 4.48.3–7) that Theodosius disguised himself as a common traveller in order to locate the
position of the enemy. He holds that this tale "tient plus du roman d'aventures que de la réalité
historique" (448 n. 195).

Epitoma, a text with which Theodosius I is generally believed to have been familiar (although it is obviously impossible to tell if *any* emperor actually read it). Near the end of *Epit.* 3.25, Vegetius points out the dangers associated with believing that a routed enemy is incapable of launching a counter-attack:

> frequenter iam fusa acies dispersos ac passim sequentes reparatis uiribus interemit. numquam exultantibus maius solet euenire discrimen quam cum ex subita ferocia in formidinem commutantur (*Epit.* 3.25.8–9).

While this piece of advice firmly belongs to the milieu of conventional set-piece engagements (witness *acies*), the principles noted by Vegetius hold true in all forms of ancient warfare. If the *Epitoma* had been read by Theodosius, two possible interpretations ensue: either a) Theodosius was a rather poor student;[25] or b) the incident in the marshes was little more than a fabrication invented by those hostile to the memory of the Christian emperor. That Theodosius was able to best the 'pagan' enemy at the Frigidus after having suffered a serious reversal in the initial engagement would appear to eliminate the first possibility. Alternatively (and, it must be said, far less realistically), Theodosius had learnt from his supposed blunder at the marshes and was able to turn his previous misfortune to his advantage by employing the barbarians' tactic at the subsequent battle of the River Frigidus.[26]

However, it might well be noted that Claudian, in the *De Quarto Consulatu Honorii*, makes Theodosius warn his son Honorius of the dangers associated with prematurely assuming that the enemy has been vanquished:

> multis damnosa fuere
> gaudia; dispersi pereunt somnoue soluti;
> saepius incautae nocuit uictoria turbae (*IV. Cons. Hon.* 334–336).

The above might initially prompt one to suggest that the emperor was imparting the fruits of his experience.[27] Yet, if Theodosius really had been guilty of succumbing to the unwarranted *gaudia* that the poet describes, Claudian's verse would have been in relatively poor taste.[28] Whatever we may think of Claudian, we should not take him for a fool – any reference to an imperial débâcle would not have been pleasing to the court. Thus it is most fitting to view the lines above as a relatively meaningless exercise in rhetoric. And if a contemporary historical allusion *must* be established (and this is by no means necessary), it would surely be enough to view lines 334–336 as an anachronistic reference to Theodosius' victory over the forces of Eugenius, an event which had already been described in the *De Tertio Consulatu Honorii*.

---

[25] If *Epit.* 3.25.8–9 were indeed written after this event, Vegetius must have been not only tactless but also bent on self-immolation.

[26] This option, however, hardly seems worth entertaining, especially when some doubt remains with regard to the authenticity of the incident in the marshes near Thessalonica.

[27] Cf. Richardot 1998, 144–146.

[28] In any case, Theodosius appears to connect his observation regarding complacency with siege-warfare. In the previous lines, the emperor is made to say *si longa moretur / obsidio, tum uota caue secura remittas / inclusumue putes* (Claud. *IV. Cons. Hon.* 332–334).

Zosimus' 'testimony' regarding castramentation, or the lack of it, warrants comparison with the verse of Claudian, who seems to imply that Roman armies – *contra* Vegetius – were protected by the traditional temporary defences when encamped in the field. Of course, the essential difference between the two writers is one of time. Unlike the sixth-century pagan apologist, Claudian lived and wrote during the time of which he treats. The poet's description of the battle of the River Frigidus (394)[29] differs markedly from the tradition recorded by Zosimus, and presumably his principal informational source for the period, viz., Eunapius. Apart from the miraculous wind that Claudian relates and Zosimus fails to record, the latter author's description of Eugenius' camp differs in many respects to that of the poet. Zosimus (4.58.4) describes a camp that is unprotected and vulnerable to conventional rather than 'divine' attack. That Eugenius' troops, who clearly did not expect the enemy to mount a counter-attack, saw fit to relax their guard immediately reminds us of the supposed laxity of the imperial troops near the marshes of Thessalonica.[30] As discussed above, Zosimus largely attributes the emperor's victory to the pagan forces' over-confidence. Claudian, however, gives much of the credit to the almighty wind that poured down from the north into the faces of the enemy. In this, he seems to borrow elements from descriptions of Hannibal's victory over the Romans at Cannae (216 B.C.),[31] and, in particular, that fanciful version of the engagement penned by Silius Italicus.[32] The significant part of the *De Tertio Consulatu Honorii* reads as follows:

> te[33] propter et Alpes
> inuadi faciles cauto nec profuit hosti
> munitis haesisse locis: spes inrita ualli
> concidit et scopulis patuerunt claustra reuulsis (*III. Cons. Hon.* 89–92).

[29] Theodosius had suffered a serious tactical reversal in the first engagement with Eugenius' army, which was commanded by Arbogast (Zos. 4.58.2–3). He then launched a full-scale attack against Eugenius' camp before dawn and caught the enemy's troops, over-confident after the first day's success, completely unawares (Zos. 4.58.4). Eugenius was put to death and Arbogast later committed suicide (Zos. 4.58.5–6). According to this tradition, it is Theodosius' perseverance and ability to re-group his forces, combined with the usurper's military indolence, that carried him to victory. The Christian writers, however, attributed his victory to a divine *turbo uentorum* that caused the pagan soldiers' *tela* to fly back and transfix those who threw them; see August. *De civ. Dei* 5.26; Oros. 7.35.17–18; Rufin. *H.E.* 11.33; Socrat. *H.E.* 5.25; Sozom. *H.E.* 7.24; Theod. *H.E.* 5.25. Claudian, at *III. Cons. Hon.* 93–98, also mentions the wind. On the battle, see Seeck/Veith 1913, 451–467.

[30] See Zos. 4.49.1–2.

[31] Flor. 1.22.16, 1.38.15; Front. *Strat.* 2.2.7–8; Livy, 22.43.10–11, with 22.46.8–9. The Byzantine account of Leo is of a similar nature; see *Strat.* 14.4. Polyaenus (8.10.3) mentions nothing of the dust and focuses, instead, on the dazzling effect of the sun. Cf. Plut. *Mar.* 26.3–5; Veg. *Epit.* 3.14.1–3.

[32] In the *Punica*, Silius Italicus writes of the wind (*turbo*: 9.509, 9.523; description: 9.491–523) that helped the Carthaginian weapons but made the Roman missiles fly backwards (9.506–510). More on the wind is found at *Pun.* 10.202–207.

[33] Claudian credits the divine intervention to Honorius rather than to Theodosius I, which is perfectly understandable given the sycophantic genre that he pursues.

This, then, is no surprise attack on sleeping troops. There is no element of sub-terfuge or cunning here. Arbogast, contrary to what Zosimus says at 4.58.4, even seems to have been given time to arrange his *acies* (line 94).

Claudian's verse, although generally fanciful in nature, is clear on one point: the enemy possessed a defensible bastion, much like that which would have housed the legions of old whilst on campaign. This is also asserted by Seeck and Veith: "ein befestigtes Lager mit Palisaden und hölzernen Türmen".[34] We might reasonably expect Theodosius' men to have been similarly protected. After all, it is the divine *uentus* that unexpectedly batters Eugenius' fortifications and brings them crashing down. According to Claudian, if the wind had not blown, Theodo-sius' men would have found it difficult to extirpate the 'pagan' forces. While one cannot tell how long Eugenius and Arbogast had occupied their position, it hardly seems possible that they had intended the camp to be a permanent structure. Rather, the site that Claudian describes was probably a traditional camp (i.e., a *Marschlager*) constructed in the manner of those advocated by Vegetius, and also Hyginus in his *De metatione castrorum*. Here, at least, is reasonably compelling evidence that the Western army was capable of building its own defences as late as 394.

It is relevant to mention that the same poet, writing early in Honorius' reign, records that, while the army under the leadership of Stilicho was a model of discipline, the eunuch consul Eutropius was responsible for its decay. Yet Claudi-an writes that *non commoda castris / eligitur regio*, and that *uicibus custodia nullis / aduigilat uallo* (*In Eutrop.* 2.417–419). Even in the midst of the most vitriolic language, Claudian does not think to say that the decadence promoted by Eutropius put an end to the construction of camps upon the completion of each day's march (which is surely the type of camp that Claudian envisages[35]), or that the soldiers refused to place the traditional palisade and rampart (*uallum*) around their makeshift nocturnal lodgings. This is highly significant in the context of Vegetius' assertion regarding the loss of these abilities.

Orosius, who wrote his Christian apology not long after Claudian, also makes mention of the western troops' field-craft during Theodosius' reign. At 7.35.3, he writes that Andragathius, *comes* of Maximus, barricaded all the Alpine passes in order to prevent Theodosius from reaching Aquileia. Orosius (7.35.3) seems to have believed that this was a significant achievement: *omnes incredibiliter Al-pium ... aditus communisset*. The verb *communire*[36] usually carries the force of

---

[34] Seeck/Veith 1913, 460.

[35] That this is so is demonstrated by the fact that Claudian, in his discussion of eastern military discipline, describes the laxity that characterized Roman troops in the field (*In Eutrop.* 2.409–422).

[36] See Lewis & Short, s.v. 1. *communio* I; *OLD*, s.v. *communio* 1. In this context, Defarrari (1964, *ad loc.*) translates the verb as "he had fortified". Arnauld-Lindet (1990–1991, *ad loc.* [vol. 3]) concurs: "il avait fortifié". Caesar uses *communire* in order to describe the establish-ment of fortified positions such as *castella* (*BGall.* 1.8.2) and *castra* (*BCiv.* 1.42.4; *BGall.* 5.49.7). Other classical writers use *communire* in a similar fashion: *castella*: Nep. *Alcib.* 7.4; *Milt.* 2.1; *castra*: Livy, 2.32.4, 21.32.11, 42.58.1; see also Sall. *Iug.* 66.1: *conmunire suos locos*.

constructing barricades rather than merely safeguarding a position with troops (which might initially be suggested by Orosius' reference to *copiae largissimae militum*).[37] Of course, the worth of Orosius' historical testimony is often difficult to establish. Yet, on this occasion, there appears to be no reason why we should dismiss his use of *communire*. One might hold, therefore, that Andragathius did in fact secure *omnes ... Alpinum ... aditus* with palisades, ditches and sharpened stakes, and that this was done *cum largissimis militum copiis* (7.35.3).[38]

In the context of a general decline in military discipline (to which Vegetius surely alludes when he mentions that Roman encampments were no longer protected by rampart and palisade) and the concomitant reliance upon federate armies rather than units of a recognizably Roman form, it is worth adding that discipline in the ranks seems to have been maintained right up until Adrianople. Ammianus records that, in 377, Frigeridus' men were marching in wedge-shaped formations: *congregatusque in cuneos* (31.9.3).[39] Before the battle of Adrianople itself, Valens' host is described as advancing in a square formation: *agmine quadrato incedens* (Amm. Marc. 31.12.4). These types of formations are found throughout the *Res Gestae*. Note, too, the wildly divergent traditions relating to the discipline of Theodosius' armies.[40] Christian writers, such as Jordanes and Orosius, saw Theodosius I as a champion of the Catholic faith and speak highly of his martial abilities. According to Jordanes, military discipline, which had decayed under the Arian Valens, was soon restored to a high level: *militaremque disciplinam mox in meliori statu reposita ignauia priorum principum* (*Get.* 27.139).[41] We are also informed that *saeueritate et liberalitate blanditiaque sua remissum exercitum ad fortia prouocaret* (*Get.* 27.139).[42]

The pagan Zosimus, on the other hand, was vehemently opposed to Theodosius (which is not surprising given the emperor's anti-Christian bias) and thus characterizes his army as a mere shadow of its predecessors: "the army soon diminished and became virtually non-existent" (4.29.1).[43] For Zosimus, discipline had become a thing of the past during the reign of Theodosius.[44] Once

---

[37] *OLD*, s.v. *communio* 1b: "to strengthen or secure (with a garrison)".

[38] However, Merobaudes, in his second *Panegyricus* (from the reign of Valentinian III), writes that Aëtius overcame a formidable barbarian stronghold by building enormous siege towers: *texitur in turres abies et uincere [muros] / iussa renitentes exterret culmin[e pinnas]* (*Pan. II*, 168–169). But this hardly matters for us – Vegetius nowhere claims that contemporary soldiers are incapable of fabricating machines of war. Unfortunately, there is no mention of temporary camps being built in Merobaudes' few remaining works.

[39] Note the unusual use of the accusative. Cf. Amm. Marc. 31.10.4: *conferti in praedatorios globos*.

[40] As Williams and Friell (1994, 176–177) point out, "the descriptions of the army in action which Ammianus gives us, at Adrianople and elsewhere, reveal a competence and spirit which would not have been out of place in any of the conquering armies of the early empire".

[41] = *MGH:AA* 5.1, 94–95.

[42] = *MGH:AA* 5.1, 95.

[43] Translation of Ridley 1982, *ad loc.*

[44] At 4.31.1, Zosimus writes that the army lacked discipline and that no distinction was made between Roman soldiers and their barbarian allies; at 4.31.2, he describes the confusion that was prevalent in the legions.

again, it is important to note that Zosimus' perception of the military situation under Theodosius may ultimately derive from a hostile anti-Theodosian pagan senatorial tradition. It is possible that Eunapius, who was presumably Zosimus' principal source for the period in question, had seized upon this negative tradition, perhaps in the form of the pro-pagan Latin source already mentioned. Despite this, the state of discipline was probably no worse under Theodosius than it had been under any other fourth-century emperor. What is more, no firm evidence exists to suggest that the art of castramentation had been abandoned in the late fourth century. Indeed, even Zosimus admits that, when needed, Theodosius' army could be returned to a state of readiness without any great effort.[45]

2. ATTITUDES TO EMPIRE

As will be seen, the anonymous author of the *De Rebus Bellicis* proposed a return to an offensive military policy that had been largely forgotten after Trajan's death. The *optimus princeps* was arguably the last Roman emperor to effect any significant magnification of the Empire. Hadrian, Trajan's successor, decided that the Empire was not to be limitless. Rather, it had reached its optimum size during the Flavian era; and it is notable, too, that Augustus, after the Teutoburger-wald disaster of A.D. 9, seems to have believed that additional conquest was unnecessary. Moreover, Tacitus writes that Augustus advised that the Empire should remain *intra terminos* (*Ann.* 1.11.4). Hadrian's reign, therefore, was one of consolidation, a time to establish a series of readily defensible borders. No more would Roman resources be 'wasted' on foreign conquest, a feature of Hadrian's rule which has met with the general approbation of many modern authorities. A.R. Birley, for one, believes that Trajan's imperialist policy, which so pleased the *uiri militares*,[46] was not only "anachronistic" but also "contrary to the interests of the state".[47] Hadrian's more pacific policy, as a consequence, was an entirely sensible change.

But was peace the gel that held the Empire together? Sekunda theorizes that the Roman "institutionalisation of violence ... fostered a thirst for violence in all forms of social activity, and more particularly a lust for war".[48] He adds that Roman military assertiveness "tended to paralyse the capacity of Rome's enemies to resist her effectively".[49] Thus while Trajan's martial vigour elevated Rome to the zenith of her power, the defensive policies of his successors – at least according to Sekunda's premise – may have foreshadowed her eventual demise.

---

[45] In one instance, for example, Zosimus (4.45.3–4) describes the preparations for the coming war against the usurper Maximus.

[46] Cf. Pliny, *Pan.* 15.5: *in praesentia quidem, quisquis paulo uetustior miles, hic te commilitone censetur.* In a summary of Fronto's thoughts on the topic, Davies (1968, 83) writes that "Hadrian's policy was peace and dummy weapons, Trajan's war and real ones".

[47] A.R. Birley 1974, 16; see also id. 1997, 78.

[48] Sekunda 1996, 42. On this theme, see also Garlan 1972, 199–200; Hopkins 1983, 1–2.

[49] Sekunda 1996, 42.

This, of course, is a broad generalization, but it is nevertheless a useful position from which to initiate further discussion. Naturally, it must be remembered that the nature of the barbarian enemy, i.e., those peoples who lived to the north of Rome's *limites*, had changed immeasurably since the times of Marius, Caesar, and even Trajan. Several of the various peoples had confederated in order to pose a more determined threat to Roman security. The two military forces, i.e., that of Rome within and that of the enemies without, were now closer in terms of numbers, organization and general military prowess than ever before. In this section, we will investigate the manner in which Vegetius relates to more or less contemporary writers in order to divine his position on the status of Empire, and to nominate the circumstances that may have caused him to reach his views.

Perhaps the most interesting work that warrants juxtaposition with Vegetius' *Epitoma* – at least in terms of military policy – is the *De Rebus Bellicis*. This work was written by an unknown author ('the Anonymus') and consists of a series of suggestions for reforming the Empire. No one knows if this petition was ever read by the emperors (its intended audience), or if it was simply ignored and consigned to the imperial archives by an unsympathetic civil servant. Despite its title, which is almost certainly not that of the original, the Anonymus' *libellus* (prol. 2)[50] deals with a range of matters, from imperial financial policy, the currency, provincial administration and the army, to matters of domestic jurisprudence. Of particular interest are his descriptions of various mechanical contrivances, inventions which, in the Anonymus' opinion, might be of use to the Roman army.[51]

Who was the Anonymus? At *DRB* prol. 6, he excludes himself from the highest echelons of society.[52] Despite this, his use of *clausulae* suggests a reasonable degree of education.[53] Although the Anonymus was apparently not a man of *summa nobilitas* or *affluentia* (*DRB* prol. 6), he surely possessed some means given that he was a man of leisure.[54] While some have seen him as a retired *uir militaris*,[55] Thompson's belief that "there is no need to suppose that he was anything other than a knowledgeable civilian" could well be correct.[56] The statement *dicent melius qui usu bella cognoscunt* (*DRB* 12.4) is important. Warfare was such a staple of military service in the Anonymus' day that it is difficult to believe that, if he were a *uir militaris*, he could have possibly reached retirement age without ever having witnessed bloodshed. In terms of his birthplace, Seeck initially noticed an eastern emphasis and pointed out that the only foreign peoples mentioned by name are the Persians (*DRB* 12.1 [*Parthicae*], 19.4 [*Persae*]) and

---

[50] At prol. 9 and 17, the Anonymus calls his work an *oratio*. *Libellus*, however, is the customary term for a petition; see Millar 1977, 240–252 (especially 242), 541–544.

[51] Coloured drawings, presumably meant to aid the reader in constructing the machines, accompanied the descriptions; see Thompson 1952, 6–11; Ireland 1979, 39ff.

[52] According to Schneider (1910, 327), "der Verfasser ist ein Privatmann".

[53] Thompson (1952, 4) believes that this "indicates some years of study". He also cites instances where the language of the Anonymus suggests knowledge of classical Latin authors.

[54] *DRB*, prol. 16: *otio persuasus, non adeo a rerum commoditatibus peregrinus.*

[55] Ireland (1979, 150), for one, thinks so.

[56] Thompson 1952, 5.

[57] Seeck 1894b, 2325.

the Arabs (*DRB* 16.2).[57] Moreover, the only specific geographical feature that the Anonymus mentions is the Danube.[58] Further evidence is provided by analysis of the various military 'inventions'. The Anonymus' scythed chariots would have been of little – if any – use in the West (chapters 12–14).[59] The artillery devices (chapters 7–8) designed for use against fortified cities and bastions (*DRB* 6.4) also suggest an eastern orientation, as does his concern with the Sassanian foe – the Anonymus makes his anti-Persian sentiments very clear at *DRB* 19.4.[60] With regard to the date, the *terminus post quem* is indisputable, for the Anonymus mentions and criticizes Constantine by name at *DRB* 2.1. It is generally agreed, too, that the work was written before Adrianople in 378.[61] The author addressed his work to a plurality of emperors (*DRB* prol. 1, 8), who had a plurality of sons (*DRB* prol. 8), and who had suppressed a plurality of usurpers (*DRB* 2.6). The joint reign of Valentinian and Valens seems to fit these three specific criteria.[62]

With these things having been established, let us see how his views on the maintenance of Empire differ from those of Vegetius, who most certainly wrote after Adrianople. In one section, the author proposes a return to the glorious days of old, a time when no nation could threaten the Roman *imperium* with impunity:

> quietem pacis lacerant inopinatis incursibus. ergo huiusmodi nationes, quae aut talibus subsidiis aut ciuitatum castellorumque moenibus defenduntur, diuersis et nouis armorum sunt machinis prosequendae (*DRB* 6.3–4).

Still, we should not confuse the Anonymus' policy ideas with the imperialist objectives of leaders such as Caesar and Trajan, even if he *did* intend to harry and eventually conquer the enemy with his wondrous military devices. He advocates, for instance, that an unbroken line of forts, which should be constructed at intervals of one mile and have solid walls and powerful turrets, could help to protect the borders of the Empire:

[58] At *DRB* 18.5, we read that the *ballista fulminalis* can shoot across the width of the Danube, a river *famosus pro magnitudine*; see Reinach 1922, 213; Seeck 1894b, 2325; Stevens 1979, 130.

[59] The Anonymus (*DRB* 18.8) also mentions that his scythed chariots should be used *per aperta camporum*. Such machines, as Vegetius (*Epit.* 3.24.2) points out, require dry and level plains – geographical features not readily associated with the West.

[60] Although he mentions troops moving through icy regions and dense woods (*DRB* 19.2), such conditions were (and indeed still are) certainly found in the East, especially in the Transylvanian area. The "sehr unbehülflich" style of the Anonymus has also been used to demonstrate that he was an easterner (Seeck 1894b, 2325), but this does not convince. On his style, see Ireland 1979, 150; Paschoud 1967, 119; Reinach 1922, 213; Syme 1968, 113; Thompson 1952, v; Wiedemann 1979, 142–143.

[61] *DRB* 6.1–3 suggests this; see Cameron 1979, 1; Seeck 1894b, 2325; Thompson 1952, 1–2. As Cameron (1979, 1) relates, the Anonymus "wrote at a time when barbarians, however threatening, could at any rate be assumed to live *beyond* the imperial frontiers".

[62] See Bonamente 1981, 9–49; Cameron 1979, 6–7; Elton 1996, 269; Seeck 1894b, 2325; Thompson 1952, 1–2; Tomlin 1989, 249. But some have preferred Constantius II (Mazzarino 1951, 72–109) and Theodosius I (Berthelot 1900, 172; Oman 1905, 19 and n. 2). Reinach (1922, 212) strangely rejects the belief that the Anonymus wrote before Adrianople.

est praeterea inter commoda rei publicae utilis limitum cura ambientium ubique latus imperii; quorum tutelae assidua melius castella prospicient, ita ut millenis interiecta passibus stabili muro et firmissimis turribus erigantur (*DRB* 20.1).

The Anonymus, it should be noted, does not appear to be describing a continuous and totally preclusive frontier barrier like Hadrian's Wall, a defensive line which, incidentally, also has milecastles.[63] Furthermore, he believed that his system of frontier defence could be achieved *sine publico sumpto* and that the *castella* should be constructed and manned, not by imperial troops, but by local militias formed by nearby landowners (*possessores*) (*DRB* 20.2). This, of course, was not a particularly novel idea. Many *centenaria* (a *centenarium* was a type of tower) from northern Africa have yielded inscriptions showing that they, too, were constructed at the expense of the surrounding landholders.[64]

Although the Anonymus does not seem to promote imperialist expansion *per se*, he does advocate that war should be waged on the barbarian side of the *limites*, i.e., away from Roman territory. He makes his general feelings clear from *DRB* 18.7. The foe, once bested in set-piece engagements, must be pursued relentlessly, either by land or by sea. He thus envisages a cohesive war-machine. In particular, it seems that the Anonymus, as pointed out above, was particularly keen to prosecute a war against the Persians. Once again, the various chariot-type vehicles and other *machinae* that he describes could only have been used with any effect in the East – they would have been virtually useless with respect to countering Rome's Germanic enemies. The question, of course, is whether the Anonymus' proposed course of action was feasible. Though highly debatable, one could contend that, at the time of composition, we find perhaps the last window of opportunity for Rome to go on the offensive.

Attitudes change after the Anonymus' period. By the Theodosian era, expansionist desires are still expressed, but they seem more the product of wishful thinking than any real hope. Symmachus remarks that Theodosius will include Persian captives and spoils from conquered Babylon in his triumphal parade: *uester triumphus Arsacidas post tergum reuinctos et gazas uictae Babylonis accipiet* (*Rel.* 9.3). Although Theodosius I did celebrate a triumph on 12 October 386 (after the partition of Armenia), a parade which obviously did not include treasure from Babylon, Symmachus nevertheless entertains the thought that the Empire may yet vanquish the 'Old Enemy' at some point in the future, however distant that might have seemed. In the book of the *HA* containing the lives of Carus, Carinus and Numerian, the writer tells us that Rome's destiny is to conquer once again the land of Persia. He alludes to the success of Galerius against Narses in 298:

[63] Johnson 1979, 69.

[64] *CIL* 8.22774 from Tripolitania (Henchir-el-Gueciret) records the building of *turris*. See also *CIL* 8.9725 and 8.21531, both of which inscriptions refer to the rebuilding of a *castram* [*sic*] at Ammi Mûsa in the former province of Mauretania Caesariensis, and *CIL* 8.19328, which concerns the construction of *turres* at Ain et-Tîn.

licet plane ac licebit (per sacratissimum Caesarem Maximianum constitit) Persas uincere atque ultra eos progredi, et futurum reor, si a nostris non deseratur promissus numinum fauor (*Car.* 9.3).[65]

The writer says this in order to dispel the belief *ut Romanus princeps Ctesifontem transire non possit*, something which he ascribes to human *timiditas* rather than to divine displeasure (*Car.* 9.1–2). If it is accepted that the *HA* was written by one man towards the end of the fourth century, we see, in the passage presented above, that fanciful and essentially delusional hopes were still maintained for the eventual chastening of Persia, and even states beyond that realm (witness *atque ultra*).[66] Of particular interest is that the statement expresses the personal opinion of the author. It was hardly written with a view to aggrandizing an exalted individual.

In Claudian's panegyrical verse, he initially maintains – albeit only in a rather ostensible fashion – the now formulaic hope that the Empire might expand. But, as wars against the barbarians began to be fought with much greater frequency *within* the borders of the Empire, statements regarding imperial expansion, although still relatively frequent, begin to take on an even more strongly formulaic flavour, to the extent that Claudian almost seems to admit their nonsensical nature – and then they finally stop.

Although, at the beginning of Honorius' reign,[67] one might still believe that the Empire could deal with the rampaging barbarians, the incessant warfare between imperial units and rebellious *foederati* must have taken its toll on Roman morale. Thus Claudian could write, in his panegyric on the brother consuls Probinus and Olybrius[68] (while Theodosius I was alive and in control of a unified Empire), that *Impetus* and *horribilis Metus* set wars afoot, *siue petat [Roma] Parthos seu cuspide turbet Hydaspen* (*Cons. Olyb. et Prob.* 77–80).[69] According to Roma, with Probinus and Olybrius as consuls, Scythian Araxes will become

[65] This is found in the section on Carus. After having advanced <C>*tesifontem usque* (*Car.* 8.1), Carus fell ill and died of some unspecified illness beneath a thunderous sky. Carus' *cubicularii* subsequently set fire to the emperor's tent, and a rumour afterwards circulated that a lightning-bolt had put an end to Carus' life (*Car.* 8.5–7). But the source does not inspire confidence.

[66] Cf. the risible prophecy of the *haruspices* recorded at *HA Tac.* 15.2–3, i.e., that a descendant of Tacitus and Florian would be born *qui det iudices Parthis ac Persis, qui Francos et [h]Alamannos sub Romanis legibus habeat, qui per omnem Africam barbarum non relinquat, qui Taprobanis praesidem inponat, qui ad Iuuernam insulam proconsulem mittat, qui Sarmatis omnibus iudicet, qui terram omnem, qua Oceano ambitur, captis omnibus gentibus suam faciat*; and, if that is not enough, that he would restore power to the senate and die without an heir after living one hundred and twenty years. Given that this prince was not expected to arrive until *post mille annos*, little faith, quite understandably, was put in the prophecy; on this, see *Tac.* 15.4–5, 16.4, with Honoré 1987, 176.

[67] It is of interest that, at *Cons. Stil.* 1.148–149, Claudian writes that the Empire was at peace upon Theodosius' death: *nulli barbariae motus; nil turbida rupto | ordine temptauit nouitas.* This statement, of course, is of an essentially hyperbolical value.

[68] The Anicii entered upon their consulship on 3 January 395.

[69] See also Claud. *Cons. Olyb. et Prob.* 83–84: *ipsa [Roma], triumphatis qua possidet aethera regnis, | adsilit innuptae ritus imitata Mineruae.*

Rome's vassal, as will both banks of the Rhine (*Cons. Olyb. et Prob.* 160–161). Furthermore, the Persians will be conquered by Roman standards, and the Ganges will bisect Roman cities (*Cons. Olyb. et Prob.* 161–163). This sort of imagery continues into the early years of Honorius' reign. In the first book of the *In Rufinum*, written shortly after Honorius' accession, the young emperor will subdue Medes and overcome Indians, while *reges* will pass *sub iuga* (1.374–375). Likewise, in the *De Tertio Consulatu Honorii* of 396, it is predicted that the *unanimi fratres* will conquer the entire world (*III. Cons. Hon.* 189–190). Claudian predicts the sack of Babylon, the Parthians (read Persians) driven headlong into flight, Bactria conquered, and the Ganges under Roman control (*III. Cons. Hon.* 201–203).[70] This sort of language continues into 398, the year in which Claudian makes Theodosius I say to Honorius that the future emperor is master of India, and is obeyed by Medes, Arabs and the Chinese (*IV Cons. Hon.* 257–258). Upon refusing Honorius' plea to join him in the suppression of tyranny in the West, the emperor consoles his son as follows:

> uos [i.e., Honorium et Arcadium] impacatus Araxes,
> uos celer Euphrates timeat, sit Nilus ubique
> uester et emisso quidquid sol imbuit ortu (*IV. Cons. Hon.* 387–389).

Moreover, Claudian himself states that Honorius will be victorious *trans Rheni cornua*, and that his brother Arcadius will be *captae spoliis Babylonos*[71] *onustus* (*IV. Cons. Hon.* 652–653). Perhaps the last instance of this kind of language is found in the third book of the *De Consulatu Stilichonis* of 400, where we read that there will never be any temporal limit to the Empire: *nec terminus umquam / Romanae dicionis erit* (159–160).

Yet, in the *De Sexto Consulatu Honorii*, written just four years later, one finds a marked absence of the forms of praise discussed above. This panegyric, like the *De Bello Gothico*, focuses on wars waged in the West, and specifically Stilicho's campaigns against the Visigoths of Alaric. With the Italian peninsula under siege, it must have made little sense to introduce the standard clichés, viz., that the conquest of India and China was imminent, and that Roman standards would soon traverse the Ganges – the world had become a very small place indeed to Claudian and his contemporaries. Thus we see the Roman world-view change within the space of a mere decade. Now the emphasis was not on emulating Trajan, but on saving his ashes from barbarian depredation.

Vegetius' attitude is markedly different to that of the Anonymus, the author of the *HA*, and the thoughts expressed in Claudian's earlier court poetry. Vegetius hardly seems to be advocating any kind of aggressive military policy, even in the most panegyrical sections of the *Epitoma*. In this, he was not particularly novel. Indeed, this kind of thought, despite the panegyrical whimsies discussed above, was more or less the product of Adrianople's aftermath. Ammianus, for one,

---

[70] Note, too, Claud. *III. Cons. Hon.* 209–211: *uestri iuris erit, quidquid complectitur axis. / uobis rubra dabunt pretiosas aequora conchas, / Indus ebur, ramos Panchaia, uellera Seres.*

[71] Presumably in imitation of the Greek genitive inflection Βαβυλῶνος, though some MSS. preserve *Babylonis*.

censures Valentinian I for building garrison-camps (*praesidiaria castra*) across the Danube (29.6.2). He writes that the emperor carried this out *in ipsis Quadorum terris quasi Romano iuri iam uindicatis* (Amm. Marc. 29.6.2), which seems a bitter reflection on the fact that impending chaos had only recently flowed *trans flumen Histrum* (Amm. Marc. 29.6.2). Elsewhere, Ammianus (29.4.1) suggests that it is more sensible to check the barbarians by means of frontier defences than to defeat them in the field.

But this need not necessarily mean that the sober thoughts of Ammianus (writing under Theodosius I) and Vegetius were exactly akin on this topic. The frontier policy of both writers might be described as passive and reactionary, and thus perhaps ostensibly suited to the time of Theodosius I. Still, while Ammianus merely states that the Empire need not expand, especially when its present borders are indefensible, Vegetius envisages a time when barbarian attack on fortified positions within the Empire was the norm rather than the exception. It is worth noting that this had obviously occurred in the East almost immediately after Adrianople, but did not really become commonplace in the West until *after* Theodosius I's reign. The civil wars waged between Theodosius and the two western usurpers Maximus and Eugenius do not seem to have involved any great amount of civilian bloodshed, and the major engagements of these wars took place away from urban dwellings – these were campaigns waged between generals and their followers rather than between a predatory 'foreign' power and its intended victims. It is in an eternally besieged West where barbarian forces roam at will that the *Epitoma*'s content becomes a matter of contemporary relevance. Once again, a post-Theodosian date seems attractive.

While the Anonymus and the author of the *HA* appear keen to fight the Persians, it would be difficult to prove that Vegetius had any such interest. If, as seems relatively clear, Vegetius wrote from a western perspective, he obviously would not have been particularly interested in matters of an eastern nature. Vegetius' views on the current state of the Empire are especially evinced in book 4 of the *Epitoma*. In all, he devotes thirty chapters (1–30), in addition to a discursive preface, to the precepts of siege warfare. Some might see Vegetius' interest in siege-craft as indicative of an eastern interest, particularly when one recognizes that the Sassanian Persians were adept at this technical aspect of war. But, if the text were written after 410, as this volume argues, siege-craft would also have been of obvious relevance to a western audience. Our view on the importance of siege-craft in the Late Empire is perhaps more a reflection of Ammianus than anything else, for the author of the *Res Gestae* makes these operations a salient feature of his work. By the fifth century, however, the long-term presence of barbarian armies in the West would have meant that siege warfare had become a staple of military conflict.

Although Vegetius states, at *Epit.* 4 prol. 8, that he has treated of this subject not only so that Roman cities might be better protected, but also so that those of the enemy might be destroyed,[72] it is clear that most of his discussion on siege

---

[72] Veg. *Epit.* 4 prol. 8: *rationes quibus uel nostrae ciuitates defendendae sint uel hostium subruendae ex diuersis auctoribus in ordinem digeram.*

warfare deals with defence. It is difficult to be sure, but Vegetius' evocation of *ciuitates hostium subruendae* and not *urbes hostium subruendae* seems more consonant with attacking smaller settlements of Germanic/Gothic barbarians than besieging the much older metropolises of the Near East. It will be well to mention, once again, that the epitomator, although he sometimes uses *ciuitates* and *urbes* quite interchangeably, seems to hold that *urbs* is the more prestigious term.[73]

To return to our theme, Vegetius, in chapters 13–17 of book 4, deals with the various *machinae* that might be used to attack a city. Yet, unlike the Anonymus, he appears to do this more out of pedantry than because he has any desire to inculcate a spirit of aggression – Vegetius sees his *opus* as a relatively complete manual on terrestrial warfare (especially that involving infantry) and so leaves no stone unturned. In chapter 24, he explains the way in which a city might be penetrated by the construction of underground passages, while, in chapter 28, he describes the means by which besiegers might protect themselves from the sudden onrush of an armed party emanating from walls. All the attacking and (in the case of chapter 28) defensive gambits that he describes, in addition to the *machinae* that make these manoeuvres possible, are discussed, not so much that the reader might be able to attack a fortified position, but so that the reader might know with what equipment his own walls might be pierced or undermined. Vegetius, then, is anxious to relate the secrets of offensive siege-craft, which he obviously gleaned from sources such as Caesar and Frontinus, in order that the besieged might successfully anticipate the actions of the enemy.

To conclude this discussion of Vegetius and his views on military aggression and defence, it is worth recalling Goffart's view that the text, as a whole, evokes a world that appears to be already "more medieval than classical".[74] In no part of the *Epitoma* does this appear more evident than in the digressions on siege warfare. As seems evident, the reign of Theodosius I is highly significant for many reasons. But what could truly be described as epoch-making is Theodosius' destruction of the very fabric of the old Principate by envisaging the formal partition of the Empire. Various dates are often bandied about as points from which one can begin to see a medieval Europe emerging: 286 (the beginning of Diocletian's tetrarchic 'Dominate'); 312 (Constantine's victory over Maxentius); 378 (Adrianople); and, of course, 476 (Romulus Augustulus' deposition). Yet the year 395 deserves more attention than it usually receives, for it is with Theodosius the Great's death that the Augustan ideal of imperial unity also perishes, especially in a geographical sense.

Although Cameron is undoubtedly correct to state that "Contemporaries could scarcely have noticed or anticipated the significance of the demarcation",[75]

---

[73] Thus the imperial honorand, at *Epit.* 4 prol. 3, founds *urbes* rather than the mere *ciuitates* built by 'lesser' rulers.

[74] Goffart 1977, 100. Note his assertion that "Vegetius is all too well aware … that, when he refers to the *populus Romanus*, he is speaking of an entity belonging to the distant past, from which he dissociates himself".

[75] Cameron/Long/Sherry 1993, 3.

especially since the Empire had been jointly ruled for over a century,[76] the full effect of Theodosius' decease did not take long to manifest itself. Classical motifs prevailed in the arts, most notably in verse and in its plastic forms, but the citizen's *Weltanschauung* became dramatically attenuated. While a highborn western Roman may still have cherished the idea that he belonged to a pan-Mediterranean political entity, his common sense must have told him that the *limites* were closing in, and, with that concrete realization, the fortune of those in Antioch and Alexandria surely became a concern of little moment. Vegetius seems to fall into this category. While he may follow the hollow line that his *imperator inuictus* is the lord of the whole Roman world, the content of the *Epitoma* shows that his main interest lay in the West. Secular writers of the Theodosian age, in general, still viewed themselves as part of the classical world and its now outmoded and increasingly irrelevant traditions. Witness Ammianus, Pacatus and Symmachus. This quickly changes after 395. Whereas Claudian is often regarded as the last of that classical tradition, he is, in many ways, also the first of a new tradition. Indeed, he might be thought of as a bridge between the two, i.e., a link between the 'classical' world,[77] and that which came thereafter.

Although Vegetius need not be equated with Claudian in terms of his literary merits, he, like the poet, became a spokesman for his era. The traditional forms remain, but they now take on the appearance of a shallow and almost entirely mannered veneer that is not difficult to penetrate. The 'western' orientation emerges, irrespective of the authors' concerted attempts to maintain, more often than not, the fiction of imperial unity. Of course, Vegetius drew his material on siege-warfare from sources belonging to the classical world. However, in his dissemination and presentation of the material, he seems to have read these accounts through eyes more familiar with a fragmented and increasingly insular society rather than through eyes that can visualize the epic conflicts described by Polybius, Livy and Arrian. Thus Vegetius provides us with familiar pictures, but with different frames. It is only through our investigation and understanding of these frames that we can draw closer to Vegetius' world. Naturally, no hard evidence can be furnished to support these claims. But one need not look beneath the classical rhetoric for too long to see that we are now dealing with a very different era indeed.

---

[76] With the obvious exceptions of Constantine the Great (324–337), Julian (361–363), Jovian (363–364) and Theodosius the Great (394–395).

[77] Note Levy's observation (1948, 87) that, apart from magic, Claudian's poems "reflect virtually every other aspect of classical culture"; and the opinion of Rolfe (1919, 141), who notes that Claudian's description of "the machinery of the pagan religion ... in full working order ... is not surprising in one who has so thoroughly assimilated the language and spirit of the great writers of pagan Rome". On this theme, see also Moore 1910, 108–115.

3. VEGETIUS AND *MARE PACATUM*

Vegetius only begins to deal with maritime matters from *Epit.* 4.31.[78] *In toto*, he devotes sixteen chapters to naval warfare.[79] Under the heading *Praecepta belli naualis*, Vegetius explains why he has not hitherto written on the subject:

> terrestris proelii rationibus absolutis naualis belli residua, ut opinor, est portio; de cuius artibus ideo pauciora dicenda sunt quia iam dudum pacato mari cum barbaris nationibus agitur terrestre certamen (*Epit.* 4.31.1).

That Vegetius mentions conflict on land with 'barbarian' nations would seem to preclude the possibility that the *Epitoma* was written in the latter half of the reign of Theodosius I (as argued previously). In addition, the reference *iam dudum pacato mari*, as will be seen directly below, could possibly indicate that the work was written in the first half of the fifth rather than in the final decade of the fourth century.

Baatz, however, considers the opposite to be true. He therefore writes as follows: "Das [referring to *iam dudum pacato mari*] konnte man wohl nicht mehr schreiben, nachdem die Vandalen im Mittelmeer als Seemacht aufgetreten waren, womit etwa seit 420 zu rechnen ist".[80] This, argues Baatz, can only mean that Vegetius' *Epitoma* was dedicated to Theodosius I.[81] The words *iam dudum pacato mari*, according to this scholar, could not possibly have been written after the Vandal acquisition of "Seemacht".[82] Now, it is thought that the Vandals had begun to construct a fleet as early as 419, a quest facilitated, as Moss points out, by "ready access to the sea and the ships which were moored in [Spain's] ... ports".[83] Moreover, the subsequent conquest of Carthage, Rome's principal port in Africa, would have allowed the Vandals to augment their existing fleet with the maritime resources and experience of this ancient maritime city.[84]

---

[78] Vegetius does mention the word *classis* at *Epit.* 2.1.4. On Vegetius' sources for naval matters, see Lammert 1931, 798–800; id. 1940a, 285–288; id. 1940b, 89–95; Sander 1928, 908–10; id. 1931, 395–399; id. 1956, 153–172. I have touched upon Vegetius and aspects of naval warfare elsewhere (Charles 2005a, 275–299; id. 2005b, 181–193).

[79] At times, there have been references to five books of the *Epitoma* (the fifth comprising the *Praecepta belli naualis*). Very few manuscripts (e.g., Paris Latin 6503) treat *Epit.* 4.31–46 as a separate section. Moreover, no recent modern edition preserves any firm division between the sections on siege-craft and naval warfare. But cf. Rubio 1973, 215–219, who concludes that the section on naval warfare could have been "un tratado independiente".

[80] Baatz 1997, 5.

[81] Baatz 1997, 5, see also 9. Cf. Hermann 2000, 259, where Baatz's *termini* are accepted, as is his assignment of the text to the reign of Theodosius I.

[82] *Cod. Theod.* 9.40.24 (419), which describes *naues* being sold to the barbarians (witness *barbaris*), is generally thought to refer to the Vandals. Cf. *Cod. Theod.* 7.16.3 (420), which deals with *merces inlicitae* being exported *ad nationes barbaras*. For a general overview of Vandal sea-power, see von Waldeyer-Hartz 1937, 137–147.

[83] Moss 1973, 725. See also Morazzani 1966, 539–561; Orlandis 1977, 31. But note that Reddé (1986, 648) holds that the ships captured in Spain were mere "barques de pêche". On the literary evidence pertaining to the Vandals in Spain, see Morales Belda 1969, *passim*.

[84] On this, see Morazzani 1966, 550.

On the other hand, Courtois attempts to prove that there was no Vandal 'navy' as such. Indeed, he writes of "la disparition presque totale des vaisseaux longs" in late antiquity[85] and believes that the Vandal fleet was merely a collection of transport ships.[86] Reddé readily agrees.[87] Despite this, it is extremely difficult to believe that the galley had died out, as Courtois seems to suggest (or does "la disparation presque totale" concede that galleys may still have existed in very limited numbers?).[88] And, if the galley no longer existed, which seems highly unlikely given that it was the premier naval vessel on the Mediterranean from *c.* 1200 B.C. until the battle of Lepanto in the late sixteenth century,[89] there was certainly no reason why construction of such vessels would not have been resumed when the need arose.[90]

To return to the problem at hand, Milner essentially agrees with Baatz, and states, in defence of his supposition that Vegetius was writing towards the end of the reign of Theodosius I, that the Vandals had "acquired a naval capability by A.D. 419".[91] This date, a year earlier than Baatz's, was presumably influenced by *Cod. Theod.* 9.40.24 of September 24, 419, where an imperial pardon is granted to those *qui conficiendi naues incognitam ante peritiam barbaris tradiderunt.*[92] *Cod Theod.* 9.40.24, as stated above, almost certainly relates to Vandal activity in Spain. According to Moss, this strengthens "the case for a Vandal war-fleet rather than only transports".[93] Thus both Milner and Baatz hold that the *Epitoma* was written *before* the Vandals took to the sea, and they use this as a factor in support of an earlier dating. Sabbah is of a similar opinion yet favours a date before 425. He seems to think that the real issue is not merely the Vandal acquisition of a naval capability – which seemingly occurred in 419 – but the beginning of "[les] premiers actes de piraterie maritime commis par les Vandales".[94] Chastagnol, however, contends that *Epit.* 4.31, which he believes could not have been written after "la piraterie maritime qui a accompagné la prise de possession progressive

---

[85] Courtois 1964, 206. *Contra* Courtois, see Kienast 1966, 124ff. Cf. Guillerm 1993, 19.

[86] Courtois 1964, 207. But cf. Hocker 1995, 90: "some [of Genseric's ships] must have been swift galleys".

[87] Reddé 1986, 650.

[88] See Guillerm 1993, 143. Procopius associates the ram (witness the present participle of ἐμβάλλειν) with the Vandals in his description of a naval battle of 467 (*Vand.* 3.6.21). Likewise, Zosimus (5.21.3) asserts that Fravitta, in 400, sank a barbarian vessel with the ram of his flagship, which πλοῖον is described as χαλκέμβολον. At 5.20.3, Zosimus calls the imperial ships Λίβερνα (*sc.* πλοῖα), a term which usually refers to galleys; but cf. Charles 2005b, 181–193.

[89] On later oared vessels, see Gardiner 1995, chs. 7, 12; Anderson 1962, chs. 6, 8–9.

[90] See Moss 1973, 726.

[91] Milner 1996, xxviii.

[92] Starr (1989, 80) provides an explanation for the decree: "it is noticeable that ... the [federate] barbarians were carefully kept away from the seacoast, which still supported some commerce; imperial edicts even banned training the Germans in the building of ships".

[93] Moss 1973, 725 n. 137.

[94] Sabbah 1980, 139. Sabbah (1980, 145) reiterates this opinion elsewhere: "la paix qui règne sur mer ... convient au règne de Théodose".

de l'Afrique par les Vandales", means that the *terminus ante quem* of the text "peut être ramené à 440 environ".[95] Sirago maintains a similar opinion.[96]

It is difficult to understand why Chastagnol and Sirago choose *c.* 440 as the date after which the Mediterranean was no longer safe for Roman shipping, especially since Vandal maritime power demonstrably commenced some years earlier.[97] In general, Chastagnol and Sirago's reasoning is quite logical, if, of course, the words of our author are taken at face value. In sum, Vegetius writes that the sea has been peaceful for some time, a statement which, at first glance, precludes the possibility that the *Epitoma* was written after the commencement of Vandal piracy. As this piracy first occurred near the beginning of Valentinian III's reign, most scholars have thought it entirely reasonable to use *Epit.* 4.31.1 as evidence against a dating under this emperor. Still, the phrase causes some disquiet, especially as the chapter in which it is found is of an essentially panegyrical nature.[98]

The solution to the problem may, in part, lie in the word *pacato*. Although the adjective *pacatus* may simply mean 'peaceful',[99] there is no reason to exclude the possibility that, in this instance, *pacatum* is the past participle passive of *pacare*, which means 'to bring into a state of peace', i.e., 'to pacify'.[100] Thus the sea in

---

[95] Chastagnol 1974, 59; see also Sirago 1961, 465ff.

[96] Sirago (1961, 465–466) holds that "Vegezio scrive ... prima del 439, presa di Cartagine da parte dei Vandali, epoca in cui si ripresero le ostilità per mare, mentre Vegezio riconosce che al suo tempo i mari sono tranquilli".

[97] Of relevance is that Jordanes (*Rom.* 320 [*MGH:AA* 5.1, 41]) and Marcellinus Comes (*Chron.* 400 [*MGH:AA* 11, *Chron. min.* 2, 66]) refer to a naval action against a rebellious *comes* called Gaina or (more correctly) Gaïnas in 400. Philostorgius (*H.E.* 11.8), Socrates (*H.E.* 6.6.2) and Sozomen (*H.E.* 8.4.10) also describe the incident, as do Zosimus (5.21) and the *Chronicon Paschale* (400–401 = Dindorf, *Chron. Pasch.* 567, lines 12–19). After terrorizing Constantinople, Gaïnas fled to the Hellespont, where *piratico ritu uiuebat* (Jord. *Rom.* 320). Still, this supposed *bellum nauale* (Marcell. *Chron.* 400) was probably of relatively trivial consequence, although Socrates (*H.E.* 6.6.36–37) records that Eusebius Scholasticus and Ammonius wrote verse on the conflict. Socrates holds that the barbarians were ἀποροῦντες πλοίων and in the process of crossing the Hellespont in σχεδίας συμπήξαντες (*H.E.* 6.6.32) when the Roman fleet appeared (*H.E.* 6.6.32–34) – he makes no mention of piracy. The form that these σχεδίας took is problematic, though Zosimus (5.21.2) tell us that they could embark both men and horses. Philostorgius' epitome also mentions σχεδίας and that the imperial commander Fravitta encountered them νηΐτῃ στόλῳ (*H.E.* 11.8). The Goths, assailed by both a strong wind and the Romans (cf. Zos. 5.21.2–3, which ignores the wind but records that a powerful current prevented the barbarian craft from being steered), perished in great numbers. Thus Gaïnas' naval activity posed no real threat to the Empire's maritime security and cannot really be used to contradict Vegetius' claim that the sea has been peaceful *iam dudum*. On Gaïnas' rebellion, see Cameron/Long/Sherry 1993, *passim*; Clover 1979, 65–76; Heather 1988, 152–172; Paschoud 1971–1979, 151–169 (vol. 3.1); Mazzarino 1942, 211–225.

[98] See Goffart 1977, 86, who holds that the phrase reflects the official attitude to naval matters.

[99] Cf. Cic. *De Or.* 1.8.30: *in pacatis tranquillisque ciuitatibus*; id. *Lig.* 2.4: *in prouincia pacatissima*; Caes. *BGall.* 5.24.7: *in pacatissimam et quietissimam partem*.

[100] Goffart (1977, 86–87) appears to agree with such a translation for *pacatus*; see also Milner 1996: *ad loc.*: "pacified"; Müller 1997, *ad loc.*: "befriedet". Stelten (1990, *ad loc.*) prefers "peaceful", while Guiffrida Manmana (1997, *ad loc.*) and Formisano (2003, *ad loc.*) provide comparable translations in Italian.

Vegetius' *Epitoma* had been "pacified", a translation which preserves the verbal force of the participle. Such an interpretation, as will be seen below, eminently fits the historical context of the fifth century, and, more specifically, the reign of Valentinian III. Let us propose the following: in the years following the Vandal acquisition of territory in northern Africa, the sea had not been peaceful, but, by the time of Vegetius' composition of the text, the Mediterranean had been supposedly returned to a tranquil state and was thus *pacatum*. The *iam dudum*, of course, represents a problem, and one would hesitate to provide any translation for these two words other than 'for a long time', or something of that nature.[101] But how long ago, exactly, is *iam dudum*, and was this phrase deliberately used by Vegetius in order to relegate a comparatively recent event to a more distant past? If this were so, the phrase would appear to have a largely rhetorical and hyperbolical value.

It behoves us to recall, albeit briefly, the historical background. A confederation of the Asding Vandals and a portion of the Alans, numbering some 80,000 persons and led by Genseric, crossed the Strait of Gibraltar to Mauretania and Africa in 429.[102] Meeting with little if any resistance,[103] they sacked Hippo Regius in 430 and established a kingdom not far from modern Tunis. Valentinian III's government, being unable to eject the foreign invaders,[104] was eventually forced to recognize the Vandals as *foederati* in 435 and was compelled to grant them land between Sitifensis in eastern Mauretania and the newly established border of western Africa Proconsularis.[105] Vegetius, if he were writing at this time, would have had just cause to follow the 'official' line and claim that the sea was *pacatum*. But *iam dudum pacatum*? This will be explained in due course.

Peace between Roman and Vandal proved short-lived. Conflict was renewed on 19 October 439, the day when Genseric broke the treaty with a surprise attack on Carthage.[106] In the following year, the Vandals began their devastating raids on Sicily.[107] It is odd that few modern scholars see the real significance of these attacks. The depredations were not merely the result of a base lust for booty.

---

[101] *OLD*, s.v. *dudum*: 1b: "(w. *iam*, also written *iamdudum*, *iandudum*) some while ago now".

[102] See Isid. *Hist. Goth.* 74 (*MGH:AA* 11, *Chron. min.* 2, 297); Prosp. 1321 (*MGH:AA* 9, *Chron. min.* 1, 474). For commentary, see Courtois 1964, 169–170; Schmidt 1953, 81–83; Sirago 1961, 279–311.

[103] Cf. Morazzani 1966, 542. Procopius (*Vand.* 3.3.25, 3.3.30) and Jordanes (*Get.* 33.167 [*MGH:AA* 5.1, 101–102]) record that Boniface, who had fallen out with Valentinian III, had invited the Vandals into Africa. This is rejected by Moss (1973, 725 n. 129), who also notes that those letters of Augustine dealing with the matter (viz., *Ep.* 229, 231) "do not offer evidence either way".

[104] On this, see Gil Egea 1997, 108.

[105] Isid. *Hist. Goth.* 74 (*MGH:AA* 11, *Chron. min.* 2, 297).

[106] See *Chron. Pasch.* 439 = Dindorf, *Chron. Pasch.* 583, lines 5–6; Salv. *Gub.* 6.12. For modern discussion, see Courtois 1964, 211–212.

[107] The danger posed by the Vandal fleet at the time was recognized officially in *Nov. Valent.* 9 (440). The *Chronicon Paschale* incorrectly places Genseric's raids on Sicily in the same year as his capture of Carthage (439 = Dindorf, *Chron. Pasch.* 583, lines 6–7).

Rather they were prosecuted in order to force Rome into granting further territorial concessions.[108] The real intent, therefore, was to cut off Rome from every last *modius* of grain issuing from the southern shores of the Mediterranean. For the first time in centuries, a non-Roman power had gained naval superiority in the western half of the Middle Sea and was using that superiority to starve the Roman people into submission.[109] Possibly for the same reasons, or simply to create widespread terror, Sardinia and the coastline of southern Italy also fell prey to looting expeditions in the same year, as is described by Salvianus (*Gub.* 6.12). Friendly relations were not restored until 442, when a second treaty was agreed upon by the two combatants.[110]

If Vegetius were writing a) some time after the first peace and before the sack of Carthage in 439, or b) shortly after the conclusion of the second peace in 442, Goffart provides a neat summary of the political context in which our author must have found himself: "the Mediterranean was 'pacified' as long as the imperial court regarded it to be".[111] Certainly, it would have been impolitic for Vegetius to write otherwise, especially if his work was to be viewed by those who had formulated the policy of Vandal conciliation and accommodation.[112] Thus Vegetius, writing under Valentinian III, may have used the phrase *pacato mari* with a degree of legitimacy.[113] E. Birley, who also prefers a Valentinian dating of the *Epitoma*,[114] writes that "the age not merely of Aëtius but also of Merobaudes seems to fit the background of Vegetius – specifically, after the treaty of peace with the Vandals in 442".[115] Quite so, but one cannot immediately exclude, however, a date near the beginning of Valentinian's reign. Certainly, the appearance of *iam dudum pacato mari* before the sack of Carthage would not have appeared as ridiculous as it seems in a context *post* 442.

To add weight to the above, one would do well to consider the second *Panegyricus* of the soldier-orator Merobaudes, a man active during the reign of Valentinian III. This panegyric was apparently written in order to praise the achieve-

---

[108] Gil Egea (1997, 110) credits the 'barbarians' with a much greater degree of intelligence than they are usually accorded.

[109] See Raven 1969, 154–155.

[110] See Prosp. 1347 (*MGH:AA* 9, *Chron. min.* 1, 479); Merob. *Pan. II*, 24–29; see also Prosp. 1342, 1344, 1346 (*MGH:AA* 9, *Chron. min.* 1, 478–479). For modern commentary, see Clover 1966, 78–88; Courtois 1964, 171–173; Schmidt 1953, 88–89; Stein 1959, 324–325 (vol. 1). Procopius, writing in the sixth century, conflates the treaties of 437 and 442 (*Vand.* 3.4.12–13). The information that he records, as Clover (1971, 52–53) suggests, is placed "in the context of Aspar's withdrawal from Africa, which occurred in 434, and which caused Valentinian to negotiate with Geiseric [*sic*] in 435" – i.e., the first treaty.

[111] Goffart 1977, 87.

[112] This policy of appeasement would culminate, after widespread depredation of the western Mediterranean, in the Vandal sack of Rome in 455; see Evag. *H.E.* 2.7; Isid. *Hist. Goth.* 75–77 (*MGH:AA* 11, *Chron. min.* 2, 297–298); Prosp. 1375 (*MGH:AA* 9, *Chron. min.* 1, 483–484).

[113] See Goffart 1977, 86.

[114] Although Goffart (1977, 86–87) does not specifically nominate a year (or years), he seems to prefer a date after 442. He does write, however, that the *Epitoma* "is unlikely to have been written ... within the years 437–442".

[115] E. Birley 1988, 68.

ments of Aëtius, consul in 432, 437 and 446, and famous for his victory against the Huns in 451.[116] The object of *Panegyricus II*, which is not preserved in its entirely, is to demonstrate that the Empire is at peace, a state propagated by the general's prudent conduct. From line 52, a *diua nocens*[117] (probably one of the Furies) complains that she has been "driven from the waves".[118] This 'Fury', we might assume, is a personification of the barbarian terror, and, in particular, the unnamed Vandal menace. The closest reference to this people occurs as far back as line 24 (sixty-two verses are missing between Vollmer's line 49 and 50[119]):

> insessor Libyes quamuis fatalibus armis
> ausus Elissaei solium rescindere regni
> milibus Arctois Tyrias conpleuerat arces (*Pan. II*, 24–26).

This should not surprise, for Merobaudes, writing at a time of amicable relations between Vandal and Roman,[120] would have understood that the recent strife should officially be forgotten. This explanation, too, effectively answers Sirago's query regarding the absence of the Vandals from the *Epitoma*.[121] While veiled references to the *insessor Libyes* and the *milia Arctoi* in Merobaudes' *panegyricus* were necessary in order to magnify Aëtius' diplomatic achievement, they would have had no place in a text that, if we adhere to the notion that it was possibly written under Valentinian III, indirectly criticizes the military and diplomatic policy of the Romano-Gallic general. Moreover, a lack of any specific reference to the Vandals in Merobaudes' work only serves to emphasize the magnitude of the danger. One might compare Augustus' reduction of his enemies to a *factio* (*RG* 1.1), and his claim, in reference to Sextus Pompeius, that he had freed the sea *a praedonibus* (*RG* 25.1).

Next, we are told that the *diua nocens*, driven aloft by the winds, finds herself near the icy abode of Enyo, who *texerat annosa refugum sub pace f[urorem]* (*Pan. II*, 62).[122] When the goddess perceives Enyo, driven to despair by the general rejoicing of humankind, she leaps down and rouses her with these words: *"quis miseros, germana, tibi sopor ob[ruit artus*[123] */ pace sub inmensa?"* (*Pan. II*, 71–72). Although Aëtius' second consulship was in 437, i.e., some five years before the treaty of 442, Merobaudes' second *Panegyricus* is believed to have been composed after this event. Clover dates the work to 446,[124] as does Oost

---

[116] According to Clover (1971, 41), "lines 106–107 of the poem indicate that the object of praise – and perhaps the recipient of the epistolary dedication – was Aëtius".

[117] These words do not appear until line 69. The section of the text where the immortal figure of the *diua nocens* would have been introduced (there appears to be a substantial lacuna after line 49) has not survived.

[118] Merob. *Pan. II* 52–53: the *diua* laments *"depellim[ur undis] / nec terris regnare licet"*.

[119] See Vollmer 1904, 12–13.

[120] *nunc [insessor Libyes] hostem exutus pactis proprioribus arsit / Romanam uincire fidem Latiosque parentes / adnumerare sibi sociamque intexere prolem* (Merob. *Pan. II*, 27–29).

[121] Sirago 1961, 472.

[122] Translation of Clover 1971, 14.

[123] Reconstruction of Vollmer 1904, *ad loc.*

[124] Clover (1971, 41) writes that "the poet probably delivered [the second panegyric] or a

after some initial hesitation.[125] Although it has been argued that the panegyric in question should be dated before the second treaty, i.e., during the years 433–439, Clover is confident that the text should be dated after this event, and that it should be associated with Aëtius' third consulship.[126] If this is so, the *annosa pax* that the poet introduces should be regarded as especially significant. Evidently, Merobaudes' language refers "to [an] enduring peace [rather] than to a recent treaty",[127] an opinion augmented by the reference to a *pax inmensa*.

Therefore, the *annosa pax*, referred to after the second treaty of 442, is more or less congruent with Vegetius' troublesome *iam dudum pacato mari*. In view of this, it may be concluded that a state of continuing and seemingly perpetual calm upon the waves was the 'official' position of the western Roman court at a time when the Mediterranean had only recently been rendered *pacatum*.[128] Vegetius, however, insists that the present situation of maritime tranquillity should not be taken as an excuse to neglect the fleet. Thus he advocates, at *Epit.* 4.31, a return to the naval system that had served Rome well during the glory years of the *pax romana*.

Now, if the text in question *was* written during the reign of Theodosius I, i.e., at a time when the Mediterranean was still *mare nostrum*, why would the author have needed to address the issue of naval warfare in detail? The problem of maintaining possession and control of *mare nostrum* did not come about until the advent of Vandal sea power during the reign of Valentinian III. Perhaps Vegetius was sapient enough to recognize that amicable relations between Vandal and Roman could not last. And, if Rome was to tame a sea-borne Vandal power, the only avenue to victory would be to secure command of the sea-lanes once again. If this is the case, Vegetius might be considered a prophet of the destruction that was to issue from Rome's policy of Vandal accommodation. Indeed, it might not be entirely unwise to suggest that the *Praecepta belli naualis*, which finds itself unhappily appended to a quite lengthy discussion on siege warfare, was a last-minute addition to the *Epitoma* prompted by the author's growing disquiet at the Vandal situation.[129]

---

form of it on 1 January, 446, when Aëtius began his third consulship". This opinion is supported by Sirago (1961, 356 n. 3), who writes that "Abbiamo ... il suo poema sul II consolato di Aezio (*Pan.* II)". Cf. Vollmer 1904, 10.

[125] Oost 1983, 280; cf. 240 and n. 115 of the same work.

[126] According to Clover (1971, 52), "There can be little doubt that Merobaudes refers ... to the treaty of 442 and its ramifications". Oost (1983, 280) is similarly emphatic with regard to his assignment of *Pan. II* to 446. Yet he writes earlier (1983, 240 n. 115) that "*Pan. I* may refer to [Aëtius'] ... third consulship in 446".

[127] Goffart 1977, 87 n. 103.

[128] Goffart (1977, 87) leans toward such a conclusion.

[129] Vegetius may have been stirred by a real concern for the maintenance, or rather restoration, of traditional Roman naval power: *Romanus ... populus pro decore et utilitate magnitudinis suae non propter necessitatem tumultus alicuius classem parabat ex tempore sed ne quando necessitatem sustineret semper habuit praeparatam* (*Epit.* 4.31.2).

CONCLUSION:
NAVIGATING BETWEEN THE *TERMINI*

It is obviously difficult to divine a precise date for a work such as the *Epitoma Rei Militaris*. To begin with, almost nothing of any real worth is known about the author. What is even more frustrating is that internal signifiers found in the text itself do not always provide evidence that is beyond dispute. At the risk of sounding post-modern, the initial thesis that the text was *not* addressed to Theodosius I has in itself perhaps led to some distortion of the material contained within this volume. Thus we have created *a* Vegetius fabricated according to the present arrangement of material and data. He is thus a Vegetius who must necessarily differ in certain respects from those created by others. It is to be hoped that the effect of this appropriation has been minimal, and that our treatment of the author and his world accords, as much as possible, with orthodox historical methodology.

Despite this, it is not altogether incorrect to say that supposedly 'firm' evidence for a dating under Theodosius I can be dismissed as either subjective or, in some cases, entirely mistaken. 'Evidence' of sorts for this contention *may* exist, at least in the eyes of some, but there is no one piece of internal information that makes a later date impossible. The door is open. Conversely, while emphasis has been given in this discussion to demonstrating that Vegetius' treatise finds its most comfortable historical niche in an early- to mid-fifth-century context (i.e., a date before 450), it must be pointed out that none of the pieces of 'evidence' arraigned to support this contention is *completely* unassailable. At an individual level, each of the points raised to demonstrate that the *Epitoma* was not addressed to Theodosius I carries minimal persuasive force. In fact, it is possible to arrange these pieces of evidence in order of their import, from the barely relevant to the quite significant. Thus it is only in its collective state that the 'evidence' amounts to something of interest. Of course, it remains to be said that a disquisition of this nature should hopefully stimulate further debate on this controversial topic.

It has been shown that little doubt should remain that the *Epitoma* is a product of the Western Empire. This certainly helps matters, for we can more or less dismiss Arcadius and Theodosius II from the list of possible candidates. Certainly, the text displays an almost total disregard for oriental matters, and the frequent references to the city of Rome and its early history is telling. Although this does not automatically exclude Theodosius the Great from contention, one might expect some kind of *real* indication that Vegetius' emperor was the effective ruler of both *partes imperii*. If the text had been addressed to Theodosius I during his first imperial journey to the West, some mention of Valentinian II or – at the very least – multiple *imperatores* would be expected. In any case, attempts to show that Vegetius' *imperator inuictus* did, in fact, command both East and West are groundless. Indeed, they are based on an imperfect understanding of the nature of the panegyrical language of the era. Study of contemporary panegyric, and specifically the *laudationes* of Claudian and Sidonius Apollinaris, clearly demonstrates that the western ruler continued to be styled the ruler of all lands in Latin literature. Although Claudian (especially in his earlier works) does not ignore the fact that the East was ruled from Constantinople rather than Milan or Ravenna, he is, in many passages, often forgetful of the dual nature of the divided Empire. By the time of Sidonius, writing not long after the death of Valentinian III, the division between East and West had become so complete that the poet does not hesitate to give his honorands power over all 'Roman' lands, and even some that lie beyond the easternmost border of the Empire.

No one seemed particularly willing to admit the fragmented state of the Roman world, especially if there was no real need to do so. In addition, the lack of reference to multiple Augusti does not correspond to the evidence provided by literature from the reign of Theodosius the Great. Theodosius appears to have been anxious to preserve the fiction of the collegiality of the *principes*. Strictly speaking, he was merely one of their number, and not even the most senior one at that (at least while Valentinian II was alive). And if Vegetius ignored Valentinian II, he also ignored Theodosius' son Arcadius, who had already been proclaimed Augustus by the time that Theodosius entered the West in order to take control after Maximus' usurpation. Literature of this era rarely fails to mention plural Augusti. Of especial import is that Pacatus, who delivered a panegyric to Theodosius after the emperor's restoration of his 'senior' colleague, not only mentions the young western Augustus but also refers to Theodosius' princely offspring.

It has been this volume's hope that a detailed and cohesive investigation of the various contemporary references made by Vegetius might show that the work was unlikely to have been addressed to Theodosius the Great. Vegetius' claim (*Epit.* 1.20.2–3) that armour was abandoned under Gratian is an important factor. It is relatively demonstrable that Roman infantry wore defensive protection up until the battle of Adrianople, and beyond. Vegetius' statement, therefore, is obviously an exaggeration – it seems reasonably clear that infantry armour was worn by at least some units throughout the period in question. *Epit.* 1.20.2–5 thus seems to have wider significance. It is effectively a call to reduce Rome's reliance on barbarian *foederati*, the infantry of which groups may not have always been protected by cuirass and helmet. It is unlikely that this sort of plea would have been made during Theodosius' time. This is for two reasons. First, it is doubtful whether Vegetius would have dared to criticize Theodosius' ostensible policy of philobarbarism. Second, and more importantly, the use of federate armies *en masse* had only just begun in Theodosius' reign. What one might term 'regular' Roman infantry units, such as the *legiones palatinae* and the *auxilia palatina*, still existed in appreciable numbers. This is attested, in some way at least, by the information recorded in the enigmatic *Notitia Dignitatum*. It was not until the fifth century that Roman military strategy was reduced to manipulating the federate *nationes* that had been allowed to remain within the Empire. Vegetius' anti-barbarian polemic, which is thinly disguised although not often recognized, has far more relevance in a fifth-century context.

In terms of naval warfare, Vegetius' mini-treatise on such matters, which appears in book 4 of the *Epitoma*, also has more relevance in a fifth-century world, and specifically after the Vandal acquisition of northern Africa. Vegetius' claim that the sea (*mare*) was *pacatum* need not exclude a date under Valentinian III, as some have contended, for the contemporary poet and orator Merobaudes demonstrates that similar language could pertain to the conclusion of treaties with the Vandals. Other military references, such as the reference to the *Iouiani* and *Herculiani*, the lost art of castramentation (which again seems part of Vegetius' anti-barbarian polemic rather than a true reflection of the contemporary abilities of 'Roman' troops), and the supposed reduction of the number of *legiones* (read non-federate infantry), also point to a date later than Theodosius I.

Debate on the date of the work's composition aside, the present study hopes to have shown that Vegetius should also be seen as a source for his own age and cultural milieu rather than merely as a compendium of earlier times. Indeed, it is profitable to view him as a source for the opinions and values of a particular class of late-Roman society, viz., the landed gentry – if this term is not too anachronistic – of the Latin-speaking West. If we look solely at those sections of the text relating to contemporary affairs, most notably the *praefationes* and the final chapter of each of the individual books,[1] we find an author well-versed in the standard panegyrical machinery, and one whose *modus operandi* closely follows the established methods of addressing an imperial honorand. If Vegetius were indeed a *comes*, as some of the manuscripts would have us believe, how could he have acted otherwise? We must accept that the epitomator was only too happy to present a distorted version of the truth in order to facilitate the acceptance of the more challenging aspects of his material. By accepting this veneer for what it is, it becomes far easier to discern, by means of a comparison of language used by others who addressed the Augusti, whether he wrote for a martial figure like Theodosius I, or a palace-bound dilettante like Valentinian III. This is where the contextual treatment offers insights into the nature of Vegetius' approach that more conventional historical analysis usually discounts or deems of little importance. And it is only by evaluating the *Epitoma* as *literature*, however slight its artistic merit, that similarities with other contemporary works emerge.

Even if one were to maintain doubts about a fifth-century date, it seems clear that, in the face of so much controversy, it is inadvisable (and rather unnecessary) for historians who use Vegetius for purposes other than the history of the last century of the Western Empire to provide a precise date for the *Epitoma*. For example, there is no need for someone discussing the auxiliary forces of the Principate to pigeonhole Vegetius in the late fourth century – and specifically during the reign of Theodosius the Great – simply because this is what appears in standard reference works such as the *OCD*, or the appropriate volume of Pauly-Wissowa's *RE*. The confident tone of these assertions belies the complex nature of the debate. The uninformed reader, not aware of the problems, simply accepts

---

[1] In book 4, of course, more attention needs to be paid to *Epit.* 4.30.5–6, where Vegetius draws his discussion of siege-warfare to a close, in addition to *Epit.* 4.31.1, where he begins his *Praecepta belli naualis*.

the author's assertion in the belief that there must be some inscription or literary notice that says something along the lines of *Flauius Vegetius Renatus sub patre Arcadii et Honorii libros numero IIII de rebus militaribus scripsit*. But no such thing exists. In such cases, i.e., where there is obviously nothing to be gained from providing a firm date, it seems preferable to state simply that the *Epitoma* was written between 383–450, and that a more precise date is open to conjecture.

In sum, it is only by means of the accumulated weight of pieces of 'evidence' large and small that a balance of probability may be established. That balance of probability, at least according to the material presented *supra*, leans decidedly in favour of a date at some time in the first half of the fifth century, and specifically one under Valentinian III. In fact, if one were to consider this accumulated evidence, as much as objectivity allows, it seems that the *least likely* of our six main imperial contenders is Theodosius I. While most of this 'evidence' for a fifth-century date, as I am only too happy to admit, is gleaned from a more or less subjective analysis of the few snippets of contemporary relevance that Vegetius provides, more concrete indicators, especially in the form of Vegetius' references to the *pedites nudati*, *mare pacatum* and the twin legions (the *Iouiani* and the *Herculiani*), seem to be decidedly at odds with a dating under Theodosius the Great. Moreover, apart from the very beginning of his reign, Theodosius' relationship with the barbarians was amicable. The Goths even fought with him as allies. Vegetius, however, says that war is currently being waged on land *cum barbaris nationibus*. This hardly seems appropriate for Theodosius I's reign, especially for the years in which some scholars imagine that the *Epitoma* must have been composed. Thus it is only when Vegetius' work is juxtaposed with the available corpus of Latin (and even some Greek) literature that we gain a clearer picture of Vegetius' cultural, literary and historical milieu.

BIBLIOGRAPHY

Adams, J.N., 1972, "On the Authorship of the *Historia Augusta*", *CQ* n.s. 22, 186–194.

– 1984, "Pelagonius, Eumelus and a Lost Latin Veterinary Writer", in Sabbah, G. (ed.), *Textes médicaux latins antiques* (Centre Jean Palerne, Mémoires V), Saint-Étienne, 7–32.

– 1992, "Notes on the Text, Language and Content of Some New Fragments of Pelagonius", *CQ* n.s. 42, 489–509.

– 1995, *Pelagonius and Latin Veterinary Terminology in the Roman Empire*, Leiden/New York/Cologne, 1995.

Albrecht, M. von, 1994, *Geschichte der römischen Literatur: von Andronicus bis Boethius. Mit Berücksichtigung ihrer Bedeutung für die Neuzeit*, 2 vols., Munich.

Alföldi, A., 1943, *Die Kontorniaten. Ein verkanntes Propagandamittel der stadtrömischen heidnischen Aristokratie in ihrem Kampfe gegen das christliche Kaisertum*, Budapest.

– 1959, "Cornuti: A Teutonic Contingent in the Service of Constantine the Great and its Decisive Role in the Battle at the Milvian Bridge", *DOP* 13, 169–179.

Alston, R., 1994, "Roman Auxiliary Pay from Caesar to Diocletian", *JRS* 84, 113–123.

Anderson, R.C., 1962, *Oared Fighting Ships: From Classical Times to the Coming of Steam*, London.

Anderson, W.B. (trans.), 1936–1965, *Sidonius. Poems and Letters*, 2 vols. (Loeb Classical Library), London/Cambridge, MA.

Andersson, A., 1937, *Studia Vegetiana*, Uppsala.

Angliviel de la Beaumelle, L., 1974, "Remarques sur l'attitude d'Ammien Marcellin à l'égard du christianisme", in *Mélanges d'histoire ancienne offerts à William Seston*, Paris, 15–23.

Arnaud-Lindet, M.-P. (ed. & trans.), 1990–1991, *Orose. Histoire contre les païens*, 3 vols. (Collection Budé), Paris.

Baatz, D., 2000, "Vegetius' Legion and the Archaeological Facts", in Brewer, R.J. (ed.), *Roman Fortresses and their Legions*, London/Cardiff, 149–157.

– and Bockius, R., 1997, *Vegetius und die römische Flotte*, Mainz.

Bachrach, B.S., 1973, *A History of the Alans in the West*, Minneapolis.

Baldini, A., 1999, "Un'ipotesi su una tradizione occidentale post-flavianea", in Paschoud, F. (ed.), *Historiae Augustae Colloquium Genevense* (Historiae Augustae Colloquia, n.s. VII), Bari, 15–33.

Baldwin, B., 1978, "Festus the Historian", *Historia* 27, 197–217.

Barnes, T.D., 1968, Review of J.W. Eadie: *The Breviarium of Festus*, *JRS* 58, 263–265.

– 1978, *The Sources of the* Historia Augusta (Collection Latomus 155), Brussels.

– 1979, "The Date of Vegetius", *Phoenix* 33, 254–257.

– 1995, "The Sources of the Historia Augusta (1967–1992)", in Bonamente, G. and Paci, G. (eds.), *Historiae Augustae Colloquium Maceratense* (Historiae Augustae Colloquia, n.s. III), Bari, 1–34.

– 1998, *Ammianus Marcellinus and the Representation of Historical Reality*, Ithaca/London.

Barrow, R.T. (ed. & trans.), 1973, *Prefect and Emperor*, Oxford.

Baynes, N.H., 1926, *The Historia Augusta: Its Date and Purpose*, Oxford.

Bennett, J., 1991, "*Plumbatae* from Pitsunda (Pityus), Georgia, and Some Observations on their Probable Use", *JRMES* 2, 59–63.

– 1997, *Trajan: Optimus Princeps: A Life and Times*, London/New York.

Berthelot, M., 1900, "Sur le traité *de rebus bellicis* qui accompagne la *Notitia Dignitatum* dans les manuscrits", *JS*, 171–177.

Bertrand-Dagenbach, C., 1990, *Alexandre Sévère et l'*Histoire Auguste (Collection Latomus 208), Brussels.

Birley, A.R., 1971, *Septimius Severus*, London.

–   1974, "Roman Frontiers and Roman Frontier Policy: Some Reflections on Roman Imperialism", *TAASDN* 3, 13–25.

–   1983–1984, "Magnus Maximus and the Persecution of Heresy", *BJRUL* 66, 13–43.

–   1997, *Hadrian: The Restless Emperor*, London/New York.

–   forthcoming, "Rewriting Second- and Third-Century History in Late Antique Rome: The *Historia Augusta*", in *Proceedings of the XIIth Congress of the Fédération internationale des associations des études classiques (FIEC), Ouro Preto, August 2004*.

Birley, E., 1988, "The Dating of Vegetius and the *Historia Augusta*", in Id. (ed.), *The Roman Army: Papers 1929–1986*, Amsterdam, 58–68 = 1985, *Bonner Historia-Augusta-Colloquium 1982/83*, Bonn, 57–67.

Bishop, M.C., 2002, *Lorica Segmentata, Vol. I. A Handbook of Articulated Plate Armour* (*JRMES* Monograph No. 1), Duns.

–   and Coulston, J.C.N., 1993, *Roman Military Equipment from the Punic Wars to the Fall of Rome*, London.

Blackman, D.R. and Betts, G.G., 1989, *Concordantia in Vegetii Opera*, Hildesheim/Zürich/New York.

Bleckmann, B., 1995, "Bemerkungen zu den *Annales* des Nicomachus Flavianus", *Historia* 45, 83–99.

–   1997, "Honorius und das Ende der römischen Herrschaft in Westeuropa", *HZ* 265, 561–595.

Bloch, M., 1945, "A New Document of the Last Pagan Revival in the West, 393–394 A.D.", *HThR* 28, 199–244.

Blockley, R.C., 1975, *Ammianus Marcellinus. A Study of his Historiography and Political Thought*, Brussels.

–   1998, "Warfare and Diplomacy", in Cameron, A. and Garnsey, P.G., *CAH²* XIII, Cambridge, 411–436.

Boak, A.E.R., 1974, *Manpower Shortage and the Fall of the Roman Empire in the West*, Westport, CT.

Bonamente, G., 1981, "Considerazioni sul *De rebus bellicis*", *AFLM* 14, 9–49.

Bonanni, S., 1981, "Ammiano Marcellino e i barbari", *RCCM* 23, 125–142.

Born, L.K., 1934, "The Perfect Prince According to the Latin Panegyrists", *AJPh* 55, 20–35.

Brandt, H., 1988, *Zeitkritik in der Spätantike. Untersuchungen zu den Reformvorschlägen des Anonymus De rebus bellicis*, Munich.

Brennan, P., 1996, "The *Notitia Dignitatum*", in Gros, P. (ed.), *Les littératures techniques dans l'antiquité romaine*, Geneva, 147–178.

–   1998, "The User's Guide to the *Notitia Dignitatum*: The Case of the *Dux Armeniae* (*ND Or.* 38)", *Antichthon* 32, 34–49.

Buck, D.F., 1988, "Eunapius of Sardis and Theodosius the Great", *Byzantion* 58, 36–53.

Burns, T.S., 1994, *Barbarians within the Gates of Rome: A Study of Roman Military Policy and the Barbarians, ca. 375–425 A.D.*, Bloomington/Indiananopolis.

Bury, J.B., 1919, "Justa Grata Honoria", *JRS* 9, 1–33.

Calderone, S., 1973, "Teologia politica, successione dinastica e consecratio in età costantiniana", in den Boer, W. (ed.), *Le culte des souverains dans l'empire romain*, Geneva, 213–261.

Cameron, A., 1964, "Christianity and Tradition in the Historiography of the Late Empire", *CQ* 58, 316–328.

–   1969a, Review of J. W. Eadie: *The Breviarium of Festus*, *CR* n.s. 19, 305–307.

–   1969b, "Theodosius the Great and the Regency of Stilico", *HSPh* 73, 247–280.

–   1970, *Claudian: Poetry and Propaganda at the Court of Honorius*, Oxford.

– 1971, Review of R. Syme: *Ammianus and the Historia Augusta*, *JRS* 61, 255–267.
– 1977, "Paganism and Literature in the Late Fourth Century", in Id. (ed.), *Christianisme et formes littéraires de l'antiquité tardive en Occident*, Bern, 1–40.
– 1979, "The Date of the Anonymus *De Rebus Bellicis*", in Hassall, M.W.C. (ed.), *De Rebus Bellicis Part I: Aspects of the De Rebus Bellicis* (BAR International Series 63), Oxford, 1–10.
– 1988, "Flavius: A Nicety of Protocol", *Latomus* 47, 26–33.
– 1998, "Education and Literary Culture", in Cameron, A. and Garnsey, P.G., *CAH*² XIII, Cambridge, 665–707.
– 1999, "The Last Pagans of Rome", in Harris, W.V. (ed.), *The Transformations of Urbs Roma in Late Antiquity* (JRA Supplement 33), Portsmouth, 109–121.
– and Long, J., with Sherry, L., 1993, *Barbarians and Politics at the Court of Arcadius*, Berkeley/Los Angeles/Oxford.
— 2004, "Vergil Illustrated between Pagan and Christians: Reconsidering the 'Late-4th c. Classical Revival', the Dates of the Manuscripts, and the Places of Production of the Latin Classics", *JRA* 17, 502–525.
Camões, L. de, 1973, *Os Lusiadas*, ed. Pierce, F., Oxford.
Campbell, B., 1984, *The Emperor and the Roman Army, 31 B.C.–A.D. 235*, Oxford.
– 2002, *War and Society in Imperial Rome 31 BC–AD 284*, London/New York.
Campenhausen, H. von, 1929, *Ambrosius von Mailand als Kirchenpolitiker*, Berlin/Leipzig.
Camus, P.-M., 1967, *Ammien Marcellin: témoin des courants culturels et religieux à la fin du IVᵉ siècle*, Paris.
Capitani, U., 1980, "Una Presenza di Vitruzio in Vegezio", *Maia* 32, 179–185.
Caprino, C., *et al.*, 1955, *La colonna di Marco Aurelio*, Rome.
Cesa, M. and Sivan, H., 1990, "Alarico in Italia: Pollenza e Verona", *Historia* 39, 361–374.
Chadwick, N.K., 1958, "The Name Pict", *SGS* 8, 146–176.
Chantraine, P., 1984, *Dictionnaire étymologique de la langue grecque*, Paris.
Charles, M.B., 2002, "*Caluus Nero*: Domitian and the Mechanics of Predecessor Denigration", *AClass* 45, 19–49.
– 2003, "Vegetius on Armour: The *Pedites Nudati* of the *Epitoma Rei Militaris*", *AncSoc* 30, 127–167.
– 2004a, "*Mattiobarbuli* in Vegetius' *Epitoma Rei Militari*: The *Iouiani* and the *Herculiani*", *AHB* 18, 109–121.
– 2004b, "Mons Graupius Revisited: Tacitus, Agricola and Auxiliary Infantry", *Athenaeum* 92, 129–140.
– 2004c, Review of M.D. Reeve, *Vegetius. Epitoma Rei Militaris*, *BMCR* 2004, 11.16.
– 2005a, "Transporting the Troops in Late Antiquity: *Naves Onerariae*, Claudian and the Gildonic War", *CJ* 100, 275–299.
– 2005b, "Vegetius on *Liburnae*: Naval Terminology in the Late Roman Period", *SCI* 24, 181–193.
Chastagnol, A., 1960, *La préfecture urbaine à Rome sous le Bas-Empire*, Paris.
– 1970, *Recherches sur l'Histoire Auguste, avec un rapport sur les progrès de la Historia-Augusta-Forschung depuis 1963*, Bonn.
– 1974, "Végèce et l'Histoire Auguste", in *Bonner Historia-Augusta-Colloquium 1971*, Bonn, 59–80.
Cheesman, G.L., 1914, *The Auxilia of the Roman Imperial Army*, Oxford.
Cherry, D., 2001, *The Roman World: A Sourcebook*, Malden, MA/Oxford/Carlton.
Christiansen, P.G., 1966, "Claudian versus the Opposition", *TAPhA* 97, 45–54.
– 1997, "Claudian: A Greek or Latin?", *Scholia* 6, 79–95.
Clemente, G., 1968, *La 'Notitia Dignitatum'*, Cagliari.
Clover, F.M., 1966, *Geiseric*, diss., University of Chicago.
– (trans.), 1971, *Flavius Merobaudes: A Translation and Historical Commentary*, Philadelphia.

–   1979, "Count Gaïnas and Count Sebastian", *AJAH* 4, 65–76.

Colgrave, B., 1940, *Two Lives of Saint Cuthbert: A Life by an Anonymous Monk of Lindisfarne and Bede's Prose Life*, Cambridge.

Collingwood, R.G. and Myres, J.N.L., 1937, *Roman Britain and the English Settlements*[2], Oxford.

Conte, G.B., 1987, *Latin Literature: A History*, trans. Solodow, J.B., Baltimore/London.

Couissin, P., 1926, *Les armes romaines*, Paris.

Coulston, J.C.N., 1990, "Later Roman Armour, 3rd–6th centuries A.D.", *JRMES* 1, 139–160.

–   2000, "'Armed and Belted Men': The Soldiery in Imperial Rome", in Coulston, J.C.N. and Dodge, H., *Ancient Rome: The Archaeology of the Eternal City*, Oxford, 76–118.

Courtois, C., 1964, *Les Vandales et l'Afrique*, Aalen.

Cowan, R., 2003, *Imperial Roman Legionary AD 161–284*, Oxford.

Cracco Ruggini, L., 1977, "Apoteosi e politica senatoria nel IV s. d.C.: il dittico dei Symmachi al British Museum", *RSI* 89, 425–489.

Crump, G.A., 1975, *Ammianus Marcellinus as a Military Historian*, Wiesbaden.

Dahm, M. K., 1999, "A Hendiadys in the Breviarium of Festus: A 'Literary' Festus?", *Prudentia* 31, 15–22.

Dagron, G., 1969, "Aux origines de la civilisation byzantine: langue de culture et langue d'État", *RH* 241, 23–56.

Dalmasso, L., 1907, "La storia di un estratto di Vegezio. Saggio sulla fortuna dell'«Epitoma rei militaris»", *Rendiconti, Reale Istituto Lombardo di Scienze e Lettere* 2.140, 805–814.

Daly, G., 2002, *Cannae: The Experience of Battle in the Second Punic War*, London/New York.

Dante Alighieri, 1972, *La divina commedia*, ed. Grandgent, C.H., rev. Singleton, C.S., Cambridge, MA.

–   1993, *The Divine Comedy*, trans. Sisson, C.H., introd. & notes Higgins, D.H., Oxford.

Davies, R.W., 1968, "Fronto, Hadrian and the Roman Army", *Latomus* 27, 75–95.

Defarrari, J. (trans.), 1964, *Orosius. The Seven Books of History against the Pagans*, Washington, DC.

Degen, R., 1992, "Plumbatae. Wurfgeschosse der Spätantike", *HA* 23, 139–147.

De Jonge, P., 1955, "Ammianus and Vegetius", in de Jonge, P. *et al.* (eds.), *Ut pictura poesis: Studia Latina Petro Iohanni Enk septuagenario oblata*, Leiden, 99–106.

Demandt, A., 1969, "Der Tod des älteren Theodosius", *Historia* 18, 598–626.

Demougeot, E., 1951, *De l'unité à la division de l'empire romain, 395–410. Essai sur le gouvernement impérial*, Paris.

–   1975, "La *Notitia dignitatum* et l'histoire de l'Empire d'Occident au début du Ve siècle", *Latomus* 34, 1079–1134.

Den Boer, W., 1972, *Some Minor Roman Historians*, Leiden.

Dessau, H., 1889, "Über Zeit und Persönlichkeit der S.H.A.", *Hermes* 24, 337–392.

–   1892, "Über die S.H.A.", *Hermes* 27, 561–605.

DeVoto, J. G. (ed. & trans.), 1993, *Τέχνη Τακτική (Tactical Handbook) and Ἔκταξις κατὰ Ἀλανῶν (The Expedition Against the Alans)*, Chicago.

Dixon, K.R. and Southern, P., 1992, *The Roman Cavalry*, London.

Dorjahn, A.P. and Born, L.K., 1934, "Vegetius on the Decay of the Roman Army", *CJ* 30, 148–158.

Dove, C.E., 1971, "The First British Navy", *Antiquity* 45, 15–20.

Duchesne, L., 1909–1924, *Early History of the Christian Church from its Foundation to the End of the Fifth Century*, 3 vols., London.

Dunkle, J.R., 1971, "The Rhetorical Tyrant in Roman Historiography: Sallust, Livy and Tacitus", *CW* 64, 12–20.

Eadie, J.W. (ed.), 1967, *Festus. Breuiarium*, London.

Egger, R., 1929, "Der erste Theodosius", *Byzantion* 5, 27–32.

Elbern, S., 1987, "Das Gotenmassaker in Kleinasien (378 n. Chr.)", *Hermes* 115, 99–106.

Elton, H., 1996, *Warfare in Roman Europe, A.D. 350–425*, Oxford.

Ensslin, W., 1923, *Zur Geschichtsschreibung und Weltanschauung des Ammianus Marcellinus* (Klio Beiträge zur alten Geschichte 16), Leipzig.

Ehrhardt, A., 1964, "The First Two Years of the Emperor Theodosius I", *JEH* 15, 1–17.

Errington, R.M., 1996a, "The Accession of Theodosius I", *Klio* 78, 438–453.

–   1996b, "Theodosius and the Goths", *Chiron* 26, 1–27.

Ferrill, A., 1986, *The Fall of the Roman Empire: The Military Explanation*, London.

–   1991, *Roman Imperial Grand Strategy*, Lanham, MD.

Festy, M. (ed. & trans.), 1999, *Abrégé des Césars* (Collection Budé), Paris.

Feugère, M., 2002, *Weapons of the Romans*, trans. Smith, D.G., Stroud, Glos.

Fiebiger, O. and Schmidt, L., 1917, *Inschriftensammlung zur Geschichte der Ostgermanen*, Vienna.

Finch, C.E., 1962, "Codices Pal. Lat. 1571–1573 as Sources for Vegetius", *TAPhA* 93, 22–29.

Fischer, K.-D., 1981a, "Pelagonius on Horse Medicine", in Cairns, F. (ed.), *Papers of the Liverpool Latin Seminar* III, Liverpool, 285–303.

–   1981b, "The First Latin Treatise on Horse Medicine and its Author Pelagonius Saloninus", *Medizinhistorisches Journal* 16, 215–226.

–   1991, "*Genera huius morbi maleos numero VII*: eine Infektionskrankheit (*Malleus*) und ihre Unterarten im Spiegel des antiken veterinärmedizinischen Schrifttums", in Sabbah, G. (ed.), *Le latin médical: la constitution d'un langage scientifique*, Saint-Étienne, 351–366.

Fornara, C.W., 1992, "Studies in Ammianus Marcellinus", *Historia* 41, 328–344.

Formisano, M. (trans.), 2003, *P. Flavio Vegezio Renato. L'arte della guerra romana*, Milan.

Förster, J.W., 1879, *De Fide Flavii Vegetii Renati*, Bonn.

–   1895, *Quaestiones Vegetianae*, Rheydt.

Foraboschi, D., 1987, "Economia e guerra nel *De rebus bellicis*", in *Studi di antichità in memoria di Clementina Gatti*, Milan, 111–127.

Frank, R.I., 1969, *Scholae Palatinae: The Palace Guards of the Later Roman Empire*, Rome.

Frend, W.H.C., 1984, *The Rise of Christianity*, Philadelphia.

Gabriel, R.A. and Boose, D.W., 1994, *The Great Battles of Antiquity. A Strategic and Tactical Guide to Great Battles that Shaped the Development of War*, Westport, CT/London.

Galdi, M., 1922, *L'epitome nella letteratura latina*, Naples.

Galletier, E. (ed. & trans.), 1955, *Panégyriques latins* III (Collection Budé), Paris.

Gardiner, R. (ed.), 1995, *The Age of the Galley: Mediterranean Oared Vessels since Pre-Classical Times*, London.

Garlan, Y., 1972, *La guerre dans l'antiquité*, Paris.

Gasparini, N., 1972, "La morte di Teodosio padre", in Sordi, M. (ed.), *Contributi dell'Istituto di storia antica* I, Milan, 180–197.

Gatier, P.-L., 1998, "Les inscriptions grecques et latines de Samra et de Rihab", in Humbert, J.-B. and Desreumaux, A. (eds.), *Fouilles de Khirbet es-Samra, Jordanie. I. La voie romaine; le cimetière; les documents épigraphiques*, Paris, 359–431.

Gauld, W.W., 1990, "Vegetius on Roman Scout-boats", *Antiquity* 64, 402–406.

Gemoll, A., 1872, "Exercitationes Vegetianae", *Hermes* 6, 113–118.

Gibbon, E., 1994, *The History of the Decline and Fall of the Roman Empire*, 3 vols., ed. Womersley, D., Harmondsworth.

Gigli, G., 1946, "La flotta e la difesa del Basso Impero", *RAL* 8.1, 3–43.

–   1947, "Forme di reclutamento militare durante il basso impero", *RAL* 8.2, 268–289.

Gil Egea, M.E., 1997, "Piratas o estadistas: la política exterior del reino vándalo durante el reinado de Genserico", *Polis* 9, 107–129.

Gilliver, C.M., 1999, *The Roman Art of War*, Stroud, Glos./Charleston, SC.

Giuffrida Manmana, C., 1981, "Per una datazione dell'*Epitoma rei militaris* di Vegezio: politica
    e propaganda nell'età di Onorio", *SicGymn* 34, 25–56.
–   (trans.), 1997, *Flavio Vegezio Renato: Compendio delle istituzioni militari*[2], Catania.
Gladys, M., 1960, "Claudian, an Intellectual Pagan of the Fourth Century", in Lawler, L.B.,
    Robathan, D.M. and Korfmacher, W.C. (eds.), *Studies in Honor of B. Ullman. Presented to
    him on the Occasion of his Seventy-fifth Birthday*, Saint Louis, 69–80.
Gnecchi, F., 1912, *I medaglioni romani*, 2 vols., Bologna.
Gnilka, C., 1976, "Dichtung und Geschichte im Werk Claudians", *FMS* 10, 96–123.
Goffart, W., 1977, "The Date and Purpose of Vegetius' *De Re Militari*", *Traditio* 33, 65–100 =
    1989, *Rome's Fall and After*, London/Ronceverte, 45–80.
–   1980, *Barbarians and Romans, A.D. 418–584*, Princeton.
Goldsworthy, A., 2000, *Roman Warfare*, London.
–   2003, *The Complete Roman Army*, London.
Gordon, C.D., 1974, "Vegetius and His Proposed Reforms of the Army", in Evans, J.A.S. (ed.),
    Polis and Imperium: Studies in Honour of Edward Togo Salmon, Toronto, 35–55.
Grant, M., 1971, *Gladiators*, Harmondsworth.
Green, R.P.H., 1991, *The Works of Ausonius*, Oxford.
–   (ed.), 1999, *Decimi Magni Ausonii Opera* (Bibliotheca Oxoniensis), Oxford.
Gregory, T.E., 2005, *A History of Byzantium*, Malden, MA/Oxford/Carlton, Vic.
Grosse, R., 1913, "Das römische-byzantinische Marschlager vom 4.–10. Jahrhundert", *ByzZ* 22,
    90–121.
–   1920, *Römische Militärgeschichte von Gallienus bis zum Beginn der byzantinischen Themen-
    verfassung*, Berlin.
Grumel, V., 1951, "L'Illyricum de la mort de Valentinien Ier (375) à la mort de Stilicon (408)",
    REByz 9, 5–46.
Guillerm, A., 1993, *La marine de guerre antique*, Paris.

Haase, G.H.C., 1860, "De latinorum codd. mss. subscriptionibus commentatio cum Hrabani
    Mauri, ut videtur, ad Lotharium Imperatorem et Theodori Gazae ad Antonium Panormitam
    epistolis et carmine Brunosis", in *Index lectionum in universitate Vratislaviensi per hiemem
    a. MDCCCLX. a die XV. mensis octobris habendarum*, Breslau, 3–24.
Hanslik, R., 1942, "Pacatus" (2), *RE* XVIII.2, 2058–2060.
Hardie, A., 1983, *Statius and the Silvae: Poets, Patrons and Epideixis in the Graeco-Roman
    World*, Liverpool.
Harmand, J., 1986, "L'armement défensif romain de métal dans le nord-ouest de l'empire, de la
    conquête au Ve siècle", *Caesarodunum* 22, 189–203.
Harries, J., 1984, "Prudentius and Theodosius", *Latomus* 43, 69–84.
Hartke, W., 1938, "Zwei chronologische Fragen um Nicomachus Flavianus", *Klio* 31, 430–436.
–   1951, *Römische Kinderkaiser. Eine Strukturanalyse römischen Denkens und Daseins*, Ber-
    lin.
Harvey, P. (ed.), 1937, *The Oxford Companion to Classical Literature*, Oxford.
Hassall, M.W.C., 1979, "The Inventions", in Hassall, M.W.C. (ed.), *De Rebus Bellicis Part I:
    Aspects of the De Rebus Bellicis* (BAR International Series 63), Oxford, 77–95.
Heather, P., 1986, "The Crossing of the Danube and the Gothic Conversion", *GRBS* 27, 289–
    318.
–   1988, "The Anti-Scythian Tirade of Synesius' *De Regno*", *Phoenix* 42, 152–172.
–   1991, *Goths and Romans 332–489*, Oxford.
–   1998, "Themistius: A Political Philosopher", in Whitby, M. (ed.), *The Propaganda of
    Power: The Role of Panegyric in Late Antiquity*, Leiden/Boston/Cologne, 125–150.
–   and Moncur, D. (ed. & trans.), 2001, *Politics, Philosophy, and Empire in the Fourth
    Century. Select Orations of Themistius*, Liverpool.
Heimsoeth, F. (ed.), 1843, "C. Fr. Heinrichii reliquiae nonnullae criticae", *RMPh* 2.2, 531–543.

Hermann, F.X., 2000, Review of D. Baatz and R. Bockius: *Vegetius und die römische Flotte*, *Gymnasium* 97, 259.

Hocker, F.M., 1995, "Late Roman, Byzantine, and Islamic Galleys and Fleets", in Gardiner, R. (ed.), *The Age of the Galley: Mediterranean Oared Vessels since Pre-Classical Times*, London, 86–100.

Hoepffner, A., 1936, "La mort du magister militum Théodose", *REL* 14, 119–129.

Holmes, N., 2002, "Metrical Notes on Vegetius' *Epitoma Rei Militaris*", *CQ* n.s. 52, 358–373.

Honoré, T., 1987, "Scriptor Historiae Augustae", *JRS* 77, 156–176.

Hopkins, K., 1983, *Death and Renewal. Sociological Studies in Roman History Volume 2*, Cambridge.

Hoppe, K., 1927, "Die commenta artis medicinae veterinariae des Pelagonius", *Veterinärhist. Jahrb.* 3, 189–219.

– 1928, "Pelagoniusstudien", *Veterinärhist. Jahrb.* 4, 1–40.

– 1933, "Mulomedicina", *RE* XVI.1, 503–513.

Ireland, R.I. (ed. & trans.), 1979, *De Rebus Bellicis: The Text*, in Hassall, M.W.C. (ed.), *Aspects of the De Rebus Bellicis. Papers presented to E.A. Thompson* (BAR International Series 63), Oxford.

Jähns, M., 1966, *Geschichte der Kriegswissenschaften vornehmlich in Deutschland* I, New York/Hildesheim, repr. of 1889 edn.

James, S., 1984, "Britain and the Late Roman Army", in Blagg, T.F.C. and King, A.C. (eds.), *Military and Civilian in Roman Britain. Cultural Relationships in a Frontier Province* (BAR British Series 136), Oxford, 161–186.

Johne, K.-P., 1976, *Kaiserbiographie und Senatsaristokratie. Untersuchungen zur Datierung und sozialen Herkunft der Historia Augusta*, Berlin.

Johnson, J.S., 1979, "Frontier Policy in the Anonymus", in Hassall, M.W.C. (ed.), *De Rebus Bellicis Part I: Aspects of the De Rebus Bellicis* (BAR International Series 63), Oxford, 67–75.

Jones, A.H.M., 1960, *Studies in Roman Government and Law*, Oxford.

– 1964, *The Later Roman Empire 284–602*, 3 vols., Oxford.

– Martindale, J.R. and Morris, J., 1971–1992, *The Prosopography of the Later Roman Empire*, 4 vols., Cambridge.

Jones, B.W., 1992, *The Emperor Domitian*, London.

Jones, C.W., 1932, "Bede and Vegetius", *CR* 46, 248–249.

Josephs, A. and Caballero, J., 1992, *Federico García Lorca: La casa de Bernarda Alba*[19], Madrid.

Jullian, C., 1884, "La carrière d'un soldat au quatrième siècle", *Bulletin Épigraphique* 4, 1–12.

Junkelmann, M., 1986, *Die Legionen des Augustus. Der römische Soldat im archäologischen Experiment*, Mainz.

Kaufmann, G., 1872, "Wurde Theodosius von Gratian zunächst zum Magister Militum und erst nach einem Siege über die Sarmaten zum Kaiser ernannt?", *Philologus* 31, 473–480.

Keenan, J.G., 1973–1974, "The Names Flavius and Aurelius as Status Designations in Later Roman Egypt", *ZPE* 11, 33–63 and *ZPE* 13, 283–304.

– 1983, "An Afterthought on the Names Flavius and Aurelius", *ZPE* 53, 245–250.

Kennedy, D.L., 2000, *The Roman Army in Jordan*, London.

– and MacAdam, H., 1985, "Some Latin Inscriptions from the Azraq Oasis, Jordan", *ZPE* 60, 97–107.

Kidd, B.J., 1922, *A History of the Church to A.D. 461*, 3 vols., Oxford.

Kienast, D., 1966, *Untersuchungen zu den Kriegsflotten der römischen Kaiserzeit*, Bonn.

Knowles, C., 1954, "Jean de Vignay, un traducteur du XIVe siècle", *Romania* 75, 353–383.

Koep, L., 1958, "Die Konsekrationsmünzen Kaiser Konstantins und ihre religionspolitische Bedeutung", *JbAC* 1, 94–104.

Krentz, P. and Wheeler, E.L. (trans.), 1994, *Polyaenus: Stratagems of War*, 2 vols., Chicago.

Kubitschek, W., 1925, "Legio (der späteren Zeit)", *RE* XII.2, 1829–1837.

Lacarra, J.M., 1945, "Textos navarros del Códice de Roda", *Estudios de Edad Media de la corona de Aragón* 1, 193–275.

Ladner, G.B., 1976, "On Roman Attitudes toward Barbarians in Late Antiquity", *Viator* 7, 1–26.

Lammert, F., 1930, "Mattiobarbuli", *RE* XIV.2, 2323.

– 1931, "Zu Vegetius' Epitome rei militaris IV 1–30", *PhW*, 27 June (no. 26), 798–800.

– 1940a, "Die älteste erhaltene Schrift über Seetaktik und ihre Beziehung zum Anonymus Byzantinus des 6. Jahrhunderts, zu Vegetius und zu Aineias' Strategika", *Klio* 33, 271–288.

– 1940b, "Ennius, Livius XXI 49–51 und Vegetius De re militari IV 32", *WS* 58, 89–95.

Lang, C., (ed.), 1867, *Flavi Vegeti Renati Epitoma rei militaris* (Bibliotheca Teubneriana), Stuttgart/Leipzig.

– (ed.), 1885, *Flavi Vegeti Renati Epitoma rei militaris*[2] (Bibliotheca Teubneriana), Leipzig.

Lauffer, S., 1971, *Diokletians Preisedikt*, Berlin.

Legge, M.D., 1953, "The Lord Edward's Vegetius", *Scriptorium* 7, 262–264.

Lenski, N., 1997, "*Initium mali Romano imperio*: Contemporary Reactions to the Battle of Adrianople", *TAPhA* 127, 333–352.

Levy, H.L., 1948, "Claudian's Neglect of Magic as a Motif", *TAPhA* 79, 86–91.

Lindsay, H., 1993, "Two New Texts from the 4th Century A.D.", Reviews of Eutropius: *Breviarum*, trans. H.W. Bird and Vegetius: *Epitome of Military Science*, trans. N.P. Milner, *Classicum* 19, Oct. 40–41.

Lippold, A., 1968, "Herrscherideal und Traditionsverbundenheit im Panegyricus des Pacatus", *Historia* 17, 228–250.

– 1980, *Theodosius der Große und seine Zeit*, Munich.

Löfstedt, L., 1976, "La réduplication synonymique de Jean de Meun dans sa traduction de Végèce", *NPhM* 77, 449–470.

Lommatzsch, E. (ed.), 1903, *Vegetii Digesta artis mulomedicinae libri* (Bibliotheca Teubneriana), Leipzig.

Lőrincz, B., 2002, *Onomasticon Provinciarum Europae Latinarum* IV, Vienna.

MacCracken, H.N., 1913, "Vegetius in English: Notes on the Early Translations", in *Anniversary Papers by Colleagues and Pupils of G.L. Kittridge*, Boston/London, 389–403.

MacDowall, S., 1994, *Late Roman Infantryman 236–565 A.D.*, London.

Mackail, J.W., 1920, "Ammianus Marcellinus", *JRS* 10, 103–118.

MacMullen, R., 1960, "Inscriptions on Armour and the Supply of Arms in the Roman Empire", *AJA* 64, 23–40.

– 1980, "How Big was the Roman Imperial Army?", *Klio* 62, 451–460.

Maenchen-Helfen, O.J., 1955, "The Date of Ammianus Marcellinus' Last Books", *AJPh* 76, 384–399.

– 1973, *The World of the Huns*, Berkeley.

Magie, H. (trans.), 1921–1932, *The Scriptores Historiae Augustae*, 3 vols. (Loeb Classical Library), London/Cambridge, MA.

Malcovati, E., 1942, "I breviari del IV secolo", *AFLC* 21, 5–11.

Malosse, P.-L., 1997, "Libanius on Constantine Again", *CQ* n.s. 47, 519–524.

Mango, C., 1985, *Le développement urbain de Constantinople (IVᵉ–VIIᵉ siècles)*, Paris.

Mann, J.C., 1976, "What was the Notitia Dignitatum For?", in Goldburn, R. and Bartholomew, P. (eds.), *Aspects of the Notitia Dignitatum* (BAR Supplementary Series 15), Oxford, 1–9.

Marcone, A., 1981, "Il «De re militari» di Vegezio", *SRIC* 1, 121–137.

Martin, G., 1960, "Claudian, an Intellectual Pagan of the Fourth Century", in Lawler, L.B.,

Robathan, D.M. and Korfmacher, W.C. (eds.), *Studies in Honor of B. Ullman. Presented to him on the Occasion of his Seventy-fifth Birthday*, St. Louis, 69–80.

Matthews, J.F., 1971, "Gallic Supporters of Theodosius", *Latomus* 30, 1073–1099.

– 1975, *Western Aristocracies and the Imperial Court*, Oxford.

– 1983, "Ammianus' Historical Evolution", in Croke, B. and Emmet, A.M. (eds.), *History and Historians in Late Antiquity*, Sydney/Oxford/New York, 30–41.

– 1986, "Ammianus and the Eternity of Rome", in Holdsworth, C. and Wiseman, T.P. (eds.), *The Inheritance of Historiography, 350–900*, Exeter, 17–29.

– 1989, *The Roman Empire of Ammianus*, Baltimore.

Maxfield, V.A., 1986, "Pre-Flavian Forts and their Garrisons", *Britannia* 17, 59–72.

Mazzarino, S., 1942, *Stilicone. La crisi imperiale dopo Teodosio*, Rome.

– 1951, *Aspetti sociali del quarto secolo*, Rome.

– 1956, *Trattato di storia romana* II, Rome.

Meyer, P., 1896, "Les anciens traducteurs français de Végèce, et en particulier Jean de Vignai", *Romania* 25, 401–423.

Mezzabotta, M.R., 2000, "Aspects of Multiculturalism in the *Mulomedicina* of Vegetius", *Akroterion* 45, 52–64.

Millar, F., 1977, *The Emperor in the Roman World: 31 B.C.–A.D. 337*, Ithaca, NY.

Milner, N.P. (trans.), 1996, *Vegetius: Epitome of Military Science*[2], Liverpool.

Mócsy, A., 1964, "Der Name Flavius als Rangbezeichnung in der Spätantike", in *Akte des IV. internationalen Kongresses für griechische und lateinische Epigraphik*, Vienna, 257–263.

– et al., 1983, *Nomenclator: provinciarum Europae Latinarum et Galliae Cisalpinae cum indice inverso* (Dissertationes Pannonicae 3.1), Budapest.

Moore, C.H., 1910, "Rome's Heroic Past in the Poems of Claudian", *CJ* 50, 108–115.

Momigliano, A., 1977, "Pagan and Christian Historiography in the Fourth Century A.D.", in Id. (ed.), *Essays in Ancient and Modern Historiography*, Oxford, 107–140.

Mommsen, T., 1965, *Gesammelte Schriften* VIII, *Epigraphische und numismatische Schriften* I, Berlin/Dublin/Zürich, repr. of 1913 edn.

Montross, L., 1960, *War Through the Ages*[3], New York/Evanston/London.

Morales Belda, F., 1969, *La marina vándala: los Asdingos en España*, Barcelona.

Morazzani, A., 1966, "Essai sur la puissance maritime des Vandales", *BAGB* 4.1, 539–561.

Moss, J.R., 1973, "The Effects of the Policies of Aetius on the History of Western Europe", *Historia* 77, 711–731.

Müller, F.M. (ed. & trans.), 1997, *Publius Flavius Vegetius Renatus. Abriß des Militärwesens*, Stuttgart.

Naudé, C.P.T., 1984, "The Date of the Later Books of Ammianus Marcellinus", *AJAH* 9, 70–94.

Neumann, A.R., 1965, "Publius (Flavius) Vegetius Renatus", *RE Suppl.* X, 992–1020.

Nicasie, M.J., 1998, *Twilight of Empire. The Roman Army from the Reign of Diocletian until the Battle of Adrianople*, Amsterdam.

Niebuhr, B.G., 1824, *Fl. Merobaudis carminum panegyrique reliquiae*[2], Bonn.

Nixon, C.E.V. (trans.), 1987, *Pacatus. Panegyric to the Emperor Theodosius*, Liverpool.

O'Donnell, J.J., 1979, *Cassiodorus*, Berkeley/Los Angeles/London.

O'Flynn, J.M., 1983, *Generalissimos of the Western Roman Empire*, Edmonton.

Ogilvie, R.M. and Richmond, I., 1967, *Cornelii Taciti de Vita Agricolae*, Oxford.

Ogilvy, J.D.A., 1967, *Books Known to the English, 597–1066*, Cambridge, MA.

Olajos, T., 1966, "Merobaudes Müvei", *Antik Tanulmányok* 13, 172–188.

Oman, C., 1905, *A History of the Art of War: The Middle Ages from the Fourth to the Fourteenth Century*, London.

Önnerfors, A., 1991, "Zu Person und Werk des Publius Flavius Vegetius Renatus", *Vetenskaps-societetens i Lund, Årsbok 1991*, Lund, 142–173.

– (ed.), 1995, *Vegetii Epitoma rei militaris* (Bibliotheca Teubneriana), Stuttgart/Leipzig.

Oost, S.I., 1962, "Count Gildo and Theodosius the Great", *CPh* 57, 27–30.
–   1964, "Aëtius and Majorian", *CPh* 59, 23–29.
–   1965, "Some Problems in the History of Galla Placidia", *CPh* 60, 1–10.
–   1983, *Galla Placidia Augusta: A Biographical Essay*, Chicago/London.
Opelt, T., 1960, "Epitome", *RLAC* Lief. 138, 944–973.
Orlandis, J., 1977, *Historia de España. La España visigótica*, Madrid.

Paniagua Aguilar, D. (trans.), 2006, *Flavio Vegecio Renato. Compendio de técnica militar*, Madrid.
Paschoud, F., 1967, *Roma aeterna. Études sur le patriotisme romain dans l'Occident latin à l'époque des grandes invasions*, Rome.
–   (ed. & trans.), 1971–1979, *Zosime. Histoire nouvelle*, 3 vols. (Collection Budé), Paris.
–   1975, *Cinq études zur Zosime*, Paris.
–   1991, "L'Histoire Auguste et Dexippe", in Bonamente, G. and Duval, N. (eds.), *Historiae Augustae Colloquium Parisinum* (Historiae Augustae Colloquia, n.s. I), Macerata, 217–269.
–   1900, "Nicomaque Flavien et la connexion byzantine (Pierre le Patrice et Zonaras): à propos du livre récent de Bruno Bleckmann", *AntTard* 2, 71–82.
–   2000a, "Symmaque, Jérôme et l'Histore Auguste", *MH* 57, 173–182.
–   2000b, *Zosime. Histore nouvelle*, vol. I² (Collection Budé), Paris.
–   (ed. & trans.), 2001, *Histoire Auguste. Vies de Probus, Firmus, Saturnin, Proculus et Bonose, Carus Numérien et Carin*, vol. V.2 (Collection Budé), Paris.
–   2005, "Biographie und Panegyricus: Wie spricht man vom lebenden Kaiser?", in Vössing, K. (ed.), *Biographie und Prosopographie. Internationales Kolloquium zum 65. Geburtstag von Anthony R. Birley* (Historia Einzelschriften 178), Stuttgart, 103–118.
Passerini, A., 1946–1985, "Legio", *Diz. Epigr.* IV.2, 549–628.
Peachin, M., 1985, "The Purpose of Festus' Breviarium", *Mnemosyne* 38, 158–161.
Pellegrino, M. (ed.), 1961, *Paulino di Milano. Vita di S. Ambrogio*, Rome.
Perea Yébenes, S., 2004, "*Cornicularius seu princeps*. La transformación de la función y del «Rangordnung» del *cornicularius* en tiempos de Valentiniano I", in Le Bohec, Y. and Wolff, C. (eds.), *L'armée romaine de Dioclétien à Valentinien Ier. Actes du Congrès de Lyon (12–14 septembre 2002)*, Paris, 451–472.
Phillips, T.R. (ed.), 1985, *The Military Institutions of the Romans*, translation of Vegetius by Clark, J., Westport, CT, first published London 1767.
Piganiol, A., 1972, *L'Empire chrétien (325–395)*², Paris.
Planck, M., 1877, *Der Verfall des römischen Kriegswesens am Ende des vierten Jahrhunderts n. Chr. Eine Kriegsgeschichtliche Studie nach Vegetius*, Stuttgart.
Platnauer, M. (trans.), 1922, *Claudian*, 2 vols. (Loeb Classical Library), London/Cambridge, MA.
Polverini, L., 2001, "Ancora la *Historia Augusta*", *Athenaeum* 89, 615–620.

Ramsay, W., 1867, "Vegetius", in Smith, W. (ed.), *Dictionary of Greek and Roman Biography and Mythology*, 3 vols., London, 1235–1236.
Rankov, B., 1994, *The Praetorian Guard*, London.
Raven, S., 1969, *Rome in Africa*, London.
Rebuffat, R., 1978, "Végèce et le télégraphie Chappe", *MEFRA* 90, 829–861.
Reddé, M., 1986, *Mare Nostrum: les infrastructures, le dispositif et l'histoire de la marine militaire sous l'empire romain*, Rome.
Reeve, M.D., 1995, "Editorial Opportunities and Obligations", *RFIC* 123, 479–499.
–   1998, "Notes on Vegetius", *PCPhS* 44, 182–218.
–   2000, "The Transmission of Vegetius's *Epitoma Rei Militaris*", *Aevum* 74, 243–354.
–   (ed.), 2003, *Vegetius. Epitoma Rei Militaris* (Bibliotheca Oxoniensis), Oxford.
Reinach, S., 1922, "Un homme à projets du Bas-Empire", *RA* 5.16, 205–265.

Reyniers, F., 1938, "Végèce et l'instruction des cadres et de la troupe dans l'armée romaine", *RMG* 2, 759–773.

Rice, D.T., 1959, *The Art of Byzantium*, New York.

Richardot, P., 1998, "La datation du De Re Militari de Végèce", *Latomus* 57, 136–147.

–   2003, "La tradition moderne du *De re militari* de Végèce (XVᵉ–XVIIIᵉ siècles)", in De-fosse, P. (ed.), *Hommage a Carl Deroux. Tome V: Christianisme et Moyen Âge, Néo-latin et survivance de la latinité*, Brussels, 537–544.

Richmond, I.A., 1963, *Roman Britain*[2], Harmondsworth.

Richter, H., 1865, *Das weströmische Reich, besonders unter dem Kaisern Gratian, Valentinian II. und Maximus (375–338)*, Berlin.

Ridley, R.T. (trans.), 1982, *Zosimus. New History*, Canberra.

Robert, L., 1940, *Les gladiateurs dans l'orient grec*, Paris.

Rolfe, J.C., 1919, "Claudian", *TAPhA* 50, 135–149.

–   (trans.), 1950–1952, *Ammianus Marcellinus*, rev. edn., 3 vols. (Loeb Classical Library), London/Cambridge, MA.

Rosen, K., 1982, *Ammianus Marcellinus*, Darmstadt.

Rossi, L., 1971, *Trajan's Column and the Dacian Wars*, trans. Toynbee, J.M.C., London.

Rowell, H.T., 1967, "Ammianus Marcellinus, Soldier-historian of the Late Roman Empire", in Taft Semple, L. and Blegen, C.W. (eds.), *Lectures in Memory of Louise Taft Semple 1961–1965*, Princeton.

Rubio, L., 1973, "El ms. *Scorialensis* L.III. 33: nuevos datos para una futura edición del *Epitoma Rei Militaris* de Vegetius", *Emerita* 41, 209–223.

Sabbah, G., 1980, "Pour la datation théodosienne du De Re Militari de Végèce", in *Centre Jean Palerne, Mémoires* 2, Saint-Étienne, 131–155.

–   2004, "L'armée romaine de Dioclétien à Valentinien Iᵉʳ. Les sources littéraires", in Le Bohec, Y. and Wolff, C. (eds.), *L'armée romaine de Dioclétien à Valentinien Iᵉʳ. Actes du Congrès de Lyon (12–14 septembre 2002)*, Paris, 31–41.

Sablayrolles, R., 1984, "Bibliographie sur l'Epitoma rei militaris de Végèce", in *Cahiers du groupe de recherches sur l'armée et les provinces* III, Paris, 139–146.

Samberger, C., 1969, "Die 'Kaiserbiographie' in den Res Gestae des Ammianus Marcellinus. Eine Untersuchung zur Komposition der ammianeischen Geschichtsshreibung", *Klio* 51, 349–482.

Sander, E., 1927, "Zu Vegetius II 19; 21", *PhW* 15 Oct. no. 41/42, 1278–1280.

–   1928, "Zu Vegetius IV, 38; 41", *PhW* 21 July no. 29, 908–910.

–   1929, "Frontin als Quelle für Vegetius", *PhW* 5 Oct. no. 40, 1230–1231.

–   1930, "Die historischen Beispiele in der Epitome des Vegetius", *PhW* 2 Aug. no. 31, 955–958.

–   1931, "Die Quellen von IV, 1–30 der Epitome des Vegetius", *PhW* 28 Mar. no. 13, 395–399.

–   1932, "Die Hauptquellen der Bücher I–III der epitoma rei militaris des Vegetius", *Philologus* 87, 369–375

–   1939, "Die Germanisierung des römischen Heeres", *HZ* 160, 1–34.

–   1956, "Die Quellen des Buches IV 31–46 der Epitome des Vegetius", *RMPh* 99, 153–172.

–   1957, "Zur Rangordnung des römischen Heeres: die Flotten", *Historia* 6, 347–367.

Sanders, H.A., 1897, *Quellencontamination in 21. und 22. Buche des Livius*, Berlin.

–   1904, "The Lost Epitome of Livy", in Id. (ed.), *Roman Historical Sources and Institutions*, New York/London, 149–260.

Schamp, J., 2001, "Claudien le «Paphlagonien», poète d'Alexandrie", *Latomus* 60, 971–991.

Schanz, M., 1881, "Zu den Quellen des Vegetius", *Hermes* 16, 137–146.

–   1914, *Geschichte der römischen Literatur. Bis zum Gesetzgebungswerk des Kaisers Justinian*[2] IV.1, Munich.

Schenk, D., 1930, *Die Quellen der Epitoma rei militaris des Flavius Renatus Vegetius*, diss., Erlangen/Leipzig.

Schenk von Stauffenberg, A., 1947, *Das Imperium und die Völkerwanderung*, Munich.

Schlumberger, J., 1974, *Die Epitome de Caesaribus. Untersuchungen zur heidnischen Geschichtsschreibung des 4. Jahrhunderts n. Chr.*, Munich.

– 1985, "Die verlorenen Annalen des Nicomachus Flavianus: Ein Werk über Geschichte der römischen Republik oder der Kaiserzeit?", in *Bonner Historia-Augusta-Colloquium 1982/ 83*, Bonn, 305–329

Schmidt, L., 1953, *Histoire des Vandales*, trans. del Medico, H.E., Paris.

– 1969, *Die Ostgermanen*², Munich, repr. of 1941 edn.

Schneider, R., 1910, "Vom Büchlein De Rebus Bellicis", *NJKA* 13, 327–342.

Schöner, C., 1888, "Studien zu Vegetius", *Programm der Königlichen bayerischen Studienanstalt zu Erlangen zum Schluss des Schuljahres 1887/88*, Erlangen, 3–44.

Schröder, B.-J., 1999, *Titel und Text: zur Entwicklung lateinischer Gedichtüberschriften: mit Untersuchungen zu lateinischen Buchtiteln, Inhaltsverzeichnissen und anderen Gliederungsmitteln*, Berlin/New York.

Schwabe, L. 1913, s.v. "Vegetius", in Teuffel, W.S. *et al.* (eds.), *Geschichte der römischen Literatur*² III, Leipzig, 317.

Sebesta, J.L., 1978, "On Stilicho's Consulship: Variations on a Theme by Claudian", *CB* 54, 72–75.

Seeck, O., 1876, "Die Zeit des Vegetius", *Hermes* 11, 61–83.

– (ed.), 1883, *Q. Aurelii Symmachi quae supersunt* (*MGH:AA* 6.1), Berlin.

– 1894a, "Ammianus" (4), *RE* I.2, 1845–1852.

– 1894b, "Anonymi" (3), *RE* I.2, 2325.

– 1912, "Gerontius" (6), *RE* VII.1, 1270.

– and Veith, G., 1913, "Die Schlacht am Frigidus", *Klio* 13, 451–467.

Sekunda, N., 1984, *The Army of Alexander the Great*, London.

– 1996, *Republican Roman Army 200–104 B.C.*, London.

Selem, A., 1964, "Considerazioni circa Ammiano ed il cristianismo", *RCCM* 6, 224–261.

Settis, S. (ed.), 1988, *La colonna traiana*, Turin.

Sherwood, F.H., 1980, *Studies in Medieval Uses of Vegetius'* Epitoma rei militaris, diss., University of California, Los Angeles.

Shrader, C.R., 1976, *The Ownership and Distribution of Manuscripts of the* De re militari *of Flavius Vegetius Renatus before the Year 1300*, diss., Columbia University.

– 1979, "A Handlist of Extant Manuscripts Containing the *De re militari* of Flavius Vegetius Renatus", *Scriptorium* 83, 280–305.

– 1981, "The Influence of Vegetius' *De re militari*", *Military Affairs* 45, 167–172.

Silhanek, D.K., 1972, *Vegetius' 'Epitoma', Books 1 and 2: A Translation and Commentary*, diss., New York University.

Singleton, C.S., 1975, *Dante Alighieri. The Divine Comedy: Paradiso, 2. Commentary*, Princeton.

Sirago, V.A., 1961, *Galla Placidia e la trasformazione politica dell'Occidente*, Louvain.

Sivan, H.S., 1985, "An Unedited Letter of the Emperor Honorius to the Spanish Soldiers", *ZPE* 61, 273–287.

——— 1996, "Was Theodosius I a Usurper?", *Klio* 78, 198–211.

Spaulding, O.L., 1933, "The Ancient Military Writers", *CJ* 29, 657–669.

Speidel, M.A., 1992, "Roman Army Pay Scales", *JRS* 82, 87–106.

Speidel, M.P., 1965, *Die Equites Singulares Augusti: Begleittruppe der römischen Kaiser des zweiten und dritten Jahrhunderts*, Bonn.

– 1973, "The Pay of the Auxilia", *JRS* 63, 141–147.

– 1975a, "The Rise of Ethnic Units in the Roman Imperial Army", *ANRW* II.3, 202–231.

– 1975b, "Vegetius on Trumpets", *AClass* 18, 153–155.

–   1987, "The Later Roman Field Army and the Guard of the High Empire", *Latomus* 46, 375–
     379 = Id., 1992, *Roman Army Studies: Volume Two*, Stuttgart, 379–384.
–   1994, *Riding for Caesar: The Roman Emperor's Horse Guards*, Cambridge, MA.
Springer, M., 1979, "Vegetius im Mittelalter", *Philologus* 123, 85–90.
Stein, E., 1959, *Histoire du Bas-Empire*², 2 vols., trans. Palanque, J.-R., Amsterdam.
–   1962, *Untersuchungen zum Officium der praetorianer Präfektur*², Amsterdam.
Stephenson, I.P., 1999, *Roman Infantry Equipment: The Later Empire*, Stroud, Glos.
Stelten, L.F., 1968, "Vegetius and the Military", *CB* 44, 70–71.
–   (ed. & trans.), 1990, *Flavius Renatus Vegetius. Epitoma Rei Militaris*, New York.
Stevens, C.E., 1957, "Marcus, Gratian, Constantine", *Athenaeum* 25, 316–347.
–   1979, "Summing Up", in Hassall, M.W.C. (ed.), *De Rebus Bellicis Part I: Aspects of the De
     Rebus Bellicis* (BAR International Series 63), Oxford, 129–131.
Stoian, I., 1967, "À-propos de la conception historique d'Ammien Marcellin", *Latomus* 26, 73–
     81.
Straub, J., 1943, "Die Wirkung der Niederlage bei Adrianopel auf die Diskussion über das
     Germanenproblem in der spätrömischen Literatur", *Philologus* 49, 255–286.
–   1952, *Studien zur Historia Augusta*, Bern.
Stroheker, K.F., 1970, *Der senatorische Adel im spätantiken Gallien*, Darmstadt, repr. of 1948
     edn.
Syme, R., 1958, *Tacitus*, 2 vols., Oxford.
–   1968, *Ammianus and the Historia Augusta*, Oxford.
–   1971a, *Emperors and Biography: Studies in the Historia Augusta*, Oxford.
–   1971b, *The Historia Augusta: A Call of Clarity*, Bonn.
–   1972, "The Composition of the Historia Augusta: Recent Theories", *JRS* 62, 123–133.
–   1983, *Historia Augusta Papers*, Oxford.

Tavender, L., 1972, "Camouflage in the First British Navy", *Antiquity* 46, 320–322.
Testi Rasponi, A., 1926, "Analecta ravennatia, I: Frammenti poetici di Merobaude", *FR* 31, 43–
     47.
Teuffel, W.S., 1892, *History of Roman Literature*, 2 vols., rev. Schwade, L., trans. Warr,
     G.C.W., London.
–   1913, *Geschichte der römischen Literatur* III⁶, Leipzig.
Thesaurus linguae latinae, 1900–1964, 10 vols., in many parts, Leipzig.
Thompson, E.A., 1947, *The Historical Work of Ammianus Marcellinus*, Cambridge.
–   (ed. & trans.), 1952, *A Roman Reformer and Inventor: Being a New Text of the Treatise De
     Rebus Bellicis*, Oxford.
–   1956, "Zosimus on the End of Roman Britain", *Antiquity* 30, 163–167.
–   1966, "Ammianus Marcellinus", in Dorey, T.A. (ed.), *Latin Historians*, London, 143–157.
Thorpe, L., 1952, "Mastre Richard: A Thirteenth-century Translator of the "De Re Militari" of
     Vegetius", *Scriptorium* 6, 39–50.
Tomlin, R.S.O., 1989, "The Late-Roman Empire", in Hackett, J. (ed.), *Warfare in the Ancient
     World*, New York, 222–249.
–   1990, "The Army of the Late Empire", in Wacher, J. (ed.), *The Roman World* I, London/
     New York, 107–135.
–   2000, "The Legions in the Late Empire", in Brewer, R.J. (ed.), *Roman Fortresses and their
     Legions*, London/Cardiff, 149–157.
Toynbee, P., 1968, *A Dictionary of Proper Names and Notable Matters in the Works of Dante*,
     rev. Singleton, C.S., Oxford.
Tränkle, H., 1962, "Ammianus Marcellinus als römischer Geschichtsschreiber", *A&A* 11, 21–
     33.

Urbainczyk, T., 1998, "Vice and Advice in Socrates and Sozomen", in Whitby, M. (ed.), *The*

Propaganda of Power: The Role of Panegyric in Late Antiquity, Leiden/Boston/Cologne, 299–319.

Várady, L., 1961, "New Evidences on Some Problems of the Late Roman Military Organization", *AAntHung* 9, 333–396.

Vera, D., 1981, *Commento storico alle* Relationes *di Quinto Aurelio Simmaco*, Pisa.

Viré, G., 1998, "La description de la morve dans la *Mulomedicina Chironis* et dans la *Mulomedicina* de Végèce", in Deroux, C. (ed.), *Maladie et maladies dans les textes latins antiques et médiévaux. Actes du Ve Colloque International 'Textes médicaux latins' (Bruxelles, 4–6 septembre 1995)*, Brussels, 260–275.

Vollmer, F. (ed.), 1904, *Merobaudes: quae supersunt* (in *MGH:AA* 14), Berlin, 1–20.

Wace, A.J.B. and Traquair, R., 1909, "The Base of the Obelisk of Theodosius", *JHS* 29, 60–69.

Waldeyer-Hartz, H. von, 1937, "Die Seeherrschaft der Wandalen", *Marine Rundschau* 42, 137–147.

Wallace-Hadrill, A., 1995, *Suetonius: The Scholar and His Caesars*², London.

Ward, J.H., 1974, "The *Notitia Dignitatum*", *Latomus* 33, 397–434.

Watson, G.R., 1969, *The Roman Soldier*, London.

Webster, G., 1985, *The Roman Imperial Army*³, London.

Wheeler, E.L., 1983, "The *Hoplomachoi* and Vegetius' Spartan Drillmasters", *Chiron* 13, 1–20.

–   2004, "The Legion as Phalanx in the Late Empire", in Le Bohec, Y. and Wolff, C. (eds.), *L'armée romaine de Dioclétien à Valentinien Ier. Actes du Congrès de Lyon (12–14 septembre 2002)*, Paris, 309–358.

White, H.G.E. (trans.), 1919–1921, *Ausonius*, 2 vols. (Loeb Classical Library), London/Cambridge, MA.

Wiedemann, T., 1979, "Petitioning a Fourth-century Emperor: The *De Rebus Bellicis*", *Florilegium* 1, 140–150.

–   1992, *Emperors and Gladiators*, London/New York.

Williams, S. and Friell, G., 1994, *Theodosius: The Empire at Bay*, London.

Wisman, J.A., 1979, "L'*Epitoma rei militaris* de Végèce et sa fortune au Moyen Âge", *MA* 85, 13–31.

Wölfflin, E. von, 1902, "Epitome", in Id. (ed.), *ALL* XI, Leipzig, 333–344, 445–454.

–   1904, "Das Breviarium des Festus", in Id. (ed.), *ALL* XIII, Leipzig, 68–97, 173–180.

Wolfram, H., 1988, *History of the Goths*, trans. Dunlap, T.J., Berkeley/Los Angeles/London.

Wytzes, J., 1977, *Der letzte Kampf des Heidentums in Rom*, Leiden.

Zaffagno, E., 1991, "*I prologhi della* Mulomedicina *di Publio Vegezio Renato*", in Santini, C. and Scivoletto, N. (eds.), *Prefazioni, prologhi, proemi di opere scientifiche latine* I, Rome, 259–291.

Zuckerman, C., 1991, "Cappadocian Fathers and the Goths", *T&MByz* 11, 473–486.

–   1994, "Aur. Valerianus (293/305) et Fl. Severinus (333), commandants en Arabie, et la forteresse d'Azraq", *AntTard* 2, 83–88.

–   1994, "Sur la date du traité militaire de Végèce et son destinataire Valentinien II", *SCI* 13, 67–74.

INDEX NOMINVM ET RERVM

The names of emperors and major usurpers are as commonly used. Other names are listed as per *PLRE*; thus 'Virius Nicomachus Flavianus' appears under 'Flavianus, Virius Nicomachus'.

HISTORIA-EINZELSCHRIFTEN

Herausgegeben von **Kai Brodersen, Mortimer Chambers, Martin Jehne, François Paschoud**
und **Aloys Winterling**

---

85. **Werner Huß: Der makedonische König und die ägyptischen Priester.** Studien zur Geschichte des ptolemaiischen Ägypten. 1994. 238 S., kt. 6502-3
86. **Gerold Walser: Studien zur Alpengeschichte in antiker Zeit.** 1994. 139 S. u. 10 Taf., kt. 6498-9
87. **David Whitehead** (ed.): **From Political Architecture to Stephanus Byzantius.** Sources for the Ancient Greek Polis. 1994. 124 S., 11 Abb., kt.

6572-6
(zugleich: Papers from the Copenhagen Polis Centre, Vol. 1)
88. **Bernhard Kremer: Das Bild der Kelten bis in augusteische Zeit.** Studien zur Instrumentalisierung eines antiken Feindbildes bei griechischen und römischen Autoren. 1994. 362 S., kt. 6548-1
89. **Joachim Szidat: Historischer Kommentar zu Ammianus Marcellinus Buch XX-XXI. Teil III: Die Konfrontation.** 1996. 293 S., kt.
(vgl. Bde. 31 u. 38) 6570-2
90. **Odile De Bruyn: La compétence de l'Aréopage en matière de procès publics.** Des origines de la polis athénienne à la conquête romaine de la Grèce (vers 700–146 avant J.-C.). 1995. 226 S., kt.

6654-9
91. **Lothar Wierschowski: Die regionale Mobilität in Gallien nach den Inschriften des 1. bis 3. Jahrhunderts n. Chr.** Quantitative Studien zur Sozial- und Wirtschaftsgeschichte der westlichen Provinzen des Römischen Reiches. 1995. 400 S., kt. 6720-1
92. **Joachim Ott: Die Beneficiarier.** Untersuchungen zu ihrer Stellung innerhalb der Rangordnung des Römischen Heeres und zu ihrer Funktion. 1995. 246 S., kt. 6660-0
93. **Andrew Drummond: Law, Politics and Power.** Sallust and the Execution of the Catilinarian Conspirators. 1995. 136 S., kt. 6741-6
94. **Heinrich Schlange-Schöningen: Kaisertum und Bildungswesen im spätantiken Konstantinopel.** 1995. VIII, 189 S., kt. 6760-7
95. **Mogens Herman Hansen and Kurt Raaflaub** (ed.): **Studies in the Ancient Greek Polis.** 1995. 219 S., kt. 6759-1
(zugleich: Papers from the Copenhagen Polis Centre, Vol. 2)
96. **Martin Jehne** (Hg.): **Demokratie in Rom?** Die Rolle des Volkes in der Politik der römischen Republik. 1995. VII, 141 S., kt. 6860-4
97. **Valerie M. Warrior: The Initiation of the Second Macedonian War.** An Explication of Livy Book 31. 1996. 118 S., kt. 6853-6
98. **Raimund Friedl: Der Konkubinat im kaiserzeitlichen Rom.** Von Augustus bis Septimius Severus. 1996. 417 S., kt. 6871-0
99. **Christopher Tuplin: Achaemenid Studies.** 1996. 226 S., kt. 6901-4
100. **Marlis Weinmann-Walser** (Hg.): **Historische Interpretationen.** Gerold Walser zum 75. Geburtstag dargebracht von Freunden, Kollegen und Schülern. 1995. 212 S. m. 3 Taf., kt. 6739-3
101. **Leonhard A. Burckhardt: Bürger und Soldaten.** Aspekte der politischen und militärischen Rolle athenischer Bürger im Kriegswesen des 4. Jahrhunderts v. Chr. 1996. 300 S., kt. 6832-1
102. **Julia Heskel: The North Aegean Wars, 371–360 B.C.** 1997. 186 S., kt. 6917-5
103. **Lukas Thommen: Lakedaimonion Politeia.** Die Entstehung der spartanischen Verfassung. 1996. 170 S, kt. 6918-2
104. **Luisa Prandi: Fortuna e realtà dell'opera di Clitarco.** 1996. 203 S., kt. 6947-2

105. **Jerzy Linderski** (ed.): **Imperium sine fine:** T. Robert S. Broughton and the Roman Republic. 1996. X, 234 S. u. 1 Taf., kt. 6948-9
106. **Karl Christ: Griechische Geschichte und Wissenschaftsgeschichte.** 1996. 238 S. m. 7 Taf., kt. 6915-1
107. **Eric W. Robinson: The First Democracies:** Early Popular Government Outside Athens. 1997. 144 S., kt. 6951-9
108. **Mogens Herman Hansen / Kurt Raaflaub,** (ed.): **More Studies in the Ancient Greek Polis.** 1996. 196 S., kt. 6969-4
(zugleich: Papers from the Copenhagen Polis Centre, Vol. 3)
109. **Victor Parker: Untersuchungen zum Lelantischen Krieg.** 1997. 189 S., kt. 6970-0
110. **Ulrich Gotter: Der Diktator ist tot!** Politik in Rom zwischen den Iden des März und der Begründung des Zweiten Triumvirats. 1996. 316 S., kt. 6815-4
111. **François Paschoud / Joachim Szidat,** (Hg.): **Usurpationen in der Spätantike.** Akten des Kolloquiums „Staatsstreich und Staatlichkeit", 6.–10. März 1996, Solothurn/Bern. 1997. 174 S., kt.

7030-0
112. **Ulrich Huttner: Die politische Rolle der Heraklesgestalt im griechischen Herrschertum.** 1997. IX, 385 S., kt. 7039-3
113. **Robert E. A. Palmer: Rome and Carthage at Peace.** 1997. 152 S., kt. 7040-9
114. **Hans Beck: Polis und Koinon.** Untersuchungen zur Geschichte und Struktur der griechischen Bundesstaaten im 4. Jahrhundert v. Chr. 1997. 320 S., kt. 7117-8
115. **Heinz Bellen: Politik – Recht – Gesellschaft.** Studien zur Alten Geschichte. Hg. von Leonhard Schumacher. 1997. VIII, 323 S., 24 Taf., kt.

7150-5
116. **Carsten Drecoll: Die Liturgien im römischen Kaiserreich des 3. und 4. Jh. n. Chr.** Untersuchung über Zugang, Inhalt und wirtschaftliche Bedeutung der öffentlichen Zwangsdienste in Ägypten und anderen Provinzen. 1997. 401 S., kt.

7151-2
117. **Thomas Heine Nielsen** (ed.): **Yet More Studies in the Ancient Greek Polis.** 1997. 258 S., kt.

7222-9
118. **Gerold Walser: Bellum Helveticum.** 1998. 192 S., kt. 7248-9
119. **Frank Bernstein: Ludi publici.** Untersuchung zur Entstehung und Entwicklung der öffentlichen Spiele im republikanischen Rom. 1998. 408 S., kt. 7301-1
120. **Robert J. Buck: Thrasybulus and the Athenian Democracy.** The Life of an Athenian Statesman. 1998. 141 S., kt. 7221-2
121. **Gocha R. Tsetskhladze,** (ed.): **The Greek Colonisation of the Black Sea Area.** Historical Interpretation of Archaeology. 1998. 336 S. m. 44 Abb., kt. 7302-8
122. **Josef Wiesehöfer** (Hg.): **Das Partherreich und seine Zeugnisse.** Beiträge des internationalen Colloquiums, Eutin (27.–30. Juni 1996). 1998. 570 S. m. zahlr. Abb., kt. 7331-8
123. **Jeffrey D. Lerner: The Impact of Seleucid Decline on the Eastern Iranian Plateau.** 1999. 139 S., kt. 7417-9
124. **Attilio Mastrocinque: Studi sulle guerre mitridatiche.** 1999. 128 S., kt. 7418-6
125. **Fabio Mora: Fasti e schemi cronologici.** La riorganizzazione annalistica del passato remoto romano. 1999. 425 S., kt. 7191-8

126. **Karl-Ernst Petzold: Geschichtsdenken und Geschichtsschreibung.** Kleine Schriften zur griechischen und römischen Geschichte. 1999. 629 S., kt. 7458-2

127. **Martin Zimmermann, (Hg.): Geschichtsschreibung und politischer Wandel im 3. Jh. n. Chr.** Kolloquium zu Ehren von **Karl-Ernst Petzold** (Juni 1998) anläßlich seines 80. Geburtstags. 1999. 244 S., kt. 7457-5

128. **Alexander Yakobson: Elections and Electioneering in Rome.** A Study in the Political System of the Late Republic. 1999. 251 S., kt. 7481-0

129. **Ralf Urban: Gallia rebellis.** Erhebungen in Gallien im Spiegel antiker Zeugnisse. 1999. 165 S., kt. 7383-7

130. **Markus Sehlmeyer: Stadtrömische Ehrenstatuen der republikanischen Zeit.** Historizität und Kontext von Symbolen nobilitären Standesbewußtseins. 1999. 319 S., kt. 7479-7

131. **Karl-Joachim Hölkeskamp: Schiedsrichter, Gesetzgeber und Gesetzgebung im archaischen Griechenland.** 1999. 343 S., kt. 6928-1

132. **Gary Forsythe: Livy and Early Rome.** A Study in Historical Method and Judgment. 1999. 147 S., kt. 7495-7

133. **Dirk Henning: Periclitans res publica.** Kaisertum und Eliten in der Krise des Weströmischen Reiches 454/5–493 n.Chr. 1999. 362 S., kt. 7485-8

134. **Hartwin Brandt (Hg.): Gedeutete Realität.** Krisen, Wirklichkeiten, Interpretationen (3.–6. Jh. n. Chr.). 1999. 151 S., kt. 7519-0

135. **Richard W. Burgess: Studies in Eusebian and Post-Eusebian Chronography.** 1. The Chronici canones of Eusebius of Caesarea: Structure, Content, and Chronology, AD 282–325. 2. The Continuatio Antiochiensis Eusebii: A Chronicle of Antioch and the Roman Near East during the Reigns of Constantine and Constantius II, AD 325–350. 1999. 358 S., kt. 7530-5

136. **Christoph R. Hatscher: Charisma und res publica.** Max Webers Herrschaftssoziologie und die Römische Republik. 2000. 263 S., kt. 7523-7

137. **Boris Dreyer: Untersuchungen zur Geschichte des spätklassischen Athen 323–ca. 230 v. Chr.** 1999. 487 S., kt. 7531-2

138. **Pernille Flensted-Jensen (ed.): Further Studies in the Ancient Greek Polis.** 2000. 256 S., kt. 7607-4

139. **Stanisław Mrozek: Faenus.** Studien zu Zinsproblemen zur Zeit des Prinzipats. 2001. 124 S., kt. 7617-3

140. **Maria H. Dettenhofer: Herrschaft und Widerstand im augusteischen Principat.** 2000. 234 S., kt. 7639-5

141. **Bernhard Linke / Michael Stemmler (Hg.): Mos maiorum.** Untersuchungen zu den Formen der Identitätsstiftung und Stabilisierung in der römischen Republik. 2000. VII, 319 S., kt. 7660-9

142. **Loren J. Samons II: Empire of the Owl.** Athenian Imperial Finance. 2000. 358 S., kt. 7664-7

143. **Gregor Weber: Kaiser, Träume und Visionen in Prinzipat und Spätantike.** 2000. XIV, 585 S., geb. 7681-4

144. **Martin Ostwald: Oligarchia.** The Development of a Constitutional Form in Ancient Greece. 2000. 96 S., kt. 7680-7

145. **Hilmar Klinkott: Die Strapienregister der Alexander- und Diadochenzeit.** 2000. 130 S., kt. 7701-9

146. **Karl-Wilhelm Welwei: Polis und Arché.** Kleine Schriften zu Gesellschafts- und Herrschaftsstrukturen in der griechischen Welt. Hg. von **Mischa Meier.** 2000. 427 S., geb. 7759-0

147. **Lene Rubinstein: Litigation and Cooperation.** Supporting Speakers in the Courts of Classical Athens. 2000. 296 S., kt. 7757-6

148. **Pierre Sánchez: L'Amphictionie des Pyles et de Delphes.** Recherches sur son rôle historique, des origines au IIe siècle de notre ère. 2001. 574 S., geb. 7785-9

149. **Fritz Gschnitzer: Kleine Schriften zum griechischen und römischen Altertum.** Bd. 1: Frühes Griechentum: Historische und sprachwissenschaftliche Beiträge. Hg. von **Catherine Trümpy** und **Tassilo Schmitt.** 2001. XXXI, 364 S., kt. 7805-4

150. **Eckard Lefèvre: Panaitios' unnd Ciceros Pflichtenlehre.** Vom philosophischen Traktat zum politischen Lehrbuch. 2001. 226 S., kt. 7820-7

151. **Giuseppe Zecchini: Cesare e il mos maio-rum.** 2001. 180 S., kt. 7863-4

152. **Leone Porciani: Prime forme della storiografia greca.** Prospettiva locale e generale nella narrazione storica. 2001. 156 S., kt. 7869-6

153. **Maria R.-Alföldi: Gloria Romanorvm.** Schriften zur Spätantike. Zum 75. Geburtstag der Verfasserin am 6. Juni 2001. Hg. von **Heinz Bellen** und **Hans-Markus von Kaenel.** 2001. XI, 381 S. m. zahlr. Abb., geb. 7918-1

154. **Karen Piepenbrink: Ordnungskonzeptionen in der attischen Demokratie des vierten Jahrhunderts v. Chr.** Eine vergleichbare Untersuchung zum philosophischen und rhetorischen Diskurs. 2001. 262 S., kt. 7848-1

155. **Peter Siewert (Hg.): Ostrakismos-Testimonien I.** Die Zeugnisse antiker Autoren, der Inschriften und Ostraka über das athenische Scherbengericht aus vorhellenistischer Zeit (487–322 v. Chr.). In Zusammenarbeit mit **Stefan Brenne, Birgitta Eder, Herbert Heftner** und **Walter Scheidel.** 2002. 555 S., geb. 7947-1

156. **Jyri Vaahtera: Roman Augural Lore in Greek Historiography.** A Study of the Theory and Terminology. 2001. 194 S., kt. 7946-4

157. **Marietta Horster: Bauinschriften römischer Kaiser.** Untersuchungen zu Inschriftenpraxis und Bautätigkeit in Städten des westlichen Imperium Romanum in der Zeit des Prinzipats. 2001. X, 496 S., geb. 7951-8

158. **Michael Lovano: The Age of Cinna: Crucible of Late Republican Rome.** 2002. 188 S., kt. 7948-8

159. **Lothar Wierschowski: Fremde in Gallien – „Gallier" in der Fremde.** Die epigraphisch bezeugte Mobilität in, von und nach Gallien vom 1. bis 3. Jh. n.Chr. (Texte – Übersetzungen – Kommentare). 2001. 526 S., geb. 7970-9

160. **René S. Bloch: Antike Vorstellungen vom Judentum.** Der Judenexkurs des Tacitus im Rahmen der griechisch-römischen Ethnographie. 2002. 260 S., kt. 7971-6

161. **Sabine Panzram: Stadtbild und Elite: Tarraco, Corduba und Augusta Emerita zwischen Republik und Spätantike.** 2002. Ca. 370 S., geb. 8039-2

162. **Thomas Heine Nielsen (ed.): Even more Studies in the Ancient Greek Polis.** 2002. 294 S., kt. 8102-3 (zugl.: Papers from the Copenhagen Polis Centre, Vol. 6)

163. **Sophia Aneziri: Die Vereine der dionysischen Techniten im Kontext der hellenistischen Gesellschaft.** Untersuchungen zur Geschichte, Organisation und Wirkung der hellenistischen Technitenvereine. 2003. 542 S., kt. 8126-9

164. **Gregor Weber / Martin Zimmermann (Hg.):**

Propaganda – Selbstdarstellung – Repräsentation im römischen Kaiserreich des 1. Jhs n. Chr. 2003. 355 S., kt.   8251-8

165. **Eckhard Meyer-Zwiffelhoffer: Πολιτικῶς ἄρχειν.** Zum Regierungsstil der senatorischen Statthalter in den kaiserzeitlichen griechischen Provinzen. 2002. 369 S., kt.   7648-7

166. **Pamela-Jane Shaw: Discrepancies in Olympiad Dating and Chronological Problems of Archaic Peloponnesian History.** 2003. 280 S., kt. 8174-0

167. **Fritz Gschnitzer: Kleine Schriften zum griechischen und römischen Altertum.** Bd. 2: Historische und epigraphische Studien zur Alten Geschichte seit den Perserkriegen. Hg. von **Catherine Trümpy.** 2003. XXX, 519 S., kt.   8037-8

168. **Rainer Bernhardt: Luxuskritik und Aufwandsbeschränkungen in der griechischen Welt.** 2003. 422 S., geb.   8320-1

169. **Christoph R. Hatscher: Alte Geschichte und Universalhistorie.** Weltgeschichtliche Perspektiven aus althistorischerSicht. 2003. 144 S. m. 7 Abb., kt.   8321-8

170. **Claudia Ruggeri: Gli stati intorno a Olimpia.** Storia e costituzione dell'Elide e degli stati formati dai perieci elei (400–362 a.C.). 2004. 244 S., kt. 8322-5

171. **Franca Landucci Gattinoni: L'arte del potere.** Vita e opere di Cassandro di Macedonia. 2003. 184 S., kt.   8381-2

172. **Christopher Tuplin (ed.): Xenophon and his World.** Papers from a conference held in Liverpool in July 1999. 2004. 524 S. m. 2 Ktn. u. 4 Taf., geb.   8392-8

173. **Alexander Weiß: Sklave der Stadt.** Untersuchungen zur öffentlichen Sklaverei in den Städten des Römischen Reiches. 2004. 265 S., kt.   8383-6

174. **Gerald Kreucher: Der Kaiser Marcus Aurelius Probus und seine Zeit.** 2003. 298 S., kt.   8382-9

175. In Vorbereitung

176. **Anthony Francis Natoli; The Letter of Speusippus to Philip II.** Introduction, Text, Translation and Commentary. With an Appendix on the Thirty-First Socratic Letter attributed to Plato. 2004. 196 S., kt.   8396-6

177. **Karl-Wilhelm Welwei: Res publica und Imperium.** Kleine Schriften zur römischen Geschichte. Hg. von **Mischa Meier** u. **Meret Strothmann.** 2004. 328 S., geb.   8333-1

178. **Konrad Vössing: Biographie und Prosopographie.** Internationales Kolloquium zum 65. Geburtstag von Anthony R. Birley . 2005. 146 S., 2 Taf., kt.   8538-0

179. **Vera-Elisabeth Hirschmann: Horrenda Secta.** Untersuchungen zum frühchristlichen Montanismus und seinen Verbindungen zur paganen Religion Phrygiens. 2005. 168 S., kt.   8675-2

180. **Thomas Heine Nielsen (ed.): Once Again: Studies in the Ancient Greek Polis.** 2004. 202 S., kt.   8438-3

181. **Gideon Maier: Amtsträger und Herrscher in der Romania Gothica.** Vergleichende Untersuchungen zu den Institutionen der ostgermanischen Völkerwanderungsreiche. 2005. 363 S., kt.
                                              8505-2

182. **David Whitehead/P. H. Blyth: Athenaeus Mechanicus, On Machines (Περὶ μηχανημάτων).** Translated with Introduction and Commentary. 2004. 236 S., kt.   8532-8

183. **Wolfgang Blösel: Themistokles bei Herodot: Spiegel Athens im fünften Jahrhundert.** Studien zur Geschichte und historiographischen Konstruktion des griechischen Freiheitskampfes 480 v. Chr. 2004. 422 S. m. 2 Ktn., geb.   8533-5

184. In Vorbereitung

185. **Stephan Berrens: Sonnenkult und Kaisertum von den Severern bis zu Constantin I (193–227 n. Chr.).** 2004. 283 S. m. 2 Taf., kt.   8575-5

186. **Norbert Geske: Nikias und das Volk von Athen im Archidamischen Krieg.** 2005. 224 S., kt.
                                              8566-3

187. **Christopher L.H. Barnes: Images and Insults.** Ancient Historiography and the Outbreak of the Tarentine War. 2005. 170 S., kt.   8689-9

188. **Massimiliano Vitiello: Momenti di Roma ostrogota: aduentus, feste, politica.** 2005. 162 S., kt.   8688-2

189. **Klaus Freitag/Peter Funke/Matthias Haake (Hg.): Kult – Politik – Ethnos.** Überregionale Heiligtümer im Spannungsfeld von Kult und Politik. 2006. Ca. 280 S., kt.   8718-6

190. **Jens Uwe Krause / Christian Witschel (Hg.): Die Stadt in der Spätantike – Niedergang oder Wandel?** Akten des internationalen Kolloquiums in München am 30. und 31. Mai 2003. 2006. 492 S. m. 42 Abb. kt.   8810-7

191. **Heinz Heinen: Vom hellenistischen Osten zum römischen Westen.** Ausgewählte Schriften zur Alten Geschichte. Hg. v. **Andrea Binsfeld** u. **Stefan Pfeiffer.** 2006. XX–VIII, 553 S. m. Frontisp. u. 34 Abb., geb.   8740-7

192. **Andrea Jördens, Hg.: Wirtschaft und Gesellschaft im spätantiken Ägypten. Kleine Schriften Itzhak F. Fikhman.** Hrsg. unter Mitarb. v. **Walter Sperling.** 2006. XVIII, 380 S. m. Frontisp. u. 2 Farbktn., geb.   8876-3

193. **Adalberto Giovannini: Les relations entre états dans la Grèce antique** du temps d'Homère à l'intervention romaine (ca. 700-200 av. J.-C.). 2007. Ca. 420 S., kt.   8953-1

194. **Michael B. Charles: Vegetius in Context.** Establishing the Date of the *Epitoma Rei Militaris*. 2007. 205 S., kt.   8989-0

195. **Clemens Koehn: Krieg – Diplomatie – Ideologie.** Zur Außenpolitik hellenistischer Mittelmeerstaaten. 2007. Ca. 260 S., kt.   8990-6

196. **Kay Ehling: Untersuchungen zur Geschichte der späten Seleukiden (164–63 v. Chr.).** Vom Tode des Antiochos IV. bis zur Einrichtung der Provinz Syria unter Pompeius. 2007. Ca. 320 S. m. 1 zweifbg. Kte. u. 1 Falttaf. in einer Tasche.
                                              9035-3

197. **Stephanie L. Larson: Tales of Epic Ancestry.** Boiotian Collective Identity in the Late Archaic and Early Classical Periods. 2007. Ca. 220 S., kt.
                                              9028-5

FRANZ STEINER VERLAG STUTTGART